Dick Mills
THE
PROPHET'S
MANTLE

Declaring the Heart of God

Dr Michael H Yeager

All rights reserved. No part of this book is allowed to be reproduced, stored in a retrieval system, or transmitted by any form or by any means-electronic, mechanical, photocopy, recording, or otherwise-without prior written permission of the copyright owner, except by a reviewer who wishes to quote brief passages in connection with a review for inclusion in a magazine, website, newspaper, podcast, or broadcast. All Scripture quotations, unless otherwise indicated, are taken from the King James Authorized Version of the Bible.

This book contains some information from non-copyrighted public sources found online, plus there are stories based on the author's real-life teachings and experiences.

Copyright © 2024 Dr Michael H Yeager

All rights reserved.

ISBN: 9798301086625

DEDICATION

To those who yearn, who are genuinely hungry and thirsty to live in the realm of the supernatural, this book is for you. To those who have already tasted the glories of the heavenly realm, this is dedicated to you. To the bride of Jesus Christ, who is called to delve deeper, to soar higher, and to journey farther than ever before, this dedication stands as a **Testament**. It is only by the unmerited grace of our Lord, obtained through unwavering FAITH in JESUS CHRIST, that we can hope to achieve His divine will on this earth. As we face the adversary, Satan, and the powers of darkness, may we always remember our purpose and calling.

Dick {Betty} Mills (1922-2012)

CONTENTS

ACKNOWLEDGMENTS

1	Chapter One	1
2	Chapter Two	19
3	Chapter Three	40
4	Chapter Four	61
5	Chapter Five	79
6	Chapter Six	99
7	Chapter Seven	122
8	Chapter Eight	143
9	Chapter Nine	163
10	Chapter Ten	186

ACKNOWLEDGMENTS

These Sermons, Teachings and Experiences from **Dick Mills** have been **MODERNIZED** for those who truly hunger and thirst after all that God has made available through the life, ministry, sufferings, death, and resurrection of Jesus Christ. My prayer is that not only will your life be touched by these **divine Truths**, but you yourself will truly step into that realm where all things are possible .God is not a respecter of people, what he did for **Dick Mills**, he desires to do for you and me. May you experience wonderful **transform**ation and divine healing.

These true stories and Sermons have been modernized to make them more understandable and descriptive in our modern vernacular. All the Sermons have been compiled from sermons of Dick Mills. Jesus Christ is the same yesterday today and forever. What he did for Dick, he will do for you and me!

DICK MILLS

Step into the remarkable life and ministry of Dick Mills, a modern-day prophet whose legacy of faith and scriptural wisdom continues to resonate today. In *The Prophet's Mantle*, readers are invited to discover the extraordinary journey of a man who devoted himself to declaring the heart of God through the living Word. Born in 1922 with an insatiable passion for the Bible, Dick Mills memorized thousands of verses by heart, equipping him with a wellspring of divine truth that became the foundation of his ministry.

CHAPTER ONE

Dick Mills: A Life Anchored in God's Word and Prophetic Ministry

Dick Mills was a prophetic minister whose life reflected an unwavering love for Scripture and a unique ability to share God's promises through personalized prophecy. Born in 1922, Mills grew up immersed in the Word of God, developing an extraordinary capacity to memorize thousands of Bible verses. This profound knowledge became the cornerstone of his ministry, enabling him to offer encouragement and guidance rooted in Scripture for over six decades.

The Beginning of a Unique Ministry

Mills' ministry began in the 1940s, a time when the world was reeling from war and searching for hope. Armed with his love for God's Word, he traveled extensively, ministering in churches, conferences, and gatherings. His gift was remarkable: the ability to recall specific Bible verses on the spot and apply them directly to a person's life. These were not generic words but "personalized promises" that often-met people at the exact point of their need.

This ministry was not about predicting the future but proclaiming God's eternal truth. Mills often reminded those he ministered to of the promise found in *Isaiah 55:11 (KJV):* **"So shall my word be that goeth forth out of my mouth: it shall not return unto me void, but it shall accomplish that which I please, and it shall prosper in the thing whereto I sent it."**

Prophetic Encouragement Rooted in the Bible

Mills believed that every prophetic word should align with Scripture. His ministry emphasized that the Bible is not a relic of the past but a living source of comfort, wisdom, and healing. He frequently referenced *Hebrews 4:12 (KJV):* **"For the word of God is quick, and powerful, and sharper than any twoedged sword."** This conviction made his prophetic words not only inspiring but deeply rooted in biblical truth.

Testimonies abound from individuals whose lives were transformed by a verse or promise Mills spoke over them. Some found healing from physical illnesses, others received clarity in times of confusion, and many experienced a renewed faith in God's ability to intervene in their lives.

A Humble Teacher and Mentor

In addition to his public ministry, Mills was a mentor to countless pastors and leaders, sharing insights into the prophetic gift with humility and grace. He often taught that prophecy should be used to uplift and encourage the body of Christ, as instructed in *1 Corinthians 14:3*

(KJV): **"But he that prophesieth speaketh unto men to edification, and exhortation, and comfort."**

Mills' approach was never about showmanship. Instead, he used his gift to point people to Jesus, the ultimate fulfillment of all Scripture. His gentle spirit and commitment to God's Word earned him respect across denominations, making him a beloved figure in the Christian community.

A Legacy of Faith and Hope

Mills authored several books, including *God's Word for You*, where he expounded on the practical application of Scripture in everyday life. He demonstrated how God's promises can transform situations, bring healing, and ignite faith. His teachings often reflected *Jeremiah 29:11 (KJV):* **"For I know the thoughts that I think toward you, saith the Lord, thoughts of peace, and not of evil, to give you an expected end."**

Though he passed away in 2012, Dick Mills' legacy lives on through his writings, teachings, and the countless lives he touched. His life is a testimony to the transformative power of God's Word and the importance of a ministry anchored in Scripture. Mills reminds us that prophecy, when aligned with God's Word, carries the power to heal, restore, and guide believers in their walk with Christ.

Healing Through the Word

A central theme of Mills' ministry was the power of Scripture to bring healing—physical, emotional, and spiritual. Just as Jesus healed the lepers in **Luke 17:12-14 (KJV)**—**"And as they went, they were cleansed"**—Mills' words often acted as a catalyst for restoration. He believed that the promises of God are as effective today as they were in biblical times.

In every verse he shared, Mills pointed people back to Jesus, the ultimate healer and redeemer. His life serves as a profound example of how one person, wholly dedicated to God's Word, can inspire multitudes to believe in the unchanging power of Scripture.

A Legacy of Faith: The Impact of Aimee Semple McPherson on Dick Mills and Beyond

On the evening of March 10, 1933, Long Beach, California, was shaken by a devastating earthquake that claimed 120 lives and caused widespread destruction. Amid the chaos, 11-year-old Dick Mills witnessed an extraordinary act of compassion that would leave a lasting mark on his life. Aimee Semple McPherson, the founder of the Foursquare Church, quickly mobilized Angelus Temple to aid the victims.

While government agencies struggled to respond, McPherson rallied volunteers to load their cars with food, clothing, and other supplies, urging them to help people they didn't even know. Survivors often shared how this effort provided the only assistance they received in the aftermath of the disaster. For Mills, this act of Christ-like love embodied **Matthew 25:40 (KJV): "Verily I say** unto you, Inasmuch as ye have done it unto one of the least of these my brethren, ye have done it unto me."

Early Influences and Sister's Impact

Mills' family attended the Foursquare church in Stockton, California, where his mother often played piano for services. She once played at a crusade hosted by McPherson, affectionately known as "Sister." The event attracted both supporters and skeptics, including pastors who came to challenge her ministry. Yet, time and again, the Spirit of God would move powerfully, transforming critics into allies.

One of these skeptics was Dr. Price, a Congregational pastor from Stockton. Initially resistant to Pentecostal teachings, Dr. Price attended one of McPherson's meetings intending to oppose her. However, the conviction of the Holy Spirit overwhelmed him. When McPherson extended an invitation for salvation, Dr. Price stood boldly, declaring, *"I'm the worst sinner in the place!"* That night, he experienced a profound filling of the Holy Spirit, igniting a ministry of divine healing that reflected the power of God's Word, as seen in **Luke 4:18 (KJV): "The Spirit of the Lord is upon me, because he hath anointed me to preach the gospel to the poor; he hath sent me to heal the brokenhearted, to preach deliverance to the captives."**

This testimony deeply inspired Mills, affirming the transformative power of God's grace and truth.

Preparing for Ministry

After serving in the Air Force during World War II, Mills enrolled at L.I.F.E. Bible College (now Life Pacific University) in Los Angeles, a school founded by McPherson. Here, he prepared for a lifetime of pastoral and evangelistic ministry, surrounded by future leaders like Harold Helms, who would pastor Angelus Temple, and Chuck Smith, the founder of Calvary Chapel.

Mills also met his wife, Betty, a nurse at St. Vincent Medical Center. Betty introduced him to a nun who cherished memories of McPherson's visits to the hospital. The nun showed Mills a Bible that McPherson had gifted her, a symbol of her dedication to supporting women in ministry and uplifting others through God's Word.

Standing Firm Amid Challenges

In 1952, Mills pastored the Foursquare church in Oceanside, California. To support his young family, he worked at Camp Pendleton alongside Marines who initially mocked him for pastoring a church founded by a woman. The ridicule was relentless until their foreman intervened, recounting how McPherson had personally advocated for fair pay for Los Angeles firefighters, including his father. Her efforts had directly improved their livelihoods, earned the foreman's respect and silencing the mockery.

This story reinforced the profound impact of McPherson's ministry, not only on Mills' life but also on countless others who benefitted from her Christ-centered advocacy.

A Lasting Legacy

McPherson's ministry, rooted in the love and compassion of Jesus Christ, served as a guiding example for Mills. Her life reflected **James 1:27 (KJV): "Pure religion and undefiled before God and the Father is this, To visit the fatherless and widows in their affliction, and to keep himself unspotted from the world."**

For Mills, these experiences solidified his calling to serve God wholeheartedly. Through his ministry and prophetic gift, he carried forward the legacy of faith and compassion modeled by McPherson, pointing others to the redemptive power of Jesus.

Reflecting on her influence, Mills often quoted **Psalm 126:3 (KJV): "The Lord hath done great things for us; whereof we are glad."** Her life, intertwined with his, stood as a testimony to the transformative power of the Gospel and the enduring impact of a life wholly surrendered to God.

To God be the glory—great things He has done!

"When the Saints Come Smiling In: A Journey of Faith and Joy"

In the heart of Cortez, Colorado, under the vast blue skies where the pinto beans were ripe for harvest, a young preacher named Dick Mills stood before his congregation. It was the kind of place where the land worked the people as much as they worked it, with days stretching long under the sun. Here, the services started at nine every evening, a time when the locals, weary from their 14-hour labors in the fields, would drag themselves into the sanctuary, not with the vigor of saints marching in, but rather as saints dragging in.

Dick, fresh from Bible school, was full of zeal and a desire to lift spirits. He looked out at the tired faces, some of which hadn't cracked a smile all morning. "This isn't a mortuary," he thought, "it's a place of life and healing." So, with a playful tone, he encouraged, "Come on folks, show me your teeth!" A farmer, catching the jest, cheekily removed his false teeth, flashing them with a grin that broke the stern atmosphere, making three of the seven unsmiling faces snicker. Five more to go, Dick thought, feeling the joy of the Lord as a balm.

He then turned the congregation towards interaction, urging them to affirm each other with, "I don't care what your neighbors are saying about you. I like you." This simple act of kindness was a reflection of Jesus' love, who healed and uplifted all who came to Him, regardless of their societal standing or condition.

Dick shared his love for Greek and Hebrew word studies, mentioning how such studies could be invigorating or overwhelming, but today's study was particularly fitting. He spoke of the Greek word meaning to give oneself continually to prayer, embodying not just routine but an energized, enduring commitment to spiritual life. "Let's not just say prayers," he echoed, "Let's pray prayers." This was about perseverance in faith, much like Jesus encouraged His disciples to persist in prayer, as seen in Luke 18:1, "And he spake a parable unto them to this end, that men ought always to pray, and not to faint."

The story of Pat Robertson and his wife Dee Dee brought a personal touch. Dee Dee's enthusiasm for Dick's daily devotions became a morning ritual that even stirred Pat from his sleep. Here was the essence of community in faith, sharing and celebrating the word together, much like Jesus shared His teachings with His followers, fostering a community of believers.

In this narrative, Dick Mills wasn't just preaching; he was living out the message of Jesus, who came not only to heal physical ailments like leprosy but also to mend the wearied spirit. Like when Jesus cleansed the leper in **Matthew 8:2-3, "And, behold, there came a leper and worshipped him, saying, Lord, if thou wilt, thou canst make me clean. And Jesus put forth his hand, and touched him, saying, I will; be thou clean. And immediately his leprosy was cleansed."** Dick's mission, like Jesus', was to rejuvenate the soul, to bring smiles where there were none, and to remind everyone that in God's house, there is always room for joy.

Reviving Joy: The Ministry and

Humor of Brother Dick Mills

Brother Dick Mills carried a profound love for God's Word and an infectious sense of humor that often broke through the toughest of congregations. His ministry wasn't only about prophecy or theology; it was about meeting people where they were and inviting them into the joy and freedom of God's presence.

A Mortuary or a Sanctuary?

Mills often reminded people, with a twinkle in his eye, that the church wasn't a place for solemn faces. He shared an instance when he noticed seven people in the congregation who hadn't smiled throughout the entire service. He couldn't resist addressing it:

"This is not a mortuary; it's a sanctuary!" he said, his voice echoing with humor.

He urged the congregation to turn to their neighbors and say, "I don't care what your neighbors are saying about you. I like you." The ripple of laughter broke the tension, and even the most stoic among them cracked a smile. Mills believed in the healing power of joy, reflecting **Proverbs 17:22 (KJV): "A merry heart doeth good like a medicine."**

Fresh Out of Bible School

Fresh out of Bible school, Mills found himself in Cortez, Colorado, during pinto bean harvest season. It was a challenging time to hold revival meetings, as farmers were working 14-hour days in the fields. The services began late at night, and by the time Mills stepped up to preach, the congregation was utterly exhausted.

With his characteristic humor, Mills joked about their theme song: "When the Saints Come Dragging In." Despite the weary crowd, Mills' enthusiasm and light-hearted spirit managed to energize the room.

Once, in an effort to lift their spirits, he encouraged everyone to smile. One farmer took the challenge literally, removing his false teeth and holding them up for Mills to see. The room erupted in laughter. For Mills, this moment illustrated the simple truth of **Psalm 16:11 (KJV): "In thy presence is fulness of joy; at thy right hand there are pleasures for evermore."**

Energized Endurance: A Life of Prayer and the Word

Brother Mills loved diving into the depths of Scripture, often weaving Greek and Hebrew word studies into his teachings. He was passionate about the transformative power of prayer and the Word of God. Referencing **Acts 6:4 (KJV): "But we will give ourselves continually to prayer, and to the ministry of the word,"** he explained how the phrase **"give ourselves continually"** in Greek conveys a sense of energized endurance, stamina, and perseverance.

Mills didn't just teach people to say prayers; he inspired them to pray prayers—with fervor and faith. His devotional writings became a source of encouragement for countless believers, including Pat Robertson and his wife, Dede. Mills recalled Robertson sharing how Dede kept one of his devotionals by her bedside, reading it each morning and joyfully sharing its insights with her husband.

Breaking Down Barriers

For Mills, the message of Jesus was never confined to the pulpit; it was alive in the laughter, joy, and connections he fostered. His ability to bring levity to serious moments didn't diminish the gravity of the Gospel but instead illuminated its beauty. Like Jesus healing the ten lepers in **Luke 17:12-19 (KJV)—"And it came to pass, as they went, they were cleansed"**—Mills believed in the power of transformation, both physical and spiritual.

He often said, "God loves you too much to leave you the way you are," urging people to step into the healing and joy found in Christ. His ministry reflected a deep belief that the church should be a sanctuary of hope and renewal, where people could encounter the living God.

A Legacy of Joy and Faith

Brother Dick Mills left behind a legacy of unwavering faith and light-hearted encouragement. His life and ministry embodied **Romans 15:13 (KJV): "Now the God of hope fill you with all joy and peace in** believing, that ye may abound in hope, through the power of the Holy Ghost."

Through his humor, biblical insight, and passion for prayer, Mills reminded believers of the joy of the Lord, which truly is our strength. To those who encountered him, he was not just a preacher but a messenger of hope and laughter, pointing always to Jesus, the source of all joy and healing.

Experiences of Dr Michael H Yeager

God Revealed My Wife in a Prophetic Vision

In 1975, I had just given my heart to Jesus and was wholeheartedly seeking to serve Him. Around this time, God wove together an incredible story that would forever change my life. A woman named Billie Deck, along with her daughter, had met a young man at a Christian meeting. That young man began attending their weekly Bible studies until he left to join the Navy.

While stationed on the remote island of Adak, Alaska, this man invited Billie to minister to a small group of hungry believers. Obeying the Lord's leading, Billie traveled to the Aleutian Islands in February 1977, where she stayed for three weeks, pouring into the lives of those who were desperately seeking God.

When the young man's tour in the Navy ended, he returned to Virginia and lived with Billie for a time. One day, he brought me—Michael Yeager—to meet her. I was a new believer, fiery and passionate about Jesus, but still discovering the fullness of His plans for my life. That day, standing in Billie's kitchen, God used her in a way I'll never forget.

As we talked, Billie suddenly began to prophesy over me. Her words were precise and anointed, and I could sense the Holy Spirit moving. She spoke of my calling to ministry and the future God had prepared for me. Then, she paused, her eyes focused as if she were looking beyond the natural. "I see your wife," she said, her voice steady with conviction. She described a beautiful blonde woman, detailing her features with astonishing clarity. I stood there, stunned. At that time, I had no idea who this woman was, but her words planted a seed of faith in my heart.

Fast forward to the spring of 1978. God orchestrated a divine encounter that brought Kathleen May Schooley into my life. Kathleen was the lead singer at Valley Forge Christian College, and the moment we met, I knew she was the one Billie had seen in her vision. She fit the description perfectly—not just in appearance, but in spirit. It was as if God had handpicked her for me, which, of course, He had.

From the beginning, our connection was undeniable. Kathleen and I quickly fell in love, and by August of that year, we were married. Shortly after, we attended Rhema Bible Training Center in Oklahoma, deepening our understanding of God's Word and preparing for the work He had called us to. After completing our training, we served as missionaries in Germany for nine months, witnessing God move in extraordinary ways.

Over the years, Billie and her ministry, Cedars of Lebanon, remained a pivotal part of our spiritual family. Her obedience to God and prophetic insight played a critical role in my journey. Reflecting on this miraculous chain of events, I see the hand of Jesus in every detail, guiding and shaping my life according to His divine purpose.

The Bible declares, *"**Trust in the Lord with all thine heart; and lean not unto thine own understanding. In all thy ways acknowledge him, and he shall direct thy paths"*** (Proverbs 3:5-6 KJV)**. God used Billie to direct my path, leading me to Kathleen, the woman He had chosen for me long before I ever knew her. Together, Kathleen and I have served Jesus faithfully, sharing His love and power with countless people.

This testimony reminds me that God is intimately involved in every aspect of our lives. He knows our needs, our desires, and our destinies. Just as He revealed Kathleen to Billie through a vision, He can guide anyone who seeks Him with an open heart. Jesus is the Good Shepherd, and His plans for us are always for our good and His glory. *"**For I know the thoughts that I think toward you, saith the Lord, thoughts of peace, and not of evil, to give you an expected end"*** (Jeremiah 29:11 KJV)**.

To this day of November 23rd, 2024, Kathleen and I stand as living proof of God's faithfulness, walking out the future He spoke through Billie all those years ago.

Dr Michael H Yeager

A Prophecy Fulfilled: The Miracle of a Child

Bill and Pam were a beloved couple in our church. They had been married for over eight years and longed deeply for children. Their hearts ached with the desire to fill their home with the laughter of a little one, but after years of trying, their hopes seemed dashed. Extensive medical tests revealed devastating news: both of them had physical conditions that made having children impossible. It wasn't just one obstacle; it was two. Their pain was palpable, and though they loved God, they struggled to hold on to hope.

One Sunday morning, during a service filled with worship and the presence of the Holy Spirit, God began giving me prophetic words for individuals in the congregation. I remember seeing Bill and Pam sitting together, their heads slightly bowed, a quiet desperation etched into their faces. Then, suddenly, I felt the unmistakable nudge of the Holy Spirit. I called them forward, and as they approached, I saw a vision—a beautiful picture of their future.

Looking directly at them, I declared, "I see you holding a baby. Within one year, you will have a child. And not only that, but you will both be involved in children's ministry." The moment the words left my mouth, both

Bill and Pam broke down in tears. They wept openly, lifting their hands in praise to God, clinging to the promise. I could see their faith stirring, even as doubt tried to wrestle its way in. They knew, just as Abraham and Sarah did, that this was a promise from God that defied every natural law.

The Bible says of Abraham, ***"Who against hope believed in hope, that he might become the father of many nations, according to that which was spoken, So shall thy seed be"* (Romans 4:18 KJV).** Bill and Pam decided to believe like Abraham, trusting that the One who promised was faithful to fulfill.

That very week, they acted on their faith. They chose one of the bedrooms in their home and began transforming it into a nursery. They painted the walls with soft, warm colors, cleaned every corner, and filled the space with love and anticipation. Then, they started buying baby clothes, even though there was no natural sign of a child coming. Their actions declared their faith louder than words ever could.

Months passed, and my wife and I left for Germany to serve in ministry. While we were overseas, we continued to pray for them, trusting that God was working His miraculous plan. When we returned, we ran into someone who knew Bill and Pam. With a broad smile, they shared the incredible news: everything I had prophesied had come to pass. Bill and Pam had welcomed a beautiful baby boy into their family—within the exact time frame God had revealed. Even more, they were now actively serving in children's ministry, pouring into the lives of young ones with the same love and faith they had clung to during their journey.

The fulfillment of God's promise in their lives reminds me of **Romans 4:19-21, where it says,** *"And being not weak in faith, he considered not his own body now dead, when he was about an hundred years old, neither yet the deadness of Sara's womb: He staggered not at the promise of God through unbelief; but was strong in faith, giving glory to God; and being fully persuaded that, what he had promised, he was able also to perform"* **(KJV).** Bill and Pam's faith mirrored Abraham's. They didn't waver, even when the odds were stacked against them. They believed that the God who promised was able to perform it—and He did.

Their story is a powerful reminder that Jesus is the same yesterday, today, and forever (Hebrews 13:8). What He did for Abraham and Sarah, and what He did for Bill and Pam, He can do for anyone who dares to trust Him. If God has spoken a promise to your heart, don't stagger in unbelief. Instead, stand strong in faith, giving glory to God, knowing that He is faithful to bring it to pass.

CHAPTER TWO
Breaking Chains: Joy, Restoration, and Receiving a Word from the Lord

Brother Dick Mills had a way of making people laugh while pointing them to the profound truths of God's Word. His ministry was a unique blend of humor, biblical insight, and the power of the Holy Spirit, aimed at breaking spiritual chains and bringing freedom.

Joy in Unexpected Lessons

Mills' teachings often came wrapped in humor. He loved to tackle real-life topics with a lighthearted touch, addressing marriage, relationships, and personal struggles with the wisdom of Scripture.

He once quipped about a chapter in his marriage series called "Ministering to Your Husband's Ego." He joked that many wives seemed more inclined to crush their husbands' egos than build them up. *"I've heard women say their husbands strut around the house like they're waiting for a vacancy in the Trinity,"* he chuckled.

His humor was always rooted in a deeper purpose—to bring healing and understanding to relationships. He often referenced **Ephesians 5:33 (KJV):** *"Nevertheless let every one of you in particular so love his wife even as himself; and the wife see that she reverence her husband."*

The Run to Freedom

One of Mills' most memorable events took place at Jack Cambridge's church, where the Lord impressed upon him to lead the congregation in a physical act of faith—a "Run to Freedom." He believed that by running laps around the sanctuary while proclaiming God's promises, people could break free from addictions, depression, and suicidal thoughts.

Mills shared three powerful verses that inspired this act, including **Hebrews 12:1 (KJV):** *"Let us lay aside every weight, and the sin which doth so easily beset us, and let us run with patience the race that is set before us."*

The response was overwhelming. As the congregation ran, people testified to being delivered from alcohol, tobacco, drugs, and other strongholds. Mills laughed as he recalled the scene: *"Half the church was running, including half the staff!"* The event was a joyous reminder that God's power to deliver is alive and active.

A Word from the Lord

Mills frequently reminded his audience that receiving a word from God didn't require perfection. *"You don't have to have it all together,"* he said. *"God has a word for you, and that word can change your life."*

He illustrated this truth by pointing to stories in Scripture where Jesus met people in their brokenness and transformed their lives. One such example was the ten lepers in **Luke 17:12-14 (KJV)**: *"And as they went, they were cleansed."* Jesus didn't require them to be perfect; He met them where they were and brought healing.

Mills emphasized that God's word is living and powerful, capable of cutting through every situation. He often cited **Isaiah 55:11 (KJV)**: *"So shall my word be that goeth forth out of my mouth: it shall not return unto me void, but it shall accomplish that which I please, and it shall prosper in the thing whereto I sent it."*

Chains Broken and Lives Transformed

Through his humorous anecdotes and Spirit-led teachings, Mills created an environment where people felt free to embrace God's grace and healing. Whether addressing the struggles of marriage or leading a congregation in a "Run to Freedom," he carried the assurance that God's word never fails.

Mills' life and ministry were a testament to the transforming power of Jesus Christ. He reminded everyone that no matter their circumstances, God's word could break chains, heal wounds, and bring restoration. His message echoed the words of **Psalm 30:11 (KJV):** *"Thou hast turned for me my mourning into dancing: thou hast put off my sackcloth, and girded me with gladness."*

An Invitation to Freedom

Mills often concluded his teachings with an invitation to experience the joy and freedom found in Jesus. His humor, paired with his deep faith, inspired countless people to run their race with perseverance, knowing that God's word would sustain them every step of the way.

Through his unique ministry, Mills left a legacy of laughter, faith, and freedom—pointing always to the one who sets us free: Jesus Christ.

Gideon's Call: From Fear to Valor

Have you ever felt like you had nothing going for you? Like the odds were stacked against you, and you were just trying to get by without being noticed? That's exactly where Gideon was when God called him, and his story in Judges 6 is one of my favorites. It's a story of transformation, where God takes a timid, fearful man and turns him into a mighty warrior.

Hiding in Fear

Picture this: Gideon is threshing wheat, but not out in the open like you'd expect. Instead, he's by a winepress, hiding from the Midianites. **Judges 6:11 (KJV)** sets the scene perfectly: *"And there came an angel of the Lord, and sat under an oak which was in Ophrah, that pertained unto Joash the Abiezrite: and his son Gideon threshed wheat by the winepress, to hide it from the Midianites."*

The Midianites were oppressors, raiding Israel's land and leaving the people in constant fear. Gideon was trying to survive, just like everyone else. There was no boldness, no courage, no hint of heroism—just a man doing what he could to avoid trouble.

A Word That Changes Everything

But then, in verse 12, the angel of the Lord appears to Gideon and says something that must have sounded completely ridiculous: *"The Lord is with thee, thou mighty man of valour."* Can you imagine Gideon's reaction? A "mighty man of valor"? He was anything but! If I were in his shoes, I might've laughed or looked around to see if the angel was talking to someone else.

But that's the incredible thing about God. He doesn't see us as we are; He sees what we can become. Gideon was stuck in fear, but God called him a warrior because that's who He created Gideon to be.

A Covenant Relationship

The book of Judges paints a picture of Israel's ups and downs over a 400-year period. At their best, they were in covenant relationship with God, protected and thriving. **Judges 2:18 (KJV)** summarizes it well: *"And when the Lord raised them up judges, then the Lord was with the judge, and delivered them out of the hand of their enemies all the days of the judge."*

But as they prospered, they often became complacent, turning away from God to worship idols. It's a cycle we see over and over: covenant, prosperity, complacency, and then oppression. Each time, God raised up a judge to deliver them, and Gideon was one of those judges.

Called in Weakness

Gideon's first response to the angel's declaration reveals just how little he thought of himself. In **Judges 6:15 (KJV)**, he says: *"Oh my Lord, wherewith shall I save Israel? behold, my family is poor in Manasseh, and I am the least in my father's house."* He saw himself as insignificant, but God had a different perspective.

This reminds me of how Jesus healed the ten lepers in **Luke 17:12-14**. These men were outcasts, considered unclean and untouchable by society. Yet, Jesus didn't see their leprosy—He saw their potential for restoration. He told them to go show themselves to the priests, and as they went, they were healed. God doesn't wait for us to have it all together before He moves in our lives. He meets us in our brokenness and transforms us as we walk in obedience.

Obedience Unlocks Transformation

Gideon's story is a testament to what can happen when we respond to God's call, even in fear and doubt. The angel's words, *"The Lord is with thee,"* were the key. Gideon didn't have to rely on his own strength; God's presence would empower him.

The same is true for us. When God calls us, it's not because we're qualified—it's because He is. **Philippians 4:13 (KJV)** says: *"I can do all things through Christ which strengtheneth me."* Like Gideon, we may feel weak and unworthy, but God's strength is made perfect in our weakness.

Breaking the Cycle

Gideon's obedience broke the cycle of fear and oppression in Israel. He tore down idols, rallied an army, and led Israel to victory—all because he trusted the word of the Lord. His story reminds us that God's plans for us are far greater than anything we can imagine. As **Jeremiah 29:11 (KJV)** assures us: *"For I know the thoughts that I think toward you, saith the Lord, thoughts of peace, and not of evil, to give you an expected end."*

Your Word from the Lord

Just like Gideon, you don't have to have it all together to receive a word from the Lord. God speaks to us in our hiding places, in our fears, and in our doubts. His word has the power to change everything—not because of who we are, but because of who He is.

If you're feeling unworthy or insignificant, remember this: God sees you through the eyes of grace. He calls you by what you can become, not by what you are. Step out in faith, trust His word, and watch Him transform your life, just as He did for Gideon. To God be the glory!

From Fear to Freedom: Gideon's Journey with God

Let me tell you a story about how fear, oppression, and desperation can turn into courage and faith when God steps in. Gideon's story in Judges 6 is a powerful example of what happens when God calls someone who feels inadequate and gives them a purpose that changes everything.

A Nation in Crisis

At this point in history, Israel was in deep trouble. They had turned away from God, worshiping idols and breaking their covenant with Him. God compared their idolatry to adultery, calling it spiritual harlotry. When Israel turned to idols, the covenant was broken, and God was no longer bound to protect them. As a result, their enemies—the Philistines and Midianites—rose up and brutalized them.

The Philistines had taken away all the farming tools, leaving Israeli farmers completely dependent on their oppressors. If a farmer wanted to work his field, he had to go to a Philistine warehouse to requisition tools. A couple of Philistine soldiers would deliver the tools, stand guard all day while the farmer worked, and then take the tools back at sunset. It was humiliating and restrictive, designed to keep the Israelites powerless.

But the Philistines weren't the worst of it. The Midianites were even crueler. During harvest season, when the crops were ripe, they would sweep in and destroy everything—burning the wheat, corn, barley, rye, olives, and grapes. They didn't just raid the harvest; they decimated the food supply for the entire year.

Hiding in Desperation

This was the world Gideon lived in. His people were traumatized, hungry, and hopeless. Gideon himself was no warrior; he was simply trying to survive. He found a little strip of land near an oak forest where he could thresh wheat in secret, using a winepress instead of an open threshing floor to hide from the Midianites.

Imagine the scene: a narrow piece of land behind the farmhouse, tucked away near the trees. There's a winepress, an olive press, and a small threshing floor, all in close proximity. Gideon is there, working in fear, just trying to prepare enough food for a meal.

God Steps In

And that's when it happens. The angel of the Lord comes through the forest and appears to Gideon. **Judges 6:12 (KJV)** records the moment: *"And the angel of the Lord appeared unto him, and said unto him, The Lord is with thee, thou mighty man of valour."*

It must have sounded absurd to Gideon. Mighty man of valor? He was hiding, not fighting. But God doesn't see us as we are; He sees us as He intends us to be.

Gideon's fear and doubt poured out immediately. He questioned God's presence, His promises, and even His care for Israel. **Judges 6:13 (KJV)** says: *"O my Lord, if the Lord be with us, why then is all this befallen us? and where be all his miracles which our fathers told us of?"*

But the angel didn't argue. Instead, he gave Gideon a word that would change everything. **Judges 6:14 (KJV)** says: *"Go in this thy might, and thou shalt save Israel from the hand of the Midianites: have not I sent thee?"*

Transformation Through Obedience

Gideon wasn't chosen because of his strength or courage—he was chosen because God wanted to show His power through him. Just like Jesus healing the ten lepers in **Luke 17:12-14 (KJV),** where they were healed ***"as they went,"*** Gideon's transformation came as he obeyed God.

He tore down idols, built an altar to the Lord, and eventually led a small army of 300 men to defeat the Midianites. God didn't need a mighty warrior; He needed someone willing to trust Him.

Lessons for Us

Gideon's story reminds us that God's call isn't based on our qualifications. It's about His purpose and power. If you feel inadequate, remember what God told Gideon: ***"Surely I will be with thee"*** **(Judges 6:16 KJV).**

When Jesus healed the lepers, He didn't wait for them to prove their worthiness. He simply gave them a command, and as they obeyed, they were cleansed. God meets us in our fear, our doubt, and our brokenness, and He calls us to step out in faith.

Gideon's transformation from a timid man hiding in a winepress to a victorious leader shows us what's possible when we trust God. No matter how small or weak we feel, God can use us to accomplish great things when we listen to His word and follow His lead.

A Call to Action

Like Gideon, we live in a world that often feels oppressive and overwhelming. But God's promise remains: *"I will never leave thee, nor forsake thee"* **(Hebrews 13:5 KJV).** If He can use a fearful man like Gideon to deliver a nation, He can use you to make a difference right where you are.

So, what's holding you back? Step out of the winepress, trust God's word, and let Him work through you. The same God who called Gideon calls you today.

From Wimp to Warrior: The Transforming Power of God's Word

There's something almost humorous about how God works sometimes. I mean, look at Gideon. This guy wasn't exactly your picture of bravery. He was timid, fearful, and more concerned about getting through his next meal than standing up to the enemy. If Gideon had a theme song, it wouldn't have been Willie Nelson's "Help Me Make It Through the Night." It would've been, "Help Me Make It Through the Wheat."

And yet, when the angel of the Lord appeared to him, He didn't call him timid or fearful. **Judges 6:12 (KJV)** says: *"And the angel of the Lord appeared unto him, and said unto him, The Lord is with thee, thou mighty man of valour."* Imagine that! The angel's words must have sounded like a joke to Gideon.

A Word That Changes Everything

At that moment, Gideon was anything but mighty. If anything, you could've called him a wimp, a nerd, a square, or even a mama's boy—maybe all four rolled into one. Yet, the angel delivered a word straight from heaven, calling him a mighty warrior.

Why would a holy angel from a holy God bring a holy word to someone who looked like a first-class coward? Because God doesn't define us by where we are right now—He sees who we're becoming.

When the angel spoke those words, Gideon wasn't yet a warrior, but he was on his way to becoming one. Jesus often did the same thing. He didn't just see people in their brokenness; He spoke life and destiny into them. Take the ten lepers in **Luke 17:12-14 (KJV)**. They were outcasts, unclean, and hopeless. But Jesus said, ***"Go shew yourselves unto the priests."*** As they obeyed His word, they were cleansed. The power wasn't in who they were—it was in the word He gave them.

Seeds of Fulfillment

Jesus taught that every word from God carries the seeds of its own fulfillment. In **Matthew 13:23 (KJV)**, He explained: ***"But he that received seed into the good ground is he that heareth the word, and understandeth it; which also beareth fruit, and bringeth forth, some an hundredfold, some sixty, some thirty."***

When the angel told Gideon he was a mighty man of valor, it wasn't a description of his present reality—it was a declaration of his future. That word began a process in Gideon's life, and if you read the next few chapters of Judges, you'll see the results. Gideon went on to win four consecutive victories, leading Israel to freedom from their oppressors.

It's the same for us. When God gives us a promise, it may not reflect where we are right now, but it reveals where we're headed. The key is to hold onto that word, let it take root in your heart, and trust God to bring it to pass.

Becoming Who God Says You Are

Think about it: God sees you not as you are, but as the person you're becoming. You may feel weak, broken, or unworthy, but He sees a conqueror. **Romans 8:37 (KJV)** reminds us: *"Nay, in all these things we are more than conquerors through him that loved us."*

If I could, I'd fast-forward your life to just before Jesus returns. Imagine yourself then—having overcome fear, doubt, insecurity, and all the battles you're facing now. You'd see someone strong, courageous, and victorious. That's who God sees when He looks at you today.

A Glorious Church

The Bible tells us that Jesus is coming back for a glorious church, not a defeated one. **Ephesians 5:27 (KJV)** says: *"That he might present it to himself a glorious church,* *not having spot, or wrinkle, or any such thing; but that it should be holy and without blemish."*

Gideon's story reminds us that the journey from fear to glory isn't about our own strength—it's about trusting the One who calls us. The word God gives you today might feel far from your reality, but it's a promise of who you're becoming in Him.

Moving Forward

So, where are you on your journey? Maybe you feel like Gideon—hiding in fear and wondering how you'll make it through the day. Let me remind you that God has a word for you, too. It's not about who you are right now; it's about who He's shaping you to be.

Hold onto that word, just as Gideon did. Trust that God's promise carries the power to fulfill itself and let Him lead you into victory. Before you know it, you'll look back and see how far He's brought you.

After all, He's not just calling you to survive—He's calling you to thrive. And like Gideon, you're on your way to becoming exactly who He's called you to be.

From Dr Michael H Yeager

A Prophetic Word Fulfilled: You Will Become an Attorney

It was during one of our regular Bible studies in Salisbury, Maryland, that the Spirit of God spoke through me in an unexpected way. We were gathered at the home of a sister in Christ named Rosemary. As I finished ministering, my eyes turned to her, and I felt a stirring within me—a word of wisdom that could only come from the Holy Spirit.

"Rosemary," I said, "you are going to become an attorney."

She looked at me, visibly taken aback. "What?" she responded, almost laughing at the absurdity of it.

"You're going to become an attorney," I repeated confidently. The words weren't my own; they were from the Lord. She was a high-ranking official in Washington, D.C., at the time, serving as the Director of National Security Training for FEMA. Her career was well-established and on a trajectory that seemed far removed from the legal field. Naturally, she was puzzled by the prophecy. "I don't understand," she admitted.

"It's okay," I told her. "If it's of God, it will happen."

We never discussed it again. I continued leading Bible studies at her home with my wife and others for a season, but eventually, life took us in different directions, and we lost touch. I hadn't given the prophetic word another thought—until about four years later, when I found myself in urgent need of a good attorney.

I started flipping through the phone book, searching for legal help. That's when my eyes landed on her name—

Rosemary McDermott, Attorney at Law. My jaw dropped. Could this be the same Rosemary? I dialed the number listed, and when she answered, I could barely contain my amazement.

"Rosemary," I said, "how did you become an attorney?"

She laughed softly, her voice warm with familiarity. "Do you remember the word you gave me that day at my house?" she asked. "After you spoke it, something ignited in my heart—a desire to pursue law. I couldn't shake it. I applied to Regent University's School of Law, and four years later, I passed the bar and became a licensed attorney."

Her words left me in awe. What had seemed impossible that day in her living room had become a reality. God had planted a seed in her heart through the prophetic word, and Rosemary, like Mary, had responded with faith. ***"Be it unto me according to thy word"*** **(Luke 1:38 KJV).**

As Rosemary shared her journey, she explained how God had not only guided her to Regent University—a top-ranked Christian law school—but also equipped her to succeed. She later became a respected attorney, licensed in both Pennsylvania and Maryland. Her legal career blossomed, and she even served two years as a judge in Frederick County, Maryland. Rosemary's life became a testament to the faithfulness of Jesus and His ability to orchestrate His plans perfectly.

This story reminds me of the lepers in **Luke 17:12-14**. When Jesus encountered ten lepers, they cried out,

"Jesus, Master, have mercy on us." He didn't heal them instantly. Instead, He told them, *"Go shew yourselves unto the priests."* It was as they went in obedience to His word that they were cleansed. Rosemary's journey mirrors this principle. She stepped out in faith, acting on the word of the Lord, and as she moved forward, God fulfilled His promise.

Rosemary's testimony is a powerful reminder of the impact of the spoken word of God. *"So shall my word be that goeth forth out of my mouth: it shall not return unto me void, but it shall accomplish that which I please, and it shall prosper in the thing whereto I sent it"* **(Isaiah 55:11 KJV).** Her faith, combined with God's divine timing, brought about a transformation that continues to inspire everyone who hears her story.

Looking back, I marvel at how God orchestrates even the smallest details of our lives. Through obedience and faith, Rosemary walked into her destiny, proving once again that nothing is impossible with Jesus. Whether healing leprosy, fulfilling a prophetic word, or opening doors that seem permanently shut, He is faithful to do what He has promised.

Mike and His Three Sons: A Prophetic Word Fulfilled

Not long after Kathleen and I were married, a prophetic phrase began to come out of my mouth: *"Mike and his three sons."* I wasn't consciously saying it, yet it would slip into conversations repeatedly, almost like a divine echo. I wanted daughters as well, but those words—*"Mike and his three sons"*—seemed to carry a weight far beyond my own desires. Little did I know, God was planting a promise in my heart, one that would come to pass exactly as spoken.

In time, that prophecy unfolded perfectly. Our first son, Michael David Yeager, was born on May 3, 1981. Two years later, on December 15, 1983, our second son, Daniel Judson Yeager, arrived. Then, on August 3, 1986, our third son, Steven Joel Yeager, completed the trio. The words I had spoken without fully understanding were now my reality. God had given us three sons, and with them, a sense of divine purpose.

But God, in His goodness, wasn't done blessing us. He also gave us two daughters: Stephanie Joy, born on February 18, 1988—exactly 32 years after my own birth—and Naomi Rachel, born on February 16, 1996. Naomi was our precious gift for only a short while before she went home to be with the Lord in 2000. Her time with us was brief but deeply impactful, a reminder of the eternal hope we have in Jesus.

I still marvel at how God orchestrated the births of our children. I even had the privilege of delivering two of my sons, Daniel and Steven, because the midwife couldn't make it in time. Those moments were unforgettable, filled with awe at the miracle of life and the realization that God's hand was on each of them.

Before my children were even born, I knew in my heart that God had a purpose for their lives. I wasn't interested in forcing them into ministry or pushing them toward a specific calling, but I carried an unshakable confidence that they would be used mightily for the gospel. The scripture God impressed upon my heart was **Isaiah 59:21:** ***"As for me, this is my covenant with them, saith the Lord; My Spirit that is upon thee, and my words which I have put in thy mouth, shall not depart out of thy mouth, nor out of the mouth of thy seed, nor out of the mouth of thy seed's seed, saith the Lord, from henceforth and forever"*** **(KJV).**

From the day each of them was born, Kathleen and I made a deliberate choice to saturate their lives with the Word of God. In those days, it was common for families to rely on television to entertain their children, but we decided early on that this would not be the case in our home. The filth and corruption pouring out of the TV were not going to shape our children's minds. Instead, we invested in biblically sound teachings and wholesome entertainment—first on cassette tapes and VHS, and later on CDs and DVDs as technology advanced.

Our home was filled with the Word of God. Our children woke up to it, carried it with them throughout the day, and fell asleep to it at night. This intentional focus on scripture created an environment where the presence of Jesus was tangible and His truth became the foundation of their lives. As a result, we avoided many of the struggles that families face today. God's Word took root in their hearts, shaping their character and guiding their decisions.

The story of my children reminds me of the ten lepers healed by Jesus in **Luke 17:12-19.** All ten were cleansed as they obeyed His command to go show themselves to the priests, but only one returned to give thanks. Like that one, I find myself overwhelmed with gratitude for what the Lord has done. His promises are true, and His faithfulness endures. *"And whatsoever we ask, we receive of him, because we keep his commandments, and do those things that are pleasing in his sight"* **(1 John 3:22 KJV).**

Through the prophetic words He spoke and fulfilled, the Lord has shown me time and again that He is trustworthy. Whether it's the gift of three sons, the blessing of daughters, or the promise of generational faith, God is faithful to do what He has spoken. And for that, I give Him all the glory.

CHAPTER THREE
THE PROMISE, THE PROBLEM, AND THE PERFORMANCE: TRUSTING GOD'S PROCESS

Have you ever thought about how God sees you? Not as you are now, but as you're becoming? That's what makes His promises so powerful. Just before the coming of the Lord, He says His church will be *glorious*, *admirable*, and *magnificent*. It's hard to grasp sometimes, especially when we're caught in our struggles and shortcomings, but God is working on us, shaping us for His purpose.

A Glorious Church

Ephesians 5:27 (KJV) says Jesus is coming back for *"a glorious church, not having spot, or wrinkle, or any such thing; but that it should be holy and without blemish."* When we hear that, it's easy to think, *That's not me. I've got too many flaws.* But here's the truth: God isn't finished with us yet. He's less concerned with where you are now and more focused on what you're becoming.

The Promise and the Performance

Luke 1:45 (KJV) gives us a powerful reminder: *"And blessed is she that believed: for there shall be a performance of those things which were told her from the Lord."* Did you catch that? There *shall* be a performance of everything God has promised.

It's important to say this out loud sometimes, to remind yourself: *There shall be a performance of all the things God has promised me.* But here's the part we often overlook—between the promise and the performance, there's the problem.

The Problem: The Space Between

The space between what God promised and when it comes to pass is where patience is tested. This interval of time can feel like a wilderness, full of trials and unanswered questions. **Hebrews 10:36 (KJV)** tells us: *"For ye have need of patience, that, after ye have done the will of God, ye might receive the promise."*

Patience isn't easy. My grandmother used to say, *"Patience is a virtue, seldom found in women and never found in men."* That always got a laugh, but it's true—we all struggle with waiting on God.

Patience is about trust. It's knowing that even though you can't see it yet, God is faithful to complete what He started. Just as a farmer plants a seed and waits for the harvest, we must hold onto God's promises, trusting Him to bring them to fruition.

Jehovah: The Eternal God

Let's take a moment to think about the One who makes these promises. His name is Jehovah, derived from the Hebrew *YHVH*, which means *"the self-existing One."* **Revelation 1:8 (KJV)** declares: *"I am Alpha and Omega, the beginning and the ending, saith the Lord, which is, and which was, and which is to come, the Almighty."*

God doesn't operate within the constraints of time. He is eternal, without beginning or end. This means that when He makes a promise, it's already fulfilled in His eternal plan. We might be stuck in the *now*, but God sees the *then*.

From Promise to Glory

Think about the ten lepers Jesus healed in **Luke 17:12-14 (KJV).** They were outcasts, living in the "problem" of their disease. But Jesus gave them a promise: *"Go shew yourselves unto the priests."* It didn't make sense at first; they were still leprous when He spoke. But as they obeyed His word, they were cleansed. The promise led to the performance.

It's the same with us. God's word carries the power to fulfill itself, but we must trust Him in the waiting. **Philippians 1:6 (KJV)** reminds us: *"Being confident of this very thing, that he which hath begun a good work in you will perform it until the day of Jesus Christ."*

Embracing the Process

If we could fast-forward our lives to just before Jesus returns, imagine the transformation we'd see. We'd look back and realize that the trials, fears, and uncertainties were all part of the process. God was using them to shape us into the glorious, victorious people He's called us to be.

The next time you feel stuck between the promise and the performance, remember this: God is faithful. He's working on you, even when you can't see it. The waiting, the problem, and the patience—it's all part of His plan to bring you into the fullness of His promises.

So hold on to His word. Trust the process. And know that there *shall* be a performance of all He has promised. To Him be the glory forever and ever!

God Is Already There: Trusting the Eternal One in the Face of Uncertainty

Time is something we all wrestle with. We live in it, we're shaped by it, and we often feel trapped by its limits. Our lives are divided into three parts: the past, the present, and the future. The past feels familiar, filled with memories and moments we can reflect on. The present is tangible, something we engage with through our senses. But the future? That's the great unknown.

While the future may be closed to us, it's not closed to God. He's already there. **Isaiah 65:24 (KJV)** gives us this incredible promise: *"And it shall come to pass, that before they call, I will answer; and while they are yet speaking, I will hear."* God is eternal, unbound by time. He exists in the past, the present, and the future all at once, and that truth changes everything.

Facing Next Friday

I once heard a story about a man who went to his pastor in absolute despair. "Pastor," he said, "it's all over for me next Friday."

The pastor asked, "What do you mean it's all over for you?"

The man explained, "The factory I've worked at for 15 years is shutting down, and I'll be out of a job. I'm already two payments behind on my car, so I'm losing it next Friday. And I'm five payments behind on my house, so I'll lose that too. Next Friday, everything ends for me."

The pastor grabbed him by the shoulders and said, "Don't worry about next Friday. God is already there!"

I love that reminder. Whatever we're facing, whether it's next week's paycheck, next month's rent, or even next year's uncertainty—God is already there. He's gone ahead of us, working things out in ways we can't yet see.

A Word for Gideon

This is exactly what the angel of the Lord was trying to show Gideon. When the angel called him a *"mighty man of valour"* in **Judges 6:12 (KJV)**, Gideon didn't feel like one. He was still hiding, trying to scrape together a meal. But God wasn't speaking to who Gideon was at that moment—He was speaking to who Gideon was becoming.

In the same way, God sees beyond our current circumstances. He doesn't just see the struggle; He sees the victory He's already preparing.

Abraham's Impossible Promise

Think about Abraham. God promised him descendants as countless as the stars in the sky and the sand on the seashore. **Genesis 22:17 (KJV)** says: *"That in blessing I will bless thee, and in multiplying I will multiply thy seed as the stars of the heaven, and as the sand which is upon the sea shore."*

But let's not forget—when God made this promise, Abraham was nearly 100 years old and didn't have a single child. Can you imagine? God asks Abraham to count the stars, and Abraham likely thinks, *How can this be possible?* Yet, God's promises don't depend on our circumstances; they depend on His eternal power.

Just as Jesus healed the ten lepers in **Luke 17:12-14 (KJV)**—telling them to go show themselves to the priests before the healing even happened—God often gives us a word that requires faith before fulfillment.

Trusting God's Timing

The truth is, there's always an interval between the promise and its fulfillment. That's the place where we have to trust God the most. It's the space where doubt, fear, and impatience creep in. But **Psalm 37:25 (KJV)** reassures us: *"I have been young, and now am old; yet have I not seen the righteous forsaken, nor his seed begging bread."*

When you're tempted to worry about what's coming, remind yourself: God is already there. He's working in your future while you're still living in the present.

From Fear to Faith

Just like Gideon and Abraham, you might feel like the odds are stacked against you. You might feel unqualified, unprepared, or overwhelmed. But remember this: God doesn't call you based on where you are; He calls you based on where He's taking you.

Whatever your "next Friday" looks like, take heart. The same God who gave Abraham a son in his old age and turned Gideon into a mighty warrior is with you. Trust Him, obey His word, and walk in faith.

And don't forget: God is already there.

When God's Promise Seems Impossible: Trusting His Word Beyond Logic

Have you ever received a promise from God that seemed utterly ridiculous? So out of reach that it felt more like a joke than reality? That's exactly how Sarah felt when she overheard God telling Abraham he would be the father of many nations. She was 75 years old, well past the age of childbearing, and her response was laughter. **Genesis 18:12 (KJV)** says: *"Therefore Sarah laughed within herself, saying, After I am waxed old shall I have pleasure, my lord being old also?"*

You can almost hear her skepticism. It's as if she's saying, *Really, God? At my age?* But what Sarah didn't realize in that moment was that God specializes in making the impossible possible.

The Promise That Defied Nature

Abraham was 90 years old when God promised he would become the father of many nations. Sarah was 75, and her hope of having children had long since faded. Yet, God's word stood firm. **Genesis 18:14 (KJV)** gives us a powerful truth: *"Is any thing too hard for the Lord?"*

Even as Sarah doubted and laughed, God saw what they could not. His promise wasn't limited by their physical reality. He wasn't concerned with biology, time, or logic. He was—and is—God, the Creator of life itself.

A Modern Perspective

I remember ministering at a Christian fertility clinic in eastern Pennsylvania, run by Dr. William Cooper. It was fascinating to see the ways science and faith could intersect. My wife and I were there to minister to his staff, but he couldn't help explaining the process of in vitro fertilization.

At the time, I was 69, and my wife was 63. As he described how even we could potentially have a baby through the process, I looked at my wife, and she looked at me. We both had a moment of *Are we really into this?*

We laughed at the thought of making it into the Guinness Book of Records. Then my wife spoke up: *"I think I'll just stick to playing with my grandchildren."*

The whole experience gave me a small glimpse into what Abraham and Sarah might have felt. The idea of having a child at their age seemed absurd. And yet, God's promise wasn't dependent on their ability or understanding—it was dependent on His power.

God's Timing and Our Faith

God's promises often require us to stretch our faith. They push us beyond what we can see or comprehend. Abraham had to wait years before God's promise of a son was fulfilled. But **Romans 4:20-21 (KJV)** says: *"He **staggered not at the promise of God through unbelief; but was strong in faith, giving glory to God; And being*** *fully persuaded that, what he had promised, he was able also to perform."*

That's the kind of faith God calls us to—faith that doesn't waver, even when the circumstances seem impossible.

An Unexpected Encounter

I'll never forget a moment that reminded me of God's intentionality in the smallest of things. I was on a United commuter flight to San Francisco, sitting in seat 8D. The flight attendant was making her way down the aisle with a tray of orange juice, serving passengers with routine efficiency.

When she reached my row, she stopped and just stared at me. No expression, no words—just stared. At first, I was completely unsettled. My mind started racing: *Is my tie crooked? Do I have food stuck in my teeth? Is my hair a mess?*

The silence was deafening. It was one of those moments where you feel exposed, unsure of what's happening. But then she spoke.

God's Subtle Reminders

Her words weren't profound or lengthy, but they reminded me of something I often tell others: God is always working, even when we don't understand it. Just as He used a staring flight attendant to catch my attention, He uses the unexpected to draw us closer to Him.

Abraham and Sarah didn't understand how God would fulfill His promise. Sarah laughed, Abraham wondered, and yet God remained faithful. When Isaac was finally born, their laughter turned to joy. **Genesis 21:6 (KJV)** says: *"And Sarah said, God hath made me to laugh, so that all that hear will laugh with me."*

Trusting His Promise

God's promises may seem laughable at times, but they are always reliable. Whether it's a baby born to a 90-year-old father, lepers healed as they walked in obedience **(Luke 17:14 KJV),** or your own impossible situation, His word never fails.

So, the next time you feel like Sarah—doubting, laughing, or even dismissing what God has spoken—remember this: His promises don't depend on your ability; they depend on His faithfulness. And what He has promised, He is fully able to perform.

Trust Him. Even when it seems impossible, He's working it out in ways you can't imagine. *"Is any thing too hard for the Lord?"* The answer is always no.

Tears, Promises, and Salvation: Trusting God for a Family's Redemption

Sometimes, the most powerful reminders of God's faithfulness come in the simplest moments. Let me tell you about an encounter I had on a flight that brought me face-to-face with the incredible way God works through His promises—even when it feels like the waiting will never end.

An Unexpected Reminder

I was sitting on a commuter flight, minding my own business, when the flight attendant stopped dead in her tracks and just stared at me. No smile, no words—just a long, intimidating look. My mind raced. *Is my tie crooked? Are my shoes mismatched?* I even thought of a pastor I once knew who showed up to church with one blue shoe and one gray shoe. When the congregation laughed, he tried to save face by saying, "Don't worry, folks, I have another pair just like this at home!"

The flight attendant finally spoke: "I know you. You're Dick Mills."

She went on to explain how, six years earlier, I had ministered at her church, First Baptist Church in Benicia, California. She reminded me that I had given her five scriptures about her husband's salvation. At the time, her husband was living a wild and ungodly life. Their family was scandalized, their children embarrassed, and she was heartbroken.

"I want to tell you," she said, "those promises you gave me became my lifeline. For years, I bathed that piece of paper in tears. It was all I had when I felt like giving up.

But last October, my husband got saved! His conversion has been glorious!"

Her face lit up as she spoke, and then she added, "I still have that piece of paper in my bag. Would you like to see it?"

The Power of Promises

As she walked up the aisle to retrieve it, my mind drifted back to another encounter I had years ago at a gospel banquet in Pittsburgh. There was an Italian woman in a green dress seated at one of the tables. I felt the Lord prompting me to call her forward and declare, *"Instant salvation for every member of your family, right now!"*

When she came up, she explained her situation: she had 14 children, all rebellious, and a husband who was causing her endless grief. She was the only Christian in her family and felt utterly alone. I gave her a word from the Lord, along with a few scriptures, including **Luke 19:9 (KJV):** *"This day is salvation come to this house, forsomuch as he also is a son of Abraham."*

I'll never forget her face as she clung to that promise.

The Interval of Tears

What strikes me in both stories is the interval of waiting. Between the promise and the performance, there's often a season of tears. The flight attendant talked about how she would hear horror stories about her husband's behavior and wonder if the promise would ever come to pass. Yet, those scriptures became her anchor. She would read them, weep over them, and find fresh courage to keep believing.

Psalm 126:5-6 (KJV) says: *"They that sow in tears shall reap in joy. He that goeth forth and weepeth, bearing precious seed, shall doubtless come again with rejoicing, bringing his sheaves with him."*

God's promises are the precious seed we carry during the difficult seasons. We may cry as we wait, but His Word is unchanging, and the harvest is guaranteed.

A Word for You

Think about what happened in **Luke 19:9**. When Jesus declared, *"This day is salvation come to this house,"* it wasn't just a statement; it was a transformation. Zacchaeus, the man Jesus spoke to, was a tax collector—despised and corrupt. Yet, at Jesus' word, his life and household were forever changed.

Maybe you're like that flight attendant or the Italian woman in the green dress. You're holding onto a promise for a family member who seems far from salvation. You've prayed, you've cried, and you're wondering if it will ever happen. Let me encourage you: God's Word does not return void **(Isaiah 55:11, KJV)**.

If Jesus could heal the ten lepers in **Luke 17:12-14**, telling them to act on His word even before they saw evidence of healing, then He can certainly transform your situation. As they went, they were cleansed. As you continue to trust and pray, God is working behind the scenes.

The Paper in Her Bag

When the flight attendant returned with that tear-stained piece of paper, I was reminded of the faithfulness of God. Those scriptures had been her lifeline, and now, they were a testimony. Her husband's salvation wasn't just a personal victory—it was proof that God's promises are sure.

Closing Thoughts

God's promises are like seeds planted in the soil of our faith. They may take time to grow, and the waiting may bring tears, but the harvest is coming. If you're praying for a loved one's salvation, hold onto Luke 19:9: *"This day is salvation come to this house."*

Keep trusting, keep praying, and keep believing. Your tears are watering the seeds, and God is faithful to bring the harvest. To Him be all the glory!

From Dr Michael H Yeager
Stabbed in the Face with a knife Multiple Times by a demon possessed women!

This is an amazing story of divine deliverance but also of

answered Prayer. You will read about the husband who was married to this demon-possessed woman most of his life, crying out to God for her deliverance. What so strange is I do not BELIEVE the husband was even saved, and yet God heard his Prayers. Not only did she get delivered, but she was born again, and he was also.

An Evangelist shared how the Lord had laid upon his heart to go to Pennsylvania to open up an evangelistic outreach center in Mount Union, Pennsylvania. He invited me to go to Pennsylvania with him and his wife to open this evangelistic outreach.

I perceived in my heart that I needed to go with them. I planned to fly back to Wisconsin, where he and his wife would pick me up as they went through. However, before I left Alaska, the spirit of God had one more assignment for me: a precious demon-possessed woman needed to be set free and saved.

One Sunday, we decided to attend a small church along the road to Fairbanks. I was the first to enter this little, old, rustic church. When I went through the sanctuary doors, I immediately noticed a strange, little, elderly lady across from me - sitting in the pews.

She turned her head and stared right at me with the strangest look I had ever seen. I could sense immediately there was something demonic about her. Out of the blue, this little old lady jumped up, got out of the pew, and ran out of the church. At that moment, I perceived that God wanted me to go and cast the devils out of her.

When the service was over, I asked the pastor who that

elderly lady was. He said she was not a member of his church, but she came once in a great while. He also told me that she lived with her husband in a run-down house on a dirt road. I asked him if it would be okay to go and see her. (I knew in my heart that God had sent me there to help bring deliverance) He said he had no problems with this, especially since she wasn't a part of his church.

We followed the directions the pastor gave us, and when we arrived at the house, it was exactly as the pastor had described it to us. It was run-down, and the yard was overflowing with old furniture and household items. It reminded me of the TV show "Sanford and Son" - but it probably had ten-times more junk in the yard!

I do not know how the old couple survived the winters in Alaska in such a poorly built house. As we got out of the car, a little old man met us outside. It was her husband. He was thanking God as he walked toward us from his house. As he walked towards us with a loud excited voice, he said: **You are sent of God, and you are here to help my wife! I believe at that moment he saw the glory of God on us!**

When I heard him say this, I simply said yes, where is she? He pointed down this path going through all of the junk in the yard. He then informed us that his wife was in their summer kitchen.

So, we walked down this path, going past broken-down washing machines, dryers, and many other items that were just pure junk. We entered a block summer kitchen through a screen door that led into a room. When I entered the summer kitchen, I could see his wife was over at a large utility sink. Her back was to me, but I could see she was peeling carrots over her kitchen sink. What was extremely strange is that she was peeling the carrots with a huge, scary-looking butcher knife.

As I stood there, looking at the back of her head, I began to speak to her about Jesus. Out of the blue, she turned her head like it was on a swivel to look at me. I could hardly BELIEVE my eyes! It was like I was watching a horror movie! Not only did her head swivel on her body without her body turning, but this little lady's eyes were glowing a bright red.

I rubbed my eyes at that moment, thinking that I must be imagining this. I looked again, and No, I did not imagine this.... her head had swiveled - without her body moving - and her eyes were glowing red.

FEAR immediately filled my heart as she looked at me with the big knife ... a butcher's knife ... in her hand. Immediately, I came against the spirit of FEAR in my heart by quoting the Holy Scriptures: **"For God hath not given me the spirit of FEAR; but of power, and of love, and of a sound mind" 2 Timothy 1:7.**

I began to preach the gospel of Jesus Christ to her. Pastor than a natural human being could move, she swung her whole body around and ran at me. Her face was filled with great rage and hate. It was not a human face that I was looking at, but the devils. During this whole event, the evangelist is right behind me, watching this happen.

The knife was still in her right hand when she spun around and came at me. She leaped through the air when she was about 5 feet away from me. Her little body hit my body. At that very moment, she wrapped her small skinny legs around my waist.

It was a demonic power that enabled her to do that which is superhuman. With her legs tightly wrapped around my waist and her left hand grabbing the back of my she lifted her right hand and started hitting me in the face, very hard, fast, and multiple times. I could feel the pressure of her hitting me on the left side of my face.

As she was hitting me in the face, a divine unction rose in my heart, and out of my mouth came these words: "In the Name of Jesus!" I spoke this with great authority and power. It was not me but the Holy Ghost inside of me speaking out of my mouth.

The minute I came against this attack, **"In The Name of Jesus"** she was ripped off me, picked up by an invisible power, and flung across the room about 10-feet or more. She flew through the air. The Evangelist who was there can testify to this story! She slammed very hard against the bare block wall of her kitchen and slipped down to the floor.

Amazingly when she hit the wall, she was not hurt! I went over to her, continuing to cast the demons out of her In the Name of Jesus. Once I perceived that she was free and in her right mind, I lead her in a sinners Prayer. I then asked God to fill her with the Holy Ghost! God answered this Prayer right then and there. Her husband came into the kitchen, and we led him to the Lord and into the baptism of the Holy Ghost!

After all, was completed I asked her how she had become demon-possessed? She told us her terrible story.

Her uncle had repeatedly molested and raped her when she was a very young girl. She thought she was free from him when he got sick and died. But then he began to visit her from the dead, continuing to molest and rape her at night.

To her, it was physical and real. She did not know it was a familiar spirit disguised as her uncle. This had gone on for over fifty years! But now, sweet, beautiful peace had come upon her, completely changing her countenance.

She was a brand-new person in Christ, finally free - after almost fifty years of torment. She and her husband began to go to church with us - until I left Alaska. I remember that we took them to see a singing group called the Davis family at a local church, visiting Alaska on a missionary trip.

Years later, the evangelist who visited this lady with me heard me retelling the story at a church, about how the woman kept punching me forcefully with her right hand. At the end of the service, he came and informed me that I was not telling the story correctly. I wondered if he thought I was exaggerating. He said that he was standing behind me when she jumped on top of me and began to hit me with her right fist.

But he informed me, it wasn't her hand she was slapping me with, but she still had the large butcher's knife in her hand, and he saw her stabbing me in the face with this knife. Repeatedly! He said he knew that I was a dead man because nobody could survive being stabbed in the face repeatedly with a large butcher knife.

He expected to see nothing but blood, but instead of

seeing my blood everywhere, he saw that there was not even one mark on my face where the knife was hitting me. I did feel something hit my face repeatedly, but I thought it was her hand! Instead, it was her knife, and it could not pierce my skin! Thank God for God's love, His mercy, and His Supernatural Divine Protection.

I am convinced that if I had not been walking with God in His holiness and obedience with Gods Glory on me, the devil in that little old lady would have stabbed me to death. Many people in the body of Christ are trying to deal with demonic powers when they are out of the Father's will.

When we move in the Holy Ghost, obedience, and absolute love for Jesus Christ - no power in hell can hurt us!

My God hath sent his angel, and hath shut the lion's mouths, that they have not hurt me: forasmuch as before him innocence was found in me; and also before thee, O king, have I done no hurt (Daniel 6:22).

CHAPTER FOUR

The Power of a Word: Trusting God's Promises Through Time and Faith

Let me tell you about an Italian lady I'll never forget. She was one of those people whose faith could light up a room—or scorch it, depending on the circumstances. Her story is proof of how powerful a word from God can be, even when it seems impossible.

A Fiery Faith

After receiving a promise of salvation for her entire family, this lady didn't waste any time. She went straight home, lined her family up in the kitchen, and held up that piece of paper with the scriptures I had given her.

She didn't ask; she declared: *"You're all going to get saved. You might as well surrender now."*

One of her teenage kids, full of sass, asked, *"How do you know?"*

Her response was unwavering: *"Because I got a word, that's how."*

The next night, I was ministering at Jimmy Lyon's Full Gospel Chapel in Greencastle, and her husband came in with tears in his eyes. He threw his arms around me and said, *"She walked in, pronounced it, and it happened. I can't explain it, but she believed, and now we're all saved."*

Timing Is in God's Hands

Now, I can't tell you why her family saw their promise fulfilled in 24 hours while another woman waited years. I've seen situations like Mary's, where she received a word about carrying the Messiah, and nine months later, the promise was fulfilled.

Then there's Joseph, who had a vision at 18 while tending his father's sheep but didn't see it fulfilled until he was 30 and ruling in Egypt. Or Jesus Himself, who prophesied the destruction of Jerusalem in 35 AD, a word that wasn't fulfilled until 65 AD.

The truth is, God's timing doesn't always make sense to us. But whether it's quick or takes decades, His word never fails. Isaiah 55:11 (KJV) promises: *"So shall my word be that goeth forth out of my mouth: it shall not return unto me void, but it shall accomplish that which I please, and it shall prosper in the thing whereto I sent it."*

The Fulfillment of Promises

One thing I've learned is that all promises from God are conditional—not in a legalistic way, but in the sense that they require faith and trust. Hebrews 11:6 (KJV) reminds us: *"But without faith it is impossible to please him: for he that cometh to God must believe that he is, and that he is a rewarder of them that diligently seek him."*

What's fascinating is how faith manifests differently in each person. The Italian woman took a bold, no-nonsense approach, while others may quietly hold onto their promise for years, praying and trusting in God's perfect timing.

God's Timing, Not Formulas

I've seen people try to box God into formulas: *If you do this, then God will do that.* But God isn't a vending machine. He's the Creator of the universe, and His ways are higher than ours.

When the ten lepers came to Jesus in Luke 17:12-14 (KJV), He told them to go show themselves to the priests. They weren't healed right away, but *"as they went, they were cleansed."* The timing of their healing required obedience and faith.

The same is true for us. Sometimes the promise unfolds as we take each step in faith, trusting God with the outcome.

Trusting Beyond Understanding

I've learned to take my hands off the process and simply trust God. When He gives a promise, I hold onto it, knowing it will be fulfilled in His way and in His time.

Just like the Italian woman who saw her family saved in a single day, or Joseph who waited years for his dream to come to pass, every fulfillment is a testimony to God's faithfulness.

If you're holding onto a promise today, remember this: God's word is true, His timing is perfect, and He is always working behind the scenes. As 2 Corinthians 1:20 (KJV) says: *"For all the promises of God in him are yea, and in him Amen, unto the glory of God by us."*

So don't give up. Whether the fulfillment comes in 24 hours or 24 years, trust that God's word will accomplish exactly what He said it would. Let Him write the story, and you'll see His glory in ways you never imagined. To Him be all the praise!

One by One: Trusting God's Promise for Your Family

I'll never forget the time I was ministering in Milwaukee at a Catholic church that had recently experienced the outpouring of the Holy Spirit. It was one of those beautiful moments where you could feel God's presence filling every corner of the sanctuary. As I stood there, I noticed a woman in the congregation and felt the Lord urging me to call her out.

When she came forward, she looked at me with eyes full of hope and said, "I have 12 kids. The youngest is three, and the oldest is 21. Will they ever come to know Jesus?"

I didn't have an exact timeline to give her, but I knew God's promise was sure. So I told her, *"All 12 of them may not come in at once, but they will come in one by one."* I handed her my address and encouraged her to keep me updated.

The Power of a Promise

Over the next seven years, I received cards from her regularly. Each time one of her children gave their life to Christ, she'd write to tell me. Finally, in the seventh year, she wrote, *"The last one is in! Not only that, but they're full of the Holy Ghost and heading into ministry."*

What a testimony! That mother held onto God's word, trusting that He would bring it to pass.

God's Faithfulness Is Unchanging

There's something deeply comforting about the promises of God. Numbers 23:19 (KJV) assures us: *"God is not a man, that he should lie; neither the son of man, that he should repent: hath he said, and shall he not do it? or hath he spoken, and shall he not make it good?"*

When God gives a promise, you can bank on it. It doesn't matter how long it takes or how impossible it seems—His word is true.

Waiting for the Fulfillment

Between the promise and its fulfillment, there's often a period of waiting. It's not easy, but Habakkuk 2:3 (KJV) gives us this encouragement: *"For the vision is yet for an appointed time, but at the end it shall speak, and not lie: though it tarry, wait for it; because it will surely come, it will not tarry."*

I've seen families wait for years, praying and believing for their loved ones to come to Christ. It's not a passive waiting; it's active, filled with prayer, faith, and expectation. This mother in Milwaukee didn't sit idly by—she prayed over the promises of God and trusted in His timing.

Claiming the Word

One of the most powerful things we can do as believers is to claim God's promises for ourselves. Ezekiel 12:28 (KJV) declares: *"Therefore say unto them, Thus saith the Lord God; There shall none of my words be prolonged any more, but the word which I have spoken shall be done, saith the Lord God."*

When you hear a promise in Scripture or receive a word from the Lord, take hold of it. Isaiah 27:5 (KJV) says: *"Let him take hold of my strength, that he may make peace with me; and he shall make peace with me."*

It's as simple as saying, *"Lord, I'll take it."* When a verse speaks to your heart, claim it in faith and trust God to fulfill it.

Releasing the Word

As I ministered that night in Milwaukee, I encouraged the congregation to release words of faith, wisdom, healing, and love over one another. We prayed together, declaring in the name of Jesus that God's promises would come to pass.

Holding up my Bible, I reminded them, *"When you hear a promise that speaks to you, claim it for yourself. Say, 'I'll take it.'"* It's a small act of faith, but it can move mountains.

The Fulfillment Is Coming

If you're waiting on a promise from God—whether it's for your family, your health, or another area of your life—remember this: God's timing is perfect. He sees the end from the beginning, and He is faithful to bring His word to pass.

Just like the lepers in Luke 17:12-14 (KJV), who were healed *"as they went,"* the fulfillment of your promise may unfold step by step. Keep walking in faith, trusting that God is working behind the scenes.

A Word for You

Take courage from that mother's story in Milwaukee. She didn't see all 12 of her children saved overnight, but one by one, God brought them into His kingdom. If He did it for her, He can do it for you.

Hold onto His promises, pray without ceasing, and declare His word over your situation. Say it with me: *"There will be a performance of those things promised me by the Lord."* And when He fulfills it, you'll have a testimony that points back to His faithfulness and glory.

To God be the glory for the great things He has done and will do!

Rejuvenation and Restoration: Becoming a Joy Bringer in God's Kingdom

The Lord gave me a word one day, and it wasn't just for a single person—it was for all of us. It was about *rejuvenation*, not some return to a second childhood, but a renewal of strength, vitality, and purpose. It's something I believe every believer can claim because it's rooted in God's Word, and His promises are true.

Renewed Like the Eagle

Take **Psalm 103:5 (KJV):** *"Who satisfieth thy mouth with good things; so that thy youth is renewed like the eagle's."* That's a promise you can grab hold of. Picture the majestic eagle soaring high, strong and untethered, renewed by the winds beneath its wings. That's what God promises us—strength and renewal, no matter our age or circumstance.

Isaiah 40:31 (KJV) echoes this truth: *"But they that wait upon the Lord shall renew their strength; they shall mount up with wings as eagles; they shall run, and not be weary; and they shall walk, and not faint."* It's not about sitting in a rocking chair, clipping coupons, and waiting for life to pass you by. It's about claiming mountains, walking boldly in faith, and fulfilling the purpose God has placed on your life.

I told this to a dear doctor one day, and he received it wholeheartedly. I could see the fire in his eyes as he embraced the word that his youth would be renewed like the eagle's. He wasn't ready to retire—he was ready to re-fire!

Fresher Than a Child's

Another scripture that stands out is **Job 33:25 (KJV):** *"His flesh shall be fresher than a child's: he shall return to the days of his youth."* Dermatologists might talk about the purity of a baby's skin, but this promise goes deeper. It's about restoration, not just of the body but of the spirit. It's a return to the vigor of youth—a supernatural rejuvenation that comes from God alone.

When I shared this, I asked the crowd, *"How many of you will take this promise for yourself?"* Hands shot up across the room. It's a simple act of faith: when you hear a word from God, you claim it.

A Vision of Freedom

I remember speaking to a woman named Dotie. The Lord gave me a vision for her life—a picture of the impact she would have.

In the vision, she was standing in a dark room filled with professional women—secretaries, office managers, and executive assistants. These women were sitting in a circle, their hands bound with chains, weighed down by their struggles. They were bitter, complaining about their broken marriages, unfulfilled lives, and deep dissatisfaction.

Then Dotie walked in, and the atmosphere shifted. She boldly declared, *"I've come in the name of the Lord."* At her words, the lights came on, and the chains fell off their hands. She began to tell them the good news of Jesus, the kind that sets souls free.

As she spoke, they raised their hands in reverence and submission to God. The Holy Spirit fell upon them, filling their hearts and transforming their lives. Women who had never experienced joy were suddenly filled with it, and it was all because Dotie had been obedient to the Lord's call.

A Joy Bringer

The word I received for Dotie was that she would be a *joy bringer*—someone who carries the light of Christ into the darkest places and restores hope to those who have never known anything good.

This is what God calls us all to do in our unique ways. Whether it's speaking life into someone's broken marriage, bringing healing to the wounded, or sharing the gospel with those in bondage, we are called to be carriers of His joy.

The Good News That Breaks Chains

Jesus demonstrated this when He healed the ten lepers in **Luke 17:12-14 (KJV)**. These men were outcasts, living in isolation and despair. But Jesus didn't just see their condition—He spoke into their future. He told them to go show themselves to the priests, and *"as they went, they were cleansed."*

The chains of leprosy fell away, just as the chains in Dotie's vision fell off those women. It's a powerful reminder that the Word of God doesn't just inform—it transforms.

Claiming the Promises

If there's one thing I've learned, it's this: when you hear a promise from God, you don't sit back and wonder if it's for you—you claim it. **Isaiah 27:5 (KJV)** says: *"Let him take hold of my strength, that he may make peace with me; and he shall make peace with me."*

So take hold of His strength. Declare, *"I'll take it!"* Whether it's rejuvenation, healing, or the restoration of joy, God's promises are yours for the taking.

Closing Thoughts

Dotie's story is a reminder that God calls each of us to be joy bringers in our own way. Whether it's through a word of wisdom, a word of faith, or simply living out His love, we have the power to make an eternal impact.

And don't forget: His promises are not delayed. **Ezekiel 12:28 (KJV)** assures us: *"There shall none of my words be prolonged any more, but the word which I have spoken shall be done."*

So stand on His Word, trust His timing, and let Him use you to bring light, freedom, and joy to a world in need. To God be the glory!

Beauty for Ashes: Becoming a Joy Bringer in the Kingdom of God

Have you ever met someone who's given life their best shot only to feel like everything went up in smoke? I've encountered so many people who sit in the ashes of their dreams, full of bitterness and regret, wondering if there's any hope left.

One young lady came to me with a story like that. She said, *"I got married, gave it my all, and now I'm left with* nothing but ashes. I'm broken, bitter, and I don't know how to move forward."

As she spoke, the Lord gave me a word for her. I looked at her and said, *"Isaiah 61:3 tells us that God gives beauty for ashes, the oil of joy for mourning, and the garment of praise for the spirit of heaviness."*

She paused, her eyes filling with tears. It wasn't just words—it was a promise that her story wasn't over.

Joy in the Midst of Mourning

God specializes in turning mourning into joy. **Psalm 30:11-12 (KJV)** says: *"Thou hast turned for me my mourning into dancing: thou hast put off my sackcloth, and girded me with gladness; To the end that my glory may sing praise to thee, and not be silent. O Lord my God, I will give thanks unto thee for ever."*

I shared this scripture with her, and I could see hope start to flicker in her heart. She didn't need to stay in those ashes forever. God was ready to lift her out, to replace her mourning with dancing and her bitterness with gladness.

I told her, *"The Lord has called you to be a joy bringer. Imagine going through life bringing joy to people who feel like they have nothing left."*

Joy to the Frozen Chosen

The Lord then gave me a picture of her ministering to people who seemed to have it all together on the outside but were empty on the inside—religious people who had a form of godliness but lacked the life of the Spirit.

I told her, *"You'll be called to go into formal churches, places where the fire has gone out, and bring the good news of Jesus. You'll bring the joy of the Lord to people who have been stuck in tradition, frozen in routine."*

I laughed and added, *"If you get a call from the 'First Church of the Frigidaire,' don't say no! Go down there, bring the fire of the Holy Ghost, melt the icicles, and warm the people up. Get those frozen chosen on fire for God!"*

Isaiah 58:12 (KJV) describes this kind of ministry: **"And they that shall be of thee shall build the old waste places: thou shalt raise up the foundations of many generations; and thou shalt be called, The repairer of the breach, The restorer of paths to dwell in."**

What an incredible calling—to rebuild, restore, and bring life where there's been nothing but waste and ruin.

From Dr Michael H Yeager

Snatched from the Flames: A Family's Redemption

It was a typical Sunday morning when Mary, one of the mothers in our church, came forward for prayer. As she stood before me, her face reflected a mix of hope and desperation. She had been interceding for her family for years, and that day, the Spirit of the Lord moved mightily. As I laid hands on her, a prophetic word came forth, clear and undeniable: *"All your children will be saved, and your husband too. But he will be as one snatched from the flames of hell."*

Mary wept as the words took root in her heart, though at the time, none of us knew the full extent of what God was setting in motion. Years passed before the prophecy began to unfold, but when it did, it became a testimony of the faithfulness of Jesus and the power of persistent prayer.

Mary's Testimony

A Husband Saved at the Brink of Eternity
"My name is Mary J. Rockwell," she later recounted. "When Pastor Mike prayed over me that morning, he said, 'Your prayers have reached the throne room of heaven. You will live to see all your children serve the Lord, and your husband will be saved, but it will happen at the very end.' At the time, I clung to those words, even though my husband seemed so far from salvation.

"Years later, my husband, at age seventy-two, was diagnosed with cancer caused by exposure to chemicals during his service in the Marines in Vietnam. I had assumed he knew the Lord, but as he lay on his deathbed, it became clear that he did not. I told him, 'I could lay hands on you until you're bald, but you need to cry out to Jesus for yourself.' Yet he couldn't even say the name Jesus—it was as though something was blocking him. I recognized it as a demonic stronghold.

"I called a local pastor to pray with him. The pastor helped him see that his understanding of salvation was incorrect. Soon after, my husband called me, his voice trembling with emotion. He said, 'I've received Jesus Christ as my Lord and Savior.' His only regret was that he hadn't done more for the Lord during his life. Not long after, he slipped into eternity. It was exactly as Pastor Mike had prophesied—he was snatched from the flames at the very end. Three people who had been present when Pastor Mike prayed for me years earlier called me, reminding me of the prophecy and asking if my husband had been saved. I told them it was just as spoken."

Healing for a Mother in a Coma

Mary also shared another miraculous encounter. "Years ago, my mother was critically ill and in a coma in a hospital in New York. Pastor Mike prayed over me before I left Maryland and told me to lay hands on her and declare, 'I command all tormenting mental spirits to leave her now in Jesus' name.'

"When I arrived, her condition was dire. The doctors had given up hope, and my sister was already making funeral arrangements. I waited until the room cleared, pulled the curtain around us, and did exactly as Pastor Mike instructed. As I clapped my hands and declared, 'Now,' I felt a surge of power flow through me. By the next morning, the IVs were removed, the swelling in her face was gone, and she was sitting up, eating breakfast. The doctors were astonished. She was discharged that very day and went on to live several more years."

Children Coming to Christ

"Pastor Mike's words about my children also continue to unfold. At the time of the prophecy, I had four children, and I have already seen two of them come to know the Lord. I hold fast to the promise that all four will serve Him before my time on this earth is done."

God's Faithfulness in Prophecy

Mary's story is a powerful reminder of God's ability to fulfill His promises, no matter how impossible the circumstances may seem. Her husband's salvation mirrors the words of Jude 1:23, *"And others save with fear, pulling them out of the fire; hating even the garment spotted by the flesh"* (KJV). God's mercy reached him at the final moment, showing that no one is beyond the reach of His grace.

Her mother's miraculous healing echoes the power of Jesus when He healed the lepers in Luke 17:14. Jesus told them to go show themselves to the priests, and as they obeyed, they were cleansed. Likewise, Mary's obedience to speak the word of God over her mother brought about a divine intervention.

Persevering in Prayer

Mary's unwavering faith demonstrates the importance of persevering in prayer and trusting in God's timing. Her story reminds us of **Isaiah 55:11,** *"So shall my word be that goeth forth out of my mouth: it shall not return unto me void, but it shall accomplish that which I please, and it shall prosper in the thing whereto I sent it"* **(KJV).**

The same Jesus who healed lepers, saved Mary's husband, and restored her mother is still working miracles today. Mary's testimony stands as a testament to the power of prayer, prophecy, and the unwavering love of Christ for every soul. For those who are praying for loved ones, take heart. The same God who fulfilled His promise to Mary will fulfill His promises to you.

CHAPTER FIVE
A Glory Yet to Come

As we talked, I reminded her that her life wasn't over. Far from it. **Haggai 2:9 (KJV)** promises: *"The glory of this latter house shall be greater than of the former, saith the Lord of hosts: and in this place will I give peace."*

I told her, *"The glory of your latter days will exceed anything you've experienced before. There are unfulfilled tasks in your life, things yet to be done, and God is going to complete the work He started in you."*

Bringing Beauty to Broken Places

This young woman's story reminds me of how Jesus ministered to the brokenhearted and outcasts. **In Luke 17:12-14 (KJV),** ten lepers came to Jesus for healing. They were outcasts, living in the ashes of their disease and rejection. But Jesus didn't just see their condition—He saw their potential. He told them to go show themselves to the priests, and as they went, they were cleansed.

The same Jesus who healed the lepers is still in the business of bringing beauty for ashes. Whether you're the one sitting in the ashes or the one called to minister to others, His power to restore and renew is limitless.

Claiming the Promise

If you're feeling stuck in a season of ashes, claim the promise of **Isaiah 61:3**. Say it out loud: *"Lord, I receive Your beauty for my ashes, Your joy for my mourning, and Your garment of praise for my spirit of heaviness."*

And if you feel the Lord calling you to be a joy bringer, don't hold back. Whether it's in formal churches, your community, or your own family, step out in faith and let Him use you to bring His joy to a hurting world.

A Prayer for Joy

As we closed that conversation, I asked her—and others in the room—to hold hands and pray together. We declared:

"In the name of Jesus, we release the oil of joy, the garment of praise, and the fire of the Holy Spirit. Lord, make us joy bringers to a world in need, and help us rebuild the broken places for Your glory."

If you're reading this, I want to encourage you: God is not done with you yet. Whether you're rebuilding from ashes or bringing joy to others, His glory will shine through your life. Trust Him, step into your calling, and watch Him do what only He can do.

To God be the glory for the beauty He brings from ashes!

Guided by the Word and Spirit: A Prophetic Word for the Next Generation

Praise the Lord! There's something powerful about seeing the Lord's hand on someone's life, especially when He begins to reveal His plans for them. I recently had the privilege of ministering to two young men, Jonathan and Benjamin, and the words God gave for them were so encouraging that I believe they can inspire all of us.

A Word for Benjamin

Benjamin stood first, and as I looked at him, the Lord brought **Isaiah 45:2-3 (KJV)** to mind: *"I will go before thee, and make the crooked places straight: I will break in pieces the gates of brass, and cut in sunder the bars of iron: And I will give thee the treasures of darkness, and hidden riches of secret places."*

I shared with him, *"Benjamin, the Lord has His hand on you, and He's already preparing the way. By the time you step into the place God has called you to, everything will be ready. The crooked paths will be made straight, the obstacles will be removed, and the resources you need will be waiting for you."*

The Lord showed me that Benjamin wouldn't need to go forward in fear or compulsion. **Isaiah 52:12 (KJV)** says: *"For ye shall not go out with haste, nor go by flight: for the Lord will go before you; and the God of Israel will be your rereward."* I explained, *"Benjamin, everywhere you go, you'll feel the momentum of God's presence carrying you forward. He'll be both your advance guard and your rear guard."*

Then came **Isaiah 55:12 (KJV):** *"For ye shall go out with joy, and be led forth with peace: the mountains and the hills shall break forth before you into singing, and all the trees of the field shall clap their hands."* I told him, *"Benjamin, your journey will be marked by joy and peace. Even creation will seem to rejoice with you as you walk in God's purpose."*

I couldn't help but smile as I added, *"I don't know where God is sending you, but I know it won't be West Texas!"*

The first two letters in the word *gospel* are *go,* and I reminded him that the gospel compels us to move. *"Take the 'go' out of the gospel,"* I said, *"and all you're left with is standing around having a spell. But Benjamin, you're called to go—and the Lord is going with you."*

A Word for Jonathan

Next, I turned to Jonathan. For him, the Lord impressed **Isaiah 30:21 (KJV):** *"And thine ears shall hear a word behind thee, saying, This is the way, walk ye in it, when ye turn to the right hand, and when ye turn to the left."* I told him, *"Jonathan, the Lord will guide you with* *clarity. When you're unsure which way to go, His voice will be there, directing your steps."*

Job 33:14-16 (KJV) also came to mind: ***"For God speaketh once, yea twice, yet man perceiveth it not. In a dream, in a vision of the night, when deep sleep falleth upon men, in slumberings upon the bed; Then he openeth the ears of men, and sealeth their instruction."***

I shared, *"Jonathan, the Lord will speak to you in ways that may surprise you—through dreams, visions, and the whispers of His Spirit. Be attentive, because He's always speaking."*

Isaiah 58:11 (KJV) gave further confirmation: ***"And the Lord shall guide thee continually, and satisfy thy soul in drought, and make fat thy bones: and thou shalt be like a watered garden, and like a spring of water, whose waters fail not."*** I told him, *"Jonathan, the Lord's guidance won't just be occasional—it will be continual. He'll sustain you in every season, even in times of drought, and you'll become a source of life and refreshment for others."*

The Two Witnesses

The Lord also gave a word about how He leads us: through the Word and the Spirit. **Isaiah 8:20 (KJV)** says: ***"To the law and to the testimony: if they speak not according to this word, it is because there is no light in them."***

I explained, *"Jonathan, these are your two safeguards. Every direction you receive will be confirmed by the Word of God and the testimony of the Holy Spirit. If the two don't align, it's not from Him. But when the Word and the Spirit agree, you can step forward with confidence, knowing you're walking in God's will."*

A Calling for All of Us

As I ministered to Benjamin and Jonathan, I realized their words weren't just for them—they were for all of us. Whether we're called to go out with joy, like Benjamin, or to receive continuous guidance, like Jonathan, the Lord's promises remain the same: He will go before us, He will guide us, and He will equip us for the journey ahead.

Trusting His Word

Just like the ten lepers in **Luke 17:12-14 (KJV),** who were healed as they obeyed Jesus' instruction to show themselves to the priests, we must trust the Word of the Lord even when we don't see the outcome yet. The lepers didn't wait for their healing to appear—they walked in obedience, and as they went, they were cleansed.

Benjamin and Jonathan's stories remind us to trust God's Word and Spirit to lead us, to prepare the way, and to sustain us. Wherever He calls us, He goes with us, ensuring that His plans for us will succeed.

So, whether you're like Benjamin, ready to go with joy, or like Jonathan, seeking continual guidance, remember: the Lord's promises are true, and He will never fail you. Let His Word and Spirit lead you every step of the way. To Him be the glory!

Guided by Confirmation: Building a Home Filled with God's Presence

Mistakes often come from impulsive decisions—acting on an impression without waiting for confirmation. I've seen it time and again. Someone rushes forward because they felt an urgency, but they didn't pause to seek clarity or wisdom. The Bible makes it clear that guidance from the Lord comes with confirmation. It's not doubt to wait; it's wisdom.

Isaiah 28:16 (KJV) says, *"He that believeth shall not make haste."* And **Isaiah 1:18** reminds us of God's approach: *"Come now, and let us reason together."* These verses teach us that the Lord doesn't rush us into decisions. Instead, He provides clear guidance—often more than once.

The Wisdom of Confirmation

When you feel led to act, seek God's confirmation. **Proverbs 1:23 (KJV)** says, *"Turn you at my reproof: behold, I will pour out my spirit unto you, I will make known my words unto you."* God's Spirit and His Word always work together to provide clarity. **Isaiah 59:21 (KJV)** reaffirms this: *"My spirit that is upon thee, and my words which I have put in thy mouth, shall not depart."*

Jesus Himself emphasized the power of His words, saying in **John 6:63 (KJV),** *"The words that I speak unto you, they are spirit, and they are life."* When we seek confirmation through the Word and the Spirit, we can move forward in confidence, knowing that our steps are guided by Him.

A Word for Jonathan and Benjamin

I recently ministered to two young men, Jonathan and Benjamin. As I shared with them, I declared that they would be *"full of the Spirit"* and *"full of the Word,"* and that their lives would be marked by balance. **Ephesians 6:17 (KJV)** reminds us to *"take the sword of the Spirit, which is the word of God."* And **Acts 10:44 (KJV)** gives us a beautiful picture: *"While Peter yet spake these words, the Holy Ghost fell on all them which heard the word."*

To Jonathan and Benjamin, I said, *"The Word and the Spirit will always guide you in harmony, ensuring that your steps are sure and your path is clear."*

A Word for Joe and Judy

Then I turned to a couple named Joe and Judy. The Lord gave me a powerful word for their home, one that I believe can resonate with all of us.

John 12:32 (KJV) says, *"And I, if I be lifted up from the earth, will draw all men unto me."* I told them, *"In your marriage, your conduct, your lifestyle, and your home, Christ will be lifted up. He will draw people to you—not because of what you do, but because of who He is in you."*

Proverbs 3:33 (KJV) adds: *"The curse of the Lord is in the house of the wicked: but he blesseth the habitation of the just."* I encouraged Joe and Judy to expect a special blessing on their home, one that would make it a beacon of light in their neighborhood.

People Will Be Drawn

I asked them, *"Have you ever wondered how the animals came to Noah's ark?"* **Genesis 49:10 (KJV)** gives us the answer: *"The sceptre shall not depart from Judah, nor a lawgiver from between his feet, until Shiloh come; and unto him shall the gathering of the people be."* Just as the animals were drawn by the Spirit of God, so will people be drawn to your home when Christ is enthroned in your hearts.

I jokingly added, *"Judy, you might want to dust off Betty Crocker's cookbook because you're going to be doing a lot of entertaining! People will come from all directions, like a 360-degree compass, to find the love and light in your home."*

A Home Filled with God's Presence

Psalm 142:7 (KJV) speaks of God's daily renewal: *"Bring my soul out of prison, that I may praise thy name: the righteous shall compass me about; for thou shalt deal bountifully with me."* I declared over their home that every day would bring a fresh infilling of the Holy Spirit, making their house a place of joy, peace, and the presence of the Lord.

Job 11:18-19 (KJV) paints a beautiful picture of what their home would be like: *"And thou shalt be secure, because there is hope; yea, thou shalt dig about thee, and thou shalt take thy rest in safety. Also thou shalt lie down, and none shall make thee afraid; yea, many shall make suit unto thee."*

I told them, *"Your home will be filled with love, laughter, light, and the Lord. It will be a refuge for those seeking hope and a sanctuary for those in need of His presence."*

A Word for All of Us

As I ministered to Joe and Judy, I could see how their word could apply to everyone. Who doesn't want a home filled with the Spirit, guided by the Word, and overflowing with love and joy?

If that's your desire, claim these promises for yourself. Say, *"I'll take that!"*

Remember, the Lord's guidance always comes with confirmation. He won't rush you into mistakes. Instead, He invites you to seek Him, to be led by His Word and Spirit, and to create a life and home that glorify Him.

To God be the glory for the beautiful things He's doing in our lives and homes!

A Home of Glory: How God Uses Your Life and Marriage for Evangelism

Sometimes, the Lord gives us a vision of what He wants to do through our homes, our marriages, and even our struggles. I was ministering recently, and the Lord gave me a word so full of hope and promise that it felt like it wasn't just for the couple standing before me—it was for all of us.

A Home That Draws Others

The Bible tells us in **Proverbs 3:33 (KJV):** *"The curse of the Lord is in the house of the wicked: but he blesseth the habitation of the just."* I shared with the couple, *"There's a cloud of glory over your home—a canopy of blessing, just as **Isaiah 4:5 (KJV)** describes. It's not just a house; it's a beacon, a signal to everyone in your neighborhood that there's a King living here, and His name is Jesus."*

This isn't about just surviving life in a subdivision or being another household on the block. No, God has bigger plans. I told them, *"Your home is going to be a missionary outpost, an evangelistic center, and a place of refuge for those seeking hope. People are going to come to you—not because you're chasing them, but because the Holy Spirit is drawing them."*

That's the beauty of how God works. He turns ordinary places—our homes, our kitchens, our living rooms—into extraordinary places of ministry.

A Marriage That Preaches

I told them something I firmly believe: *"Your marriage is going to be a tool for evangelism."* When people see the love of Christ reflected in your relationship, it becomes a testimony. **John 12:32 (KJV) says:** ***"And I, if I be lifted up from the earth, will draw all men unto me."***

I explained, *"Your marriage is lifting up Jesus, and it's drawing people to Him. That's the kind of home the Lord is building—a place where people can knock on the door and meet the King."*

Strength in the Struggle

The last three and a half years had been difficult for this couple. I felt the need to speak to their challenges, to interpret their experiences through the lens of God's purpose. Philippians 1:12 (KJV) came to mind: *"But I would ye should understand, brethren, that the things* which happened unto me have fallen out rather unto the furtherance of the gospel."

I told them, *"The struggles you've faced weren't random. Satan's been throwing everything he has at you, trying to knock you out of the game. But God has used every attack to strengthen your faith, deepen your determination, and give you clarity about the future."*

Exodus 1:12 (KJV) paints a beautiful picture of this principle: **"But the more they afflicted them, the more they multiplied and grew."** I shared with them, *"Every time the enemy has fought against you, God has turned it around for your good. Your faith is stronger now than it was three and a half years ago, and your relationship is closer than ever. What Satan meant to divide, God has welded together."*

Healing from Painful Relationships

Not every struggle comes from outside attacks. Sometimes, the wounds come from within our circle—from relationships that let us down or promises that were never kept.

I felt led to speak about a specific relationship from their past. *"About three years ago,"* I said, *"someone made promises to you that were never fulfilled. Two years ago, you realized those promises weren't going to happen, and it's consumed your time, energy, and resources."*

Psalm 66:12 (KJV) came to mind: **"Thou hast caused men to ride over our heads; we went through fire and**

through water: but thou broughtest us out into a wealthy place."

I reassured them, *"God is bringing you out of that painful season. He's restoring what was lost, and He's freeing you to step fully into what He's called you to do. That chapter is over, and the Lord is leading you into a new season of purpose and joy."*

A Word for All of Us

As I ministered to this couple, I couldn't help but feel that their story is a word for all of us. Whether you're navigating challenges in your marriage, waiting for God to fulfill a promise, or healing from disappointment, His plans for you are good.

Isaiah 4:5 reminds us that His glory rests over our homes like a canopy. **Proverbs 3:33** assures us that His blessing is upon the habitation of the just. And **Exodus 1:12** promises that every attack of the enemy will only serve to strengthen and multiply what God is doing in your life.

Claiming the Promise

If you want this for your home, your marriage, your life, simply say, *"I'll take that!"* Declare it over your family: *"Our home will be a place of love, light, laughter, and the Lord. It will be a refuge, a beacon, and a testimony to God's goodness."*

And remember this: God doesn't waste your struggles. Every trial, every setback, and every disappointment is being used to prepare you for what's ahead. Trust Him, lift Him up, and let Him use your life to draw others to Himself.

To God be the glory for the incredible things He's doing in our homes and hearts!

From Dr Michael H Yeager

Pamela Healed of TMJ: A Testimony of God's Power

It was a typical day at our church when the Spirit of the Lord stirred within me in a way I've come to recognize. I had just finished delivering the message, and as I prepared to wrap up the service, the Lord interrupted my thoughts with a clear instruction: *"Call for Pamela Flickinger."*

Pamela was working with the children's church that day, so I asked someone to fetch her. I wasn't sure why the Lord had impressed her name upon my heart, but I've learned to trust His leadership without question. Moments later, Pamela walked into the sanctuary, looking a little puzzled as she approached the front.

As she stood before me, the word of knowledge came to me. I looked at her and said, "Pamela, you have TMJ." I had no natural way of knowing this, but the Lord revealed it to me in that moment. For those unfamiliar, TMJ—or temporomandibular joint disorder—affects the jaw joint and can cause significant pain and discomfort.

The jaw struggles to move freely, and even basic actions like chewing or speaking can become excruciating.

Pamela's eyes widened slightly, but before she could respond, I added, "I'm going to pray for you, and in three days, it will be completely gone and never come back."

With that, I laid my hands on her and prayed. I commanded the TMJ to leave her body in the name of Jesus, declaring healing over her jaw and muscles. The presence of the Lord was tangible, but Pamela simply nodded and returned to the children's ministry after the prayer.

I didn't think much about it after that day. To be honest, it completely slipped my mind over the years. But God doesn't forget His promises or the words He speaks.

Years later, Pamela and I were catching up, and she brought up that moment in the sanctuary. "Pastor Mike," she said, her voice full of gratitude, "do you remember the day you called me out of children's church and prayed for me?"

I admitted that I didn't, so she reminded me. "I had TMJ," she said, "and I didn't know why you had called for me until you said it. You prayed for me and told me it would be gone in three days—and it was. From that day to now, over 30 years later, I've never had another problem with it."

I was speechless for a moment, marveling at God's faithfulness. It was exactly as I had spoken, not because of me, but because of Jesus. The Bible declares, **"He sent** *his word, and healed them, and delivered them from their destructions"* **(Psalm 107:20 KJV).** God had sent His word through me that day, and Pamela's healing was permanent.

This testimony reminds me of the ten lepers in **Luke 17:12-19**. When Jesus told them to show themselves to the priests, they were healed as they went. One of them, seeing he was cleansed, turned back to glorify God. Like that leper, Pamela's story is a testament to God's healing power and His desire to make us whole.

Jesus hasn't changed; **He is the same yesterday, today, and forever (Hebrews 13:8).** Whether it's leprosy, TMJ, or any other affliction, His power to heal remains limitless. All it takes is faith to believe and obedience to act. Pamela's healing was not only a miracle but a reminder that no matter how great or small the need, God cares for His children.

To this day, her testimony encourages me to continue stepping out in faith, speaking what God reveals, and trusting Him to do what only He can do. If He can heal leprosy with a touch or TMJ with a prayer, there's nothing too hard for Jesus. As it says in **Jeremiah 32:27,** *"Behold, I am the Lord, the God of all flesh: is there any thing too hard for me?"*

Precise Prophetic Word to a Rodeo Clown

I'll never forget the day God gave me a precise prophetic word for a rodeo clown. It was during one of our church services when a married couple came forward for prayer. Both husband and wife worked for a youth and children's camp ministry. The husband's unique role as a rodeo clown brought joy to countless children, but I could sense there was more to their story.

As I approached them, the Spirit of God quickened me. Without hesitation, I looked at the husband and said, "In three days, you will lose your job and position with this ministry. But don't despair—God is about to open new doors of opportunity for you and your family. What seems devastating at first will lead to something far better."

The words came with such clarity and boldness that I knew they were from the Lord. The couple stood there, a mix of surprise and apprehension on their faces. I could see they were processing what had just been spoken, but they received the word with faith, trusting that God's plans are always for good.

Sure enough, just as I had prophesied, three days later, the man was called into a meeting. The ministry leaders informed him that he was being let go—effective immediately. The reason? He and his wife spoke in tongues, a practice not accepted by the non-Pentecostal organization they worked for.

It was a crushing moment for them. Their hearts ached, not only because of the job loss but because they had poured so much of themselves into the ministry. Yet, even in their pain, they clung to the prophetic word God had given them. They knew that this trial was not the end but the beginning of something new.

God's faithfulness quickly became evident. The couple was led to start their own business, and the doors of favor swung wide open. Their new venture flourished beyond anything they had imagined. What had initially seemed like a devastating loss turned into a season of unprecedented blessing.

This experience reminds me of Paul's encouragement to Timothy in **1 Timothy 4:14:** *"Neglect not the gift that is in thee, which was given thee by prophecy, with the laying on of the hands of the presbytery"* **(KJV).** Prophetic words can carry an impartation of faith, guidance, and strength, enabling us to endure trials and embrace God's plans.

Paul also told Timothy in **1 Timothy 1:18,** *"This charge I commit unto thee, son Timothy, according to the prophecies which went before on thee, that thou by them mightest war a good warfare"* **(KJV).** This couple took the prophecy spoken over them and used it as a weapon of faith. When the storm came, they didn't sink into despair—they stood firm, knowing God had already declared victory over their situation.

Reflecting on this story, I'm reminded of how Jesus healed the ten lepers in **Luke 17:12-19.** Though He told them to go show themselves to the priests, their healing came as they went in obedience to His word. Similarly, this couple's breakthrough came as they acted in faith, trusting the prophetic word that had been spoken over them.

The faithfulness of Jesus is unwavering. He sees beyond our present circumstances and speaks words of life, hope, and direction. When God speaks, His word does not return void **(Isaiah 55:11).** It accomplishes what He intends, just as it did for the rodeo clown and his wife.

This testimony stands as a reminder that even when life takes unexpected turns, we can trust in the One who holds our future. God is faithful, His plans are good, and His words are true. For those who face uncertainty, hold on to the promises of Jesus—they are your anchor in every storm.

CHAPTER SIX
From Adversity to Abundance: God's Plan to Turn It Around

Sometimes, life feels like it's breaking you apart piece by piece, and you wonder if you'll ever recover. But let me tell you—what feels like the end is often just the beginning of something incredible God is preparing for you. I've seen this truth unfold in my own life and in the lives of others.

Turning Evil into Good

Joseph understood this better than anyone. In **Genesis 50:20 (KJV)**, he told his brothers: *"But as for you, ye thought evil against me; but God meant it unto good, to bring to pass, as it is this day, to save much people alive."*

What Joseph endured—betrayal, slavery, false accusations—was painful, but God turned it into a springboard for Joseph's elevation. What others meant for evil, God used for good.

A Wealthy Place Awaits

Psalm 66:12 (KJV) beautifully describes this process: *"Thou hast caused men to ride over our heads; we went through fire and through water: but thou broughtest us out into a wealthy place."*

When I shared this verse recently, I explained, *"That wealthy place isn't just about finances—it's about abundance in every area of life. It's a place of restoration, renewal, and blessing."*

Different translations capture the richness of this promise. The New International Version says, *"a place of abundant moisture,"* while the New Century Bible calls it *"a place of larger blessings."*

The message is clear: the fire and flood you've been through weren't the end. They were the path to something greater.

Seasons of Turnaround

Ecclesiastes 7:14 (KJV) teaches us: *"In the day of prosperity be joyful, but in the day of adversity consider: God also hath set the one over against the other, to the end that man should find nothing after him."* Life's seasons offset each other—lean years make way for years of plenty, and drought gives way to rain.

Joseph endured seven years of famine before seven years of abundance. Elijah saw three and a half years of drought before the rains returned. And now, for those who've been in a season of affliction, I have good news: ***"The day of adversity has ended, and the day of prosperity has begun."***

This is turnaround time.

Finding Purpose in Pain

The last four and a half years may have felt like punishment, but let me assure you—they weren't. God wasn't angry with you, chastising you, or trying to push you away. There's only one word to describe those years: *preparation.*

Second Corinthians 1:4 (KJV) explains it perfectly: ***"Who comforteth us in all our tribulation, that we may be able to comfort them which are in any trouble, by the comfort wherewith we ourselves are comforted of God."***

God allows us to experience trials so we can minister to others who are hurting. The pain you've endured has given you credibility with those who feel broken. **Ezekiel 3:15 (KJV)** describes this heart of compassion: ***"Then I came to them of the captivity at Telabib, that dwelt by the river of Chebar, and I sat where they sat."***

Sometimes, you need to sit where others have sat to truly understand their pain.

Ministering to the Broken

The Lord gave me a picture of you ministering to those who feel like Humpty Dumpty—those who've had a great fall and feel shattered beyond repair. The world has its "king's horses" and "king's men"—psychiatrists, counselors, and self-help programs—but they can't put people back together.

But here's the good news: *Jesus puts people back together again.*

You're being called to bring hope to those who feel hopeless, to share the comfort you've received from God with others who are hurting. You'll be the one who says, *"What the world couldn't fix, Jesus can restore."*

Claiming the Promise

If you're in a season of adversity, take heart. **Psalm 66:12** assures us that the fire and flood are temporary. They're leading you to a wealthy place—a place of abundance, joy, and restoration.

Say it out loud: *"This is my turnaround time. The day of adversity has ended, and the day of prosperity has begun."*

Remember, what was meant for evil, God will use for good. And when you've been comforted by the God of all comfort, you'll be equipped to comfort others.

Jesus is the ultimate restorer. No matter how broken someone feels, He can make them whole again. Trust Him, and let Him use your story to bring hope and healing to others.

To God be the glory for every turnaround He's bringing in our lives!

Healing the Broken: Turning Trauma Into Triumph Through Jesus

Hallelujah! One of the greatest privileges we have as believers is to minister to people who are wounded, hurting, and broken. There's a mass of people out there saying, *"Nobody understands what I'm going through, and nobody even cares."* And that's where you and I step in, carrying the love and compassion of Christ, saying, *"I understand. I've been there. And I care."*

Some people's lives are so broken that even Hallmark can't write a card for what they've been through. I recently spoke over a couple who had endured more than most could imagine. I told them, *"It wasn't punishment, it wasn't anger, and it wasn't because you were out of God's will. Instead, He allowed you to taste a bitter cup so you would be uniquely qualified to minister to the Humpty Dumpties of this world."*

Ministering to the Broken

The world is full of people like Humpty Dumpty—people who've had a great fall and are sitting in their brokenness, convinced they're beyond repair. The world has tried to fix them with self-help books, therapy, and every resource imaginable, but nothing works.

But here's the good news: *Jesus puts people back together again.* **Psalm 34:18 (KJV)** promises: ***"The Lord is nigh unto them that are of a broken heart; and saveth such as be of a contrite spirit."***

When you've walked through pain and come out the other side, God gives you a unique ability to say to others, *"I've been there, and I know the One who can heal you."*

A Word for the Wounded

I declared Psalm 90:15 (KJV) over this couple: *"Make us glad according to the days wherein thou hast afflicted us, and the years wherein we have seen evil."*

I told them—and I believe it's a word for many of us—*"For every bad day you've had in the past, God is going to give you a beautiful day in the future. For every miserable month you've endured, He's going to bless you with a miracle month. And for every traumatized year, He's going to give you a triumphant year."*

How many of you can say, *"I'll take that"*? That's the kind of turnaround only God can bring.

Cast Your Cares

The woman in the couple stood and shared her testimony. She spoke of meeting me years ago in Alaska and receiving a word from the Lord: **"Casting all your care upon him; for he careth for you" (1 Peter 5:7, KJV).**

She clung to that scripture during a season of immense difficulty. Her husband, John, wasn't saved at the time and faced a life-threatening aneurysm. Through prayer and God's miraculous intervention, he survived—and later came to know the Lord.

But that wasn't the end of their challenges. When they moved to Illinois, they were thrown into a spiritual battle they hadn't been prepared for. Yet, every time they felt overwhelmed, she returned to that promise: *"Cast your cares upon the Lord."*

She testified, *"God brought us through, time and time again, because He is faithful. And I praise God for His servants who remind us of His promises."*

Warfare and Victory

Spiritual warfare is real. **Ephesians 6:12 (KJV)** reminds us: **"For we wrestle not against flesh and blood, but against principalities, against powers, against the rulers** *of the darkness of this world, against spiritual wickedness in high places."*

This couple had faced intense warfare, but through it, their faith was strengthened, their trust in God deepened, and their ministry expanded. They learned to stand firm in God's promises, even when the battle raged around them.

Comfort for Others

Second Corinthians 1:4 (KJV) says: *"Who comforteth us in all our tribulation, that we may be able to comfort them which are in any trouble, by the comfort wherewith we ourselves are comforted of God."*

God doesn't waste our pain. He uses it to equip us to comfort others who are walking through similar struggles. Just as this couple was strengthened to minister to the broken, so can you.

Turning Trauma Into Triumph

If you've experienced seasons of pain, loss, or hardship, let me encourage you: God is not done with you. He specializes in taking what was meant for evil and turning it into good **(Genesis 50:20, KJV).**

Say it with me: *"For every bad day, I'll have a beautiful day. For every miserable month, I'll have a miracle month. For every traumatized year, I'll have a triumphant year."*

This is your turnaround time. Cast your cares on Jesus, because He cares for you. Trust Him to put the broken pieces back together and use your story to bring hope and healing to others.

To God be the glory for the triumphs He's bringing out of our trials!

Casting Your Cares: Trusting in the Father's Loving Affection

Sometimes we hear a scripture so often that it begins to lose its depth, its weight, and its beauty. One of those is **1 Peter 5:7 (KJV):** *"Casting all your care upon him; for he careth for you."* It's a verse we can quote in our sleep, but have we ever truly unpacked its meaning?

As I prepared to minister recently, the Lord gave me an opportunity to share the richness of this verse. Now, before you think I'm about to get too academic, let me assure you—I'm here to make it practical and alive, not stuffy and distant.

Understanding "Casting All Your Care"

Let's start with the word *care*. In this verse, it's actually two different Greek words, each carrying its own depth and nuance.

The first *care*—"Casting all your care upon him"—is from the Greek word *merimnao*. It refers to *stresses, tensions, pressures, and distractions.*

Think about that for a moment. How many of us start the day with a well-laid plan, only to fall into bed at night wondering where the hours went and realizing we accomplished none of what we intended? That's *merimnao*. It's the freeway driver in California who says, *"I don't even know where I'm supposed to be, but I know I'm already an hour late."* It's the constant noise of life pulling you in every direction except forward.

Now here's the beauty—God invites you to cast all those distractions, tensions, and pressures on Him. Every last one.

"For He Careth for You"

The second *care* in the verse is completely different. It's a tender, fatherly care. The Greek word here carries the idea of a deep, familial affection—a father for his child.

Picture a father who's not just concerned with his child's safety but who actively wants the best for them. He's not cold or distant; he's lovingly invested. He wants to protect, provide, and nurture.

It's like when a teenager says to their parents, *"Don't you trust me?"* And the wise father responds, *"No, because you haven't earned it yet."* That's not lack of love—it's profound love. It's the kind of love that says, *"I'm not going to let you go play with rattlesnakes. I care too much for you."*

That's the kind of care God has for us. He's not just taking on our burdens—He's doing so because He's deeply, personally, and tenderly fond of us.

A Word for a Couple

As I was sharing this message, the Lord drew my attention to a couple in the congregation. I asked them to come forward, and as they stood before me, I felt the Spirit impress this truth on my heart for them.

"Casting all your distractions on Him because He is properly fond of you."

I looked at them and said, *"God is not a distant father who leaves you to fend for yourselves. He's watching over you, guiding you, and protecting you. The challenges you're facing—those tensions and distractions—aren't meant to crush you. They're opportunities to lean into His care."*

Trusting the Father's Care

Here's what I want you to take away from this. God's invitation to *cast your cares* isn't a command born out of frustration or obligation. It's a loving appeal from a Father who is deeply fond of you.

Isaiah 46:4 (KJV) promises: ***"And even to your old age I am he; and even to hoar hairs will I carry you: I have made, and I will bear; even I will carry, and will deliver you."***

When life feels overwhelming, when the distractions threaten to drown you, remember this: God is not only able to carry your burdens—He *wants* to carry them.

Take the Invitation

So, let's say it together: *"Casting all your distractions on Him, because He is properly fond of you."*

Whatever has been pulling you in a million directions, hand it over to the One who is uniquely qualified to handle it. Trust His care, His timing, and His heart for you.

And the next time you feel the weight of the world on your shoulders, picture a loving Father saying, *"Give it to Me. I've got you."*

To Him be all the glory for the peace that comes from casting every care on Him!

Keep Doing What You're Doing: Faithfulness, Expansion, and Deliverance

I've got the best news in the world for you today! It's straight from **Matthew 13:12 (KJV):** *"For whosoever hath, to him shall be given, and he shall have more abundance."*

I can't help but feel this word is for so many of you. And I especially want to speak it over the pastors and faithful servants who have been steadfast in their calling. **Matthew 25:29 (KJV)** echoes this promise: ***"For unto every one that hath shall be given, and he shall have abundance."***

If you've been faithful in what God has given you, I want you to hear this loud and clear—there's more coming. More blessing, more influence, and more opportunities to serve His kingdom.

Faithfulness Leads to Expansion

The Lord drew my attention to a couple in the congregation. As I prayed, He impressed this on my spirit: *"Because of their faithfulness, I'm going to expand their sphere of influence. They'll cooperate with Me in ministry expansion."*

Isaiah 54:2-3 (KJV) came to mind: ***"Enlarge the place of thy tent, and let them stretch forth the curtains of thine habitations: spare not, lengthen thy cords, and strengthen thy stakes; For thou shalt break forth on the right hand and on the left."***

I turned to this couple and said, *"You're going to lengthen your cords and strengthen your stakes. Your borders are about to enlarge. What you've been doing has been right, and now God is calling you to go even further."*

A Place for Deliverance

In my travels, I've often been asked, *"Where can I go for deliverance?"* It's a question that breaks my heart because there aren't many places where people can find the help they need in a safe, theologically sound environment.

I shared this with the congregation: *"I don't know of many places like this one, where people can come and find freedom. Don't you appreciate ministries like these that spend their lives setting people free?"*

Ministries like this are a gift to the body of Christ, and I encouraged them: *"Go with what you've got going for you. Do what you do best. And keep on doing it because you're doing it right."*

Staying Faithful

Faithfulness is key. I reminded them of a saying from Tennessee: *"You've got to dance with the one that brought you."* In other words, stick with what God has called you to do. Don't try to reinvent the wheel—just keep being faithful in the work He's already given you.

I encouraged the congregation to prophesy over this couple with me:

"Lengthen your cords! Strengthen your stakes! Stretch forth the curtain of your habitation! Enlarge your

borders! You're going to break out on the left hand and the right!"

I added with a laugh, *"You're breaking out all over—like measles, spreading everywhere!"*

A Word in the Middle of the Night

Let me share a story about a friend of mine who's an evangelist. He was staying at a Ramada Inn in Houston, Texas, when he got a call at 2 a.m. A man on the other end said, *"I listened to you Sunday night, and I didn't believe you. I listened to you Monday night, and I still didn't believe you. But tonight, something happened. I believe you now. Do you have a word for me?"*

My friend, pulled straight out of a deep sleep, simply said, *"Yes. Go back to bed!"*

Sometimes the word we need is simple: keep doing what you're doing. Stay faithful. Trust God to do the rest.

God's Promise for the Faithful

If you've been serving faithfully, hear this promise from **Habakkuk 2:2-3 (KJV):** ***"Write the vision, and make it plain upon tables, that he may run that readeth it. For the vision is yet for an appointed time, but at the end it shall speak, and not lie: though it tarry, wait for it; because it will surely come, it will not tarry."***

God sees your faithfulness. He knows the labor of love you've poured into His work. And He's about to expand your influence, enlarge your borders, and bless your efforts abundantly.

A Call to Action

So, what's the takeaway? Go with what you've got going for you. Do what you do best. Keep on doing what you're doing, because you're doing it right. The Lord is about to meet you right in the line of fire and take your ministry to the next level.

Let's claim the promise of **Isaiah 54:2-3:** *"Enlarge the place of thy tent, and let them stretch forth the curtains of thine habitations: spare not, lengthen thy cords, and strengthen thy stakes."*

And remember: the best is yet to come. To God be the glory for all He's doing in and through your faithfulness!

From Dr Michael H Yeager
THEY COULD NOT MOVE or SPEAK for 2 1/2 HOURS

My family and I travelled out West ministering in different churches and visiting relatives in Wisconsin. We were invited to speak at a church in Minneapolis, Minnesota. The pastor had two different churches that he pastored. One of these churches was in the suburbs, and the other one was in the heart of Minneapolis. The larger of the two churches was in the suburbs.

I was to minister at the larger church first and then immediately go to his other church downtown. The whole congregation was in the same service that morning. There were approximately 140 to 160 people including women, men, children, and babies in the sanctuary.

As I began to speak, I found myself unexpectedly speaking about the **year that King Uzia died, I saw the Lord high and lifted up, and his glory filled the Temple,** which is found in the book of Isaiah! The unction of the Holy Ghost was upon me so strong that it just flowed out of my belly like rivers of living water. To this day I do not remember everything that I said. As I was speaking, I sensed an amazing heavenly touch of God's presence on myself and everyone in the sanctuary.

The spirit of God was on me in a mighty way, and yet I was aware of the time factor. To get to Pastor Bill's sister church downtown Minnesota, I was not going to have time to lay hands on, or pray for any-one. If God were going to confirm his word with signs following, then he would have to do it without me being there.

It turns out that is exactly what God wanted to do! When I was at the limit of the amount of the time allotted to me, I quickly closed with a prayer. I did not say anything to the pastor or anyone else as I grabbed my Bible to leave the sanctuary. My family was already loaded up and waiting for me in our vehicle. As I ran out the door I perceived something strange, awesome, and wonderful was beginning to happen to the congregation. There was a heavy, amazing, and holy hush that had come upon them.

By the time I arrived at the other church, their worship had already begun. As I stood up in the pulpit to Minister God's Word, the Holy Spirit began to speak to me again, with a completely, totally different message. God did wonderful things in the sister church downtown that afternoon as I preached a message on being radically sold out and committed to Christ.

Everyone ended up falling out of their chairs to the floor on their faces, weeping and crying before the Lord. This is not something I have ever encouraged any congregation to do. I have seen this happen numerous times where I simply must stop preaching because the presence of God is so strong, and so real that people cannot stay in their seats. I would stop preaching, get on my face, and just wait on God, as he moved on the people's hearts.

After that service, we went back to our fifth wheel trailer at the local campgrounds where we were camping. Later in the day, I received a phone call from this pastor. He was acting rather strange and speaking very softly in a very hushed manner.

He asked me with a whisper: **does that always happen after you are done preaching?** I said to him, tell me what happened. He said, "As you were headed out the door, I began to melt to the floor, I could not keep standing, and I found myself pinned to the floor of the sanctuary. I could not move or speak." Now all the children (including babies) were in the sanctuary with the rest of the congregation. He said he could not move for two and a half hours. During this whole experience, he did not hear another sound in the facility. For over two and a half hours he just simply laid there not being able to move or speak a word under the presence and mighty hand of God. After two and a half hours Pastor Bill was able to move finally, and to get up.

He had thought for sure that he was the only one still left in the church. Everybody must have gone home a long time ago, and that he was there by himself. But to his complete shock and amazement, everybody was still there, laying on the floor. Nobody could move or speak for over two and a half hours! **Men, women, children and even the babies were still lying on the floor, not moving, talking, or crying!** God was in the house! The tangible, overwhelming, solemn, presence and holiness of God had come!

Pastor Bill asked me to come over to his house so we could talk about what happened that day in his church service. My family and I arrived. He invited us inside. He asked if this normally happens wherever I went. I informed him, no, but many wonderful and strange things do take place. It did not always happen, except when I get myself in a place of complete, absolute surrender and submission to Jesus Christ. This submission included not putting **ANYTHING** else but the **WORD** of God into my heart. When I simply seek the face of God, by praying, giving myself completely to the word, meditation, singing and worship, intimacy with the Father, Son, and Holy Ghost, this was the result! God is not a respecter of people, what he does for one, he will do for others.

A Prophetic Warning to an Evangelist

One sunny afternoon, an old friend of mine, an evangelist who traveled the country sharing the gospel, stopped by our church. He was in town for a series of meetings and needed a place to stay. Our church had a small apartment tucked away above the gymnasium, and I offered it to him for his brief visit. It was a perfect spot for rest and reflection.

We spent some time catching up in the church hallway, laughing and reminiscing. My son, Daniel, happened to be walking down the corridor toward us. As he approached, I noticed his steps falter. His gaze locked onto our guest, and an expression of shock and alarm spread across his face. I didn't think much of it at first, but after the evangelist retired to the apartment, Daniel came to me, visibly shaken.

"Dad," he said, his voice trembling, "unless he changes his ways, he's going to die in a car accident."

I was taken aback. "What are you talking about, Dan?" I asked.

He explained that God had given him a vision of the evangelist's death. "I saw him in a car crash, Dad. The

Lord showed me three things leading to his death: women, money, and dancing."

Daniel looked at me with pleading eyes. "You have to tell him, Dad. Warn him."

I shook my head. "No, Dan. God gave you the vision. It's your responsibility to tell him."

He was stunned. "Why not, Dad? You're the pastor. You should tell him."

But I stood firm. "Son, God entrusted this vision to you, not me. If you don't deliver the message, his blood will be on your hands."

Daniel was frustrated, and I could see the weight of the vision pressing on him. He spent the rest of the day wrestling with the responsibility, begging me repeatedly to intervene. Each time, I reminded him that it wasn't my message to deliver. By the next day, Daniel was in tears, pleading with me to tell the evangelist. Again, I refused. "Dan, God gave you the vision and the warning. You must obey Him."

Finally, Daniel relented. He asked me to pray for him as he prepared to confront the evangelist. I did, asking God to give him courage and to open the evangelist's heart to receive the warning.

About 20 minutes later, Daniel returned, his face pale but determined. I asked him how it went, and he recounted the encounter. He had knocked on the door of the apartment and was invited inside. The evangelist was in the bedroom at the end of the hallway. Daniel entered and shared the vision, warning him of the fatal car accident that would occur if he didn't repent and change his ways. As Daniel spoke, the evangelist sat on the bed, silent tears streaming down his face. He didn't say a word, only nodded.

Moments later, we heard a car engine. We stepped outside just in time to see the evangelist pulling out of the driveway, his belongings hastily packed. He left without a word, driving down the highway. It all happened so fast.

For the next year, I didn't hear from him. I often wondered if he had heeded the warning or if he had ignored it. Then, one day, we crossed paths again. He was traveling with his family now—his wife and children accompanying him everywhere he went. He didn't bring up the vision or the warning, and I didn't press him. But his actions spoke volumes. The women, money, and dancing that had once been a danger to him seemed to have been replaced by a renewed focus on his family and ministry.

I was relieved and grateful. Daniel had fulfilled his responsibility, and the evangelist had seemingly made changes in his life. It was a clear reminder of **Ezekiel 33:6:** *"But if the watchman see the sword come, and blow not the trumpet, and the people be not warned; if the sword come, and take any person from among them, he is taken away in his iniquity; but his blood will I require at the watchman's hand"* **(KJV).** Daniel had been the watchman, and he had blown the trumpet.

This experience also reminded me of how Jesus healed the ten lepers in **Luke 17:12-19**. Only one returned to give thanks, but all ten were healed as they obeyed His command to go and show themselves to the priests. In a similar way, the evangelist's decision to change his ways was a response to the warning he received. God's mercy had given him a second chance.

I often reflect on this event, grateful for the courage God gave my son and the willingness of the evangelist to listen. It's a reminder that God's ways are higher than ours and that His plans are always for our good. As **2 Timothy 2:15** says, ***"Study to shew thyself approved unto God, a workman that needeth not to be ashamed, rightly dividing the word of truth"*** **(KJV).** Daniel stepped into his calling that day, delivering a message that only he could give. It's a story of faith, obedience, and the unfailing grace of Jesus.

CHAPTER SEVEN
Prosperity with Purpose: Flowing as a Channel of Blessing

I'll never forget the moment I stood before a row of people and felt the Spirit of God stirring. It reminded me of the story in **John 5:4 (KJV):** *"For an angel went down at a certain season into the pool, and troubled the water: whosoever then first after the troubling of the water stepped in was made whole of whatsoever disease he had."*

The waters were being stirred, and I declared to those in front of me, *"This is Prosperity Row!"* I even pointed to two empty seats and said, *"Those seats are for anyone ambitious enough to step out and claim them."*

Two people immediately responded, making their way forward. I smiled and thought, *That's the kind of faith God honors—faith that acts when the opportunity arises.*

The Truth About Prosperity

There's so much confusion and controversy surrounding prosperity in the church today. To address it, I studied every instance of the word *prosperity* in Scripture. Did you know it appears 88 times in the Bible? And every single reference is conditional on one thing: *seeking the Lord.*

Psalm 34:10 (KJV) says: *"The young lions do lack, and suffer hunger: but they that seek the Lord shall not want any good thing."*

On the flip side, I also studied poverty. Is there any redemptive value in being poor? As Derek Prince once said, *"It's no sin to be broke, but it's terribly inconvenient."*

In Proverbs, poverty is consistently linked to things like laziness, neglecting the house of God, bad company, and chasing after get-rich-quick schemes. Poverty, according to Scripture, is a result of wrong living, wrong confessions, and wrong attitudes—not God's plan for His people.

Prosperity vs. Materialism

Now, let's be clear—there's a big difference between prosperity and materialism. Materialism is rooted in covetousness and greed. **Colossians 3:5 (KJV)** warns us: *"Covetousness, which is idolatry."*

What's idolatry? It's essentially an exalted form of self-love. When a man bows before an idol, he's really bowing to himself. Covetousness traps us in a cycle of selfishness, much like the Dead Sea in Israel.

The Dead Sea is notorious for being inhospitable—28% salt, no vegetation, no fish, no picnics, no life. Why? Because it has no outlet. Water flows in, but it doesn't flow out. It's stagnant, lifeless, and repugnant.

Contrast that with the Sea of Galilee, just a short distance away. It's vibrant and full of life—fresh water, thriving vegetation, families picnicking along the shore, fish teeming beneath the surface. The difference? The Sea of Galilee has an outlet. Water flows in, through, and out, keeping it fresh and alive.

Prosperity for a Purpose

God prospers His people not so they can hoard His blessings, but so they can be a channel of His love and provision. **2 Corinthians 9:8 (KJV)** says: *"And God is able to make all grace abound toward you; that ye, always having all sufficiency in all things, may abound to every good work."*

I've never met a true Christian who wanted to prosper just to heap it on their own desires. But I've met plenty who wanted to prosper so they could support the work of God—missions, ministries, and the spreading of the gospel.

God's blessings are meant to flow through us like the waters of the Sea of Galilee. When we allow His blessings to flow out to others, He continues to pour more into us.

A Call to Be a Channel

As I stood before Prosperity Row, I couldn't help but think about how God is stirring His people to step into their calling as channels of blessing. It's not about accumulating wealth for ourselves; it's about being faithful stewards of what He's given us.

Malachi 3:10 (KJV) promises: *"Bring ye all the tithes into the storehouse, that there may be meat in mine house, and prove me now herewith, saith the Lord of hosts, if I will not open you the windows of heaven, and pour you out a blessing, that there shall not be room enough to receive it."*

God wants to pour out His blessings, but He's looking for those who will let them flow.

A Prayer for Prosperity

Let's pray together:

"Lord, make us like the Sea of Galilee—alive, fresh, and full of life. Help us to be channels of Your blessing, allowing Your provision to flow through us to those in need. Teach us to seek You above all else, and to use

what You give us to further Your kingdom. In Jesus' name, amen."

So, are you ready to step out in faith? Remember, God prospers those who seek Him. And when you let His blessings flow through you, He'll pour out even more. To Him be the glory for all He's doing!

The Purpose of Prosperity: Blessing Others and Advancing God's Kingdom

Sometimes, I hear people say, *"I don't need to prosper. I just want enough to pay my bills, put food on the table, and keep gas in the car."* It sounds humble at first, doesn't it? But when you dig deeper, that mindset reveals something troubling—it's selfish.

When someone says, *"I only want enough for me,"* they're essentially saying, *"I'm not interested in missionaries, Bible translators, feeding the hungry, or supporting the work of the gospel. I'm fine as long as I have enough for myself."*

But that's not what God's prosperity is about. Prosperity isn't for selfish gain—it's about having more than enough so you can pour into others, fund missions, and support the work of God's kingdom.

The Keys to Prosperity

There are 88 scriptures in the Bible that mention prosperity, and every one of them is tied to seeking God and obeying His word. Let me share just a few of these verses with you.

1. Matthew 6:33 (KJV):

"But seek ye first the kingdom of God, and his righteousness; and all these things shall be added unto you."

I told the congregation, *"Say it with me: 'Seek first the kingdom of God and His righteousness, and all these things shall be added unto you.'"*

And then I added, *"Satan subtracts and divides, but Jesus adds and multiplies."*

2. Joshua 1:8 (KJV):

"This book of the law shall not depart out of thy mouth; but thou shalt meditate therein day and night, that thou mayest observe to do according to all that is written therein: for then thou shalt make thy way prosperous, and then thou shalt have good success."

When we meditate on God's Word and obey it, He promises to make our way prosperous.

3. 2 Chronicles 20:20 (KJV):

"Believe in the Lord your God, so shall ye be established; believe his prophets, so shall ye prosper."

Faith and trust in God bring stability, and believing His word through His servants brings prosperity.

4. 2 Chronicles 26:5 (KJV):

"And he sought God in the days of Zechariah, who had understanding in the visions of God: and as long as he sought the Lord, God made him to prosper."

Seeking God is the foundation of prosperity.

5. 2 Chronicles 31:21 (KJV):

"And in every work that he began in the service of the house of God, and in the law, and in the commandments, to seek his God, he did it with all his heart, and prospered."

Wholehearted service to God results in success and prosperity.

6. Job 36:11 (KJV):

"If they obey and serve him, they shall spend their days in prosperity, and their years in pleasures."

I told the crowd, *"All you have to do is trust and obey. Say it with me: 'Trust and obey.'"* God's promise is clear—obedience brings prosperity and joy.

Prosperity with a Purpose

I reminded everyone that prosperity is not about hoarding wealth or indulging in selfish desires. It's about being a channel of blessing. God's plan for prosperity is like the Sea of Galilee—water flows in, through, and out, bringing life and nourishment wherever it goes.

In contrast, materialism and greed are like the Dead Sea—water flows in but has no outlet, leaving it stagnant and lifeless.

"God prospers His people," I said, *"so they can support His kingdom. I've never met a Christian who wanted to prosper for selfish reasons. But I've met countless believers who want to prosper so they can give to missions, help the poor, and fund the spreading of the gospel."*

A Prophetic Word

I had the congregation stand, and I spoke over them:

"For those of you who are willing to receive God's blessings, this is your moment. The waters are being stirred, and it's time to step into your calling as a channel of His provision. You've got the keys to Fort Knox—not for selfish gain, but for advancing God's kingdom."

I turned to a group near the front and said, *"Turn around and face the congregation. Everyone else, reach your* hands toward them and say, 'Remember me when you come into your kingdom!'"

Waiting on the Promise

Before we closed, I reminded everyone that there's often a gap between receiving a promise from God and seeing it fulfilled. That waiting period is where faith grows.

Habakkuk 2:3 (KJV) says: *"For the vision is yet for an appointed time, but at the end it shall speak, and not lie: though it tarry, wait for it; because it will surely come, it will not tarry."*

God's promises are true, and His timing is perfect. Prosperity will come as you seek Him, trust Him, and walk in obedience.

Claim the Blessing

So, are you ready to step into God's plan for prosperity? Say it with me:

"I will seek first the kingdom of God and His righteousness. I will trust and obey. And I will be a channel of His blessing to the world."

Remember, God prospers those who are faithful to Him, not for their glory but for His. Let's use His blessings to reach the lost, feed the hungry, and share the gospel to the ends of the earth.

To God be the glory for the abundance He provides!

The God Who Sees: Promotions, Prophecies, and Missions Fulfilled

Let me tell you about a time when God fulfilled a prophecy right on the spot, to my complete embarrassment. It started when I was in a congregation, scanning the crowd as I often do, waiting for the Spirit to prompt me. That's when I noticed a man in a gray suit.

The Lord began to reveal something to me about this man. It wasn't the whole picture—we know in part and prophesy in part **(1 Corinthians 13:9, KJV)**—but I had enough to share. I sensed that this man was loyal, conscientious, and deserving of a promotion. A promotion, I felt, that should have happened last July but didn't. Instead, his boss had diverted the promotion and given it to a friend.

So, I stood the man up and began sharing this word, speaking scripture over him about God's favor and justice. I thought I was encouraging him, but little did I know, his boss was sitting right next to him in the pew—a non-Christian boss he had spent three years inviting to church!

The Awkward Moment

As I spoke, I noticed the man's boss pulling on his coat sleeve. He leaned in and whispered something. I couldn't hear, but I could see the man's sheepish expression. The boss's face started to turn red, and I realized I had stumbled into a very awkward situation.

The boss whispered harshly, *"Did you set me up for this? Did you tell him?"*

The man shook his head furiously. *"I've never seen this guy before in my life!"* he said, pointing at me.

That's when I started praying silently: *Lord, get me out of this!* I could feel the tension rising, and my mind was racing. I thought about the old phrase "hoof-in-mouth disease," for when you open your mouth and immediately regret it.

Instant Fulfillment

Then something amazing happened. The boss, visibly uncomfortable, threw up his hands and said to the man, *"You've got the promotion. Just get this guy off my back!"*

The man turned to me, eyes wide, and mouthed the words, *"It's happened!"* Right there, in the middle of the service, God had moved.

I laughed later, thinking about how risky my job can feel sometimes. But the Lord knows what He's doing. Even when I feel like I've stumbled, He's working all things together for good **(Romans 8:28, KJV).**

A Word for the Year

That experience reminded me of the truth found in **Isaiah 48:15**. The New International Version says: *"I, even I, have spoken; yes, I have called him. I will bring him, and he will succeed in his mission."*

Let that sink in. God speaks, He calls, He brings us along, and He ensures our success.

I shared this scripture with the congregation as a word for the year ahead. *"This promise applies to you,"* I told them. *"God has called you, and He's bringing you along. You will succeed in your mission."*

Everyone Has a Mission

One thing I believe with all my heart is that everyone has a mission. It's unique, special, and divinely assigned. And let me tell you something else—I don't buy into the idea that if you don't fulfill your mission, God will just hand it off to someone else.

God chose you for a reason. **Ephesians 2:10 (KJV)** says: *"For we are his workmanship, created in Christ Jesus unto good works, which God hath before ordained that we should walk in them."*

Your mission is part of the good works He's prepared for you. And He doesn't make mistakes.

Trusting God's Timing

If there's one thing that moment with the man in the gray suit taught me, it's that God's timing is perfect. The promotion that was delayed last July wasn't forgotten. God saw the injustice, and He made it right.

Psalm 75:6-7 (KJV) reminds us: *"For promotion cometh neither from the east, nor from the west, nor from the south. But God is the judge: he putteth down one, and setteth up another."*

If you're waiting for something—a breakthrough, a promotion, a fulfillment of God's promises—hold on. He hasn't forgotten you.

Moving Forward in Faith

As we look to the year ahead, let's hold on to the promise of **Isaiah 48:15**. Say it with me:

"God has spoken. God has called me. God is bringing me along. And I will succeed in my mission."

Whatever God has called you to do, He's equipping you for it. Whatever obstacles you're facing, He's clearing the way. Trust Him, follow Him, and step boldly into the mission He's given you.

To Him be all the glory for every success He brings!

From Dr Michael H Yeager
When the Shekinah Glory Came

In May of 1975, my sister asked me to drive her car up to Anchorage Alaska. I had just been discharged from the Navy, and she was stationed in New Mexico in the Air Force. She had received her new orders to relocate to the Air Force Base in Anchorage, Alaska. In my heart I really felt like I was supposed to go back to Wisconsin, to share Christ with the gang of men that I used to run with before I was born again.

Now, I felt like I was between a rock and a hard place, because I was committed to driving her 1973 red Maverick up the Alcan Freeway! I had just driven the Alcan the year before right at the onset of winter. From Anchorage to Mukwonago Wisconsin was 3,500 miles long. (At that time, I was only eighteen years old and not yet saved. I cover that experience in another book.)

I experienced heavy rains as I headed up through Canada on the dirt road which took me to Fairbanks. The farther I adventured, the worse it got. Some people were adventuring on taking the roads that logging trucks drove, but my sister's car was not designed for such rough terrain. I spoke to one family that had a large passenger van who had endeavored to do this. Numerous times they had to cross rivers and streams, hoping and praying they would make it across.

I had to face the fact that I could not make it up to Anchorage Alaska with my sister's car. I had to stop and turn around. The flooding was so bad that year, which they could not give any reasonable dates when the bridges and the road to Anchorage would be opened once again for public traffic. The only other option I had was to drive my sister's car back to Mukwonago, Wisconsin where my parents lived.

Looking back, I now realize that God was in this event, in order that I would share Christ with the men that I used to do drugs, alcohol, and other gang-related activities with. The spirit of God strongly convicted me, saying I told you to go back to Wisconsin.

I had from the beginning felt like I was supposed to go back to Wisconsin, but because of my commitment to my sister, I had not listen to my heart. God has a wonderful way of divinely intervening when it is necessary for his plan to be fulfilled. It reminds me of Jonah taking the ship so that he could ignore going to Nineveh. God spoke to me through this circumstance.

Revelation 3:8 I know thy works: behold, I have set before thee an open door, and no man can shut it: for thou hast a little strength, and hast kept my word, and hast not denied my name.

God's Shekinah Glory Fills the Car

I realize how incredible and insane this sounds, but it is the truth. None of the stories that I share with you about my life are fake or exaggerated. There is a Scripture that says all liars will go to hell.

Revelation 21:8 But the fearful, and unbelieving, and the abominable, and murderers, and

whoremongers, and sorcerers, and idolaters, and all liars, shall have their part in the lake which burneth with fire and brimstone: which is the second death.

I would not blame people for not believing this story. In many of my testimonies, others were present to verify exactly what happened. In this situation, I was all by myself coming out of Canada, driving my sister's 1973 red Maverick. My sister wanted me to drive her car up to Alaska from New Mexico, but when I got unto the Alcan freeway, I had to turn around because the roads were all flooded out.

As I was driving my sister's 1973 Ford Maverick when early in the morning an overwhelming hunger and thirst for God took a hold of me. To describe it with human vernacular would be almost impossible. I completely gave myself over to this deep urge to draw close to God.

James 4:8 Draw nigh to God, and he will draw nigh to you.

Zechariah 1:3 Therefore say thou unto them, Thus saith the Lord of hosts; Turn ye unto me, saith the Lord of hosts, and I will turn unto you, saith the Lord of hosts.

I came out of the mountains of Canada, Praying, singing, and worshiping God in the Spirit as the sun was at its peak in the sky above me. I am guessing it was right around 11 a.m. as I continue to pray and worship God with all my heart, as my heart was filled with an overwhelming love for the Father, and Jesus Christ.

It felt like my heart was going to come out of my chest because of the greatness of God's love for me. My Heart was filled with gratitude for the Father and the Son for snatching my soul out of hell even as I was committing suicide on the 19th birthday.

I was weeping, praying, and crying as I drove along, so much so to where I could not see where I was going any longer. Suddenly the car began to be filled with the tangible presence of the Lord. My car's inside was filling with a light, glistening, sparkly, light blue, green, silver, gold mist.

The mist became so heavy that I could not see outside of my car window. Now, you would think that my heart would be filled with fear because I could not see where I was going, but, it was the opposite. I was so overwhelmed by the Spirit of God that nothing else existed at that moment. I was so caught up in the presence of the Lord that without even thinking, I raised my hands toward heaven, taking them off my steering wheel.

In this place of deep intimate worship, Time came to a complete standstill. Here I was in my sister's 1973 red maverick driving through Canada's rugged back roads with my hands lifted towards heaven, weeping, and crying and worshiping God. I was ushered into the supernatural, incredible, mind-boggling realm of the Holy Ghost.

I remember that after what only seemed a short Time, my hands came back to the steering wheel as this divine mist, the Shekinah glory, was dissipating. To my utter amazement, I noticed that the sun, which had been in the middle of the sky when I began to experience the overwhelming presence of God, was just now barely peeking over the horizon, and it was starting to get dark. I did not check the car's mileage at that time, but I know my car had gone hundreds of miles without me driving it. Someone had driven my car for hours on end as I was caught up in the glory of God.

This total experience could have possibly been 5 to 7 hours long. It had to be Angelic beings that took complete control of my vehicle as I was lost in the Spirit! My heart was filled with joy, unspeakable and full of glory at this wondrous miracle. To this day, as I think about this experience, I can hardly grasp its reality. Not only did someone drive my car, but the vehicle should have also run out of gas.

Then a cloud covered the tent of the congregation, and the glory of the LORD filled the tabernacle (Exodus 40:34)

Healed by the Power of Jesus

When I first walked into Pastor Mike's church years ago, back in 2007 or 2008, I had no idea the impact it would have on my life. At the time, I was searching for direction, feeling lost and unsure of my path. Then I met Doc Yeager, a man whose deep relationship with God was evident in everything he did. He didn't just preach faith—he lived it. Miraculous things happened around him, not because of who he was, but because of the One he served.

By 2010, life had beaten me down. I faced a mountain of health issues that felt insurmountable. I had recently undergone surgery to remove a growth on my leg, which the doctors feared might be cancerous. My back was in constant pain from a slipped disc, so severe I couldn't turn my head in either direction. To make matters worse, my right arm was almost immobile. I had tried everything—chiropractors, therapy—but nothing brought lasting relief. It felt like my body was betraying me, and I was growing more hopeless with each passing day.

One afternoon, as I scrolled through Facebook, something unexpected happened. I accidentally clicked on an invitation to a healing service at Pastor Mike's church. It had been years since I'd stepped foot in that building, but in that moment, it felt like God was guiding my hand. I knew I had to go. I invited a few friends to join me, but none of them could make it. Looking back, I realize that night was meant to be just between me and God.

When I arrived, I felt a mixture of hope and hesitation. Doc prayed for me with a faith that seemed unshakable. As he laid hands on me, he began to speak words of knowledge that took me by surprise. "There's an issue with your liver," he said. I hadn't told him, but I had suspected something was wrong for months. Then he mentioned my right eye, saying he sensed something there as well. Again, I was floored. For weeks, I'd been telling my doctor about discomfort behind that eye, but no one had been able to figure out the cause. Doc's words confirmed what I had been struggling to articulate.

As he prayed, I felt something extraordinary—a warmth, a love, a power that could only come from Jesus. It started at the top of my head and flowed through my entire body. Suddenly, my back loosened. The pain I had carried for years vanished. I could move my head freely, lift my arm, and bend without restriction. Tears streamed down my face as I realized—I was healed.

The joy that filled me was indescribable. It wasn't just about the physical healing, though that was a miracle in itself. It was the overwhelming realization that Jesus had seen me in my pain, my doubt, and my weariness. He had chosen to intervene, to remind me of His love and power. *"But he was wounded for our transgressions, he was bruised for our iniquities: the chastisement of our peace was upon him; and with his stripes we are healed"* **(Isaiah 53:5, KJV).**

I stood before the congregation that night and shared my testimony, my heart bursting with gratitude. Doc made it clear that the healing didn't come from him. "Jesus is the healer," he said. "All the glory belongs to Him."

As I walked out of that service, I felt like a new person. My body was restored, and so was my faith. That night, I experienced the truth of **Hebrews 13:8:** *"Jesus Christ the same yesterday, and today, and forever"* **(KJV).** The same Jesus who healed lepers and the brokenhearted in the Bible is still healing today.

If you're reading this and struggling—whether it's with physical pain, emotional wounds, or a broken spirit—know that Jesus sees you. He knows your pain and longs to heal you. Trust Him. He is still in the healing business, and His love knows no bounds. Sometimes, He shows up through a prayer, a word of knowledge, or even an accidental click on Facebook. Whatever the means, He is faithful. Praise God for His endless mercy and grace.

CHAPTER EIGHT
A New Day: Walking in Prosperity, Purpose, and Power

I want to start by saying something simple but profound: *You have a mission, and nobody else in this world can fulfill it but you.*

Catherine Kuhlman once said that God called a man to do what she ended up doing, but he didn't respond, so God called her. While I respect her ministry deeply, I don't fully agree with that perspective. I believe God called Catherine Kuhlman specifically for her mission. Just as He's called you for yours.

God doesn't hand out generic missions—He designs them uniquely for each of us. And let me tell you, you *will* succeed in it if you hold on to His promises.

The Promise of Prosperity

I reminded the congregation of **Isaiah 48:15 (KJV):** *"I, even I, have spoken; yea, I have called him: I have brought him, and he shall make his way prosperous."*

I had them say it with me: *"He spoke to me. He called me. He's bringing me along. And I will make my way prosperous."* Then I asked every man to pull out his wallet and every woman to grab her coin purse. We were about to declare prosperity—not for selfish gain, but for the sake of the kingdom.

I held my Bible in my right hand and my wallet in my left, and we declared together:

"I'm going to be full of the Word, full of the Spirit, and full of blessings."

We claimed this promise for the rest of the year: to get out of debt, pay our bills, and have enough not just for ourselves but to sow into God's work.

Driving Out Poverty

Let me be clear—prosperity isn't about greed or materialism. It's about being a vessel for God's blessings. When we're full of His Spirit and His provision, we're equipped to bless others, fund missions, and spread the gospel.

I joked with the crowd, *"Let's drive those poverty demons all the way back to Salt Lake City!"* It's time to walk in the fullness of God's provision.

A New Day

As we moved into worship, the Spirit of the Lord filled the room. I began to declare a word over the congregation:

"This is the day of new beginnings. This is the day of the new thing. Remember ye not the former things, neither consider the things of old. I will do a new thing; now it shall spring forth" **(Isaiah 43:18-19, KJV).**

The Lord impressed this on my heart for everyone in the room:

"This is your new day. A day of newness in spirit, newness in your flesh, new vision, new authority, and new anointing. You will not walk in the oldness of the letter or the weakness of the flesh, but in the vitality and power of the Spirit. This is your new day, sayeth the Lord."

Moving with the Cloud

As we worshiped, we sang a song that captured the moment perfectly:

"The cloud of glory is moving. Move with the cloud. Let your spirit arise and your strength be renewed. Come, let us move together, as we follow where He leads. It's a

new day for us. New life we will receive. Move with the cloud."

God's glory is on the move, and He's calling us to follow Him into newness. This isn't a season to stay stagnant or cling to the past—it's a time to rise, renew, and move with the Spirit.

Walking in Purpose

As we closed the service, I left the congregation with this final encouragement: *"You have a mission that only you can fulfill. God has spoken to you, called you, and is bringing you along. You will succeed because He has promised it."*

Ephesians 3:20 (KJV) reminds us: ***"Now unto him that is able to do exceeding abundantly above all that we ask or think, according to the power that worketh in us."***

This is the day of new beginnings. Trust Him to bring His promises to pass in your life. Move with the cloud, step into your calling, and watch how God makes your way prosperous.

To Him be all the glory for the new thing He's doing!

Lift Up Your Eyes: Walking in Victory and Joy

Let me tell you something powerful, something life-changing. It's so simple that you might have overlooked it, but the Lord said it over and over again in His Word: *"Lift up your eyes."*

Too many people walk around with their heads down. You can see it—shoulders slumped, eyes fixed on the ground. There's nothing down there but discouragement. When your eyes are downcast, you're only looking six feet ahead, maybe even six feet under if you're not careful.

But the Bible says in **John 4:35 (KJV):** *"Lift up your eyes, and look on the fields; for they are white already to harvest."*

The Difference a Perspective Makes

Try it right now—look down at the ground. How does that feel? Heavy? Limiting? It's like a weight on your shoulders. Now, lift up your head. Look straight ahead. Look further, past the walls of this building. If the walls weren't there, your eyes could travel miles and miles into the horizon.

Lift them even higher. Look to the heavens. You can see stars thousands of miles away, the moon a quarter-million miles away. That's what happens when you lift up your eyes. Your vision expands, your spirit lifts, and you begin to see possibilities instead of limitations.

Psalm 121:1-2 (KJV) says: "I will lift up mine eyes unto the hills, from whence cometh my help. My help

cometh from the Lord, which made heaven and earth."

When you lift your eyes, you're reminded of where your help comes from—not from yourself, not from the world, but from the Lord.

A New Day for the Body of Christ

I believe with all my heart that we're entering one of the greatest days the body of Christ has ever known. This isn't just rhetoric; it's the Word of God. **Joel 2:28 (KJV)** declares: *"And it shall come to pass afterward, that I will pour out my spirit upon all flesh; and your sons and your daughters shall prophesy, your old men shall dream dreams, your young men shall see visions."*

This is that day! God is pouring out His Spirit, and we have to make up our minds—are we going to hang our harps on the willows in despair, or are we going to march forward in victory?

I've decided I want everything God has for me. I'm not settling for less, and I don't want you to either.

Shake Off Discouragement

During the service, I noticed some people just sitting there, unmoved, while others were fully engaged. I said, *"Come on, lift up your head! Don't just sit there like a bump on a log. Get up and move!"*

I shared a little humor to get folks smiling: *"My wife once asked me to dance with her after we got married. I gave it my best shot, but by the time I was done, her toes were bleeding, and she never asked me again!"*

But the truth is, you don't need to know how to dance to praise the Lord. Just move. Do something. Lift up your hands, lift up your head, and lift up your spirit.

A Physical Act of Faith

I had the congregation do something symbolic. I told them, *"Bow your head down for a moment. Now take your hand, place it under your chin, and lift your head up."*

We did it together, and I could see the change in the room. People began to smile, their posture improved, and there was a renewed sense of joy. It's amazing how a small physical act can reflect a spiritual shift.

Praise Break

I called for the musicians to play something with a beat. *"Let's not just sing; let's praise Him with all we've got!"* The atmosphere shifted as people began clapping, singing, and even dancing.

The Bible says in **Psalm 150:4 (KJV):** ***"Praise him with the timbrel and dance: praise him with stringed instruments and organs."***

It wasn't long before the entire congregation was on their feet. Even those who had been sitting silently were caught up in the joy of the moment.

A Word of Encouragement

I ended the service with this encouragement: *"This is the day of new beginnings. The Lord says in **Isaiah 43:18-19 (KJV):** 'Remember ye not the former things, neither consider the things of old. Behold, I will do a new thing; now it shall spring forth.'"*

This is your new day—a day of new vision, new strength, and new joy. Lift up your eyes, lift up your heart, and step into the newness of life that God has for you.

The River of God

We closed by singing about the river of God, a reminder of His Spirit flowing through us, refreshing and empowering us for the journey ahead. **Psalm 46:4 (KJV) says:** *"There is a river, the streams whereof shall make glad the city of God."*

So, let me leave you with this: Don't look down. Don't give in to discouragement. Lift up your eyes, look to Jesus, and walk forward in victory. This is your time, your season, and your new beginning. Hallelujah!

Food for the Soul: The Power of

God's Word in Every Season of Life

Let me tell you something: this book, the Bible, is food for your soul. And not just any food—it's the kind that satisfies your deepest hunger, nourishes your spirit, and fills you with life. I want to give you five scriptures to remind you of that truth.

The Bible is Nourishment

1. **1 Peter 2:2 (KJV):** *"As newborn babes, desire the sincere milk of the word, that ye may grow thereby."*
   The Word of God is like milk for the soul. It helps us grow, mature, and become strong in our faith.
2. **Jeremiah 15:16 (KJV):** *"Thy words were found, and I did eat them; and thy word was unto me the joy and rejoicing of mine heart."*
   Jeremiah didn't just read God's words—he consumed them. They became the joy and rejoicing of his heart, just as they can be for you.
3. **Psalm 119:103 (KJV):** *"How sweet are thy words unto my taste! yea, sweeter than honey to my mouth!"*
   Jackie Gleason used to say, *"It doesn't get any sweeter than this!"* But he must have been talking about the Bible, because nothing compares to the sweetness of God's Word.
4. **Job 23:12 (KJV):** *"I have esteemed the words of his mouth more than my necessary food."*
   Job understood that the Word of God is more vital

than even the food we eat. It sustains us in ways physical bread never can.
5. **Deuteronomy 8:3 (KJV):** *"Man doth not live by bread only, but by every word that proceedeth out of the mouth of the Lord."* Jesus Himself quoted this scripture when He was tempted in the wilderness. It's a reminder that God's Word is our true source of life.

Moment of Laughter

Now, let me share a little story to keep things light. A friend of mine was at a church so cold and lifeless it could have been nicknamed *"The First Church of the Frigidaire."* He said a man had a heart attack during the service, and when the paramedics arrived, they carried out 20 other people before finding the actual victim.

Love and Marriage: A Personal Testimony

Let me tell you about the love of my life, Betty. She's a farm girl from Southern Illinois who became a head nurse at St. Vincent's Hospital in downtown Los Angeles. I was holding a revival at her church when she walked in wearing her nurse's uniform, and let me tell you, I was immediately smitten.

My heart started racing, my knees turned to rubber, and I knew this was it. I didn't waste any time. I walked right up to her and said, *"I have a word from the Lord for you."*

She looked intrigued and said, *"You do?"*

I said, *"Yes—marry me!"*

We've been married for 44 years now, and it just gets better with time. Betty, is the love of my life!

From Dr Michael H Yeager
AN UNQUENCHABLE HUNGER FOR GOD

One time, my wife anointed all my clothes without telling me, praying that I would get hungry for God again. I hope she never does that again, because it went overboard. She anointed my clothes, my doorknob, and other things. Hunger for God is a spiritual experience.

I came home one night after counseling people. My wife was praying, **"Oh God, give me back the young man that I married who was on fire for you. Oh God, give me back that man."** When I laid my head down on the pillow, the Spirit of God hit me. I fell out of bed, weeping, wailing, and crying. I could not stop for 40 days. I couldn't eat. I didn't decide to fast; I simply couldn't eat. All I could do was drink water.

Wives, you have more power than you think. Stop nagging and start praying for your husbands. Pray fervently, saying, **"God, get that man. Oh God, in the name of Jesus, touch my husband."** Begin to anoint everything secretly as a sign of faith. The spirit of prayer hit me so strongly that all I could do was cry, pray, and drink water.

This went on for one day, two days, five days, a week, two weeks, and eventually 40 days. All I could do is pray. I only drank water!

Matthew 5:6 (KJV) says, **"Blessed are they which do hunger and thirst after righteousness: for they shall be filled."** This hunger and thirst for righteousness is what drives us to seek God with all our hearts.

My wife's prayers and actions remind me of **James 5:16 (KJV), which says, "The effectual fervent prayer of a righteous man availeth much."** Her fervent prayers brought about a profound change in me.

When we are truly hungry and thirsty for God, He responds. **Jeremiah 29:13 (KJV)** promises, **"And ye shall seek me, and find me, when ye shall search for me with all your heart."** This is the key to experiencing God's fullness and Glory—seeking Him with all our hearts.

Let's not be content with a lukewarm faith. Let's be like the prodigal son who realized his need and returned to the Father. **Luke 15:17 (KJV) says, "And when he came to himself, he said, How many hired servants of my father's have bread enough and to spare, and I perish with hunger!"** He realized his deep need and returned home.

Jesus is the only one who can satisfy our deepest hunger and thirst. **John 6:35 (KJV)** says, **"And Jesus said unto them, I am the bread of life: he that cometh to me shall never hunger; and he that believeth on me shall** never thirst."

As we seek Him with all our hearts, we will be filled with His presence, His glory, and His power. Let's be vessels full of God's glory, living testimonies of His power and love.

My experience showed me the power of prayer and the importance of spiritual hunger. May we all seek God with the same desperation and fervor, allowing Him to fill us to overflowing.

A Divine Encounter: When God Filled the House

My family and I were traveling out West, visiting churches and relatives in Wisconsin, when we were invited to minister at a church in Minneapolis, Minnesota. Pastor Bill, the leader of two congregations—one in the suburbs and the other downtown—had arranged for me to preach at the larger suburban church first and then rush to the second church in the city.

The suburban church was filled to capacity, with 140 to 160 men, women, children, and even babies in attendance. As I stood before them, I felt the Holy Spirit begin to stir. I was led to preach on Isaiah's vision of the Lord:

*"In the year that king Uzziah died I saw also the Lord sitting upon a throne, high and lifted up, and his

train filled the temple"* (Isaiah 6:1, KJV).

The words came with power, and it felt as though rivers of living water were flowing out of me. I was under such a strong unction from God that I could hardly remember the words I spoke. The presence of the Holy Spirit grew so thick that it felt like the sanctuary itself was being filled with the glory of God.

Yet, I was mindful of the time. I had to leave for the downtown church soon, and I couldn't linger to pray or minister further. In my heart, I said, *"Lord, if You're going to move, it will have to be without me."* Little did I know, that was precisely what He intended.

I closed the service with a short prayer and quietly left the sanctuary. As I walked out, an extraordinary stillness fell over the congregation—a deep, holy silence that seemed to echo heaven itself. Though I didn't fully understand what was happening, I knew God was working in a profound way.

God's Power Unleashed Downtown

I rushed to Pastor Bill's second church downtown, where the worship service had already begun. Standing at the pulpit, the Spirit led me to preach a different message. This time, I spoke about radical commitment to Jesus Christ—a total surrender of heart, soul, and life to Him.

As the Word went forth, God's presence began to move powerfully. People wept openly, some falling to their knees, while others lay prostrate before the Lord. Not one person was able to stay in their chairs. The Spirit of God swept through the room like a holy fire, touching every heart.

The Call That Changed Everything

That evening, after returning to our trailer at a nearby campground, I received a call from Pastor Bill on my cell phone. His voice was low and trembling as he asked, "Does this always happen after you preach?"

Confused, I asked him what he meant. He recounted how, after I left the suburban church, the power of God fell so heavily that he was unable to stand or even speak. He fell to the floor as I ran out the door. He lay on the floor, overwhelmed by God's presence, for two and a half hours.

When he finally managed to stand, he thought everyone else had gone home. But to his astonishment, every single person was still in the sanctuary—men, women, children, and even the babies—lying motionless on the floor in total silence. For over two hours, not a sound was heard. The presence of God had utterly consumed the room.

The Secret of the Overflow

The next day, Pastor Bill invited me to his home to discuss what had happened. Sitting across from him, he asked, "Does this kind of thing happen often?"

I explained that while I often witness the miraculous, moments like this are rare and only occur when I'm fully surrendered to Jesus. As *John 3:30* declares, *"He must increase, but I must decrease."*

The key, I told him, is being a vessel for God—a temple filled with His Spirit. This happens when we empty ourselves of all distractions and allow Him to fill us completely. It comes through prayer, continual meditating on His Word, worshiping Him with all our hearts, and living in intimate fellowship with the Father, Son, and Holy Spirit.

God is no respecter of persons. What He does for one, He will do for others. It's not about our strength, wisdom, or ability—it's about our surrender. When we yield ourselves as living sacrifices, as temples of the Holy Spirit, He will move through us in ways that leave us in awe.

A Call to Surrender

That day in Minneapolis, God showed me what He could do when we step aside and let Him take over. His glory filled not just one sanctuary, but two—transforming lives and leaving everyone in reverent wonder.

If you desire this kind of encounter with God, the invitation is simple: surrender. Seek Him with all your heart. Fill yourself with His Word. And as *2 Corinthians 4:7* reminds us, *"But we have this treasure in earthen vessels, that the excellency of the power may be of God, and not of us."*

Let the rivers of living water flow through you, and watch as the God who filled the temple of Isaiah's vision fills your life—and the lives of those around you—with His glory

A Woman Fell at My Feet Weeping

Through the years, I've seen God move in miraculous ways, especially through the gift of the word of knowledge. Yet, I yearned for a deeper and more precise manifestation of this gift. The word of knowledge, given by the Holy Spirit, reveals what no human could naturally know, piercing through the veil of the unknown to bring truth and freedom. It's a powerful expression of God's love and sovereignty, and Scripture encourages us to seek such gifts.

In Galatians, we are reminded that ministry through the Spirit is done by faith. Faith is the key that activates every gift—healing, prophecy, miracles—all rooted in the person and power of Jesus Christ. To build this faith, I immersed myself in the Word of God, because *"faith cometh by hearing, and hearing by the word of God"* **(Romans 10:17, KJV).**

One particular verse captured my heart and became a cornerstone for my faith journey:

"But if all prophesy, and there come in one that believeth not, or one unlearned, he is convinced of all,

he is judged of all: And thus are the secrets of his heart made manifest; and so falling down on his face he will worship God, and report that God is in you of a truth" (1 Corinthians 14:24-25, KJV).

This scripture resonated deeply within me. I didn't just memorize it; I meditated on it, speaking it aloud with conviction and letting it take root in my spirit. Over time, it burned brighter in my heart than the physical world around me. This, I believe, is how faith grows—like a muscle, it strengthens through intentional repetition and immersion in the Word.

Not long after, I began to notice a new sharpness in the words of knowledge God gave me. Then, one evening during a midweek service, something extraordinary happened.

A woman entered the church for the first time. She appeared to be in her fifties, someone I had never seen before. As I wrapped up my sermon, the Spirit of God impressed upon me to call her forward. She hesitated but eventually stepped up, visibly nervous.

As she stood before me, the Holy Spirit began to flow. Words came to me with a clarity that only God could provide. I looked at her and said, "You have one son and two daughters. Your daughter is married to a man who is physically abusing her, and you are consumed with fear for her safety and life."

The room fell silent. The words came forth not from my mind but from the Spirit of God, and as I spoke, I could see the weight of her burden begin to surface. Her body trembled, and then, unable to hold back her emotions, she collapsed to the floor, weeping uncontrollably.

Through her tears, she cried out, "It's true! Everything you've said is true. God is speaking through you!" Her cries were not of despair but of release. In that moment, the secrets of her heart were revealed, just as 1 Corinthians 14:25 describes. She worshiped God with her whole being, acknowledging His presence and power.

I was deeply humbled. This wasn't about me; it was a demonstration of the faithfulness and compassion of Jesus. His Word, sharper than any two-edged sword, had penetrated to the depths of her heart, bringing healing and freedom. *"For the word of God is quick, and powerful, and sharper than any two-edged sword, piercing even to the dividing asunder of soul and spirit, and of the joints and marrow, and is a discerner of the thoughts and intents of the heart"* **(Hebrews 4:12, KJV).**

That evening reminded me of the incredible potential of meditating on God's Word. When we fill our hearts with His truth, allowing it to become more real to us than the physical world, God moves through us in ways that defy explanation. The same Spirit who revealed the secrets of this woman's heart desires to work through every believer who is willing to surrender to Him.

God's gifts are not reserved for a select few. As Peter declared, *"God is no respecter of persons"* **(Acts 10:34, KJV).** What He has done through me, He can do through you. The question is, are you willing to immerse yourself in His Word and step out in faith?

That night, a woman left the church transformed—not just because her burden was acknowledged, but because she encountered the living God. Her tears were a testament to His love, and her worship was proof that His Word never returns void. Let this be a reminder to us all: when we seek Him with our whole hearts, He meets us in ways that are beyond what we could ask or think.

CHAPTER NINE
Sharing Wisdom Across Generations

A few years back, we were invited to lead a marriage seminar for a group of 50 couples—all under the age of 35. Betty and I were in our 70s, so I asked the organizer, *"How do two people in their 70s talk to 35-year-olds about love, marriage, and intimacy?"*

He shot back with a grin, *"You do what all 70-year-olds do—you talk about it!"*

That was a cheap shot, but we took the challenge because we've learned that experience speaks volumes. After all, we've been married longer than most of those folks had been alive.

The Word Sustains Every Season

Here's the truth: no matter where you are in life—young, old, single, married—the Word of God sustains you. It's your daily bread, your source of joy, and your guide for every situation.

Psalm 37:25 (KJV) says: *"I have been young, and now am old; yet have I not seen the righteous forsaken, nor his seed begging bread."*

God's Word is faithful, and it will carry you through every season of life.

Closing Encouragement

So, grab your Bible, hold it high, and say this with me:

"He spoke to me. He called me. He's bringing me along. And He's making my way prosperous!"

Whether you're reading it for the first time or the hundredth, remember that this book is food for your soul. Dive in, feast on its promises, and let it transform your life.

To God be the glory for His everlasting Word!

Through the Fire: How God Grows Us in Times of Trouble

Let me begin with a promise from **Ezekiel 12:28 (KJV)**: *"There shall none of my words be prolonged any more, but the word which I have spoken shall be done, saith the Lord God."*

Now, lift your Bible and declare it: *"None of God's promises to me shall be delayed any longer. What He has spoken will come to pass—right now!"*

Say it again: *"Right now!"*

A Word on Growth

I was told once, *"When growth stops, decay sets in."* That phrase stuck with me because it's so true. Growth isn't optional for us—it's essential. But let me tell you a funny story to illustrate this.

When I turned 70, a pastor asked me how it felt to reach that milestone. I told him, *"I think I'm getting mellow."*

He pulled out a big dictionary, flipped to the word *mellow*, and said, *"I'm not sure you want to use that word."*

I looked it up, and sure enough, one of the definitions was *"fruit that is going soft."*

I laughed and said, *"There's no soft fruit here!"*

We are meant to keep growing, spiritually and otherwise. Stagnation isn't an option. Like the hymn *Amazing Grace* says, *"Through many dangers, toils, and snares, we have already come."* God's grace has carried us this far, and His grace will carry us forward.

Lessons from the Sequoia Tree

Out in California, they have these massive Sequoia trees, some of which are over 4,000 years old. Rangers study their growth by examining their rings. Each year, the tree grows a microscopic ring, slow and steady.

One ranger explained to me how these trees survive attacks—fire, lightning, and beetles. The secret lies in a tannic acid just beneath their bark. Whenever the tree is attacked, this acid multiplies, strengthening the tree and causing it to grow faster.

He showed me a cross-section of a tree that survived a massive wildfire in 1867. Its growth rings for that year were incredibly wide. He said, *"This tree grew more in one year than it had in the last 50 because of the attack."*

The Lord used that lesson to speak to me through **Psalm 34:19 (KJV):** *"Many are the afflictions of the righteous: but the Lord delivereth him out of them all."*

Why the Attack?

Attacks come, but they're not the end of the story. Like the Sequoia tree, it's in those moments of trial that we experience the greatest growth. When fire comes, when the enemy strikes, God uses those challenges to build us stronger.

James 1:2-3 (KJV) says: *"My brethren, count it all joy when ye fall into divers temptations; Knowing this, that the trying of your faith worketh patience."*

You see, the attacks are not to destroy us but to refine us, to cause us to grow in ways we couldn't otherwise.

Your Growth is Coming

Maybe you've been through a season of fire. Maybe you've faced obstacles, roadblocks, and heartaches. Let me remind you: ***"The Lord delivers us out of them all"*** **(Psalm 34:19, KJV).**

You're not just surviving—you're growing. The trials you're enduring are preparing you for an abundant harvest. The roots are going deeper, and the branches are reaching higher.

Say it with me: *"I'm growing stronger, even in the attack."*

Hold onto God's promises. He's not just taking you through the fire—He's using it to grow you in ways you never thought possible. Hallelujah!

Breaking Through the Fire: How God Uses Adversity to Multiply Our Faith

Let me tell you something: prosperity can bring out all your vices, but adversity? That brings out your virtues. When people prosper, it's easy for pride, arrogance, and even contempt to creep in. We've all seen it—people pushing others around, flaunting their power, losing their humility. Prosperity has a way of revealing our flaws.

But adversity? Adversity does the opposite. It refines us. It exposes our dedication, our commitment, and the strength of our character. Let me illustrate this with a story about Mary and her alabaster box.

The Alabaster Box

Mary had this precious box of ointment—12 ounces of the most aromatic and costly fragrance. It was sealed, locked away. No one could benefit from it as long as it remained unbroken. People might've asked, *"What's in the box?"* and she could've explained, but nothing could compare to the moment she broke it open.

When Mary broke the alabaster box, the entire house was filled with its sweet aroma **(John 12:3, KJV)**. Imagine this: it's a hot April day, and people have just walked uphill from Jerusalem. The room is heavy with the smell of human perspiration. But then, suddenly, the air shifts. That exquisite fragrance fills the space, completely transforming it.

It's the broken places that release the aroma of our dedication to God.

Through the Fire and the Flood

Exodus 1:12 (KJV) gives us a profound truth: ***"The more they afflicted them, the more they multiplied and grew."*** The Israelites were making progress, but then the enemy came to fight them, to block their way. Yet the more the enemy came against them, the stronger they became.

Now listen to me—Satan has come against you too. Maybe he's tried to extinguish your fire, to silence your praise, to hinder your ministry. But he made a big mistake. Just like the Israelites, the more the enemy fights you, the stronger you will become.

Say to your self, *"We're still in the race. We're still on our feet!"*

The Power of Perspective

Paul understood this truth. In **Philippians 1:12 (KJV),** he wrote, *"**The things which happened unto me have fallen out rather unto the furtherance of the gospel.**"* In other words, everything Paul endured—the persecution, the imprisonments, the beatings—wasn't wasted. God used it to spread the gospel further than Paul ever could've imagined.

David said the same thing in **Psalm 66:12 (KJV):** *"**Thou hast caused men to ride over our heads; we went through fire and through water: but thou broughtest us out into a wealthy place.**"*

David wasn't sugarcoating anything. He acknowledged the pain. He described being steamrolled, trampled, and left face-down in the mud. But he also proclaimed God's faithfulness. He said, *"The Lord is bringing us out!"*

A Wealthy Place

Now let me tell you what that "wealthy place" means. Some translations call it *"a place of abundant refreshing"* or *"a place of great moisture."* It's a picture of restoration, renewal, and overflowing blessings. God doesn't just bring us through the fire—He brings us to a place better than we were before.

There's no going back to the way things were. God told Moses, **"Speak unto the children of Israel, that they go forward" (Exodus 14:15, KJV).** Forward is the only direction we're meant to go.

Your Breakthrough is Coming

You've been through the fire. You've walked through the flood. Maybe you've faced opposition that left you wondering if you could keep going. But let me remind you of this: **"The Lord delivers [the righteous] out of them all" (Psalm 34:19, KJV).**

This isn't the end—it's the beginning. God is bringing you out into a wealthy place, a place of abundant blessings and refreshing. So lift your head, hold onto His promises, and keep moving forward. The best is yet to come.

Say it with me: *"The more the enemy fights me, the stronger I become!"*

"I'm Going Through with Jesus"

"Success is not measured by attainment, accomplishment, and achievement," Booker T. Washington once said, "but by how much adversity you have been able to overcome." Those words ring truer than ever in my life. Say it with me: *Success is determined by how much adversity you've been able to get through.* Hallelujah! And let me tell you, I'm going through, because Jesus is with me.

It was a clear morning when Betty and I were driving across Nebraska, on our way to Colorado. We were pulling our 30-foot trailer, a mobile home we had called ours for 35 years as Pentecostal evangelists. We were traveling from church to church, comforting the afflicted and, yes, afflicting the comfortable—that's what an evangelist does, after all.

Out of nowhere, disaster struck. The trailer jackknifed, causing the car to break loose. It went careening over a 40-foot embankment, leaving us at the bottom of the hill in a mangled mess. Our trailer smashed against a siding, almost destroyed.

For a moment, I looked around and thought, *Is this it? Is this the end?*

But then, my eyes fell on my guitar. It was intact. I glanced at the sewing machine I had just bought for Betty—it was unharmed. I grabbed them both, one in each hand, and turned to Betty, helping her climb straight up the side of that steep ravine.

As we climbed, it felt like Satan himself was hurling every accusation he could muster: *It's over, you've lost everything. You'll never get there.* But then, out of my spirit came a melody, an old hymn by Herbert Buffum:

"Lord, I've started to walk in the light, Shining on my pathway from heaven so bright, Living each moment with Your face in view—I've started in with Jesus, and I'm going through!"

We reached the highway, battered but alive. Our car was smashed, our trailer wrecked. Yet I turned to Betty and said, "Honey, if we have to hitchhike to Colorado, we'll do it. Cars and trailers are just tin and wood—they can be replaced. But what we carry inside of us, that fire to preach the gospel to every creature, cannot be replaced!"

The words of Jesus resounded in my heart: **"Go ye into all the world, and preach the gospel to every creature" (Mark 16:15, KJV).** And in that moment, I knew we couldn't stop, no matter what obstacles Satan threw in our path.

The next night, we made it to Sterling, Colorado—somehow, some way. And as I stood there, guitar in hand, ready to preach, I thought about what it means to survive the storm. It's not just about getting through; it's about being prepared for the bigger purpose God has for you. **"Thou hast enlarged me when I was in distress" (Psalm 4:1, KJV).** The trials aren't meant to break you—they're meant to make you stronger for what's ahead.

I shared with the congregation that night a truth God had impressed on my heart: When adversity comes, it's not just the troublemakers who are being tested. It's you. ***"Keep thy heart with all diligence; for out of it are the issues of life"* (Proverbs 4:23, KJV).** You can't let bitterness take root because of what's happened to you. Bitterness will rob you of joy, anointing, and purpose.

I've seen too many people—good, God-fearing people—fall into the trap of bitterness. They get hurt, they grow angry, and before long, they're sitting at home, clipping coupons, their ministries and dreams a distant memory. They say, "I'll get even if it's the last thing I do." And often, it *is* the last thing they do. Don't let that be your story.

That night in Colorado, the Spirit of God fell on that congregation as I shared our testimony. Feet were tapping, hands were raised, and I could feel the determination rising in that room: *We're going through with Jesus.*

Because, let me tell you, the storms will come. But when you have Jesus, you can sing in the middle of them. Just like the ten lepers who cried out, "Jesus, Master, have mercy on us!" **(Luke 17:13, KJV),** and were healed as they went, so too does healing—physical, emotional, and spiritual—come when we obey His Word and keep going.

Betty and I have seen our fair share of storms. But every time, we've come out stronger. And through it all, the song in my heart remains the same:

"I've started in with Jesus, and I'm going through."

So, keep going, friend. Through every trial, through every storm—Jesus is with you, and He's more than enough. **"For with God nothing shall be impossible" (Luke 1:37, KJV).** Hallelujah!

From Dr Michael H Yeager
Healed When I Slammed My Broken Foot Down the 5th Time.

One day I had to climb our 250-foot AM radio tower to change the light bulb on the main beacon. (If you ever visit our church I will be glad to have you visit our tower) However, to climb the tower, I had to first find the keys, which I never did. Since I could not find the keys to get the fence open, I did the next best thing—I simply climbed over the fence.

This idea turned out not to be such a wonderful idea after all! With all my climbing gear hanging from my waist, I climbed the fence to the very top. At this point, my rope gear became entangled in the fencing. As I tried to get free, I lost my balance and fell backwards off the fence. Trying to break my fall, I got my right foot down underneath me. I hit the ground with my foot being turned on its side and I felt something snap in the ankle. I knew instantly I had a broken foot, my ankle.

Most normal people would have climbed back over the fence, go set up a doctor's appointment, have their foot x rayed, and then placed into a cast. But I am not a normal-thinking person, at least according to the standards of the modern-day church. When I broke my foot, I followed my routine of confessing my stupidity to God and asking Him to forgive me for my stupidity.

Moreover, then I spoke to my foot and commanded it to be healed in the name of Jesus Christ of Nazareth. When I had finished speaking to my foot, commanding it to be healed, and then praising and thanking God for the healing, there seem to be no change whatsoever in its condition.

The Scripture that came to my heart was where Jesus declared, "The kingdom of heaven suffereth violence, and the violent take it by force!" Based completely upon this scripture, I decided to climb the tower by FAITH, with a broken foot mind you. Please do not misunderstand, my foot hurt so bad I could hardly stand it. And yet, I had declared that I BELIEVED I was healed.

There were three men watching me as I took the Word of God by FAITH. I told them what I was about to do, and they looked at me as if I had lost my mind. I began to climb the 250-foot tower, one painful step at a time.

My foot hurt so bad that I was hyperventilating within just twenty to thirty feet up the tower. It literally felt like I was going to pass out from shock at any moment. Whenever I got to the point of fainting, I would connect my climbing ropes to the tower, stop and take a breather, crying out to Jesus to help me. It seemed to take me forever to get to the top.

Even so, I finally did reach the very top of the tower and replaced the light bulb that had gone out. Usually, I can come down that tower within 10 minutes, because I would press my feet against the tower rods, and then slide down, just using my hands and arms to lower myself at a very fast pace.

However, in this situation, my foot could not handle the pressure of being pushed up against the steel. Consequently, I had to work my way down very slowly. After I was down, I slowly climbed over the fence one more time. I hobbled my way over to my vehicle and drove up to the church office. The men who had been watching this unfold, were right behind me.

I hobbled my way into the front office, which is directly across the street from the radio tower. I informed the personnel that I had broken my foot, showing them my black and blue, extremely swollen foot. It did not help that I had climbed with it! I told them that I was going home to rest. At the same time, however, I told them that I BELIEVED I was healed.

Going to my house, which is directly across from the main office of the church parking lot, I made my way slowly up the stairs to our bedroom. I found my wife in the bedroom putting away our clothes. Slowly and painfully, I pulled the shoe and sock off the broken foot.

What a mess! It was fat, swollen, black and blue all over. I put a pillow down at the end of the bed, and carefully pulled myself up onto the bed. Lying on my back, I tenderly placed my broken, black, and blue, swollen foot onto the pillow. No matter how I positioned it, the pain did not cease. I just laid there squirming, moaning, and sighing.

As I was lying there trying to overcome the shock that kept hitting my body, I heard the audible voice of God. He said to me: "What are you doing in bed? God really got my attention when I heard him with my natural ears. My wife would testify that she heard nothing. Immediately in my heart I said: Lord I'm just resting. Then He spoke to my heart with the still small voice very clearly, do you always rest at this time of day? No, Lord, I replied. (It was about 3 o'clock in the afternoon)

He spoke to my heart again and said: I thought you said you were healed by MY Stripes?

At that very moment I knew it was Jesus Himself talking to me and the gift of FAITH exploded inside my heart. I said, "Lord, I am healed! Immediately, I pushed myself up off the bed, grabbed my sock and shoe, and struggled to put them back on. What a tremendous struggle it was! My foot was so swollen that it did not want to go into the shoe. My wife was watching me as I fought to complete this task.

You might wonder what my wife was doing this whole time as I was fighting this battle of FAITH. She was doing what she always does, just watching me and shaking her head. I finally got the shoe on my swollen, black, and blue foot. I put my foot down on the floor and began to put my body weight upon it. When I did, I almost passed out. At that moment, a holy anger exploded on the inside of me. I declared out loud, **"I am healed in the name of Jesus Christ of Nazareth!"** With that declaration, I took my right (broken) foot and slammed it down to the floor as hard as I possibly could.

When I did that, I felt the bones of my foot break even more. Like the Fourth of July, an explosion of blue, purple, red, white, black exploded in my brain and I passed out. I came to lying on my bed. Afterward, my wife informed me that every time I passed out, it was for about ten to twenty seconds.

The moment I came to, I jumped right back up out of bed. The gift of FAITH was working in me mightily. I got back up and followed the same process again, **"In the name of Jesus Christ of Nazareth I am healed,"** and slammed my foot down once more as hard as I could! For a second time, I could feel the damage in my foot increasing. My mind was once again wrapped in an explosion of colors and pain as I blacked out.

When I regained consciousness, I immediately got up once again, repeating the same process. After the third time this happening I came to with my wife leaning over the top of me. I remember my wife saying as she looked at me, "You're making me sick. I can't watch you do this." She promptly walked out of our bedroom and went downstairs.

The fourth time I got up declaring, **"In the name of Jesus Christ of Nazareth I am healed, "**and slammed my foot even harder! Once more, multiple colors of intense pain hit my brain. I passed out again! I got up the fifth time, angrier than ever. This was not demonic or proud anger.

This was a divine gift of violent I-will-not-take-no-for-an-answer type of FAITH. I slammed my foot down the fifth time, **"In the name of Jesus Christ of Nazareth I am healed!"** The minute my foot slammed into the floor, for the fifth time, the power of God hit my foot. I literally stood there under the quickening power of God, and watched my foot shrink and become normal.

All the pain was completely and totally gone. I pulled back my sock and all the swelling was gone! I watched as the black and blue in my foot disappear to normal flesh color. I was healed! Praise God, I was made whole! I went back to the office, giving glory to the Lord and showing the staff my healed foot.

Prophesied Tyson's Baby Boy – Born January 4th, 2024

There's something indescribably powerful about seeing God's promises fulfilled—especially when He turns the impossible into a testimony. Over the years, I've had the privilege of delivering prophetic words to couples longing for children, couples who were told by doctors that they would never conceive. Time and time again, I've stood in awe as God moved, proving that His Word is always true.

It all began in 1981 when I prophesied over a couple named Bill and Pam. They had been trying to have a child for eight long years, but every doctor they saw said it was impossible. One evening, as I prayed for them, the Spirit of the Lord came upon me, and I boldly declared, *"You will have a child, and God will use you both in a children's ministry."* Pam clung to that word, tears streaming down her face. Within a year, she was pregnant, and today, not only are they parents, but they also serve faithfully in children's ministry, just as God had promised.

Fast forward to 2021, when a similar moment unfolded. One of my church elders brought his son and daughter-in-law to a service. The young man, a member of the Air Force stationed in New Mexico, was visiting with his wife for the first time. I didn't know anything about their struggles, but as I stood before them, the Holy Spirit began to whisper to my heart.

I walked up to the couple, looked them in the eyes, and said, *"You will have a child within the next year."*

The wife immediately burst into tears. It wasn't until later that I learned how fervently they had been praying for a miracle. True to the word of the Lord, she became pregnant not long after, and in August of 2022, they welcomed a beautiful baby girl into their family.

Then, in 2023, another couple visited our church with their ten-year-old daughter. As I prayed for them, the Holy Spirit revealed to me that the wife had been enduring repeated miscarriages. I hadn't been told this beforehand, but the Spirit made it clear. With confidence in Jesus, I spoke the word of the Lord over them: *"Within the next year, you will have a healthy baby boy."*

The wife broke down, clinging to the promise of God. A few months later, they reached out to share the good news—she was pregnant. This time, she carried the baby without any complications. On January 4th, 2024, they welcomed a perfect, healthy baby boy into the world. When they brought him to church to be dedicated, it was a moment of pure joy, a tangible reminder of God's faithfulness.

These moments are why I never stop marveling at how deeply God cares for His people. He hears every cry and answers in His perfect timing. As **Psalm 37:4 (KJV)** says, ***"Delight thyself also in the Lord; and he shall give thee the desires of thine heart."***

Even within my own family, I've witnessed God's promises fulfilled. Years ago, the Lord revealed to me that my son and his wife would have two children. They waited nearly eight years, standing firm in faith, before being blessed with their first—a beautiful baby girl. Now, three years later, they are expecting their second child, due in May of 2025. God's Word never fails.

Most recently, I felt led to give another prophetic word to a young couple. I told them, *"God has heard your prayers, and He will grant you the desire of your heart."* The hope in their eyes was unmistakable. I know it won't be long before we see another miracle unfold.

These testimonies are not about me—they're about Jesus and His faithfulness. His promises remain true, just as they did when He healed the lepers in **Luke 17:12-14.** Ten lepers came to Jesus, crying out for mercy. He told them to go and show themselves to the priests, and as they went, they were healed. Faith met obedience, and the impossible became reality.

For anyone who is waiting on a miracle—whether for a child, healing, or a breakthrough—know this: Jesus sees you. He hears your prayers and is working on your behalf. Trust Him and hold fast to His promises. ***"Jesus Christ the same yesterday, and today, and forever"* (Hebrews 13:8, KJV).** What He has done for others, He will do for you. His timing is perfect, and His love for you is unshakable.

A Reprobate and an Outlaw

One Sunday morning, the Spirit of God moved in a way I'll never forget. The sanctuary was filled with the weight of His presence, and many came forward for prayer. Among those in the line was a young evangelist who had been attending our church for some time. He was eager, energetic, and seemed to have a deep hunger for God. But that morning, the Spirit of prophecy was flowing strongly, and the Lord had something to address in his life.

When I came to him, I laid my hands on him, and he immediately fell under the power of God. I continued praying for others, moving down the line, but just as I got to the third person, something stirred deeply in my spirit. The Spirit of the Lord drew me back to the evangelist lying on the floor. What happened next was not planned—it was completely under the direction of God.

I found myself standing over him, straddling him with one foot on either side of his body. Without hesitation, I reached down, grabbed the collar of his shirt with my left hand, and began slapping his face with my right. Hard. I slapped him on both cheeks, at least five times, forcefully and deliberately. It wasn't me; it was the Spirit of God moving through me. Once I was finished, I stepped away and continued praying for the others as if nothing had happened.

A short time later, I was drawn back to him again. This time, I spoke words that flowed from the Spirit of God: "Even as my servant has slapped your flesh, so you must slap your flesh. If you do not crucify your flesh, you will become a reprobate and a fugitive from the law!"

When the Spirit of God moves so strongly, it's as if I am simply a vessel. I don't fully process what I say or do in those moments. Once the service ended, I didn't give the incident much thought. But three days later, I received a phone call that would make everything clear.

One of the ladies in the church called me, weeping. She explained that her twenty-something-year-old daughter had run away with that evangelist. To my shock, she also revealed that he had been involved in an immoral relationship with another woman in the congregation. My heart broke for this mother as we prayed together over the phone, asking God to intervene.

About a month later, the same woman called me again, and this time her voice was filled with desperation. She shared that the man had physically abused her daughter. The situation had escalated further—they had gone out drinking one night and were pulled over by a police officer. In a fit of rage, the evangelist got into an argument with the officer that turned into a physical altercation. Things spiraled out of control, and he ended up grabbing the officer's revolver, pointing it at him. Realizing what he had done, he fled, leaving the officer and the young woman behind.

Word soon spread that he was running for Canada, a fugitive from the law. That was the last I heard of him, but the prophetic word spoken over him had tragically come to pass. The warning from God had been clear, yet he chose to follow the desires of his flesh rather than surrender them to Christ.

The apostle Paul wrote in **1 Corinthians 9:26-27 (KJV): "I therefore so run, not as uncertainly; so fight I, not as one that beateth the air: But I keep under my body, and bring it into subjection: lest that by any means, when I have preached to others, I myself should be a castaway."**

This scripture carries a sobering truth: even those who preach to others are not exempt from falling into sin if they do not discipline their flesh. The young evangelist had so much potential, but his refusal to crucify his flesh led to his downfall.

This story serves as a reminder for all of us. No one is immune to temptation. We must actively bring our bodies under subjection to the will of Christ, choosing daily to deny ourselves, take up our cross, and follow Him. It's not just about ministering to others—it's about living in personal obedience and holiness before God. Let us walk humbly, allowing the Holy Spirit to guide and correct us, so we do not become reprobate.

CHAPTER TEN
"Joy Comes in the Morning"

"We're not here to coast—we're here to crow!" That's what I told them that Sunday morning as the Spirit stirred in my heart. "Say it with me: *A church alive is worth the drive!*" I could feel the energy of the room shift as the congregation began to believe it, declaring to one another, "Our best days are ahead."

It wasn't always this way. When I first started calling people out during services, giving them scriptures that the Lord placed on my heart, I was in an organization that wasn't ready for it. They were steeped in tradition, predictable to the point that church was more like a 60-minute countdown to the benediction. It didn't take long for the backlash to come.

I still remember the sting of my first hate mail. I was young, living at home, not yet married, and I couldn't understand how someone could write such a nasty letter to a man who only wanted to serve Jesus. I turned to my mother and said, "How could anyone be this mean to someone as lovable as me?"

Bless her heart, she tried to help. She quoted Mark Twain, saying, "You can't drown a man who's born to hang." I didn't get it. "What does that even mean, Ma?" I asked, exasperated.

She explained, "It means you've got to toughen up. These little tests and trials are just the beginning. You've got to get ready for the big ones—the firing squads of life, the real tribulations."

Her words stayed with me, though I didn't fully grasp them until later. Over the years, I've come to see how true they were. The little things—the criticisms, the challenges—can't derail the calling God has placed on your life unless you let them. *"If thou faint in the day of adversity, thy strength is small"* **(Proverbs 24:10, KJV)**.

The truth is, weeping comes to all of us. But as **Psalm 30:5 says,** *"Weeping may endure for a night, but joy cometh in the morning."* And that morning came for me—and it's coming for you.

When the announcements started rolling in about the challenges our church had faced in recent years, my spirit grieved. I cried out to the Lord, asking, "How much more can we take?" And He answered me clearly: *"I will beat the devil at his own game. I will open the windows of heaven and pour you out a blessing, that there shall not be room enough to receive it"* **(Malachi 3:10, KJV)**.

The Lord wasn't just talking about material blessings—He was talking about souls. *"And the Lord added to the church daily such as should be saved"* **(Acts 2:47,**

KJV). I knew then that this was a season of supernatural increase, not just for me but for the body of Christ.

I turned to the congregation that day and declared, "God says He's putting this church on a 24-hour-a-day schedule of soul-winning. Salvations will happen daily. Deliverances will happen daily. Marriages will be restored daily. Blessings will overflow daily. And if you think you've been busy up until now, you haven't seen anything yet!"

The people erupted in praise, faith rising in their hearts as they repeated after me, "Salvations on a daily basis! Blessings on a daily basis! Deliverances on a daily basis!"

But this wasn't just hype. It was a promise rooted in the Word of God. **Psalm 126:5** declares, *"They that sow in tears shall reap in joy."* Every tear we had cried, every seed of faith we had sown in the hardest times, was about to yield a harvest of joy.

I want to encourage you today—no matter what you've been through, no matter how dark your night has been—joy is coming. Jesus Himself healed the lepers who cried out to Him in desperation, *"Master, have mercy on us"* **(Luke 17:13, KJV).** He didn't turn them away, and He won't turn you away either.

The trials, the hate mail, the challenges—they're nothing compared to the glory that awaits when we keep our eyes on Jesus. So, say it with me one more time: *Weeping may endure for a night, but joy comes in the morning!* Hallelujah!

"From This Day Forward: A New Beginning"

It's the dawning of a new day. My schedule has been packed—I had to cancel a campus group meeting in Phoenix and Tucson, Arizona, because of all my invites. I didn't have anything open until later in the summer, but I felt a deep stirring in my spirit. And let me be clear: it's not because of me—it's because the Lord is at work, and He's letting me be a part of what He's doing. Glory to God!

I want you to turn with me to the book of Haggai, chapter 2, verse 19. It's tucked away there in the Old Testament, but it holds a word for us today. *"Is the seed yet in the barn? Yea, as yet the vine, and the fig tree, and the pomegranate, and the olive tree, hath not brought forth: from this day will I bless you"* **(Haggai 2:19, KJV).** Did you catch that? Even though the vine isn't ripe, the fig tree hasn't produced, and the pomegranate and olive trees seem barren, God says, *"From this day forward, I will bless you!"*

There have been times in life where the results didn't seem to match the effort. The seeds we've sown felt like they remained in the barn. We labored, but the harvest didn't come when we thought it would. Maybe you've felt the same. Maybe you've prayed for healing, for breakthrough, or for restoration, and the fruit hasn't appeared yet. But let me tell you something: the God of

Haggai is still the same today. Jesus said, *"Ask, and it shall be given you; seek, and ye shall find; knock, and it shall be opened unto you"* **(Matthew 7:7, KJV).** His promises are true, and His blessings are sure.

Before we go any further, I want you to agree with Gods word! There's power in agreement. Jesus said, *"If two of you shall agree on earth as touching anything that they shall ask, it shall be done for them of my Father which is in heaven"* **(Matthew 18:19, KJV).** So as we pray together, let's release words of healing, wisdom, faith, and peace in the name of Jesus.

We're declaring today as a turning point. Like the ten lepers who cried out to Jesus in **Luke 17:13,** saying, *"Jesus, Master, have mercy on us,"* we're stepping out in faith. Jesus told those lepers to go show themselves to the priests, and as they went, they were healed **(Luke 17:14).** The healing didn't come before the act of obedience—it came in the going. And one, recognizing the miracle, returned to give glory to God, and Jesus told him, *"Thy faith hath made thee whole"* **(Luke 17:19, KJV).** That's the kind of faith we're calling on today.

Now, the Bible is the Word of God, and in it is the strength we need for today. *Isaiah 27:5* says, *"Let him take hold of my strength, that he may make peace with me; and he shall make peace with me."* Daniel experienced this firsthand when he was flat on the floor, completely drained. Yet in **Daniel 10:19,** it says, *"O man greatly beloved, fear not: peace be unto thee, be strong, yea, be strong."* And Daniel said, *"When he had spoken unto me, I was strengthened."*

If you've been feeling weak, worn out, or defeated, know this: His Word brings strength. His promises are for you. And His blessings—yes, even in the barren seasons—are already on their way.

As I prayed over a congregation one day, I could feel the Spirit of God moving. This wasn't just another Sunday service. This was a moment of prophetic significance, a time to declare, *"From this day forward, things are going to change!"*

And I want to tell you, friend, it's not too late for you either. Maybe you've been waiting for healing, just like those lepers. Maybe you've been sowing seeds in tears, wondering when the harvest will come. But hear this: *"They that sow in tears shall reap in joy"* **(Psalm 126:5, KJV)**.

Take hold of His strength today. Believe in His Word. And declare with faith: *This is my day of new beginnings.* From this day forward, God's blessings are pouring out. Hallelujah!

"Your Best Days Are Ahead"

You've got to understand something about me—I'm not here to flatter anyone or butter them up. That's not my calling. My calling is to encourage people, to speak truth, and to build them up in the Word of God. And today, I've got a word for you that I believe is going to set someone free.

Let me start with **Psalms 37:37**, which says, *"Mark the perfect man, and behold the upright: for the end of that man is peace"* **(KJV)**. That verse has your name written all over it. It's not a word of flattery—it's a statement of fact. God isn't working in fractions or percentages with your faith. It's not 10% faith or half faith. No, He's given you a *complete faith!* Say it with me: *Complete faith.*

Take Beatrice, for example. The Lord has imparted to her a robe of righteousness, a gift from heaven itself. And with that robe comes a promise: *"From this day forward, Beatrice, you're stress-free, pressure-free, tension-free, and hassle-free!"* How many of you would say, "I'll take that!"? I can feel the Spirit of God stirring in this place as we declare that over her life—and over yours too.

The truth is, when God gets involved, He doesn't just clean the surface. He gets right into the deepest parts of us, into that "cerebral region" where the clutter and the doubts hide. Like a divine Roto-Rooter, He clears out all the junk, all the gobbledygook, and makes a way for us to walk in freedom.

I think about **Philippians 3:13,** where Paul says, *"Forgetting those things which are behind, and reaching forth unto those things which are before"* (KJV). Now, consider who's writing this. Paul—formerly Saul—was there when Stephen, a saint of God, was stoned to death. Not only was he present, but he orchestrated it. Imagine the weight of that memory when Paul came to know

Jesus. How does someone move forward with such a past?

Paul found the answer in Jesus. He learned to forget what was behind and to fix his eyes on what lay ahead. That's the message for you today. Forget the failures, the regrets, the pain. God is doing a new thing. **Isaiah 43:18-19** says, ***"Remember ye not the former things, neither consider the things of old. Behold, I will do a new thing; now it shall spring forth; shall ye not know it?"*** **(KJV)**.

Let me tell you about Jeremy. I looked at him one day and said, "Jeremy, your best days are ahead of you." The room went silent for a moment as the Word sank into his spirit. And you know what? It wasn't just for Jeremy. It's for you too. God is saying, "Stop turning back. Stop holding on to the past. Tomorrow is where it's at. I've got something new waiting for you!"

Now, let me speak directly to you, the one reading this. God isn't finished with you. Whatever you've been carrying—pain, regret, or fear—He's ready to lift it. Look at the lepers in **Luke 17:12-19**. Ten men stood at a distance, crying out, ***"Jesus, Master, have mercy on us"*** **(KJV)**. They were outcasts, marked by disease, yet Jesus didn't ignore them. He told them to go show themselves to the priests, and as they obeyed, they were healed. But here's the key—only one came back to give glory to God. And to that one, Jesus said, ***"Arise, go thy way: thy faith hath made thee whole"*** **(KJV)**.

Healing comes when we step out in faith. Wholeness comes when we give glory to God.

So today, I declare over you: *Your best days are ahead!* From this day forward, step into the new thing God is doing in your life. Forget the past, reach for what's ahead, and trust in Jesus to lead the way. And as you go, remember this: It's not about who you've been; it's about who God is making you to be. Hallelujah!

Free at Last: Breaking Every Chain"

This message, I know, is going to liberate the church. It's going to set the leadership free. It's going to release individuals from burdens they've been carrying for far too long. I want you to put your hands together, just like this—palms clasped—and listen closely.

In **Jeremiah 40:4,** the Lord declares, *"I loose thee this day from the chains which were upon thine hand."* Do you hear that? He's saying, *This day, I am breaking the chains off your soul.* Chains of financial adversity, chains of fear, chains of insecurity, chains of anger and bitterness—all of them are coming off in Jesus' name.

We're going to name these chains together, one by one. Let's call them out into the open. Say it with me:

- Financial adversity.

- **Physical suffering.**
- **Personal anxiety.**
- **Discouragement.**
- **Weariness.**
- **Fatigue.**
- **Chains of lust.**
- **Chains of pride.**
- **Chains of religious bondage.**
- **Chains of sickness and disease.**
- **Depression.**
- **Hopelessness.**

Let those words sink in as you name them. Now, raise your hands wherever you are, clasped together as if bound. And this time, you are going to declare the Word of God three times. On the third time, we'll separate our hands and proclaim, **In the name of Jesus Christ** *"Free at last! Free at last! Praise God Almighty, I'm free at last!"*

I can't help but think about the lepers in **Luke 17:12-19**. Ten of them stood afar off, crying, *"Jesus, Master, have mercy on us"* **(KJV)**. They were bound not only by disease but also by the stigma and isolation that came with it. Yet Jesus saw them. He didn't just heal their bodies—He set them free. He told them to go show themselves to the priests, and as they went, they were cleansed. But one—just one—came back, glorifying God. To him, Jesus said, *"Arise, go thy way: thy faith hath made thee whole"* **(Luke 17:19, KJV)**.

That's the kind of freedom we're stepping into today—not just healing, but wholeness.

So, I say to you today: Let the chains fall. Whatever has held you captive—be it fear, pain, or bitterness—Jesus is loosing you this day. Say it again: *Free at last, free at last! Praise God Almighty, I'm free at last!* Hallelujah! Let's give Him the praise He deserves by faith. The chains are gone, and we are stepping into a new season of freedom, wholeness, and victory in Jesus' name. Amen!

From Dr Michael H Yeager
Completely Engulfed in a Consuming Fire: Drunk in the Holy Ghost

In 1980, I began to meditate on and memorize scriptures declaring that fire cannot consume me. One scripture that stood out was Isaiah 43:2, which says, *"When thou passest through the waters, I will be with thee; and through the rivers, they shall not overflow thee: when thou walkest through the fire, thou shalt not be burned; neither shall the flame kindle upon thee."* I kept this scripture close to my heart because, back then, I kept burning myself on our wood stove.

For years, I held on to these words, and in the summer of 2011, they became more real to me than ever before when God miraculously rescued me from what should have been a deadly fire.

One particular morning, I woke up completely lost in the Holy Ghost. My mind and heart were so caught up in the presence of God, it felt as though I was totally drunk in the Spirit. In the world, they might say I was "three sheets to the wind," but I was deeply lost in God's presence. I was so heavenly-minded, I probably wasn't much earthly good at that moment! While in this state, I decided it was a perfect day to burn the large pile of brush on our property.

The brush pile was massive, towering several feet above my head. The day was hot, easily over 90°F. I took a two-gallon plastic gas container with me, intending to use it to light the brush pile. The container was so hot that visible gasoline fumes were rising from it. With me, I had one of those long-stemmed lighters you can buy at any hardware store.

Without thinking, I stepped into the pile of dry brush, which towered over me. I began to splash gasoline over the entire pile, drenching it thoroughly. The liquid gasoline reached the edges of my feet. I was so lost in the Spirit that I wasn't aware of what I was doing, just meditating on the Word of God.

My son Daniel saw what I was about to do. As I stood there with the gas container in my left hand, visible fumes rising, I reached down with the lighter in my right hand to ignite the pile. Daniel, realizing the danger, screamed, "Dad, don't!" But I was too far gone in the Spirit to fully comprehend his warning. I pulled the trigger of the lighter, and instantly, the whole brush pile exploded into flames.

I was completely engulfed in fire.

Daniel later told me that from where he stood, he couldn't even see me. I was swallowed up by the flames. But as I stood there, surrounded by fire, I felt no heat. It was as though there was an invisible shield around me, shimmering like a force field. The force field sparkled, glowing in shades of light blue, silver, gold, and glistening white.

In that moment, I thought, "Wow, this is amazing!" But then, something happened, I heard the audible voice of God say:—*You're standing in the fire, dummy! At that moment I knew I had to get out!*

Immediately, I began to backtrack, walking backward through the flames with the gas container still in my left hand. As soon as I was out of the fire, I looked down at my body, amazed. Not a single flame had touched me. My clothes were untouched, and the gas container, which should have exploded due to the fumes, remained intact. I didn't even feel the heat!

Once again, God had miraculously delivered me from my own foolishness. My son Daniel witnessed the entire event. He was shocked and amazed, thinking I was a dead man. He told me later how helpless he felt, unable to get near the fire to save me. But I reassured him that there was nothing he could have done—it was all God. The Lord had shielded me from flames that should have consumed me.

Consider this: gasoline, the most commonly known flammable liquid, has a flash point of about -50°F (-

65°C) and ignites at around 495°F (232°C). Burning gasoline can reach temperatures of 1500°F (945°C). Yet, in the midst of those flames, I was protected by God's hand.

We rejoiced and praised God for His great mercy that day. Even in my moment of carelessness, God showed His faithfulness. He protected me when nothing else could have, not even my son's desperate cries to save me. It was yet another testimony of God's goodness, reminding me—and everyone else—that when you walk through the fire, God is with you. The flames will not burn you, for His Word and His promises are true.

Engulfed in a Gasoline Tar fire.

I have experience on numerous occasions when God has divinely intervened on my behalf. I can think of at least ten Times this has happened to me.

#1 when a gang leader was trying to kill me by stabbing me to death while coming out of Chicago in his car.

#2 While saving a young man's life from a motorcycle accident.

#3 A large mule deer was going to slam into me on my motorcycle while I was headed through Canada.

#4 My wife and I rolling down a cliff in our car. My newborn son Michael was up in the air, as my wife reaches out and snatches him to her chest.

#5 My seventh-month pregnant wife, my son Michael and I were on a 450 custom Honda. Headed for guardrails, telephone pole, and a pile of rocks.

#6 Supernaturally empowered while driving a motorcycle through communist infested lands.

#7 While flying my airplane through a set of high lines.

#8 Right before I slammed my Cadillac into a concrete bridge.

#9 Preventing a young lady from burning to death when her hair caught on fire.

#10 When I was engulfed in a Raging fire.

Everything around me exploded into fire! (Tears are filling my eyes as I share this incredible story of God's protection in the midst of my stupidity.) It all began as I was stirring gasoline into a five-gallon bucket of black tar, thinning it to be spread on our Churches Steal roof! We had a thirty-gallon galvanized garbage can with an LP torch under this container melting the tar! The fumes ignited, and this massive wave of fire came rushing from about 20 feet away wholly engulfing me.

I mean I am entirely swallowed up in this gasoline and black tar fire. The two buckets of gasoline are burning at my feet. The bucket of tar and gasoline I was stirring is on fire. I had been using an excessive amount of gas to keep my hands, arms, and face free from tar. Gasoline is the only thing that would clean the black tar off me.

My clothes are completely saturated in gasoline, as well as my hands, arms and face. I'm standing there in the midst of all of this fire with no FEAR in my heart. At the same Time my mind is quickened, but Time seems to have come to a standstill! I have complete and utter peace, but still knowing that I was in big trouble.

Back in 1980, I began to memorize and meditate on Scriptures declaring that fire could not consume me.

Isaiah 43:2, "When thou passest through the waters, I will be with thee; and through the rivers, they shall not overflow thee: when thou walkest through the fire, thou shalt not be burned ; neither shall the flame kindle upon thee."

I meditated on the scriptures because I kept burning myself with our woodstove. Through the years, I have maintained these scriptures in my heart. In the summer of 2011, I had an amazing experience when God used these scriptures to come to my rescue, otherwise, I would have been burned to death.

I can honestly tell you that I did not feel the heat, flames, or the fire upon me. I grabbed a metal canister and put it over the top of the one bucket of burning gas. I quickly found another canister that I could put over the other bucket. During this Time, I'm running in and out of the fire.

I'm not thinking; I'm just moving knowing that our gymnasium and our whole church could go up in flames at any moment. We are right up against the gymnasium with a house trailer right there. The apartment and the stairs to the apartment above our gymnasium were right there. I had to get the fire out, and I mean fast! Everything was on fire, including the ground where we had spilled tar and gas.

The whole place is nothing but an infernal. During this Time, Jesse had made his way around the flames nurturing his burnt arm, which he had received standing outside of the flames! He was trying to find a water hose we had lying there to water a small garden. I'm still running in and out of the flames, trying to put out this raging fire. Jesse had been through a terrible fire in the past, being seriously hurt. I could see that he was in the midst of some shock from the fire and the heat.

Right before my very eyes, the bucket that was filled with tar and gasoline had melted at my feet to less than 8 inches high. Now the flames were getting worse, they were reaching high into the sky. The men who have been spreading the mixture of tar and Gasoline come running seeing the flames on top of our Church Sanctuary. The whole thing was nothing but a massive blaze. During this Time, brother Mark, who lives in the apartment up above, comes running out onto his apartment's deck. He sees everything that is happening.

Brother Jesse is wrestling with the water hose, trying to disconnect it from another hose to use it to fight the fire. I ran over and began to help him. And then I took the hoses from him, heading back into the fire. Praise God the water did the job even with gasoline and burning tar everywhere. We were able to douse the flames. Praise God, praise God, praise God the fire was out.

Things happened so fast at the Time that I did not even realize exactly the events that had transpired. But God in His grace and in His mercy once again protected me from my own massive stupidity. Jesse did receive burns on his right forearm. Amazingly, I did not receive one burn, not one singed hair, or even the smell of smoke on me. All of the gas that was on me, my hands, my face, and my clothes never ignited. God is so good! His Mercy Endures Forever!

Shekinah Glory at Abbot Loop Fellowship

I was doing missionary work in Dillingham, Alaska as a 19-year-old kid in 1975. I decided that I needed to rest and visit some people I knew in Anchorage, Alaska. Money was no problem because I had been making good money by working on a salmon boat during salmon season.

While I was visiting Anchorage, Alaska, I decided to visit a church someone had told me about. The name of it was Abbott Loop Fellowship. I arrived late because I had to hitchhike and walk my way there in twenty degrees below zero weather with blowing snow. I think I had to travel approximately 5 miles.

Pastor Mike, weren't you cold? Absolutely I was cold and shivering. But I would do it all over again because I was hungry for Jesus Christ. God showed up supernaturally for me in that service. As you continue to read this testimony, you will discover how God showed up and changed me forever.

You might ask, why in the world would I go through such trouble to get to that church? It's called being spiritually hungry and thirsty. I am convinced that this is one reason why I have had so many visitations from the Lord. It is because of the spiritual hunger within my heart that I have not lost since 1975. Even though it was 48 years ago when I was born again at 19, I am still just as hungry, if not hungrier now as I was back then, for Jesus.

I have always told the congregations that God has allowed me to pastor that if you ever lose your hunger for God, for Jesus, for truth, then you have lost everything. Here we are in the year 2024, and many Christians are still not going to church out of fear.

If you wondered why God is not showing up in your life, it most likely is because you do not have a hunger for him the way you need to. Get your appetite back, and you will have amazing experiences from God, for the Lord delights to reveal himself to those who are hungry for him.

Matthew 5:6 Blessed are they which do hunger and thirst after righteousness: for they shall be filled.

I entered the sanctuary late and found a chair in the last row in an amphitheater type Sanctuary. The worship was beautiful, and I found myself being caught up in the Spirit. As my eyes were closed, I smelled a beautiful fragrance in the air I had never experienced before. It smelled like some type of beautiful flower. It could have been the rose of Sharon.

My eyes were closed during this time, but I opened them as I smelled this beautiful aroma. The same glistening fog that had filled my car when I was driving through Canada began to descend upon me. Before I knew it, I could not see anyone around me. The person in front of me was probably only two feet away, but this Divine Fog was so thick I could not see them. I became lost in worshiping and praising God. To this day, I do not know if anyone else saw or smelled what I experienced on that day.

I'm telling you that I could not even see the chairs in front of me or those around me. Not only was I engulfed in this glory, but time itself ceased to exist for me. When the Glory finally lifted off me, I was standing there all alone. Everybody had left the building. Most of the lights had been turned off. I was standing all alone with my hands lifted toward Heaven. My hands had been lifted for hours with no tiredness. I can only imagine that they saw this young man caught up in worship and decided to leave me alone!

To this day, I do not know what happened in that service. I was lost in the Glory! I'm sure when everybody left the sanctuary, they just saw this young man standing with his eyes lifted towards heaven and his hands extended up towards God.

How to Live in the Miraculous!

This is a quick explanation of how to live and move in

the realm of the miraculous. Seeing divine interventions of God is not something that just spontaneously happens because you have been born-again. There are certain biblical principles and truths that must be evident in your life. This is a very basic list of some of these truths and laws:

1. You must give Jesus Christ your whole heart. You cannot be lackadaisical in this endeavour. Being lukewarm in your walk with God is repulsive to the Lord. He wants 100% commitment. Jesus gave His all, now it is our turn to give our all. He loved us 100%. Now we must love Him 100%.

My son, give me thine heart, and let thine eyes observe my ways
(Proverbs 23:26).

So then because thou art lukewarm, and neither cold nor hot, I will spew thee out of my mouth (Revelation 3:16).

2. There must be a complete agreement with God's Word. We must be in harmony with the Lord in our attitude, actions, thoughts, and deeds. Whatever the Word of God declares in the New Testament is what we wholeheartedly agree with.

Can two walk together, except they be agreed? (Amos

3:3).

For the eyes of the LORD run to and fro throughout the whole earth, to shew himself strong in the behalf of them whose heart is perfect toward him (2 Chronicles 16:9).

3. Obey and do the Word from the heart, from the simplest to the most complicated request or command. No matter what the Word says to do, do it! Here are some simple examples: Lift your hands in praise, in everything give thanks, forgive instantly, gather together with the saints, and give offerings to the Lord, and so on.

I can of mine own self do nothing: as I hear, I judge: and my judgment is just; because I seek not mine own will, but the will of the Father which hath sent me (John 5:30).

4. Make Jesus the highest priority of your life. Everything you do, do not do it as unto men, but do it as unto God.

If ye then be risen with Christ, seek those things which are above, where Christ sitteth on the right hand of God. Set your affection on things above, not on things on the earth (Colossians 3:1-2).

5. Die to self! The old man says, "My will be done!" The new man says, "God's will be done!"

I am crucified with Christ: nevertheless I live; yet not I, but Christ liveth in me: and the life which I now live in the flesh I live by the faith of the Son of God, who loved me, and gave himself for me (Galatians 2:20).

Now if we be dead with Christ, we believe that we shall also live with him (Romans 6:8).

6. Repent the minute you get out of God's will—no matter how minor, or small the sin may seem.

(Revelation 3:19).

As many as I love, I rebuke and chasten: be zealous therefore, and repent.

7. Take one step at a time. God will test you (not to do evil) to see if you will obey him. *Whatever He tells you to do: by His Word, by His Spirit, or within your conscience, do it.* He will never tell you to do something contrary to His nature or His Word!

For whosoever shall do the will of my Father which is in heaven, the same is my brother, and sister, and mother (Matthew 12:50).

Then went he down, and dipped himself seven times in Jordan, according to the saying of the man of God: and his flesh came again like unto the flesh of a little child, and he was clean (2 Kings 5:14).

ABOUT THE AUTHOR

Dr. Michael and Kathleen Yeager have served as pastors/apostles, missionaries, evangelists, broadcasters, and authors for over four decades. Doc Yeager has authored over 400 books. They flow in the gifts of the Holy Spirit, teaching the Word of God with wonderful signs and miracles following in confirmation of God's Word. In 1982, they began Jesus is Lord Ministries International, Biglerville, PA 17307.

Some of the Books Written by Doc Yeager:

"Living in the Realm of the Miraculous #1 to 5"

"I need God Cause I'm Stupid"

"The Miracles of Smith Wigglesworth"

"How Faith Comes 28 WAYS"

"Horrors of Hell, Splendors of Heaven"

"The Coming Great Awakening"

"Sinners In The Hands of an Angry GOD", (modernized)

"Brain Parasite Epidemic"

"My JOURNEY To HELL" - illustrated for teenagers

"Divine Revelation Of Jesus Christ"

"My Daily Meditations"

"Holy Bible of JESUS CHRIST"

"War In The Heavenlies - (Chronicles of Micah)"

"Living in the Realm of the Miraculous #2"

"My Legal Rights To Witness"

"Why We (MUST) Gather!- 30 Biblical Reasons"

"My Incredible, Supernatural, Divine Experiences"

"Living in the Realm of the Miraculous #3"

"How GOD Leads & Guides! - 20 Ways"

"Weapons Of Our Warfare"

"How You Can Be Healed"

Printed in Great Britain
by Amazon

1 MONTH OF FREE READING

at www.ForgottenBooks.com

By purchasing this book you are eligible for one month membership to ForgottenBooks.com, giving you unlimited access to our entire collection of over 1,000,000 titles via our web site and mobile apps.

To claim your free month visit: www.forgottenbooks.com/free442430

* Offer is valid for 45 days from date of purchase. Terms and conditions apply.

ISBN 978-0-265-36709-4
PIBN 10442430

This book is a reproduction of an important historical work. Forgotten Books uses state-of-the-art technology to digitally reconstruct the work, preserving the original format whilst repairing imperfections present in the aged copy. In rare cases, an imperfection in the original, such as a blemish or missing page, may be replicated in our edition. We do, however, repair the vast majority of imperfections successfully; any imperfections that remain are intentionally left to preserve the state of such historical works.

Forgotten Books is a registered trademark of FB &c Ltd.
Copyright © 2018 FB &c Ltd.
FB &c Ltd, Dalton House, 60 Windsor Avenue, London, SW19 2RR.
Company number 08720141. Registered in England and Wales.

For support please visit www.forgottenbooks.com

ALSACE-LORRAINE

PAST, PRESENT, AND FUTURE

BY

COLEMAN PHILLIPSON
M.A., LL.D., Litt.D.
OF THE INNER TEMPLE, BARRISTER-AT-LAW

WITH FOUR MAPS

LONDON: T. FISHER UNWIN, LTD.
ADELPHI TERRACE

First published in 1918
(ALL RIGHTS RESERVED)

DEDICATED

TO

THE RIGHT HON SIR FREDERICK SMITH, BART.
K.C., M.P.

HIS MAJESTY'S ATTORNEY-GENERAL

PREFACE

THE object of the present work is to consider the problem of Alsace-Lorraine—how it arose in the past, what its present aspects are, and what appears to be its most desirable solution for the future. To carry out this object I have adopted the following plan. First the salient features of the question are indicated; then follow a description of the provinces and of their economic position, and a brief historical outline the purpose of which is to help us to look at the entire problem dispassionately, and in due perspective, in view of the various contending claims advanced. Next I deal with the annexation in 1871, the fateful Franco-German negotiations, the regulation of numerous matters arising out of the transfer of the territory, the German view of the acquisition, the proposals made as to the status of the acquired provinces, and how their germanisation was to be effected. This is followed by an account of the solemn and moving protests of 1871; and a critical analysis of the German claims to Alsace-Lorraine, and the alleged grounds of annexation—historical association, nationality and race, language, necessity (political, economic, and military), conquest and confirmation thereof by the Treaty of Frankfort. Here are examined, too, the common assertions that the latter treaty was necessarily abrogated on the commencement of hostilities in 1914, and that the forcible acquisition of the provinces by France would be only a restoration, and not a conquest. Then I set forth the German régime in Alsace-Lorraine from 1871 down to the outbreak of the Great War, the methods adopted to bring about the *entwelschung* of the Reichsland, and the factors retarding such a consummation; the strivings and aspirations of the Alsace-Lorrainers, the rise and growth of the nationalist movement, the views and feelings in France, the *revanche* ideal, its obsolescence, and recent recrudescence. Finally, I consider the numerous solutions that have from time to time been suggested or demanded (as the case may be), *e.g.* reannexation to France, the establishment of Alsace-Lorraine as an autonomous State within the framework of the German Empire, the creation of an independent neutralised State, partition schemes, and readjustments of boundaries; also the Franco-German coal and iron problem, and the question of a plebiscite. I point out the difficulties and advantages of the various proposals, and show which is the best in the interests of justice and international peace and amity.

In the investigation of all these matters I have done my utmost on the one hand to be concise and clear, and on the other to preserve throughout an attitude —if I may say so—of judicial impartiality. " Tribuere suum cuique " : it is ever the wisest policy to follow this principle, even if it involves giving the devil his due.

COLEMAN PHILLIPSON.

4, ELM COURT, TEMPLE,
    April 13, 1918.

CONTENTS

	PAGE
PREFACE	7
REFERENCES	15

CHAPTER I

INTRODUCTORY: THE QUESTION OF ALSACE-LORRAINE STATED

Alsace-Lorraine long a bone of contention—Forcible annexation in 1871—How the question of Alsace-Lorraine has arisen—How it differs from the Near Eastern Question—Other States concerned—Different aspects of the question—German view that there is no question of Alsace-Lorraine—Relation to the present war—The " challenge-cup of Europe "—Desiderata in the solution of the question—Difficulties involved in the solution—Justice and right the fundamental consideration

pp. 19-33

CHAPTER II

DESCRIPTION OF ALSACE-LORRAINE, AND ITS ECONOMIC POSITION

Area and configuration—Minerals; climate; population—Characteristics of the people—Language—Religion—Industries—Agriculture—Exports and imports—Transport and communication; public works—Budget—Public instruction—Great progress under German rule . pp. 34-48

CONTENTS

CHAPTER III

HISTORICAL OUTLINE

Roman occupation—Germanic invasions—Union with the German Empire. (*a*) *Lorraine*: Middle Ages—Relations with France—Certain annexations to France—The Three Bishoprics—Cession to France. (*b*) *Alsace*: Middle Ages—Part of Germany till the seventeenth century—The Thirty Years War—Treaty of Westphalia (1648)—Position of Strassburg—The French Revolution.; Union with France . . . pp. 49-60

CHAPTER IV

ANNEXATION OF ALSACE-LORRAINE IN 1871

(*a*) *Military events leading to peace negotiations*: Outbreak of the war of 1870—Neutrality of the Powers—German successes—Annexation proclaimed—Capitulation of Metz—Siege of Paris—National Assembly at Bordeaux; peace signed. (*b*) *Negotiations and Arrangements as to Alsace-Lorraine*: Protests against announced annexation—Bismarck's fear of European intervention—He secures Russian support—His doubt as to territorial demands; military view—Demands made at Versailles—German resolve as to annexation—Bismarck's concession—The Preliminaries of Versailles—Negotiations at Brussels—Difficulties of the French plenipotentiaries—Negotiations transferred to Frankfort—The French plenipotentiaries—Treaty of Frankfort—Belfort—Germans affect to be disappointed—The boundary commission—Rights of inhabitants of ceded territory—Regulation of various other matters

pp. 61-85

CHAPTER V

PROPOSALS AS TO THE FATE OF ALSACE-LORRAINE AFTER ITS CONQUEST—BISMARCK'S VIEW OF THE TASK OF ASSIMILATION

Protests in Germany against the annexation—German policy as to the annexed territory—View as to neutralisation—View as to plebiscite—Division of the territory suggested—Autonomy suggested—Alsace-Lorraine made a Reichsland—Bismarck's view as to German assimilation—His doubts about Metz . . . . . pp. 86-97

CONTENTS 11

CHAPTER VI

THE PROTESTS OF 1871 AGAINST THE ANNEXATION

Declaration of Alsace-Lorraine deputies—Submitted to the National Assembly—Various other protests—Debates in the Assembly on the proposed cession—Vote on the Preliminaries—Further protest of Alsace-Lorraine deputies—Demand from Germany—Effects of the annexation

pp. 98-111

CHAPTER VII

GERMAN CLAIMS TO ALSACE-LORRAINE — ALLEGED GROUNDS OF ANNEXATION: (a) HISTORICAL GROUNDS; NATIONALITY AND RACE; LANGUAGE

Historical grounds: Ranke's view—Mommsen's view—Treitschke's view—Early treaties—Appeal to the Holy Roman Empire—Difficulties in such contentions. Racial grounds: Names as a criterion—Claim untenable—Treitschke's arrogant pretensions. Claim on ground of language: Early struggles between languages—German dialect becomes predominant—Position of the *pays messin*. Principle of nationality—Attachment of Alsace to France—Principle of public right

pp. 112-131

CHAPTER VIII

GERMAN CLAIMS TO ALSACE-LORRAINE — ALLEGED GROUNDS OF ANNEXATION: (b) NECESSITY; CONQUEST AS CONFIRMED BY THE TREATY OF FRANKFORT

Claim on ground of necessity. Economic necessity: Outlet for overcrowded Germany?—Natural deficiencies of Germany. Political necessity: German unity and the Reichsland. Military necessity: Frontier security—Mommsen on Metz. Conquest as confirmed by the Treaty of Frankfort: Prussia's territorial ambitions—Bismarck's admission in 1862—German views as to "right of conquest"—Recent growth of opinion as to conquest—Ground of illegitimacy of conquest—When conquest justified—International law as it existed in 1871. Binding force of Treaty of Frankfort—Supersession of one treaty by another

pp. 132-154

CHAPTER IX

GERMAN RÉGIME IN ALSACE-LORRAINE

Military occupation, 1870–71—Status from February 1871 to June 1871—Dictatorship, 1871–3—The imperial constitution applied, 1874—Territorial Delegacy established, 1874—Council of State established, 1879—Application of the régime—Repressive measures—New constitution, 1911—Why autonomy refused—Precautions of Germany on outbreak of the present war—Why thorough germanisation not effected—The German official classes—The German immigrants—Pan-germanism—German methods compared with French . . pp. 155–183

CHAPTER X

VIEWS AND ASPIRATIONS OF ALSACE-LORRAINE—THE NATIONALIST MOVEMENT

Protest of the Alsace-Lorraine deputies in the Reichstag, 1874—Why autonomist movement began—Aim in social and intellectual life of the people—Method of the nationalist leaders—Differentiation between autonomists and protesters—Socialist party; anti-clerical campaign—Democrats leave the Catholic party—National Union formed, 1910; its programme—Manifesto against the Constitution of 1911—"Home rule" demanded, 1913—Before present war, memory of 1871 fading in Alsace-Lorraine—Did Alsace-Lorraine desire reunion with France?—Noisseville affair; Saverne affair—Attitude of the people towards France and Germany—Distinctive personality of Alsace-Lorraine—The new generation and France—Doubtful indications as to feelings and desires of the people—Attitude of Alsace-Lorrainers at outbreak of the war—Declarations of the two Chambers, 1917—Conclusions

pp. 184–213

CHAPTER XI

VIEWS AND FEELINGS IN FRANCE AS TO ALSACE-LORRAINE

Three phases of French feeling—*Revanche* ideal—Evanescence of *revanche* ideal: contributory causes—Pacific policy of French democracy—Why *revanche* ideas were passing away—Disturbing currents in France since 1871—France and the question of nationalities—Recent national policy of France—Von Bülow's view of the French temper—French views after outbreak of the war—British view—Why France determined to recover Alsace-Lorraine—Whether recovery would be "restoration" or conquest—Status of Alsace-Lorrainers in France during the war . . . . pp. 214–234

CONTENTS 13

CHAPTER XII

SOLUTIONS SUGGESTED : (*a*) REANNEXATION TO FRANCE

Reannexation followed by referendum suggested—German pronouncements as to Alsace-Lorraine — Forcible reannexation not a true solution; inherent difficulty—Various other difficulties : Frontier—Grouping of Alsace-Lorraine within political framework of France—The language question—The legal system—The industrial organisation—The commercial system—Fiscal legislation—The religious question—The educational system—Position of immigrants and the younger generation— The previous nationalist movement—Other difficulties. Interregnum suggested for smoothing over difficulties . . . . pp. 235–250

CHAPTER XIII

REANNEXATION AND THE FRANCO-GERMAN COAL AND IRON PROBLEM

Commercial basis of the war—German declarations in 1915 as to economic needs—Coal and iron in modern war—German need of coal and iron —German demands as to Briey and Longwy—Coal resources of France and Germany—Iron ore in Lorraine—Iron resources of Germany— Effect of depriving Germany of the Lorraine ore . . pp. 251–264

CHAPTER XIV

SOLUTIONS SUGGESTED : (*b*) AUTONOMY WITHIN THE GERMAN EMPIRE

The nationalist ideal—Alsace-Lorraine can no longer remain a Reichsland —German view in 1898—Swiss view—French views—Recent German opinion—German Socialist view, 1917—Form of autonomous government—Position of Alsace-Lorraine as an autonomous State—Autonomy followed by plebiscite suggested . . . . . pp. 263–270

CHAPTER XV

SOLUTIONS SUGGESTED : (*c*) ALSACE-LORRAINE AS AN INDEPENDENT STATE

Proposed neutralisation—Suggested in 1870—German objections—Population to be consulted—Resolution of League of Peace, 1884—Form of independent government—Various matters for adjustment—Advantages of creating an independent Alsace-Lorraine : Meeting the wishes of

CONTENTS

the people—*Revanche* obviated—Fusion of Germanic and Gallic elements—Military service difficulties removed—Bond of union between France and Germany—Would be a " buffer " State. Future international co-operation and treaties . . . . . pp. 271-284

CHAPTER XVI

SOLUTIONS SUGGESTED : (*d*) PARTITION ; ALTERATION OF BOUNDARIES, ETC.

Partition proposals—Language as a basis—Suggested union of Alsace with Baden—Division among German States—Frontier rearrangement—The *pays messin* to France and the rest neutralised—Alsace-Lorraine as part of a Rhenish-Alpine Confederation—Boundary readjustment—Arbitration of the Pope suggested—Difficulties in these proposals : Division on basis of speech—Division on basis of sentiment—Division between German States—Lorraine as an independent State—Suggested confederation. The Rhine as a Franco-German boundary—Criticism of the view as to a Rhine frontier—Desideratum in fixing frontiers
pp. 285-301

CHAPTER XVII

THE QUESTION OF A PLEBISCITE

Plebiscite for Alsace-Lorraine necessary—Examples of plebiscites—Cases of annexation without a plebiscite—Anglo-American practice—Juristic opinion—Grounds of support of plebiscite—Grounds of objection to plebiscite—Each case to be considered on its merits—Alsace-Lorraine a suitable case—Prevailing views as to self-determination of peoples—Alsace-Lorraine desirous to decide its own fate—Alsace-Lorraine ever against war as a solution—Opposition to plebiscite by France, Germany, and leading Alsatians—Criticism of objections—A real difficulty : presence of immigrants and absence of emigrants—Compromise necessary—Organisation of plebiscite—Persons who should vote—Probable result—Essential condition for the future . . . . pp. 302-318

INDEX . . . . pp. 319-328

LIST OF MAPS [1]
PAGE

Structural Map of France showing Boundaries in 1870 and 1914 *Frontispiece*
Sketch-map of Alsace and Eastern Lorraine. 35
Geological Sketch-map of Alsace-Lorraine 253
The Ramparts of Paris 299

[1] For the use of these maps indebtedness is acknowledged to the Royal Scottish Geographical Society, and to Miss M I. Newbigin, the editor of its magazine.

REFERENCES

M. Alfassa, " Le fer et le charbon lorrains ' (Paris, 1916).
Count von Beust, " Aus drei Viertel Jahrhunderten " (Stuttgart, 1887).
K. Blind, " Alsace-Lorraine and William II (with personal recollections) ' ; in *Fortnightly Review*, vol. 78 (1902), pp. 257 *seq*.
J. C. Bluntschli, " Das moderne Völkerrecht " (Nördlingen, 1872). French trans. by C. Lardy, "Le Droit international codifié " (Paris, 1895).
J. E. C. Bodley, " The Church in France " (London, 1906).
——" France " ; in *Encyclopædia Britannica*, vol. x. (1910).
G. Bourdon, " L'Énigme allemande " (Paris, 1913). Eng. trans. (London, 1914).
E. Bourgeois, " The Third French Republic " ; in *Cambridge Modern History*, vol. xii. (1910), chap. v.
Prinz von Bülow, " Imperial Germany." Eng. trans. (London, 1916).
M. Busch, " Bismarck: Some secret pages of his history.' Eng. trans. 3 vols. (London, 1898).
A. J. Butler (Trans.), " Bismarck: the man and the statesman" (London, 1898).
C. Calvo, " Le droit international théorique et pratique." 6 vols. 5th ed. (Paris, 1896).
R. de Card, " Les annexions et les plébiscites dans l'histoire contemporaine " ; in *Études de droit international* (Paris, 1890).
E. J. Dillon, " Counting the cost " ; in *Fortnightly Review*, September 1917.
F. Y. Eccles, " Alsace-Lorraine " (Oxford Pamphlets, 1914–15).
A. Eckel, " La réunion de l'Alsace et de la Lorraine à la France " (Vesoul, 1894).
F. Engerand, " Les frontières lorraines et la force allemande " (Paris, 1916).

J. Favre, "Le Gouvernement de la Défense Nationale." 3 vols. (Paris, 1871–5).
P. Fiore, "Nouveau droit international public." Traduit de l'italien par C. Antoine. 3 vols. (Paris, 1880).
Florent-Matter, "L'Alsace de nos jours" (Paris, 1908).
N. Fustel de Coulanges, "L'Alsace, est-elle allemande ou française? Réponse à M. Mommsen" (Paris, 1870).
H. Galli, "Gambetta et l'Alsace-Lorraine" (Paris, 1911).
C. Gavard, "Un diplomate à Londres: Lettres et Notes, 1871–1877" (Paris, 1895).
A. Haenel, "Deutsches Staatsrecht" (1892, etc.).
G. Hanotaux, "Contemporary France." Eng. trans. 4 vols. (London, 1903).
J. Heimweh, "Droit de conquête et plébiscite" (Paris, 1896).
——— "La guerre et la frontière du Rhin" (Paris, 1895).
——— "Triple Alliance et Alsace-Lorraine" (Paris, 1892).
P. A. Helmer, "Alsace under German rule" (London, 1915).
——— "France—Alsace" (Paris, 1916).
Sir T. M. Holdich, "New political boundaries in Europe: Alsace-Lorraine"; in *New Europe*, February 8, 1917.
——— "Political frontiers and boundary-making" (London, 1916).
F. von Holtzendorff—Vietmansdorf, "Encyclopädie der Rechtswissenschaft." Ed. J. Kohler. 5 vols. (München; Leipzig, 1913–14).
B. E. Howard, "Alsace-Lorraine in its relation to the German Empire"; in *Political Science Quarterly* (New York, 1906), vol. xxi.
D. S. Jordan, "Alsace-Lorraine: a study in conquest; 1913" (Indianapolis, 1917).
F. Klein, "L'Évêque de Metz: Vie de Mgr. Dupont des Loges" (Paris, 1899).
P. Laband, "Das Staatsrecht des Deutschen Reiches." 3 vols. (Freiburg i. B., 1876–82.)
G. de Lamberty, "Mémoires pour servir à l'histoire du XVIIIe siècle," etc. 14 vols. (Amsterdam, 1734–40).
A. Lasson, "Das Culturideal und der Krieg" (Berlin, 1868).
——— "Princip und Zukunft des Völkerrechts" (Berlin, 1871).
L. de Launay, "Le problème franco-allemand du fer"; in *Revue des Deux Mondes*, July 15, 1916.
A. Laussedat, "La délimitation de la frontière franco-allemande" (Paris, 1901).

REFERENCES

H. et A. Lichtenberger, " La question d'Alsace-Lorraine " (Paris, 1915).
J. Longuet, " Alsace-Lorraine " ; in *The Nation*, January 5 and 12, 1918.
O. Lorenz, " Kaiser Wilhelm und die Begründung des Reichs, 1866–1871 " (Jena, 1902).
L. W. Lyde, " Some frontiers of to-morrow " (London, 1915).
M. Maass, " Was soll mit Elsass-Lothringen werden " (Leipzig, 1884).
G. May, " Le Traité de Francfort " (Paris, 1909).
—— " La lutte pour le français en Lorraine avant 1870." Annales de l'Est publiées par la Faculté des Lettres de l'Université de Nancy (Paris : Nancy, 1912).
E. Milhaud, " La démocratie socialiste allemande " (Paris, 1903).
T. Mommsen, " Letters on the war between France and Germany." Eng. trans. (London, 1871).
G. Monod, " Allemands et français " (Paris, 1892).
F. Naumann, " Central Europe." Eng. trans. (London, 1916).
M. I. Newbigin, " The Problem of Alsace-Lorraine " ; in *The Scottish Geographical Magazine*, March and April, 1918 (vol. xxxiv.).
J. Novicow, " L'Alsace-Lorraine : Obstacle à l'expansion allemande " (Paris, 1913).
F. A. Ogg, " The Governments of Europe " (New York, 1913).
H. Oncken, " The German Empire " ; in *Cambridge Modern History*, vol. xii., chap. vi. (Cambridge, 1910).
Général Palat, " L'alliance franco-allemande ou la guerre ' (Paris, 1914).
" Patiens," " L'Alsace-Lorraine devant l'Europe " (Paris, 1894).
C. Pfister, " La limite de la langue française et de la langue allemande en Alsace-Lorraine " (Paris, 1890).
C. Phillipson, " Termination of war and treaties of peace " (London, 1916).
C. Phillipson and N. Buxton, " The question of the Bosphorus and Dardanelles " (London, 1917).
G. Rasch, " Die Preussen in Elsass und Lothringen " (Braunschweig, 1874). French trans. (Paris, 1876).
M. Sembat, " Faites un roi, sinon faites la paix " (Paris, 1913).
H. von Treitschke, " Was fordern wir von Frankreich " (Berlin, 1870). Eng. trans. in " Germany, France, Russia, and Islam " (London, 1915).

REFERENCES

J. Valfrey, " Histoire du traité de Francfort et de la libération du territoire français " (Paris, 1874).

Villefort, " Recueil des traités, conventions, lois, décrets et autres actes relatifs à la paix avec l'Allemagne." 5 vols. (Paris, 1872–9).

A. Wagner, " Elsass und Lothringen und ihre Wiedergewinnung für Deutschland " (Leipzig, 1870).

H. Welschinger, " Bismarck " (Paris, 1900).

—— " La guerre de 1870. Causes et responsabilités " (Paris, 1910).

—— " La protestation de l'Alsace-Lorraine les 17 février et 1er mars 1871 à Bordeaux " (Paris, 1914).

L'Abbé E. Wetterlé, " Ce qu'était l'Alsace-Lorraine et ce qu'elle sera " (Paris, 1915).

S. Whitman (Ed.), " Conversations with Prince Bismarck." Collected by H. von Poschinger (London ; New York, 1900).

J. Zeller, " Origines de l'Allemagne et de l'Empire Germanique " (Paris, 1872).

" Die Bevölkerung Elsass-Lothringens ' (Strasburg, 1908).

" La neutralité de l'Alsace-Lorraine." Compte rendu de l'Assemblée générale des membres de la Ligue internationale de la paix et de la liberté. Tenue à Genève le 7 sept. 1884 (Bâle, 1884).

" Parliamentary Papers," vol. 70 (1870).

ALSACE-LORRAINE

CHAPTER I

INTRODUCTORY : THE QUESTION OF ALSACE-LORRAINE STATED

Alsace-Lorraine long a bone of contention—Forcible annexation in 1871—How the question of Alsace-Lorraine has arisen—How it differs from the Near Eastern Question—Other States concerned—Different aspects of the question—German view that there is no question of Alsace-Lorraine—Relation to the present war—The " challenge-cup of Europe "—Desiderata in the solution of the question—Difficulties involved in the solution—Justice and right the fundamental consideration.

FROM very early times Alsace-Lorraine was a bone of contention between rival races and rival sovereigns. In the numerous conflicts of the contending parties, the lands and possessions of these unhappy provinces were repeatedly subjected to destruction or pillage, and the population to all the violence of warfare, with the inevitable result that the social, intellectual, and industrial development of the country—rich as it is in natural resources and favoured in its geographical position and configuration—has been seriously hampered. Thanks to such salient features and barriers as the Rhine on the one hand and the Vosges Mountains on the other, the Alsace-Lorraine territory has constituted a border-country separating ever hostile and seemingly incompatible peoples ; and its extent and

Alsace-Lorraine long a bone of contention.

boundaries have frequently changed with the vicissitudes of war and the succession of its rulers.

At one time it extended in the north to the sea; at another time it stretched in the east to the Rhine; sometimes, again, it comprised in the west areas and towns now forming an integral part of France. At certain periods it was divided up into a duchy, counties, and free towns; and its earlier history—when it possessed neither a distinctive name nor a clearly defined area—is to be found, not in indigenous records, but in the chronicles of various foreign countries, such as France and Germany, Flanders and Burgundy. In later times it witnessed the increasing and fateful rivalry of the French and the Germanic races, and the sanguinary struggles between them, resulting in the annexation of its territory in 1871 to Germany.

Varying areas.

Now this annexation was a forcible one; it was a consequence of German victories in the field, and of a signal military humiliation on the part of the French; and it was effected without consulting the inhabitants of the conquered territory. The latter—a progressive, cultured, and a traditionally freedom-loving people—repeatedly protested against their violent dissociation from France; and the great majority of them being unable to abandon their homes and property and so remain French, in pursuance of the right of option conceded to them, were compelled against their will and against their instincts and aspirations to assume German nationality and submit to the new, trying, uncongenial, oppressive régime of German domination, which inflicted all the burdens of subjecthood, but withheld many of the most important rights and privileges of citizenship.

Forcible annexation in 1871.

ALSACE-LORRAINE

CHAPTER I

INTRODUCTORY: THE QUESTION OF ALSACE-LORRAINE STATED

Alsace-Lorraine long a bone of contention—Forcible annexation in 1871—How the question of Alsace-Lorraine has arisen—How it differs from the Near Eastern Question—Other States concerned—Different aspects of the question—German view that there is no question of Alsace-Lorraine—Relation to the present war—The " challenge-cup of Europe "—Desiderata in the solution of the question—Difficulties involved in the solution—Justice and right the fundamental consideration.

FROM very early times Alsace-Lorraine was a bone of contention between rival races and rival sovereigns. In the numerous conflicts of the contending parties, the lands and possessions of these unhappy provinces were repeatedly subjected to destruction or pillage, and the population to all the violence of warfare, with the inevitable result that the social, intellectual, and industrial development of the country—rich as it is in natural resources and favoured in its geographical position and configuration—has been seriously hampered. Thanks to such salient features and barriers as the Rhine on the one hand and the Vosges Mountains on the other, the Alsace-Lorraine territory has constituted a border-country separating ever hostile and seemingly incompatible peoples; and its extent and

<small>Alsace-Lorraine long a bone of contention.</small>

boundaries have frequently changed with the vicissitudes of war and the succession of its rulers.

At one time it extended in the north to the sea ; at another time it stretched in the east to the Rhine ; sometimes, again, it comprised in the west areas and towns now forming an integral part of France. At certain periods it was divided up into a duchy, counties, and free towns ; and its earlier history—when it possessed neither a distinctive name nor a clearly defined area—is to be found, not in indigenous records, but in the chronicles of various foreign countries, such as France and Germany, Flanders and Burgundy. In later times it witnessed the increasing and fateful rivalry of the French and the Germanic races, and the sanguinary struggles between them, resulting in the annexation of its territory in 1871 to Germany.

Varying areas.

Now this annexation was a forcible one ; it was a consequence of German victories in the field, and of a signal military humiliation on the part of the French ; and it was effected without consulting the inhabitants of the conquered territory. The latter—a progressive, cultured, and a traditionally freedom-loving people—repeatedly protested against their violent dissociation from France ; and the great majority of them being unable to abandon their homes and property and so remain French, in pursuance of the right of option conceded to them, were compelled against their will and against their instincts and aspirations to assume German nationality and submit to the new, trying, uncongenial, oppressive régime of German domination, which inflicted all the burdens of subjecthood, but withheld many of the most important rights and privileges of citizenship.

Forcible annexation in 1871.

THE PROBLEM STATED

Moreover, so far as France was concerned, she was obliged to submit to the annexation, and her consent thereto, formally recorded in the Preliminaries of Versailles and the Treaty of Frankfort, was given involuntarily—it was extracted from her by reason of superior physical force ; and so she has thenceforth felt that the arrangement made in 1871 was not, and could not be, a definitive solution, and she has long hoped for an opportunity of recovering the conquered territories, and of fulfilling the vows of *revanche*. On the other hand, Germany has repeatedly declared that she is prepared to shed the last drop of her blood rather than relinquish the provinces ; and she lays claim to them on various grounds (which will be examined later). Thus has arisen another sinister stumbling-block for Europe—the question of Alsace-Lorraine. *[How the question of Alsace-Lorraine has arisen.]*

In a previous publication [1] it was pointed out that one of the most important and most urgent questions of modern European politics is that of the Straits of the Bosphorus and Dardanelles ; that this constitutes the fundamental basis of the Near Eastern Question—a problem which for several generations Europe has endeavoured to solve by "all the arts of diplomacy, all the devices of political combinations, and all the violence of wars"; that this unsolved question has produced, with ever-increasing intensity, the dangerous misunderstanding and ill-feeling due to tortuous diplomacy, international jealousy and friction, unhealthy rivalry ; and that numerous devastating wars have inevitably resulted therefrom. The difference between the Near Eastern Question *[Difference between the Near Eastern Question and the Alsace-Lorraine Question.]*

---

[1] *The Question of the Bosphorus and Dardanelles.* By Coleman Phillipson and Noel Buxton. (London, 1917.)

and the Alsace-Lorraine Question (which may be termed the Western Question) lies in the fact that the former involves directly and intrinsically the conflicting interests of the Great Powers of Europe and their incompatibility, not only amongst themselves, but with a non-Christian Empire, whose régime, government, and institutions are entirely out of harmony with those of the rest of Europe, and are a serious obstacle to the development and application of European public law and to the promotion of international relationships conformably to such law. On the other hand, the Alsace-Lorraine Question is, in itself, less comprehensive in its scope and purport, and involves primarily, if not exclusively, first, the conflicting interests between two powerful neighbouring States, so different in civilisation, culture, and ideals, and secondly—this being the particularly distinctive differentia—the claims of a clearly defined territory with a population sharing in some of the characteristics of the rival nations, but clearly differing from both in regard to many other important qualities.

But, owing to the geographical solidarity of Europe and to the political and economic nexus of its nations— Other States indeed of the nations of the world generally concerned. —the question unavoidably affects countries other than those immediately concerned. It is therefore nowadays well-nigh impossible to "localise" a conflict between two countries, and confine its results to the contending parties; their conflict becomes indirectly a conflict also with third parties, who thus acquire the right to have a say in the matter. Moreover, the principal disputants, fearing the growing power of each other, seek, in pursuance of a precarious and factitious diplomatic policy, to ally themselves with other Powers, in order to secure sympathy and

THE PROBLEM STATED 23

material support in the event of an outbreak of hostilities. Thus the quarrel primarily between two States drags in other States, which necessarily become parties thereto. Thus with the object of maintaining the existing equilibrium threatened by the military preparations and accumulation of armaments by this or that Power, combinations are brought about, and are virtually transformed into armed camps, which are a hindrance to the social and commercial development of nations, and to the realisation of an enlightened domestic policy. All this has happened as a result of the Franco-German hostility consequent on the annexation of the two French provinces in 1871; and so not only States in their collective and representative capacity, but also citizens and subjects in their individual capacity have been, and are, affected by this territorial conquest. The masses of the populations of the world have ever been obliged to pay their blood and treasure as the price for the misguided aims and overweening ambitions of fanatical cliques and inflammatory sections of their fellow-citizens. It comes to pass, therefore, that each one of us is indirectly concerned in, because each is prejudicially affected by, such a political blunder as the seizure of Alsace-Lorraine by Germany, which has engendered a veritable European nightmare. As a recent Russian writer observes : " . . . La question de l'Alsace-Lorraine influe directement sur le train ordinaire de notre vie quotidienne par l'impôt du sang et l'impôt de l'argent." [1]

The question of Alsace-Lorraine, which arose in 1871 and has subsisted to this day, has not always possessed the same character and presented the same

[1] J. Novicow, *L'Alsace-Lorraine : Obstacle à l'expansion allemande* (Paris, 1913), p. 4.

aspects; nor has it always been maintained in the same acute form, and regarded as involving the same implications. At the time of the annexation of the provinces, the question was easier to understand and to appreciate; here was a conqueror, there was a defeated country at the mercy of the victor, who exacted the abandonment of a large slice of territory, the inhabitants of which repeatedly protested against the violent dissociation from their mother-country. The question, then, in the eyes of France, appertained to what she regarded as an illegitimate act of conquest, especially so when consummated without regard to the wishes of the local population. Neutral statesmen, such as Gladstone,[1] also felt that the predominating factor of the compulsory cession was not the alleged right of conquest on the part of Germany, or the inalienable right of property on the part of France, but the attachment of the population of the wrested provinces to France and their refusal to change their nationality and to be dragged into an alien civilisation. In the eyes of Germany, on the other hand, no Alsace-Lorraine question ever came into being; for she held that she was entitled, in virtue of her military victories, to gain possession of the territory, which she claimed to be necessary for her security, and that such possession was specifically recognised and definitively sanctified by the Preliminaries of Versailles and the Treaty of Frankfort—solemn treaties between the contending parties, who contemplated and expressly stipulated their perpetual validity. Accordingly, the majority of people now look upon the question as one that merely relates to a clearly

Different aspects of the question.

[1] Lord Morley, *Life of William Ewart Gladstone* (London, 1903). 3 vols.; vol. ii. p. 347.

THE PROBLEM STATED

defined province, which once belonged to Germany, was afterwards taken from her by France, was re-annexed by Germany in 1871, and is now claimed again by France. The issue, however, is not so simple ; for, as we shall see in the subsequent chapters, in the interval between 1871 and, say, 1914, various important changes have taken place, first, in regard to the attitude of France, secondly, in the attitude of Germany, thirdly, in the aspirations and tendencies of the Alsace-Lorrainers, and in the development of their country, and lastly, in the economic and industrial evolution of modern Europe—all of which changes cannot but have affected the situation as it existed in 1871 and in the few years immediately following, as well as the original contentions of the principal parties concerned, together with the claims of other States. Now, again, since the outbreak of the Great War in August 1914, further changes have been introduced, notably in regard to the claims of France and the view of her principal ally, Great Britain ; also in the offer of a new policy on the part of Germany towards Alsace-Lorraine, hitherto constituted as a Reichsland (imperial territory). All these considerations must be carefully taken into account in order to gain a clear conception of this Western question as it exists to-day, and as it has existed for two generations.

Whenever the question of Alsace-Lorraine has been raised since 1871, the Germans—not only their Conservative and Pan-Germanist parties, but also the more liberal sections of the people —have emphatically and indignantly declared that there was no such question at all. Thus, such a philosophical and anti-militarist writer as Professor Paulsen observed in 1907 that the

<small>German view that there is no question of Alsace-Lorraine.</small>

question of the annexed provinces cannot constitute a subject of discussion between France and Germany.¹ Germans have repeatedly asserted that the final annexation in 1871, confirmed by solemn treaties, made future transactions on the subject impossible. On the contrary, Frenchmen have reiterated the claim that there is and has been all along a question <small>French reply thereto.</small> of Alsace-Lorraine, by reason of the violent dismemberment in 1871, the repeated protests of France and the annexed population, the oppression of the Alsace-Lorrainers under German domination, and the imprescriptible right of peoples to dispose of their own destiny. The latter point has recently been emphasised in the manifesto of the French Socialist party (December 1915). Europe, too, has in general recognised the existence of the question, and has realised that the failure to effect a settlement satisfactory to all parties is fraught with serious dangers menacing the public peace. This being so, it must necessarily be concluded that the question of Alsace-Lorraine, despite the profuse German disclaimers, must also exist for Germany, whether she likes it or not. Indeed, to maintain that there was no question of Alsace-Lorraine after the conclusion of the definitive Treaty of Frankfort, May 10, 1871, is either " insolent arrogance or myopia." ² In point of fact, Germany was not insensible of its existence. We may recall that when the Hague Conference of 1899 entered on the discussion of a general treaty of arbitration, fears were aroused in Germany as to whether her adhesion to such a convention would necessitate her submitting the Alsace-Lorraine question to an international tribunal. Again, the German Emperor, realising the tension and strained relation-

¹ *La paix par le droit* (February 1907).   ² Novicow, *op. cit.*, p. 43.

THE PROBLEM STATED 27

ships with France owing to this very question, emphasised at a dinner at Berlin, January 2, 1908, that the German people must remain united in view of an approaching conflict. An attitude of this kind shows a recognition of the existence of the question—at all events, in the sense that in France at least the transaction of 1871 was not and could not be regarded as final and closed.

In these circumstances, admitting the existence of the question of Alsace-Lorraine, can it be said that it was the cause of the present war? Here we have to discriminate between the direct and immediate causes of the war, and the indirect and more distant causes. *Was the question of Alsace-Lorraine the cause of the present war?* We may say that it was not the direct and immediate cause of the war, inasmuch as before the outbreak of hostilities the relations between France and Germany were peaceable and normal, and the incidents that gave rise to the conflict between Austria and Serbia did not particularly concern France. But the moment France felt compelled to commence hostilities against Germany, the question of Alsace-Lorraine, which before was relegated to the margin of consciousness in French minds, was rapidly transferred to the focus of consciousness, and its solution, implying a reversal of the act of 1871, became an essential object of France's war. France did not, then, take up arms for the purpose of regaining possession of the lost provinces; but as soon as she entered the war it was felt that her former territories constituted an important part of the stakes.

Looking at the events from a broader point of view, it may be said with truth and accuracy that the question of Alsace-Lorraine was a proximate cause of the war, seeing that its origin lies in the forcible annexation of French territory and the humiliation inflicted on a great and proud country which could not for several generations entirely forget such a bitter experience. The result of this was the establishment of political combinations in Europe, mutually distrustful and suspicious, highly susceptible in case of the smallest friction, ready to take offence and respond with threats at the first emergency. Thus European politics was ever in a state of tension, and it needed but a spark to set ablaze the whole dangerous structure resting on such an unstable foundation. And the main cause of this condition of European politics was, at bottom, the irreconcilable character of the relationships between France and Germany, rendering impossible a friendly alliance and frank *entente* between them.

As a proximate cause of the present war.

Another contributory cause is itself a result of Germany's victory in 1870–71, and her annexation of Alsace-Lorraine—*viz.* her territorial lust and aggressiveness, and her assumption of an arrogant hegemony on the Continent. This aggressiveness has been condemned even in Germany. Thus Herr Walther Schücking, professor of international law at the University of Marburg, writing in 1908, said that nowhere can one see more clearly than in German conduct in Alsace how disastrous for the German popular mind the influence of Bismarck has been in certain respects. Though it seems impious to say so, the writer observes, yet it must be said. Bismarck was a genius from the point of view of action, but not from the point of view of thought. The German watchword should be " less Bismarck and more Schiller." Germany ought to shake off her aggressive nationalism, which

German territorial lust and aggressiveness.

THE PROBLEM STATED 29

is contrary to her true genius.[1] In this sense, then, the question of Alsace-Lorraine was the virtual cause of the war. As Dr. Fried, a distinguished German pacifist, remarked recently in a Swiss paper [2]: "Alsace-Lorraine is, after all, the cause of the war. The fight for the two provinces had determined European politics, during the past half-century, culminating in the present war." Similarly, Mr. Asquith observed at Liverpool, October 11, 1917 : " It is this act of crude and short-sighted spoliation which was the root and source of the unrest, of the unstable equilibrium, of the competition in armaments, which have afflicted Europe during the life-time of two generations, and which have culminated in the most terrible war in history." [3] At all events, whether Alsace-Lorraine is the cause of the present war or not, there is no doubt that the failure to reach an agreement on the question during the course of the hostilities was the main reason for continuing this widespread and sanguinary conflict. Thus, Baron von Kühlmann, the German Foreign Secretary, said in the Reichstag, October 9, 1917 : " After a very thorough investigation of the whole situation, according to information derived from most diverse sources, I am convinced that the great question around which the struggle of the nations centres, and for which they are shedding their blood, is not, in the first instance, the Belgian question. The question for which Europe is being turned more and more into a heap of ruins is the question of the future of Alsace-Lorraine."

Having regard to such considerations and to the fact that secular contests have centred round Alsace-

---
[1] *Friedenswarte*, February 1908 ; cited by Novicow, *op. cit.*, p 378.
[2] *Neue Zürcher Zeitung* (a Swiss independent paper), June 24, 1917.
[3] *Daily Chronicle*, October 12, 1917.

Lorraine, those provinces have sometimes been described—not, however, without an appearance of flippancy—as " the challenge-cup of Europe." Were it not for the destruction and devastation, the waste of treasure and loss of lives that these contests have brought with them, the phrase might well be admitted as being aptly descriptive of the part played by these unhappy provinces. Sometimes Belgium, sometimes the Balkan peninsula has been designated the cockpit of Europe. This designation may just as appropriately be applied to Alsace-Lorraine. Romans, Gauls, Huns, Germans, French, Austrians, Hungarians, Spaniards, Swedes, have fought on the blood-soaked soil of this small country. The old Chronicles of Thann relate how the land was devastated in the Thirty Years War. In the seventeenth century Alsace was a great battle-field of religion. The battles of the Franco-German war of 1870–71 were fought principally in Lorraine. And now, once again, a conflict—the greatest of all—rages in these provinces, where the destiny of many a nation will probably be decided.

The "challenge-cup of Europe."

Whatever settlement is eventually arrived at, it must realise at least two desiderata: first, it must take account of the principle of nationality which concerns mainly Alsace-Lorraine, together with France and Germany, as the great protagonists struggling, the one to regain her " lost children," the other to retain what she conceives to be now an integral part of herself; secondly, it must establish and assure Franco-German peace and friendship, as the vital condition indispensable for securing the real pacification of Europe, and indeed of the world. So long as Alsatian disaffection continues, the resentment of France and her nurture

Desiderata in the solution of the question.

THE PROBLEM STATED

of *revanche* ideas will remain. So long as Franco-German concealed or manifest hostility continues, the crushing burden of European armament, military expenditure, and bleeding of the populations, will subsist, and industry and commerce, social reform and education, will suffer an incalculable injury. If these suggested desiderata are realised, then Alsace-Lorraine may well serve as a conciliatory connecting-link, as a felicitous bond of union between the long hostile French and German peoples. As M. Léon Boll, the editor of the Strassburg *Journal d'Alsace-Lorraine*, said not long before the outbreak of the present war: " Let us make of Alsace-Lorraine the melting-pot in which shall be blended the double-distilled civilisation of Germanism and Latinism." [1]

To arrive at a solution satisfactory to all parties is now all the more difficult inasmuch as economic considerations at present play a predominating part. Formerly the importance of possessing Alsace-Lorraine was conceived to depend primarily on the exigencies of military strategy and territorial security. Now the mineral wealth and the fertile soil of the Reichsland, coupled with its advantageous position—in the very midst of a great net-work of communications radiating in every direction—are thought to be the main factors that stimulate the desire of the contending parties to possess it. The Pan-Germanists are fully convinced that to be deprived of the provinces would be tantamount to destroying the fondly cherished ideal of securing the economic and political domination of the Continent. Similarly, France, now less mindful than formerly of the strategic significance of the provinces, less

Difficulties involved in the solution.

[1] G. Bourdon, *L'Énigme allemande* (Paris, 1913). English translation (London, 1914); French edition, p. 417; English edition, p. 316.

susceptible also to the old vows of *revanche* (at least, apart from their recent resuscitation during the present war), attaches all the greater importance to the economic side of the question; she feels that the unrestricted possession of the natural resources of the provinces would contribute substantially to her commercial and industrial development, and to her national power and welfare. Nevertheless, it is now thought in some quarters that it is not the actual economic value of the provinces that intensifies the difficulty of the question, but the fact that their possession is now considered by the leading belligerents as symbolising the issue of the war; that is to say, that whoever keeps them will be accounted the victor. Thus, Dr. Fried, writing in June 1917, points out that, having regard to the intrinsic value of the disputed territory, common sense would suggest that the prize sought is not worth the struggle; since the enormous losses in life, property, and treasure suffered by each of the contending parties already exceed on the one hand the total value of the provinces, and on the other the total number of their inhabitants; so that the actual value of the object aimed at is no longer the main consideration. " The fight for these few square miles has now assumed the terrible meaning that their final possession at the end of the war is regarded as the certificate of victory . . . even if the so-called victor is only another loser." [1] Outside France and Germany, it is felt generally that European equilibrium and peace are jeopardised so long as France is far outstripped by Germany in material property, and—as a corollary—in the growth of population, and therefore in national power and fighting strength; and that the possession of these

[1] *Neue Zürcher Zeitung*, June 24, 1917.

THE PROBLEM STATED 33

rich provinces has contributed considerably to bringing about this difference.

All these difficulties and conflicting interests, then, must be adjusted in the ultimate settlement of the question. And, finally, the moral principle of international justice, which in the eyes of many takes precedence of strategic and economic interests, must be vindicated therein, so as to recognise the dominion of public morality and public law over the society of nations, and the subordination of might to right. For when one contemplates the question of Alsace-Lorraine as impartially and dispassionately as possible, one cannot help coming to the conclusion that to do justice to these disputed provinces and to their aggrieved people is far more important than to satisfy the economic and military demands of Germany or France, or to make amends for the humiliation of 1871 by facilitating the consummation of an oscillating or adventitious *revanche*.

Justice the fundamental point.

Having thus set forth the essential significance of, and the various implications involved in, the question before us, we have now to inquire into the diverse relevant matters for the purpose of grasping the real issue and arriving at what seems to be the best solution.

CHAPTER II

DESCRIPTION OF ALSACE-LORRAINE, AND ITS ECONOMIC POSITION

Area and configuration—Minerals; climate; population—Characteristics of the people—Language—Religion—Industries—Agriculture—Exports and imports—Transport and communication; public works—Budget—Public instruction—Great progress under German rule.

ALSACE-LORRAINE is bounded on the south by Switzerland; on the east by Baden, from which it is separated by the Rhine; on the north and north-east by the Bavarian Palatinate, the Prussian Rhine Province, and Luxemburg; on the west by France. The area of the provinces as ceded in 1871 is 5,605 square miles, that is less than one-tenth of the area of England and Wales, or a little less than the area of Yorkshire. The total area acquired by Germany constituted nearly the whole of the former Alsace, together with about one-fifth of the former Lorraine; the annexed area of Alsace alone being 3,344 square miles. The maximum length of Alsace-Lorraine from north to south is 145 miles, the maximum breadth from east to west is 105 miles, and the minimum breadth, at the line drawn through Schlettstadt, is 24 miles.

Area of Alsace-Lorraine.

The configuration of the country is varied and beautiful.[1] There are mountains and hills, valleys,

[1] As to the surface and soils of Alsace-Lorraine, see an article by Miss M. I. Newbigin, in *The Scottish Geographical Magazine*, vol. xxxiv (1918), pp. 121 seq.

Mannhei

Sarrebou

Sarre

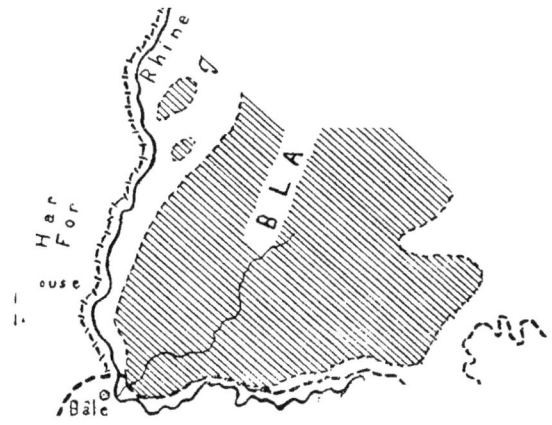
Rhine
Har
For
ouse
Bâle
B L A

Doubs

DESCRIPTION 37

rivers, plains, tablelands, lakes, forests; the hills being well wooded with fir, beech, and oak. The salient physical features may be divided roughly into three classes: mountain land, plain, and plateau. **Configuration.** First, the mountain land occupies the western half of Alsace, and consists of the Vosges range, which runs in a northerly direction from the gap or pass of Belfort (*trouée de Belfort*). A conspicuous peak of the Vosges is the Ballon d'Alsace, 4,085 feet high. Secondly, between the Vosges range and its sharp eastern slopes and the Rhine lies a plain of remarkable fertility occupying the eastern portion of Alsace. Thirdly, in the north-west there is a great undulating plateau, which descends gradually in the west to the valley of the Moselle, and is nearly co-extensive with Lorraine. From the Vosges chain beautiful valleys descend into the plain, each watered by its own stream, and all of them draining into the Ill—the only river of importance; the latter falls into the Rhine near Strassburg after a course of more than 100 miles, and is navigable below Colmar. Among the smaller streams may be mentioned the Doller, the Thur, the Lauch, the Fecht, the Weisse, the Lieprette, the Bruche, and the Zorn.

The provinces possess not only a rich soil—one of the most fertile in central Europe—but also great mineral wealth: coal, iron, copper, lead, potash, petroleum, rock-salt, silver. **Minerals.**

The climate is temperate, the temperature varying according to altitude. The mean annual temperature of Strassburg is 49·8° F., of Metz, 48·2° F. The rainfall at Strassburg is $26\frac{1}{4}$ in., Metz, $27\frac{1}{2}$ in. (The mean annual temperature of London is 50·4°, and the rainfall from $20\frac{1}{2}$ to $27\frac{1}{2}$ in.) **Climate.**

The population of Alsace-Lorraine was, in 1877,

1,548,900; in 1912, 1,886,800; in 1914, about
Population. 1,900,000. The changes and fluctuations in
the total number, due to the emigration of natives
and the immigration of Germans, will be considered
in a subsequent chapter.

The native Alsatians are neither French nor German
in character, temperament, and ideals; they are
Characteris- Alsatians, sharing certain characteristics of
tics of the the rival nations, and differing markedly
people. from both in many other qualities. There
is more friction between the Germans and the Alsatians
than between the Germans and the Lorrainers; the
latter being for the most part engaged in mines,
iron-works, and factories, and being mainly concerned
with questions of industry and capital. The Alsatians
are an optimistic, merry, religious, industrious people,
lacking in enthusiasm generally, but with democratic
and republican leanings. They are very practically-
minded, and set great store by material well-being.
In the eyes of many Germans they have something
of the Sancho Panza type in them. The Alsatian
peasantry do not regard with favour the ubiquitous
dispensations of paternalism; neither they nor the
agricultural workers of Lorraine are deeply concerned
with the broad questions of politics; both classes
alike would desire the burdens of taxation to diminish,
and, above all, they would like to be let alone
to jog along in their own quiet, cheerful, simple
manner.[1]

Both French and German are spoken by the educated
Language. classes in the towns. Apart from these, the
great majority of Alsatians speak a Germanic
dialect. In some of the Vosges valleys French pre-

[1] As to the feelings and aspirations of the people, see further *infra*, chap. x.

DESCRIPTION 39

dominates or is spoken as the mother-tongue by a considerable proportion of the inhabitants. Along the Moselle French yields to German; similarly on the banks of the Sarre and in the environs of the confluence of the two rivers Nied. In 1890 it was calculated that the French-speaking inhabitants of Alsace numbered 53,000; whilst there were 1,000,000 who spoke German or a Germanic patois.[1] French is the mother-tongue of a small portion of annexed Lorraine, notably in Metz and district (the *pays messin*). The Teutonic dialect of the north-east of Lorraine is somewhat like that of Luxemburg. Some of the recent census returns[2] (December 1, 1905) may be given as examples to show the linguistic diversity. In the district of Sarrebourg there were, in Saint-Quirin, 798 French, 221 German; in Abreschwiller, 887 French, 627 German; Lorquin, 610 French, 149 German; Heming, 316 French, 209 German. In the district of Château-Salins, there were in the canton of Dieuze 7,062 French, 4,657 German; Vic, 6,362 French, 801 German; Château-Salins, 8,868 French, 1,321 German; Delme, 7,970 French, 574 German; Albestroff, 1,831 French, 6,921 German.

It is to be noted that, after 1871, German became the official language of the country, and had to be used exclusively in all official assemblies, such as general councils, the Alsace-Lorraine Delegacy (the Landesausschuss), etc.; and from January 1, 1888, its use was made obligatory in all courts of law.

---

[1] *Cf.* C. Pfister, *La limite de la langue française et de la langue allemande en Alsace-Lorraine* (Paris, 1890), p. 14.

[2] Published by the official statistical bureau: *Die Bevölkerung Elsass-Lothringens* (Strassburg, 1908); cited by G. May, *La lutte pour le français en Lorraine avant 1870. Annales de l'Est publiées par la Faculté des Lettres de l'Université de Nancy* (Paris: Nancy, 1912), p. 21.

40   ALSACE-LORRAINE

Moreover, the teaching of French in schools was considerably reduced.¹

About three-quarters of the population of Alsace-Lorraine are Roman Catholics. Thus, according to Religion. the returns of 1904, there were 1,310,391 Roman Catholics, 372,078 Protestants, and 32,370 Jews. In 1905, out of a total civilian population of 1,733,455, there were 1,348,648 Roman Catholics, amounting to 78 per cent. Lorraine is proportionately more Roman Catholic than Alsace. In Alsace-Lorraine, unlike France, there is no separation between Church and State. Since 1871 it has remained under the régime of the French Concordat² concluded between Napoleon, as First Consul, and the Pope, July 15, 1801, whereby Roman Catholicism was allowed to be practised freely and publicly in France, subject to such regulations as the French Government might consider necessary to make in the interest of public order. The First Consul was empowered to nominate the bishops, and the Pope to confer canonical institution; whilst the bishops acquired the right of presentation to parochial cures, subject to the approval of the Government. Within certain limits Catholics were entitled to establish ecclesiastical endowments. The Concordat was supplemented by the Organic Articles (April 8, 1802), which dealt with the jurisdiction of the Holy See, ecclesiastical discipline, areas of provinces, dioceses, and parishes, liturgy, catechism, dogma, and salaries.³ The professors in the seminaries were obliged to subscribe to the Gallican Declaration made in 1682 by the

¹ The question of language, race, etc., is dealt with more fully, *infra*, chap. vii.
² As to the Concordat of 1801, see J. E. C. Bodley, *The Church in France* (London, 1906), pp. 30 *seq.*, 35 *seq.*
³ *Ibid.*, p. 41.

DESCRIPTION 41

French clergy, and to teach its doctrine. Sunday was proclaimed the official day of rest.[1] Special laws have improved the position of ministers of religion, and the founding of various religious associations has been sanctioned. Elementary schools have retained their confessional character; religious instruction is given by the teachers, and the Catholic clergy have the right of inspection, and the right to sit on the local council (the *Ortsschulvorstand*), which controls public education. In other schools, religious teaching is obligatory and is given by the clergy. The ecclesiastical budget amounted in 1910 to about 5,000,000 marks, from which Protestant ministers, as well as Catholic, were paid. The influence of the State on the Lutheran Church is greater than on the Catholic Church, inasmuch as the Government of Alsace-Lorraine nominates the president of the " Directoire " and the " Conservatoire," which are the two highest authorities of the Lutheran Church.

According to a recent estimate[2] the occupations of the people are apportioned as follows: Occupations.

Industries   . 730,952 (of whom 222,931 are women)
Agriculture . 551,654 (,,   294,051   ,,   )
Commerce and
  trade .   . 221,393 (,,   115,344   ,,   )

The principal industries are spinning and weaving. Textile goods (cotton, linen, woollen)—the amount produced in Alsace-Lorraine alone being equal to a quarter of the total produced in the whole of France—are manufactured at Mülhausen (the Manchester of Alsace) and Colmar, together with

Industries.

---
[1] J. E. C. Bodley, *op. cit.*, p. 42.
[2] L'abbé E. Wetterlé, *Ce qu'était l'Alsace-Lorraine et ce qu'elle sera* (Paris, 1915), pp. 227 *seq.*

Münster, Logelbach, Winzenheim, Türkheim, as well as in all the valleys of the Vosges; e.g. in the valley of the Doller (Massevaux and other villages), of the Thur (Wesserling, St. Amarin, Thann, Moosch, Cernay, Willer), of the Lauch (Guebviller and adjacent villages), of the Lieprette (Ste. Marie-aux-Mines and adjacent districts). Other industries are dyeing; tanning and leather goods manufacture (Strassburg; and Massevaux in the Doller Valley); the manufacture of silk, lace, machinery, glass, china ware (in Lorraine), house furniture, clocks, paper, and tobacco (at Strassburg).

Further, mining and metallurgy employ a large number of people, the principal minerals being coal, iron (in Lorraine), potash, petroleum, and argentiferous lead. The question of coal and iron will be considered later separately[1]; for the present it will suffice to state that in 1912, the coal extracted amounted to 3,538,951 tonnes (1 tonne = ·9842 ton), of the value of 39,000,000 marks; and in 1913 (the last normal year) the iron mines of annexed Lorraine produced 21,135,000 tonnes of ore,[2] of the value of nearly 56,000,000 marks.

In 1872 the total yield of coal and iron from the Alsace-Lorraine mines was 1,000,000 tonnes; so that in a period of forty years under the German régime the output has become twenty-five times as large. In 1872 some 1,500 workmen were employed in the furnaces, and turned out 200,000 tonnes of pig-iron; in 1910 there were 6,500 workmen, who produced 2,700,000 tonnes of pig-iron (3,800,000 in 1913). The production of steel increased as follows: in 1872, 180,000 tonnes; in 1910, 1,300,000 tonnes;

[1] See chap. xiii.
[2] *Comité des Forges de France.* Circulaire No. 655, p. 13; quoted by M. Alfassa, *Le fer et le charbon lorrains* (Paris, 1916).

DESCRIPTION 43

in 1913, 2,300,000 tonnes.[1] With regard to potash, we may refer to a statement made in the spring of 1916 by the *Rhenish Westphalian Gazette*, which is subsidised by Krupp's: " In Upper Alsace there are rich deposits of potash. If this region belonged to France, the German world-monopoly of potash, which lays the foreigner and especially the United States under tribute to this country, would be lost, and France would gain a notable source of wealth and also the means of providing her munitions. She would then control a powerful weapon in waging war against us. So important indeed are these potash deposits in munition-making that Germany has had to limit and control their export." The value of this mine is calculated at several thousand millions of francs. As to petroleum, the same paper says: " We have at Pechelbronn in Alsace the only large petroleum well in Germany, especially since the field of the Hanover Wietze district has greatly diminished. Thanks to Pechelbronn, Alsace has during the present war considerably assisted our economic resistance by supplying us with petroleum, benzine, and lubricating oils."

Agriculture is in a prosperous condition. The system of small holdings, favoured by the Civil Code, is established; of cultivated land of 881,569 hectares (1 acre = ·405 hectare), there are 244,988 holdings. The slopes of the Vosges are covered with extensive and fruitful vineyards; in the neighbourhood of Colmar one of the best wines is produced. Recently viticulture has undergone an enormous development. The average production of wine is 600,000 hectolitres (1 hectolitre = 22·01 gallons),

Agriculture.

[1] *Cf.* H. and A. Lichtenberger, *La Question d'Alsace-Lorraine* (Paris, 1915), pp. 101 *seq.*

of the value of about 22,000,000 marks; this amount constitutes a third of the total production of wine in Germany. The annual production of beer reaches 1,274,000 hectolitres, and that of alcohol 14,857 hectolitres.[1] Amongst the more important agricultural products may be mentioned wheat, barley, rye, oats; pulse; potatoes; tobacco; hops; hemp, flax; beet (for sugar); dairy produce, notably cheese; fruit; timber. Forestry employs many people; the forest land is extensive, nearly one-third of which belongs to the State, more than one-third to the communes, and the rest to private owners. The provinces are rich in horses, cattle, sheep, pigs, goats, hares, geese, ducks, and chickens.

As for the exports and imports of Alsace-Lorraine, we find that Germany takes by far the most important place. Thus in 1909 the provinces exported 10,248,604 tons of merchandise, of which 80 per cent. went to Germany; and of the imports, too, about 80 per cent. came from Germany. The remaining 20 per cent., both of exports and imports, was divided between Belgium, France, and Switzerland; that is, Belgium (and not France) came next to Germany.

Exports and imports.

The means of transport and communication have developed enormously under German organisation. Watercourses—canals and rivers, especially the Rhine—have been greatly improved; the traffic of the port of Strassburg has increased considerably. In 1872 there were 768 kilometres of railway lines, and 9,000 employees. There are now over 2,000 kilometres of railways, which are valued at about a milliard francs (£40,000,000), and which carried in 1909 47,000,000 passengers and

Transport and communication.

[1] Wetterlé, *loc. cit.*

DESCRIPTION 45

2,611,000,000 kilometric tonnes of goods[1]; and the number of persons employed in 1900 was 31,000. The gross receipts for 1912 amounted to 140,000,000 marks. The railway system was bought in 1871 by France from the Eastern Company for 325,000,000 francs, and was ceded to Germany in reduction of the war indemnity. The postal, telegraphic, and telephonic services have also been rapidly extended in recent years. In 1871 there were only 192 post offices, 57 telegraph offices, and 600 employees; whilst in 1909 there were 1,560 post offices, 1,329 telegraph offices, and 1,295 telephone offices, employing 8,000 persons, and despatching 441,000,000 letters and packets, 13,000,000 parcels, and 2,000,000 telegrams.[2]

The establishment of public works for purposes of irrigation, canalisation, etc., has added largely to the value of the plant of the country, and on which a sum of about 48,000,000 marks was spent between 1871 and 1904. *Public works.*

The expenditure of the State in the provinces amounted in 1872 to 31,000,000 marks, in 1880 to 47,000,000 marks, and in 1912 to 76,000,000 marks; that is, it has increased, during the forty years of German administration, from 20 marks per head of the population to 38 marks per head. The expenditure of the communes has in this interval grown in greater proportion—from 14,500,000 marks to 55,500,000 marks, that is, from 9 marks per head to 29 marks per head. Similarly, the debt of the State has increased from 3,000,000 marks to 44,500,000 marks (that is, from 2·44 m. per head to 22 m. per head), and that of the communes from 15,000,000 *Budget.*

[1] H. and A. Lichtenberger, *La Question d'Alsace-Lorraine*, p. 98.
[2] *Ibid.*, p. 99.

marks to 180,000,000 marks (that is, from about 10 m. per head to 96 m. per head).[1]

Both the expenditure and the debt—as is admitted even by critics strongly opposed to the German occupation of Alsace-Lorraine [2]—were necessary and fully justified; a bold financial policy was needed for the purposes of public organisation and economic development. The merits of German administration —activity, method, precision—are recognised by the Alsatians, though they have sometimes felt that the governing authorities might have been a little more economical in the use of public money, especially in regard to the high salaries paid to officials, who for the most part are Germans. Impartial judges, however, will agree that in order to secure competent and efficient officials it is indispensable to offer them adequate, indeed, attractive, salaries; so that the Alsatian reproach of " dispendieuse mégalomanie "[3] is not merited, at all events in this respect. A comment of striking significance here is that in 1872 the deposits in the savings banks of the provinces amounted to 7,500,000 marks, whilst in recent years they attained a total of 178,000,000 marks. Further, it is admitted that the schemes and incidence of taxation have changed for the better since the annexation of the territory.[4]

Public instruction of all grades is admirably organised and adequately endowed.[5] In regard to elementary education, there are 3,846 schools, with 4,138 masters and 4,053 mistresses and 320,000 scholars. For secondary instruction, which requires a budget of 2,000,000 to 3,000,000 marks,

Public instruction.

---

[1] Wetterlé, loc. cit.; Lichtenberger, op. cit., p. 105.
[2] E.g. Lichtenberger, ibid.
[3] Ibid., p. 107.   [4] Wetterlé, op. cit., p. 294.   [5] Ibid., p. 100.

DESCRIPTION 47

there are 15 *gymnasiums* (grammar-schools) and 13 *realschulen* (modern schools), containing 700 masters and 10,000 pupils. Excellent provision is made for technical and professional training; the School of Chemistry at Mülhausen is an institute of European reputation. Finally, the University of Strassburg— for which the annual expenditure is 1,800,000 marks— is one of the finest and best equipped on the Continent; and its organisation is universally praised and admired. In 1872 it had 47 professors and lecturers and 220 students, now it has 176 professors and lecturers and 2,200 students; and it contains a library of nearly a million volumes. There can be no doubt that the various kinds of continuation schools and technical institutes have greatly contributed to the commercial expansion and industrial prosperity of the Reichsland. As MM. Lichtenberger testify: " L'enseignement post-scolaire, les écoles d'adultes, les écoles d'apprentissage, l'enseignement technique sont admirablement organisés en Alsace et ont certainement contribué, pour une bonne part, à la prospérité industrielle du pays." [1]

Whatever disadvantages were inherent in and whatever hardships [2] resulted from the German administration, there can be no doubt that it also brought about great economic and educational progress, as well as true religious liberty. *Great progress under German rule.* We may sum up in the words of a well-known French writer: " Under the German rule, Alsace-Lorraine received an impulse which it had not known before the annexation. Schools, roads, railways, public places, monuments, factories, large shops, transformed old Alsace and French Lorraine.

[1] *Op. cit.*, p. 115.
[2] That there were many will be seen in chap. ix.

After French administration, so conventional and so nonchalant, German administration, even if still somewhat rough in its methods, seemed a wonderful fairy of initiative and intelligence, and the same comparison between the commercial bourgeoisie of France and of Germany was forced on us ; the more the one appeared conventional and timid, the more the other seemed bold and enterprising." [1]

Having now considered the nature of the question of Alsace-Lorraine and the present position of the provinces, it is necessary to set forth the principal historical facts in order to appreciate the character of the contending claims and the issues involved.

[1] G. Hervé, *L'Alsace-Lorraine* (Paris, 1913).

CHAPTER III

HISTORICAL OUTLINE

Roman occupation—Germanic invasions—Union with the German Empire. (a) *Lorraine :* Middle Ages—Relations with France—Certain annexations to France—The Three Bishoprics—Cession to France. (b) *Alsace :* Middle Ages—Part of Germany till the seventeenth century—The Thirty Years War—Treaty of Westphalia (1648)—Position of Strassburg—The French Revolution ; Union with France.

THE regions of Alsace-Lorraine inhabited by such tribes as the Rauraci and Sequani, formed part of ancient Gaul ; they extended from the Atlantic to the Rhine, and were subjected to the Roman dominion through the conquests of Julius Cæsar. For five centuries they constituted a colony of the Roman Empire, being included in the provinces of Germania Superior and Maxima Sequanorum. The results of the Roman occupation, *e.g.* the founding of towns, such as Strassburg, Metz, Verdun, Saverne, and the construction of roads and monuments, are visible in various parts of the country. To the east of the Rhine was a region of forest land inhabited by barbarians who frequently crossed over the river into the adjacent lands on depredatory enterprises, and with the help of the Roman and Gallic legions were driven back.

Early in the fifth century, however, the provinces were more extensively ravaged by bands of Goths, Alani, and other Germanic tribes, who broke in successive waves over Gaul and the Roman Empire. The former Roman colony was occupied on the south by the Alemanni, and in the north by the Franks. About A.D. 500 the Alemanni were overthrown by Clovis, the Merovingian king, at the battle of Tolbiac, and were driven beyond the Rhine, so that the territories on the left bank passed under the sway of the Franks. Immediately afterwards followed the conversion to Christianity of Clovis and thousands of his soldiers, who were baptized by Remigius, Bishop of Rheims, conformably to the victor's promise made before the great battle. Many of the old names in the conquered country were then supplanted by new ones; thus the designation Alsatia or Elsass came into use, being derived from the river Ell or Ill, which falls into the Rhine at Strassburg.

For some time during the Merovingian period it formed a duchy attached to the Austrasian kingdom, with Metz as the capital, and was governed by the successors of Duke Eticho, one of whom was St. Odilia, to whose shrine Alsatians still make pilgrimages.

Merovingian period.

Under Charlemagne it participated in the military expeditions to the interior of Germany; and at his death (A.D. 814) the Frankish empire fell to pieces, and Alsace-Lorraine, along with it, was divided into countships.

Charlemagne.

By the Treaty of Verdun (A.D. 843), the original kingdom of Lorraine passed to the Emperor Lothair I, and in A.D. 855 his second son, King Lothair, succeeded to it. It then comprised not only the territory that was afterwards designated Lorraine, but also the regions corresponding to what is now Holland and Belgium, portions of Rhenish Prussia, of Switzerland, and of the old province of Franche-Comté. A century later the entire country received the name of Lotharingia.

HISTORICAL OUTLINE 51

Towards the end of the ninth century, when the empire was divided between Charles the Bald and Louis the German, Alsace and Lorraine were united to the German Empire. Alsace was now settled by Germans of Alemannic stock, akin to those who had colonised a great part of the territories now comprised in Baden, Bavaria, and North Switzerland; and Lorraine was occupied by Franks and Franconians—the Vosges or Wasigen Mountains forming a barrier between the German-speaking and the Romance-speaking peoples. {Union with German empire.}

It will now be convenient to deal with Lorraine and Alsace separately, as for some centuries they followed different destinies.

(a) LORRAINE

At the beginning of the tenth century Lorraine was converted from a countship into a duchy. In A.D. 944 Otto the Great gave it to Conrad the Red, Duke of Franconia, and on the latter's revolt took it away again and assigned it to Bruno, Archbishop of Cologne (A.D. 954). Owing to the sedition of Lotharingian nobles, Bruno divided the duchy into Lower Lorraine (given to a Duke Godfrey, who was styled *Dux Ripuariorum*), and Upper Lorraine (given to Frederick, Count of Bar, styled *Dux Mosellanorum*). After numerous changes Lower Lorraine was assigned by the Emperor Henry V in 1106 to Godfrey, Count of Louvain, the first hereditary Duke of Brabant, and was afterwards designated Brabant. From the eleventh century the duchy of Upper Lorraine came to be known simply as Lorraine. Among its fiefs were the three ecclesiastical lordships of Metz, Toul, and Verdun— {Lorraine: Middle Ages.}

described as the Three Bishoprics—which enjoyed almost complete independence.

In 1315 Verdun and Toul placed themselves for a short time under the protection of the King of France. Metz, above all, was on terms of close friendship with France, and very cordial relations existed between the *pays messin* and Louis XI, Charles VIII, and Louis XII. When a French king was crowned at Rheims, several Messins attended and received the honour of knighthood; similarly they participated in the solemnities consequent on the death of a French sovereign. The French language was predominant in Metz.

Relations with France.

In the middle of the sixteenth century a considerable portion of Lorraine territory was definitively annexed to France. At this time Germany was much divided up, and cannot yet be described as constituting a nation.[1] Metz, Toul, and Verdun, which had long shaken off the dominion of the bishops, were governed as independent republics, recognising only a nominal suzerainty of the Emperor of the Romans. Charles V opposed the spread of Protestantism, and endeavoured by forcible measures to bring back to the Roman Catholic Church princes and communities who had adopted the reformed religion. Whereupon the Protestant princes, notably Maurice of Saxony, took up arms and appealed for protection to Henry II of France (husband of Catherine de' Medici). The latter accordingly entered into alliances with the German Reformers, towards the end of 1551, raised an army of 36,000 men (more than half of whom were German and Swiss mercenaries), and invaded Lorraine early in

Certain annexations to France.

---

[1] *Cf.* A. Eckel, *La réunion de l'Alsace et de la Lorraine à la France* (Vesoul, 1894).

HISTORICAL OUTLINE

1552. Toul readily surrendered without offering any resistance. In April 1552, Metz was occupied by Montmorency. Henry II then crossed the Vosges into Alsace, and tried to take Strassburg, but failed. He took possession, however, of Hagenau and Weissenburg, and, after recrossing the Vosges, occupied Verdun.

Thus, the three Lotharingian bishoprics, comprising the three towns and dependent territories, became part of the French dominions. In 1553 Charles V tried to retake Metz, but after a siege of two months was compelled to retire with heavy loss, before the resistance of Duke Francis of Guise. Under the Treaty of Cateau-Cambrésis, April 1559, France was obliged to surrender various conquests, but was permitted to retain the Three Bishoprics: "She lost as many provinces as she gained cities." The newly acquired territories, which were already French in language and sentiments, were rapidly assimilated to France in every other respect, and gave their new country illustrious sons (such as Marshal Fabert of Metz) who were ready to sacrifice themselves in its service.

The Three Bishoprics.

The possession of the Three Bishoprics facilitated and promoted French relations with the duchy of Lorraine generally, and paved the way for the definitive acquisition of the latter. The Duke of Lorraine was in several respects in a peculiar position. In the first place, his subjects were some of French origin and some of German; the people inhabiting the banks of the Moselle, in the neighbourhood of Nancy, Épinal, etc., spoke French, whilst those inhabiting the banks of the Sarre, near Sarreguemines, Sarrebourg, and Phalsbourg, spoke German. Secondly, he owed homage to the French sovereign for the county of Bar-le-

Duc, but the remainder of his possessions acknowledged the suzerainty of the Emperor of Germany. Thus the division of his interests and obligations affected his policy. In the reign of Duke Charles (surnamed the Great), the duchy suffered much from German bands who passed through it on their way to help the Protestants in France, as well as from disturbances due to the progress of Calvinism. His son, Henry II (the Good), expelled the invaders.

Duke Charles IV (or III), having harboured French malcontents, Louis XIII invaded Lorraine and obtained the cession of several fortresses (1631–3). The duke then abdicated and withdrew to Germany, whereupon the Parlement of Paris adjudged him guilty of rebellion, and confiscated his estates. By the Treaty of Vincennes (1661) he recovered the duchies of Lorraine and Bar, but ceded Clermont, Sarrebourg, and Phalsbourg. The following year he transferred the succession to the duchy to Louis XIV for a life-rent, but the Lorrainers refused to ratify the transaction. Lorraine was then occupied by Marshal de Créqui. The ducal estates were not restored till 1697, when, under the Treaty of Ryswick, Duke Leopold regained them, but was obliged to dismantle the fortresses of Lorraine, and to disband nearly the whole of his army. During the latter's reign great progress was made in the duchy, and French immigrants were welcomed.

French invasion.

After the death of Leopold, his heir, Francis III, was betrothed to Maria Theresa, the daughter and heiress of the Emperor Charles VI. But France opposed the union of Lorraine with the Empire. By the Treaty of Vienna (1735) the duke exchanged Lorraine for the duchy of Tuscany; the former was given to Stanislaus Leszczynski, the

Cession to France.

HISTORICAL OUTLINE 55

dethroned king of Poland and father-in-law of Louis XV, and on his death (A.D. 1766) passed to the French king conformably to the stipulations of 1735. Thus the acquisition of the territory was effected by way of a regular and legitimate cession, and not by conquest.

(b) ALSACE

After the death of Henry I, King of the Germans, Alsatia (or Elsass) was re-established as a duchy, and remained in the possession of the Hohenstaufen House till 1273, when Rudolf III of Habsburg was elected King of the Romans. (The Imperial dignity was vested in the House of Habsburg from 1438-1740, and from 1745 until the dissolution of the Holy Roman Empire in 1806.) At the beginning of the twelfth century the country was divided into the two landgraviates of Upper Alsatia (the Sundgau) and Lower Alsatia; but, owing to the continual disintegration of the great duchies and the multiplication of principalities and minor lordships in the Empire, the Emperors established numerous free towns for the purpose of combating the growing power of the princes and lesser nobles. In the latter part of the fifteenth century there were some eighty Free Imperial towns in the Empire, most of which were situated in southern or western Germany; and the traditions of freedom in Alsace go back at least to the middle of the fourteenth century, when the League of Free Cities was established (1353), at the suggestion of the Emperor Charles IV, and existed for over two centuries. It included Hagenau, Colmar, Schlettstadt, Weissenburg, Münster, Türkheim, Kaisersberg, Oberehnheim, Rosheim, and Mülhausen. Landau entered the league in 1511, but in 1523 Mülhausen

Middle Ages.

left it to join the Swiss Confederation. These " free towns" enjoyed autonomy, though not complete independence.

Till the seventeenth century Alsace was part of Germany; in the Middle Ages it was one of the cradles of German thought, civilisation, art, and architecture. In the thirteenth and fourteenth centuries the pious mystical fellowship, the "Gottesfreunde" (the "Friends of God"), with Johannes Eckhart and Johann Tauler at their head, prepared the way for the Reformation. In the earlier part of the fifteenth century, Gutenberg set up his printing-press at Strassburg; and Martin Schongauer, the leading engraver and painter of the early German School, established a school of engraving at Colmar, which produced the "little masters" of the following generation and a group of Nuremberg artists. Nearly the whole of Alsace accepted the reformed doctrines, Martin Bucer being their foremost champion in Strassburg about 1523. In 1530 the latter city joined the religious and political league known as "das-christliche Bürgerrecht," which Mülhausen had entered the year before; and through the succeeding period of Catholic persecutions and religious dissensions Strassburg was piloted by Jacob Sturm von Sturmeck, who obtained from the Emperor favourable terms for his native city at the termination of the Schmalkaldic War.

Part of Germany till seventeenth century.

In the Thirty Years War, France intervened at the instance of several German princes. After the defeat of Duke Bernhard of Saxe-Weimar at Nördlingen (1634), Richelieu demanded, as the price of his assistance, the Alsatian fortresses held by the former, and in May 1635 declared war against Spain. In 1638 Bernhard crossed the Rhine near Basle at the head of the Swedish army

Thirty Years War.

HISTORICAL OUTLINE 57

(which he commanded after the death of Gustavus Adolphus), and took possession of Alsace. But in the following year he died, and his army was taken over by France; and subsequently the French, under Condé, broke the Spanish power in the Netherlands, and under the same leader and Turenne they rolled back the leaguers through the Palatinate and Bavaria, and gained a victory at Nördlingen (1645).

In the ensuing peace negotiations France claimed the cession of Alsace in consideration of her intervention, which had saved Germany from the despotism of the Austrian house. This claim gave rise to disputes, which are reflected in the obscure text of the Treaty of Münster (Westphalia). The relevant provisions are contained in Articles 75, 76, and 89. Article 75 indicates the extent of the territory ceded to France by the Emperor, viz. the two landgraviates of Upper and Lower Alsace, Sundgau, and the prefecture of the ten free imperial towns, except Strassburg. Article 76 stipulates that the said territories shall be incorporated into France in perpetuity, and that neither any Emperor nor any Austrian prince shall ever lay claim to them. In view of this provision, which expressly confers on France the rights of sovereignty over the ceded territories, Article 89 appears to be ambiguous and contradictory. The latter lays down that the King of France is to maintain Alsace "in that liberty and possession of immediacy towards the Roman Empire which it has hitherto enjoyed" ("in ea libertate et possessione immedietatis erga Imperium Romanum qua hactenus gavisæ sunt"); and he is not to exercise royal power, but only the rights which the Emperor possessed. Thus what is conferred by Article 76 is apparently denied by Article 89; but this restriction is again

Treaty of Westphalia (1648).

modified by the subsequent clause, which says that the present declaration is not to be understood as detracting from the sovereign power recognised above ("ita tamen ut præsenti hac declaratione nihil detractum intelligatur de eo omni supremi dominii jure quod supra concessum est"). The explanation of these seeming contradictions is that the expression "ea libertate et possessione immedietatis erga Imperium Romanum" implies that the lay and ecclesiastical nobles, together with the Alsatian towns concerned, enjoyed such rights and privileges as placed them in a position of relative independence with regard to the Emperor. Thus the real purport of these difficult clauses seems to be that Alsace is ceded to the King of France, who becomes its sovereign and agrees to protect the said local rights and privileges.[1]

As to Strassburg, which was an imperial free city and an autonomous republic bound by very feeble ties to the Empire, it is not expressly mentioned as being ceded to France; but Article 89 includes it among the other imperial free cities in the provision for maintaining the liberty and "possession of immediacy towards the Emperor." However this may be, Louis XIV did not take possession of Strassburg till 1681 (when it capitulated to the French troops); though it was thought the treaty transferred it to him equally with the other towns. Two years before this, the Treaty of Nimeguen, terminating the war between the Emperor and Louis XIV, who tried to seize Holland, confirmed the annexation of Alsace to France, without making any stipulation as to the protection of local rights and liberties. By the Treaty of Ratisbon (Regensburg), 1684, Strassburg was secured to France. Shortly

Position of Strassburg.

[1] *Cf.* Eckel, *op. cit.*

afterwards hostilities were renewed, and continued till 1697, when the Peace of Ryswick was concluded, whereby the annexation of Strassburg to France was definitively confirmed. (It is of interest to recall that Louis XIV thereupon received a congratulatory communication from Frederick William, the Elector of Brandenburg, who was the direct ancestor of William II.) In 1781, when the centenary of the cession of Strassburg to France was celebrated, the mayor spoke of the peace and happiness of the town under French rule, and of its attachment and gratitude to its sovereign: " Tous les citoyens de la ville, jouissant depuis cent ans sous la domination de la France d'une tranquillité et d'une félicité inconnues à leurs aïeux, ont marqué le désir unanime de témoigner publiquement leur reconnaissance et leur attachement." [1] The French Government respected the local traditions, liberties, and customs; under its mild régime, wise administration, and moderate taxation the city prospered; the Protestant religion was tolerated, but the cathedral was restored to the Catholic worship. This progress, economic and intellectual, during the eighteenth century was not confined to Strassburg; Alsace, and indeed the whole of France, shared in it. The province was at last delivered from the invasions, ravages, devastations, and bloodshed to which it had for centuries been subjected.

The Revolution of 1789 was hailed with enthusiasm in Alsace. The acclaimed principles of liberty, and then the victories of the Empire, aroused in the province a strong French sentiment, despite Germanic culture, language, and traditions. Alsatian generals distinguished themselves, and Alsatian soldiers gave their lives in the service of France.

The French Revolution.

[1] J. Heimweh, *La Question d'Alsace*, p. 97.

It was in Strassburg that the *Marseillaise* was composed and first sung (1792). The abolition of feudalism by the National Assembly dissociated Alsace fundamentally and entirely—that is, socially and economically, as well as politically—from the still feudal Germany.

Merlin of Douai, presenting the report of the Comité Féodal, October 28, 1790, observed : " The Alsatian people has united itself to the French people because it willed to do so ; it is then its will alone, and not the Treaty of Münster, that has legitimatised this union." During the revolutionary disorders Alsace might well have found an opportunity to liberate itself from France, had it chosen to do so ; instead of that it voluntarily sealed the union with its blood.

{Union with France.}

In 1815 Austria was anxious to acquire possession again of Alsace ; but, notwithstanding the hatred and fear long inspired by France, and the obvious expediency of impeding her territorial aggrandisement, the Allies opposed such a project, as it was felt that the provinces in question had become an integral part of France and were essentially French. It is a significant fact that, though numerous nationalist movements arose in Europe during the course of the nineteenth century, none appeared in Alsace-Lorraine until after its annexation by Germany.

{Aim of Austria in 1815.}

CHAPTER IV

ANNEXATION OF ALSACE-LORRAINE IN 1871

(a) *Military events leading to peace negotiations :* Outbreak of the war of 1870—Neutrality of the Powers—German successes—Annexation proclaimed—Capitulation of Metz—Siege of Paris—National Assembly at Bordeaux; peace signed. (b) *Negotiations and Arrangements as to Alsace-Lorraine :* Protests against announced annexation—Bismarck's fear of European intervention—He secures Russian support—His doubt as to territorial demands; military view—Demands made at Versailles —German resolve as to annexation—Bismarck's concession—The Preliminaries of Versailles—Negotiations at Brussels—Difficulties of the French plenipotentiaries—Negotiations transferred to Frankfort—The French plenipotentiaries—Treaty of Frankfort—Belfort—Germans affect to be disappointed—The boundary commission—Rights of inhabitants of ceded territory—Regulation of various other matters.

(a) MILITARY EVENTS LEADING TO PEACE NEGOTIATIONS

ON the evening of July 14, 1870, when the "Ems telegram" became known in Paris, war was decided on by the Emperor Napoleon III in Council. The next morning it was announced in the Senate that the Imperial forces were ordered to mobilise, and that the Government would "take measures to safeguard the interests and the honour of France." Similar orders were issued on the evening of the same day by the King of Prussia to the armies of the North German Confederation, and mobilisation preparations were begun in South Germany immediately afterwards (July 16). The efforts of Great Britain to preserve peace, by proposing recourse to mediation conformably to Protocol XXIII of the negotiations relative to the Treaty of Paris, 1856,

Outbreak of war in 1870.

were not successful; both sides declined to entertain the proposal.[1]

The French formal declaration of war was received in Berlin on July 19; and a few days later Bismarck published (in *The Times*, July 25) the draft of a Franco-Prussian treaty, proposed by Benedetti in 1866, that Prussia should aid France to acquire Belgium in return for French support in regard to certain annexations in northern Germany. The protest of the French diplomatist that the projected treaty had been drawn up at the dictation of Bismarck failed to allay the excitement in England, where the unfortunate document was regarded as evidence of a recrudescence of French territorial ambitions. Accordingly, Lord Granville without delay concluded treaties with the belligerents (signed at London, August 9 and August 11), whereby each undertook to oppose jointly with England any violation of Belgian territory on the part of the other.[2]

Napoleon had hoped to obtain the support of Austria, Italy, and Denmark, as Powers obviously opposed to the Prussian policy of aggrandisement; but they, together with Russia, declared their neutrality. Thus France, besides being militarily unprepared—every department of her army being in a state of hopeless confusion—found herself diplomatically isolated; and in such unpropitious circumstances the campaign opened.

Neutrality of the Powers.

The operation at Saarbrücken, August 2, in favour of France, was followed by German victories at Spicheren and Weissenburg (August 4), and the decisive defeat of Marshal Macmahon's army at Wörth (August 6). After various political and

German successes.

[1] *Cf.* Earl Granville to Lord Lyons, etc., July 15, 1870: *Parliamentary Papers*, vol. lxx. (1870), p. 57: *British and Foreign State Papers* (1869–70), vol. lx. p. 833.
[2] *British and Foreign State Papers*, vol. lx. pp. 10, 13.

ANNEXATION IN 1871

military changes were hastily effected in France, the German armies followed up their successes by crossing the Vosges (August 11). On August 16-17 ensued the sanguinary engagements of Vionville, Mars-la-Tour, and Gravelotte, and on the 19th the investment of Bazaine's army in Metz was begun. On September 1 the battle of Sedan ended in the surrender of Napoleon.

Thus in the short space of one month one of the French armies was destroyed, another was locked up in Metz, and the Germans were free to march upon Paris. It was now that the victorious invaders had determined that the cession of the fortresses of Strassburg and Metz with their surrounding territories—*i.e.* Alsace and Lorraine—should be an indispensable condition of peace. After Sedan followed the fall of the Empire, the establishment of the Republic, and the constitution of a Government of National Defence. A second seat of government was set up at Tours; and, the separatist movements developing in France, Gambetta assumed the dictatorship (October 7), and for a time put an end to dissension.

In the meantime the annexation of Alsace and of Eastern Lorraine was proclaimed after the surrender (September 28) of Strassburg, the key of Alsace. A few days before (September 19), during the investment of Paris, Jules Favre had an interview with Bismarck at Ferrières; and, in reply to the latter's territorial demands, the representative of the Provisional Government declared that France would not cede an inch of her territory or a stone of her fortresses.

<small>Annexation proclaimed.</small>

On September 13 Thiers, notwithstanding his advanced age, had started on a mission to the Courts of London, St. Petersburg, Vienna, and Florence in the hope of securing their mediation, even if only for the conclusion of an armistice so that the elections might be held. But the time was ill-chosen, and he received little encouragement.

After French successes in the Loire Valley, the Germans occupied Orleans on October 11, which they afterwards lost. On October 27 Bazaine surrendered at Metz; and, after various reverses of the French in the campaign of the Loire, Orleans was recaptured by the Germans on December 4, and a panic throughout Touraine was thereby created. The seat of administration of the Provisional Government was now removed to Bordeaux.

Capitulation of Metz.

In the meantime the capital was undergoing the terrible trials of the siege; and, in these circumstances, added to the fact that Bourbaki's army was compelled to begin its disastrous retreat, Favre had an interview with Bismarck at Versailles, January 23, 1871, for the purpose of arranging the terms of a general armistice and of the capitulation of Paris.

Siege of Paris.

On January 28 a three weeks' armistice was signed; in the interval a National Assembly was to be elected and summoned for the purpose of deciding on the continuance or definitive cessation of hostilities. Gambetta was for continuing the war, and declined to accept the authority of the Paris Government to act on behalf of the country; but his policy gained few adherents, and he therefore resigned. On February 12 the National Assembly was opened at Bordeaux; the Provisional Government declared its functions at an end; Thiers was appointed head of the executive (February 17), and, together with Favre and Picard, was commissioned to conclude peace.

National Assembly at Bordeaux.

ANNEXATION IN 1871

The Preliminaries of Versailles were signed on February 26, ratified by the National Assembly on March 3, and the definitive Treaty of Frankfort was concluded on May 10, and the ratifications were exchanged at Frankfort on May 20. *(Peace signed.)*

(b) NEGOTIATIONS AND ARRANGEMENTS AS TO ALSACE-LORRAINE

It has been pointed out that in the middle of September M. Thiers sought, without success, the interposition of the British, Russian, Austrian, and Italian Governments, and that the annexation of Alsace and Eastern Lorraine was proclaimed after the capitulation of Strassburg, which took place on September 28.

Subsequently, the French resistance to the investment of the capital having unexpectedly revived with renewed vigour and determination, protests began to be made in various quarters against the German projected annexation, involving, as it was thought, a repudiation of previous treaties; and a joint intervention of the Powers was suggested to prevent the dismemberment of France. Bismarck avowed his fear of such intervention. He was anxious to end the war speedily—and particularly so, owing to the continued large German losses—by bringing up heavy artillery against Paris, instead of attempting to reduce the city by famine. "In the Council of War," he observed,[1] "Roon was the only supporter of my opinion that we should lose no time about ending the war if we wanted to make sure of stopping interference from the neutrals and their congress. . . . The delay in the decision caused me more serious dis- *(Protests against announced annexation. Bismarck's fear of European intervention.)*

[1] *Bismarck: the Man and the Statesman*, English translation (London, 1898), pp. 107, 108, 111.

quietude in the political sphere from my anxiety respecting the intervention of neutrals. . . . An intervention could only tend to deprive us Germans of the prize of victory by means of a congress. This danger, which troubled me day and night, made me feel the necessity of hastening the conclusion of peace, in order to be able to establish it without the intervention of neutrals."

However this may be, amongst European statesmen Count von Beust appears to have been the only one who made any attempt to bring about a collective intervention of the neutral Powers. On September 28, following on the appeal of M. Thiers, he sent a despatch to that effect to the Austrian ambassador in London [1]; and again on October 12 he communicated with Count Chotek, the Austrian ambassador in St. Petersburg, suggesting a European intervention in order "to moderate the demands of the conqueror and soften the bitterness of the sentiments which must crush the vanquished." [2]

But Bismarck's diplomatic skill in definitely securing the good-will of Russia made such an eventuality impossible. Russia had for some time been endeavouring to extricate herself from the difficult position imposed on her by the Treaty of Paris, 1856, and the Straits Convention of the same date.[3] Already in 1866, during the Austro-Prussian War, King William of Prussia had been assured of the friendship of the Emperor Alexander, and in return had manifested his sympathy with the determination of Russia to bring about an abrogation of the ob-

Bismarck secures Russian support.

---

[1] Count von Beust, *Aus drei Viertel-Jahrhunderten* (Stuttgart, 1887), Pt. II., pp. 361, 395.

[2] *Ibid.*, p. 397.

[3] See C. Phillipson and N. Buxton, *The Question of the Bosphorus and Dardanelles* (London, 1917), pp. 81 seq.

ANNEXATION IN 1871 67

noxious clauses of the above-mentioned treaties.[1] Now, in 1870, Bismarck sent a despatch (dated Ferrières, September 20) to Prince Reuss, the Prussian minister in St. Petersburg, declaring that King William deemed the Tsar's intended repudiation of the treaties to be justifiable, and that Prussia, in her hour of victory, would do her utmost to get not only France, but also the other signatory parties, to recognise the denunciation. Soon afterwards (October 9) Bismarck made it everywhere known that a close *entente* existed between Prussia and Russia; and then Prince Gortchakoff issued his famous circular despatch, dated October 19–31, 1870, announcing his Government's withdrawal from the restrictive articles of the Conventions of 1856.[2]

Having ensured a clear field for negotiation, Bismarck, it appears, began to feel some doubt as to the expediency of insisting on such large territorial demands as had been announced to France. Even after the conclusion of the armistice (January 28), when France was virtually at the feet of Prussia, he is reported to have been in conflict with Moltke and the military party who, in their inordinate exactions, were disposed to show little consideration and to brook no compromise. The German Emperor was obliged to intervene on at least one occasion to adjust these differences between the diplomatists on the one side and the military leaders on the other. For a considerable length of time the Chancellor adhered to the view that Germany ought not to insist on the cession of Metz and the adjacent territory, and he did not regard the military party's arguments for annexing this locality as decisive. He thought it would suffice to dismantle the fortress, and believed

<small>His doubt as to territorial demands.</small>

[1] Phillipson and Buxton, *op. cit.*, p. 103   [2] *Ibid.*, pp. 105 *seq.*

that security could be assured by constructing another strong place behind it.

"If they were to give us another milliard," he is reported to have said,[1] " we might perhaps leave Metz, and build a fortress a few miles farther back in the neighbourhood of Falkenberg, or towards Saarbrücken. . . . I do not want so many Frenchmen in our house. It is the same with Belfort, which is entirely French. But the soldiers will not hear of giving up Metz spoken of, *and perhaps they are right.*" The words italicised show, however, that Bismarck could be prevailed upon to abandon his own views in favour of others, if he was convinced that the latter would more effectively serve the interests of his country—regardless of whatever humiliation or burden might thereby be inflicted on any other country.

Influence of military circles.

The demands laid before M. Thiers by Bismarck at Versailles, February 21, 1871, included the cession of Alsace and Metz, together with the part of Lorraine constituting the Department of the Moselle, the payment of a war indemnity of 6,000,000,000 francs (which he did not think excessive),[2] and the occupation of French territory till payment was completed. He mentioned also Nancy, "which the Headquarters Staff wished to keep"; and referred to Savoy and Nice, which France might retrocede to Italy. In the long discussion that followed Thiers with difficulty suppressed his emotion; he declared that the demands were monstrous, that the exorbitant indemnity must have resulted from the dreams of military men and not from the sober

Demands made at Versailles.

---

[1] M Busch, *Bismarck: some Secret Pages of his History*, Eng. trans. 3 vols. (London, 1898), vol. i. pp. 556-7; *cf.* Ottokar Lorenz, *Kaiser Wilhelm und die Begründung des Reichs*, 1866-71 (Jena, 1902), pp. 520 seq.

[2] *Cf.* G. May, *Le Traité de Francfort* (Paris, 1909), pp. 163 seq.

ANNEXATION IN 1871 69

calculations of financiers; and he suggested to Bismarck that, if he seriously insisted on such terms, he had better take upon himself the government of France, and that the existing administration would retire.

On the following day Thiers, having come again to Versailles, asked to see the German Emperor, in the hope of getting more favourable terms from him. But the latter spoke only of the entrance of the German troops into Paris; and on other questions Bismarck had already taken precautions, for he remarked to the French representative : " The Emperor does not wish to speak of business except in the presence of his ministers." M. Thiers saw also the Crown Prince, on whom he seems to have had some effect : " The old man," says M. Hanotaux, " broken with fatigue and emotion, speaking with eloquence of the war which he had wished to avert, of the fault of the Imperial Government, of the dangers which an ill-advised peace would cause to Europe, touched the sensitive soul of the Crown Prince." [1] He declared that the abandonment of Metz would be intolerable to France, and that, if such extravagant demands were persisted in, the resumption of hostilities would become inevitable. He emphasised that the sum of the indemnity mentioned the previous day should be considerably reduced, and he opposed the entrance of German troops into the capital. The Crown Prince appeared to his entourage to be willing to renounce Metz ; but his confidential friend, General von Blumenthal, said that " it turned the heart in one's body to renounce Metz and leave Paris, looking like a fool." [2]

_{German Emperor's resolve as to annexation.}

---

[1] G. Hanotaux, *Contemporary France*, English translation, 4 vols. (London, 1903), vol. 1. p. 122.
[2] *Ibid.*

The next day (February 23), the Emperor, who did not take the same view as his son, having conferred with the Grand Duke of Baden, exclaimed excitedly that he declined to discuss the question of Metz. In the interview of Thiers and Favre with Bismarck at Versailles the Chancellor was reminded that in the preceding November he had promised that France would not be dispossessed of Metz. "What was possible in November," replied Bismarck, "is no longer possible to-day, after three months' bloodshed"; and he added that if France was not ready to give up Metz an immediate rupture of the negotiations was necessary.

<small>Bismarck's refusal to give way.</small>

On February 24 another conference was held, when Thiers expressed the firm resolve of France not to cede both Metz and Belfort. After some deliberation and consultation with Moltke and the Emperor, Bismarck announced that he would give way in regard to Belfort, and that the amount of the indemnity would be reduced by a milliard, thus leaving a sum of 5,000,000,000 francs.[1] (It may be pointed out that the reduction in what the French called the "ransom" was effected at the instance of the British Government[2]; even then, the remaining sum was the largest pecuniary indemnity ever exacted in the history of war.)

<small>Bismarck's concession.</small>

On February 26 the Preliminaries of Versailles were signed.[3] Then M. Thiers and M. Favre left Versailles for Páris. "Seated in the carriage," says

---

[1] Jules Favre, *Le Gouvernement de la Défense Nationale*, 3 vols. (Paris, 1871–5), vol. iii. p. 100.

[2] C. Gavard, *Un Diplomate à Londres : Lettres et Notes, 1871–7* (Paris, 1895), pp. 3, 4; C. Phillipson, *Termination of War and Treaties of Peace* (London, 1916), pp. 274, 275.

[3] For the complete text of the Preliminaries see Phillipson, *Termination of War and Treaties of Peace*, Appendix (J), pp. 380–83.

ANNEXATION IN 1871

M. Jules Favre, " we did not find a word to exchange during the whole journey ; my heart was so heavy that it suffocated me. Motionless, and as it were struck down, M. Thiers gave way to his emotion. From Versailles to Paris his eyes did not cease to fill with tears. He wiped them away without saying a word, but it was easy to see, from the expression of his troubled features, that he was a prey to one of the most ineffable sorrows that it is given to man to feel."[1] *(Preliminaries of Versailles.)*

The Preliminaries of Versailles disposed of Alsace-Lorraine in the following terms:

" Article I.—France renounces in favour of the German Empire all her rights and titles over the territories situated on the east of the frontier hereafter described. *(Stipulation as to Alsace-Lorraine.)*

" The line of demarcation begins at the north-west frontier of the canton of Cattenom, towards the Grand Duchy of Luxemburg, follows on the south the western frontiers of the cantons of Cattenom and Thionville, passes by the canton of Briey, along the western frontiers of the communes of Montjois-la-Montagne and Roncourt, as well as the eastern frontiers of the communes of Marie-aux-Chênes, St. Ail, Habonville, reaches the frontier of the canton of Gooze, which it crosses along the communal frontiers of Vionville, Bouxières, and Onville, follows the south-west frontier, south of the district of Metz, the western frontier of the district of Château-Salins, as far as the commune of Pettoncourt, taking in the western and southern frontiers thereof to follow the crest of the mountains between Seille and Moncel, as far as the frontier of the district of Sarreburg, to the south of Garde. The demarcation afterwards coincides with the

[1] Favre, *op. cit.*, vol. iii. p. 118.

frontier of that district as far as the commune of Tanconville, reaching the frontier to the north thereof, from whence it follows the crest of the mountains between the sources of the White Sarre and Vezouze, as far as the frontier of that canton of Schirmeck, skirts the western frontier of that canton, includes the communes of Saales, Bourg-Bruche, Colroy-la-Roche, Plaine, Ranrupt, Saulxures, and St. Blaise-la-Roche of the canton of Saales, and coincides with the western frontier of the departments of the lower Rhine and the upper Rhine, as far as the cantons of Belfort, the southern frontier of which it leaves not far from Vourvenans, to cross the canton of Delle at the southern limits of the communes of Bourogne and Froide Fontaine, and to reach the Swiss frontier skirting the eastern frontiers of the communes of Jonchery and Delle.

"The German Empire shall possess these territories in perpetuity in all sovereignty and property. An international commission, composed of an equal number of representatives of the two High Contracting Parties, shall be appointed immediately after the exchange of the ratifications of the present treaty to trace on the spot the new frontier, in conformity with the preceding stipulations.

"This commission shall preside over the division of the lands and funds, which have hitherto belonged to districts or communes divided by the new frontiers; in case of disagreement in the tracing and the measures of execution, the members of the commission shall refer to their respective Governments.

"The frontier, such as it has just been described, is marked in green on two identical copies of the map of the territory forming the Government of Alsace, published at Berlin in September 1870 by the geographical and statistical division of the Staff, and a

ANNEXATION IN 1871 73

copy of which shall be annexed to both copies of the present treaty.

"Nevertheless, the alteration of the above tracing has been agreed to by the two Contracting Parties. In the former department of the Moselle, the villages of Marie-aux-Chênes near St. Privat-la-Montagne, and Vionville to the west of Rezonville, shall be ceded to Germany. In exchange therefor France shall retain the town and fortifications of Belfort, with a radius which shall be hereafter determined upon."[1]

It was stipulated in Article VII of the Preliminaries of Versailles that the opening of negotiations for the definitive treaty of peace should take place at Brussels immediately after the ratification of the former. This formality was complied with on March 2, 1871 ; but, owing to the faulty diplomacy of the French Government—obviously due, however, to the internal disorders and to the rapid succession of military disasters—the French plenipotentiaries, Baron Baude, the minister in Belgium, and M. de Goulard, a member of the National Assembly (who were to be assisted by two commissioners), did not reach Brussels before March 19 and 24 respectively. The German delegates were Herr von Balan, the minister in Belgium, and Count von Arnim, the minister at the Papal Court, to whom were added representatives from the kingdoms of Bavaria and Würtemberg and the Grand Duchy of Baden.

Negotiations at Brussels.

The first meeting of the peace plenipotentiaries took place on March 28, when various preliminary and formal matters, such as the exchange and verification of the delegates' full powers, were transacted. The next meeting revealed the exceptional difficulties that would be met with

Difficulties of the French plenipotentiaries.

[1] Hertslet, *Map of Europe by Treaty*, vol. iii. (1875), pp. 1913, 1914.

in the course of the negotiation, owing to the attitude, methods, and tactics adopted by the German representatives. The writer may be permitted to quote on this point what he has said in a recent publication[1]: " The German plenipotentiaries were determined to exact the last ounce that could be squeezed out of the Preliminaries; indeed, they were not always very scrupulous as to whether their various exactions were juridically and equitably compatible with those Preliminaries. They were opposed to all suggestions that savoured of compromise, and refused to make any concessions even in details. They disregarded the customary procedure, whereby differences of view and partial agreements are recorded in the *procès-verbaux* or the protocols; they had recourse to the latter only when they succeeded in enforcing agreement or acquiescence in regard to the definite and final drafting of an article. They seem to have adopted, too, the practice of producing a number of propositions on diverse subjects at the same time, regardless of order, system, or intelligible classification; such a course could not but increase the difficulties with which the French delegates had to contend. Throughout the discussions the French negotiators were no match for their opponents. Several reasons may be given for this inequality. In the first place, the latter had the moral and physical support of their military victories; their troops were still on French territory, and might, at the word of command, renew their havoc against a vanquished and well-nigh helpless nation. Their verbal arguments had therefore the sanction of force behind them. They were in a position to dictate terms, and not in the humour to submit to suggested amendments thereto. They more

[1] C. Phillipson, *Termination of War and Treaties of Peace*, pp. 137, 138.

ANNEXATION IN 1871 75

than once threatened to break off negotiations. . . . Secondly, the French delegates were intrinsically inferior; they had had little diplomatic experience, and were manifestly deficient in those qualities that are indispensable in the work of negotiation—dexterity, penetration, decision.[1] Thirdly, they found themselves at a great disadvantage, in that they had received no instructions from their Government, preoccupied as it was with the internal disorders of France."[2] It appears, indeed, that they had received only one precise instruction, viz. to demand a plebiscite for the inhabitants of Alsace-Lorraine.[3]

In these untoward circumstances the discussions at Brussels continued throughout April, without arriving at definite conclusions. The German Government became more and more impatient and embittered: for it believed that the French representatives had deliberately resorted to dilatory tactics in order to bring about a modification of the Preliminaries of Versailles—indeed, Bismarck made an open charge to that effect in the Reichstag (April 24). On May 4 the negotiations at Brussels were broken off; and Bismarck and Favre agreed to meet personally at Frankfort-on-the-Main on May 6. *Negotiations transferred to Frankfort.*

The French Minister for Foreign Affairs was accompanied by M. de Goulard and M. Pouyer-Quertier, the Minister of Finance; the German Chancellor was accompanied by Count von Arnim. The difficulties of the French representatives by no means diminished in the discussions with the " man of blood and iron." On the one hand, M. Thiers *The French plenipotentiaries.*

[1] Cf. May, *op. cit*, p. 44.
[2] J. Valfrey, *Histoire du traité de Francfort et de la libération du territoire français* (Paris, 1874), Pt. I. pp. 17, 18.
[3] *Ibid.*, p. 38.

was anxious to sign the definitive peace as soon as possible, and to avoid protracted negotiations and persistent efforts to combat the German demands—indeed, hedged in on all sides and having just emerged from his conflicts with the Commune, it appeared that he was disposed to make peace at any price, if only it could be effected speedily. On the other hand, M. Favre, the first French plenipotentiary, was lacking in calmness and firmness; his terror-stricken and lachrymose disposition was not of the kind to impress Bismarck favourably and to secure concessions from him. M. Pouyer-Quertier, however, was not intimidated by the bluntness and abruptness—with the ever-underlying menace—of the Chancellor; whenever the first plenipotentiary gave him an opportunity, he examined and criticised the German claims, and—thanks to his ready Norman wit, urbanity, good sense, and undisturbed composure—he gained more than one point. Thus he prevailed on Bismarck to abandon in the Belfort district the valley of the Marcine, with a French-speaking population, whereby the most direct communication, *via* Delle, between France and Switzerland was preserved. On the same day he succeeded in obtaining the relinquishment of the commune of Villerupt (containing valuable iron-mines), which had previously been included in the territories to be ceded to Germany, in return for the latter's agreement to extend the radius of the Belfort frontier. Bismarck had just declared he would make no further territorial concessions, whereupon M. Pouyer-Quertier observed: "If you were the conquered party, I give you my word that I would not have compelled you to become a Frenchman, and here you make me a German."

"How is that?" exclaimed the Chancellor. "And

ANNEXATION IN 1871

who is talking of taking your Normandy ? I do not understand in the least."

" The matter is, however, very simple, Prince. I am one of the principal shareholders in the forges of Villerupt, and you see clearly that, in this quarter, you make me a German."

" Well, well," said Bismarck, " don't cry about it. I leave you Villerupt. But do not ask me for anything more, or I shall take it back again." [1]

The definitive treaty was signed at Frankfort on May 10. The new frontier and the relinquishment of Belfort by Germany in return for the cession of Lorraine territory by France were provided for in Article I :

Provisions of Treaty of Frankfort.

" The distance between the town of Belfort and the line of frontier such as it had been proposed during the negotiations of Versailles, and such as it is marked on the map annexed to the ratifications of the Preliminaries of the 26th February, is considered as describing the radius which, by virtue of the clause relating thereto in Article I of the Preliminaries, is to remain to France with the town and fortifications of Belfort.

" The German Government is disposed to extend that radius so as to include the cantons of Belfort, Delle, and Giromagny, as well as the western part of the canton of Fontaine, to the west of a line to be traced from the spot where the canal from the Rhône to the Rhine leaves the canton of Delle to the south of Montreux-Château, to the northern limits of the canton between Bourg and Félon, where that line would join the eastern limit of the canton of Giromagny.

[1] A. Laussedat, *La Délimitation de la frontière franco-allemande* (Paris, 1901), p. 51.

"The German Government will nevertheless not cede the above territories unless the French Republic agrees, on its part, to a rectification of frontier along the western limits of the cantons of Cattenom and Thionville, which will give to Germany the territory to the east of a line starting from the frontier of Luxemburg between Hussigny and Redingen, leaving to France the villages of Thil and Villerupt, extending between Erronville and Aumetz, between Beuvillers and Boulange, between Trieux and Lomeringen, and joining the ancient line of frontier between Avril and Moyeuvre.

"The international commission mentioned in Article I of the Preliminaries shall proceed to the spot immediately after the ratification of the present treaty to execute the works entrusted to them, and to trace the new frontier, in accordance with the preceding dispositions."

With regard to the radius round Belfort, the above article gave France the option either of maintaining the radius previously fixed at seven kilometres, or of receiving such an extension as would secure for her nearly the whole administrative district of Belfort ; but if she chose the latter alternative she was to abandon to Germany a portion of territory ten kilometres long on the Luxemburg frontier. In the former case, the enlarged zone near Belfort contained some 6,000 hectares (*i.e.* about 23 square miles), with a population of 27,000 ; in the latter case the territory to be given up in exchange comprised an area of 10,000 hectares (*i.e.* about 38 square miles), and a population of only 7,000. This arrangement appeared on the whole to be to the advantage of France ; but it involved, none the less, the abandonment to Germany of 7,000 inhabitants (who would

ANNEXATION IN 1871

have remained with France had the terms of the Preliminaries been followed), as well as an interference with the communication with Luxemburg, and the sacrifice of a very valuable mining district in the vicinity of Longwy. In the debates in the French Parliamentary Commission and in the Assembly on this proposed exchange of territory, conflicting opinions were expressed as to the expediency and advantage of the exchange. M. Thiers, however, emphasised the strategic value of Belfort, and declared that France would remain rich enough in iron, without the resources of the region near Longwy. Thiers's view prevailed, and the exchange was sanctioned.

When the territorial dispositions were published in Germany various sections of the people, including the military classes, many journalists, and deputies of the Reichstag thought that the acquisitions were inadequate, and that Bismarck had been much too moderate in his demands. In military circles Belfort above all was regretted. Many declared that the German negotiators ought to have insisted also on the cession of Burgundy and Franche Comté, and even suggested the annexation of Dunkirk; it was thought in many quarters that France had been dealt with far too leniently and considerately. <small>Germans affect to be disappointed.</small>

However this may be, when the extent and the character of the acquired territory became known more precisely in Germany, there was not a little surprise at the magnitude of the conquest, and the economic benefits secured thereby. It not infrequently happens that a party seeking to enter into an unconscionable transaction, or making exorbitant demands on another, loudly proclaims—with his tongue in his cheek—that he is <small>But really surprised at conquest.</small>

really asking too little, and that he is not at all doing himself justice in the arrangement suggested. Colonel Laussedat, who was on the delimitation commission for tracing the new frontier, observes in his work on the subject [1] that, during the negotiations, he could not but conclude that the conquerors were astonished at their success, and were dazzled by their annexation, that they scarcely believed their own eyes, and could not understand how the French could so promptly give up such a rich territory inhabited by a French population.

The work of the boundary commission took six years: it began in May 1871, and ended on April 26, 1877; and the ratifications thereof were exchanged at Metz, May 31, 1877. In the course of the topographical labours, the German commissioners disputed the soil foot by foot [2]; where the stipulations of the treaties, which were to serve as a guide, were indefinite or ambiguous they invariably claimed the benefit of the doubt, and pushed their claims to the uttermost limit possible. To the populations immediately concerned, the proceedings were throughout a source of bitter and cruel trials; the staking out of the new boundary was observed with grief and misgiving, and not always with acquiescence; for in many cases, no sooner were the poles and pegs fixed and the commissioners out of sight, than they were all pulled up; later, even

The boundary commission.

---

[1] *La Délimitation de la frontière franco-allemande*, p. 14 : " Pendant la durée des négociations auxquelles j'ai pris part au sujet du tracé définitif de cette frontière qui mutilait la France et qui, tôt ou tard, c'est mon voeu le plus cher, créera à la Prusse des ennuis inextricables et peut-être mortels, j'ai acquis la certitude que nos vainqueurs étaient stupéfaits de leurs succès, éblouis de leur conquête. Ils n'en croyaient par leurs yeux et ne comprenaient pas que nous leur eussions abandonné sitôt une si riche proie, un si merveilleux pays, des populations si françaises ! "
[2] *Ibid.*, pp. 85 *seq.*

ANNEXATION IN 1871

many boundary-stones were removed. Colonel Laussedat refers to the frequent scenes, here of despair, there of ardent patriotism, that were witnessed in the course of this sinister severance of people from their mother-country. He relates the following incident :

" It was on the boundary of the two communes of Beuvillers and Boulange. We had all arrived at the first boundary-mark, except the Mayor of Boulange. The German Commissioner, M. Hauchecorne, who had summoned him, was getting impatient, and, seeing him coming in the distance at a walking-pace, and swinging himself about :

" ' Come, Mr. Mayor, hurry up, you are late, and we are waiting for you,' he shouted to him.

" But the Mayor of Boulange, a miller by trade, if I recollect rightly, and with a breadth of shoulder I could not help admiring, seemed to slacken his pace still more ; this made the German Commissioner furious, and caused him to fall into the mistake of assuming an authoritative tone, which, by the way, was common enough with him.

" The miller did not put himself out at all, in appearance at least, but slackened his pace still more instead of hastening it ; and when he came quite close to M. Hauchecorne—

" ' Ah, there now ! ' said he calmly, and looking him full in the face, ' do you think, then, that I am in such a hurry to become a Prussian ? ' "

Besides the delimitation of the new frontier, there were various other questions that presented themselves for solution, as a result of the cession of Alsace-Lorraine. The Preliminaries of Versailles had already provided for the commercial and civil rights of the inhabitants of the annexed territory, and for their unimpeded emigration : *Rights of inhabitants of ceded territory.*

6

" Article V.—The interests of the inhabitants of the territories ceded by France, in everything relating to their commerce and their civil rights, shall be regulated in as favourable a manner as possible when the conditions of the definitive peace are settled. A certain time will be fixed during which they will enjoy particular advantages for the disposal of their produce. The German Government will put no obstacle in the way of free emigration by the inhabitants from the ceded territories, and shall take no steps against them affecting their persons or their property."

The Treaty of Frankfort afterwards stipulated as follows, with regard to the industrial produce of Alsace-Lorraine :

" Article IX.—The exceptional treatment at present granted to the produce of the industry of the ceded territories for imports into France shall be continued for six months, from the 1st March, under the conditions made with the commissioners of Alsace."

The questions of option, amnesty, archives, registers, etc., pecuniary deposits, ecclesiastical authority, navigation on rivers and canals, and canalisation of the Moselle were thus regulated by the definitive treaty :

" Article II.—French subjects, natives of the ceded territory, actually domiciled in that territory, shall up to the 1st October, 1872, and on their making a previous declaration to that effect to the competent authority, be allowed to change their domicile into France and to remain there, that right in nowise infringing the laws on military service, in which case the title of French citizen shall be maintained.

" They shall be at liberty to preserve their immovables situated in the territory united to Germany.

Option.

ANNEXATION IN 1871

"No inhabitant of the ceded territory shall be prosecuted, annoyed, or sought for, either in his person or in his property, on account of his political or military acts previous to the war. *Amnesty.*

"Article III.—The French Government shall deliver over to the German Government the archives, documents, and registers relating to the civil, military, and judicial administration of the ceded territories. Should any of the documents be found missing, they shall be restored by the French Government on the demand of the German Government. *Public records.*

"Article IV.—The French Government shall make over to the Government of the Empire of Germany within the term of six months dating from the exchange of the ratifications of this treaty [1] : (1) The amount of the sum deposited by the departments, communes, and public establishments of the ceded territories. (2) The amount of the premium of enlistment or discharge belonging to soldiers and sailors, natives of the ceded territory, who shall have chosen the German nationality. (3) The amount of security of responsible agents of the State. (4) The amount of sums deposited for judicial consignments on account of measures taken by the administrative or judicial authorities in the ceded territories." *Pecuniary deposits.*

"Article VI.—The High Contracting Parties being of opinion that the diocesan circumscriptions of the territories ceded to the German Empire must agree with the new frontier determined upon by Article I above, will consider, without delay after the ratification of the present treaty, upon the measures to be taken in common upon the subject. *Ecclesiastical authority.*

"The communities belonging either to the Re-

[1] The ratifications were exchanged at Frankfort on May 20, 1871.

formed Church or to the Augsburg Confession, established on the territories ceded by France, shall cease to be under French ecclesiastical authority.

" The communities of the Church of the Augsburg Confession established in the French territories shall cease to be under the Superior Consistories and of the Directors residing at Strassburg.

" The Jewish communities of the territories situated to the east of the new frontier shall cease to depend on the Central Jewish Consistory residing at Paris.

" Article V.—The two nations shall enjoy equal privileges as regards the navigation on the Moselle, the canal of the Marne to the Rhine, the canal of the Rhône to the Rhine, the canal of the Sarre and the navigable waters communicating with those channels of navigation. The right of floatage shall be maintained.

Navigation on rivers and canals.

" Article XIV.—Each of the two Parties shall continue on his territory the works undertaken for the canalisation of the Moselle. The common interests of the separate parts of the two departments of the Meurthe and the Moselle shall be liquidated."

Canalisation of the Moselle.

Article XVII made provision for the carrying out of such further arrangements as would be necessitated by the due execution of the Preliminaries and the definitive treaty.

To the Treaty of Frankfort were appended a number of supplementary articles concerning the purchase of French railways and other rights connected therewith, and the rectification of the frontier near Belfort. In accordance with the above-mentioned Article XVII, more than a hundred conventions were entered into between France and

Regulation of various matters.

ANNEXATION IN 1871 85

Germany.[1] It is beyond the scope of the present work to go into all these details,[2] so that we must here confine ourselves to mentioning that, by the Additional Convention[3] concluded at Frankfort, December 11, 1871, various important matters affecting the transferred territory were regulated : choice of nationality by natives resident outside Alsace-Lorraine, pensions (civil, religious, and military), execution of judgments, judicial proceedings, exchange of criminals and lunatics, guarantee of mortgage rights, restitution of all titles, documents, etc., belonging to communes detached from their former administration, diocesan circumscriptions crossed by the new frontier, patents, appointment of financial commission, export and import duties, concessions granted by France in the ceded territory, financial regulations relative to canals, railways, renewal of treaties, etc.

[1] These are contained, together with many other documents and records, in the voluminous publication of Villefort, *Recueil des traités, conventions, lois, décrets et autres actes relatifs à la paix avec l'Allemagne*, 5 vols. (Paris, 1872-79).
[2] For the various arrangements necessitated by, and the various legal and political effects consequent on, a cession of territory see Phillipson, *Termination of War and Treaties of Peace*, Pt. I., ch. iv. ; Pt. II. chaps. xi. xii. and xiii.
[3] Villefort, *Recueil*, vol. i. p. 89.

CHAPTER V

PROPOSALS AS TO THE FATE OF ALSACE-LORRAINE AFTER ITS CONQUEST—BISMARCK'S VIEW OF THE TASK OF ASSIMILATION

Protests in Germany against the annexation—German policy as to the annexed territory—View as to neutralisation—View as to plebiscite—Division of the territory suggested—Autonomy suggested—Alsace-Lorraine made a Reichsland—Bismarck's view as to German assimilation—His doubts about Metz.

WHEN it became abundantly clear, after the fall of Sedan, that the war against France was a war of *Protests in* spoliation, voices even in Germany were *Germany* *against the* raised against the policy of the victors. *spoliation.* The German Socialists protested publicly and energetically against the projected annexation of French territory. They condemned any arrangement whatever that would involve the humiliation of France and would engender lasting bitterness and an ardent desire for retaliation; they demanded that, in the very interests of the German people, an honourable peace should be granted to France.[1] On May 25, 1871, Bebel said in the Reichstag : " I protest categorically against the annexation of Alsace-Lorraine. I consider it a crime against the right of the people ; I consider it a disgraceful stain on German history." A similar protest was offered by Liebknecht. For their courageous and enlightened opposition, they were tried

[1] Cf. E. Milhaud, *La Démocratie socialiste allemande* (Paris, 1903), p. 39 ; Novicow, *op. cit.*, p. 381.

for high treason and condemned to two years' imprisonment in a fortress.

It is of special interest to recall the observations made in the autumn of 1870 by various German leading papers, as showing that it was by no means the entire German people that had become possessed of a conquering fury and territorial lust. The following may be referred to as illustrations :

The *Frankfurter Zeitung*, August 17, 1870 : " The annexation of Alsace-Lorraine is shrilly demanded by a section of National Liberals and National Democrats. The powder acts as an intoxicant on the democratic parties. They invoke the brutal right of conquest, and hardly trouble to dissimulate their claims. They do not ask, What do the Alsatians and Lorrainers say ? Do they wish to become German or remain French ? "

The *Rheinische-Westfaelische Zeitung*, August 17, 1870 : " The question of a French cession of territory is very difficult if we do not merely wish to assert the right of conquest."

The *Zukunft*, September 18, 1870 : " They tell us that Alsace-Lorraine must be taken from France. There is no surer way of turning the coming peace into an armistice until the moment when France will have recovered sufficient strength to claim the restitution of the territory we are taking. The most jingoistic Teuton will not dare to pretend that Alsatians and Lorrainers are yearning for the joys of German rule." [1]

Germany having compelled France to abandon Alsace-Lorraine, the first problem the German Govern-

---

[1] These extracts were given in the *Daily Telegraph*, October 19, 1917, and were supplied to this paper by the Ligue Patriotique des Alsaciens-Lorrains.

ment was confronted with was—what was to be done with the surrendered territory? Was it to be incorporated in the newly established German Empire, and, if so, on what basis? Was it expedient to neutralise it and constitute it a buffer State between the rival nations?

German policy as to the annexed territory.

In a speech delivered in the Reichstag, May 2, 1871, Bismarck foreshadowed the future policy that was to be adopted, and criticised certain proposals that had been advanced as against annexation, *e.g.*, the mere dismantling of the French fortresses in Alsace-Lorraine and allowing the territory to remain French; or the neutralisation of the territory. The Chancellor reported a conversation he had had before the Franco-German War with the recently deceased King William of Würtemberg. The latter declared he was for peace, but that if war broke out against France he would participate in the conflict. " Give us Strassburg," he observed to Bismarck, " and we shall be united for all eventualities; but so long as Strassburg will remain a sally-port for an armed Power, I fear my country will be invaded by foreign troops before the German Confederation will be able to help me." Thus Strassburg was thought to be the knot of the situation; so long as it was not German it would always be regarded as an obstacle on the one hand to South Germany's committing herself without reserve to German unity, and on the other hand to the development of a German national policy.

As to the suggested dismantling of the French fortresses of Alsace-Lorraine, Bismarck said he strongly objected to such an inadequate scheme. In the first place, he thought it was of little practical use in the interests of maintaining peace. Besides, the geographical configuration of the advanced bastion was

PROPOSALS AS TO ITS FATE

too near Stuttgart and Munich, so that it therefore became necessary to push it back. Further, Metz, by its topographical nature, was a place that demanded very little works to make a formidable fortress of it, and demolished works could easily be reconstructed. Secondly, political reasons were against imposing on a State restrictions interfering with its self-defence. "To constitute a condition of servitude upon foreign policy and soil is to create a very heavy burden, very annoying to the sentiments of sovereignty and independence of the country upon which it weighs."

The proposed plans to neutralise Alsace-Lorraine, Bismarck said, had many advocates amongst its population. If it were made an independent neutral State, like Belgium and Switzerland, there would thus be a chain of neutral States extending from the North Sea to the Swiss Alps, and separating France from Germany. The Germans, being accustomed to respect treaties and neutrality, would therefore be prevented from attacking the French; but the French would not be prevented from realising the plan conceived during the last war, viz. to despatch a fleet to Germany with troops for landing, or to land French troops in allied countries and afterwards invade German territory. Accordingly France would be protected against Germany by this belt of neutral States, but Germany would remain exposed to naval attacks, seeing that the German fleet was not as powerful as the French. Furthermore—and this was conceived to be a more important reason against neutralisation—neutrality is tenable only if the neutralised country is resolved to safeguard and defend it; but if Alsace-Lorraine were established as a neutral State, the strong French elements in it, French sympathies and interests, would induce it to take the side

View as to neutralisation.

of France in the event of a conflict with Germany. Hence there was only one course to adopt, viz. to subject Alsace-Lorraine to German dominion.

Treitschke, writing in 1870,[1] had already condemned (before Bismarck's definitive pronouncement) the proposal to neutralise Alsace-Lorraine. Like so many other Germans, he regarded small nations with impatience and contempt. "What is the use," he exclaimed, "of attempting to answer the suggestion that Alsace and Lorraine should form a neutral State? Has Europe not had enough of that already in the disgusting spectacle of the 'Luxemburg nation'? Only the brain of an English Manchester man, surrounded by the mists he blows from his pipe of peace, could conceive such extraordinary bubbles. No wonder that every enemy of Germany should approve of this suggestion. No better way has yet been thought of to enable France to recover all that she has lost."

To the suggestion that recourse should be had to a plebiscite for the purpose of settling the destiny of the provinces, German opinion was still more strongly opposed. Such a policy naturally finds little favour with those who repudiate democratic demands, who look upon the masses of the people as mere objects of government, and who are animated by dreams of jingoistic imperialism and territorial aggrandisement.

View as to plebiscite.

Thus Lasson, one of the leading teachers of modern Germany and a persistent advocate of the virtues and desirability of war, observes[2]: "To allow a people, and still more a fraction of a people, to decide international

---

[1] H. von Treitschke, *Was fordern wir von Frankreich?* (Berlin, 1870). An English translation of this pamphlet is included in a volume entitled *Germany, France, Russia, and Islam* (London, 1915); p. 163 (reference to the English edition).

[2] A. Lasson, *Das Culturideal und der Krieg* (Berlin, 1868).

questions, for example, which State shall control them, is as good as making the children of a house vote for their father. It is the most ridiculous fallacy that human wit has ever conceived." It may be said, on the contrary, that this comparison involves a most ridiculous fallacy. To ask the inhabitants of a given territory to decide its fate is to ask them to vote for *themselves* ; for they are more directly concerned than the sovereign whose subjects they were originally.

Von Sybel, one of the most eminent historians of Germany, writing in 1870,[1] says that a cession of territory is the natural conclusion of a war in which one side is victorious and the other defeated ; the defeated party is a debtor of a particular kind who cannot pay his debt except by abandoning a portion of his territory ; there is no longer any diplomacy, or politics, or history, if it be claimed that the payment of this debt should be subordinated to the vote of a province. In reply to this pronouncement, one may say that it rests on the fallacious basis that a defeated country necessarily becomes indebted to the victor. What if the victorious sovereign was an ambitious, unscrupulous aggressor, and the defeated country—comparatively small, powerless, and helpless—is the object of the former's covetousness, and is attacked without any provocation and without any legitimate reason ? In what sense, then, can it be said that the small, innocent country overrun and crushed by its powerful, merciless neighbour becomes indebted to it? To argue thus is indeed to resort to such a "transvaluation of values" as will make the worse appear the better reason, and will call black white and evil good.

Treitschke, in the course of a speech made in the

[1] H. von Sybel, *Deutschlands Rechte auf Elsass und Lothringen* (Leipzig, 1871).

Reichstag in 1871, acclaimed Germany's refusal to entertain the proposal of a plebiscite. "With sound German pride," he said, "we have despised the Bonapartist jugglery of universal suffrage."[1] Similarly, Herr Wagner, a professor of Göttingen, in a pamphlet published in 1870, calls the universal vote a "comedy."[2]

Division of the territory suggested. Schemes for neutralisation and plebiscite having been rejected by the mass of German opinion and by the German Government, it followed that Alsace-Lorraine was to become part of the Empire. To effect this object it was suggested in some quarters in Germany that the acquired territory should be divided between the Kingdom of Bavaria and the Grand Duchy of Baden; and the question was raised, too, in the Bundesrat. It may be recalled that after the Preliminaries of Versailles were signed by the representatives of Bavaria, Würtemberg, and Baden, Bismarck is said to have declared that "in order to efface any unpleasant recollections of the war of 1866, he intended to hand over to Bavaria the town of Weissenburg after the annexation of Alsace." "These tidings," observes M. Jules Jolly, in his *Recollections* (he was the representative of Baden, at the Versailles negotiations) "had been welcomed with lively emotion by Count von Bray, the Bavarian minister."[3]

Such distribution of Alsatian territory was afterwards objected to. Treitschke opposed not only the suggested partition of Alsace-Lorraine between Bavaria and Baden, but also the assignment of the territory entirely either to the one State or to the other—as

[1] *Germany, France, Russia, and Islam*, p. 194.
[2] A. Wagner, *Elsass und Lothringen und ihre Wiedergewinnung für Deutschland* (Leipzig, 1870).
[3] *Cf.* Ottokar Lorenz, *Kaiser Wilhelm und die Begründung des Reichs, 1866–71* (Jena, 1902), p. 525.

PROPOSALS AS TO ITS FATE 93

both these alternatives had also been brought forward ; and he proposed that the provinces should be given to Prussia. He said it was unreasonable to entrust this "outwork of Germany" to a secondary State, and doubted whether German boundaries would be safe in Bavarian hands, and whether Bavaria possessed the intellectual and political power necessary for fusing Alsace into union with herself.[1] Rather, a common diplomacy and a collective German parliament were best fitted for the work of assimilation. Prussia, however, might be an efficient master. "Prussia alone," he said, "can undertake the remorseless sweeping away of the French officials in Alsace, which is indispensable, and replace the foreign powers by vigorous home ones. Prussia alone can steadfastly maintain the state of siege which, we may easily imagine, may be necessary for a time in some of the districts of the forlorn land. . . . A powerful State, which has impressed its spirit on the inhabitants of the Rhine country and the people of Posen, will know how to reconcile the separate life of the half-French Germans."[2] "The people of Alsace have learned to despise this Germany, broken into fragments. They will learn to love us when the strong hand of Prussia has educated them."[3] But against this suggestion many objections were raised ; moreover, the Prussian monarch had declared in September 1870 that he desired no increase of territory.

A more liberal proposal was advanced in some quarters, viz. that the acquired provinces should constitute a new autonomous State within the German Empire. The German Government, however, was not disposed to adopt such a liberal and generous course. In a speech in the

Autonomy suggested.

[1] *Op. cit.*, pp. 163–6. [2] *Op. cit.*, pp. 167, 168. [3] *Op. cit.*, p. 173.

ALSACE-LORRAINE

Reichstag, Treitschke argued against the multiplication of small German States: " We have been contending vigorously, gentlemen, during many years for the unity of Germany ; we have seen, in the course of this century, hundreds of small German States collapse; we are now prepared, as men of good feeling, to respect and to spare the few States which remain, because they are no longer in a condition to be exactly injurious to the might of the German Empire. But to create a new State in addition to the already too great existing number, now when we are hard at work counteracting the German tendency to division, to form afresh a State out of the departments which never in the course of their history were a State, to cultivate a new half-German provincialism on the severely endangered frontier—that, gentlemen, I call striking our own face." [1]

Eventually it was decided to make Alsace-Lorraine simply an imperial province—a Reichsland—to be the collective property of all the German States ; for its dismemberment and division between two or more or its assignment to one of the States would have aroused jealousy and dissatisfaction in the others, and so might have imperilled the stability of the newly established confederation. It thus becomes—to use the words of a recent writer already referred to [2]—" la première colonie de la Confédération germanique," or a kind of dependency placed under the sovereign control of the Empire and administered by organs of imperial government acting independently of each and all of the federated States as such.[3] The federal constitution did not apply *ex*

(marginal note: Alsace-Lorraine made a Reichsland.)

---

[1] *Op. cit*, pp. 188–9.   [2] Wetterlé, *op. cit.*, p. 103.
[3] Cf. A. Haenel, *Deutsches Staatsrecht* (1892, etc.), vol. 1. p. 124 ; Anschütz, in F. von Holtzendorff-Vietmansdorf (Ed. J. Kohler), *Enzyclopädie der Rechtswissenschaft* (München ; Leipzig, 1913-14), 5 vols. vol. 11. p. 559.

PROPOSALS AS TO ITS FATE 95

proprio vigore to the annexed provinces; only express imperial legislation could make it applicable thereto.[1] The three main reasons that impelled the German Government to impose this status on Alsace-Lorraine were, first, the difficulty of satisfactorily fitting conquered territory into a federation of autonomous States, secondly, the danger of a subsequent French invasion in the hope of recovering it, and thirdly, the danger of internal disorder due to the discontentment and alienation of the inhabitants whose territory was annexed without consulting them.

In his speech before the Reichstag, May 25, 1871, Bismarck referred to what were deemed to be the only two practicable courses, viz. to unite Alsace-Lorraine to Prussia, or to constitute it an " immediate territory " of the Empire. He thought from the first that the second alternative was preferable, because dynastic questions would not then become mixed with political questions, and because the Alsatians would more easily assimilate to themselves the name of Germans than that of Prussians—in France it was the Prussians, not so much the Germans, who had been the detested people.

As to how Germany would assimilate the conquered country and make the population loyal Germans the Chancellor had early made up his mind. Bismarck's It is related that when he was asked in 1870 view as to German at Versailles by one William Jones, an English assimilation. quaker, how the denationalisation of Alsace would be accomplished, he replied that the children would be brought up in German schools, and the younger generation would be subjected to the discipline of the

[1] As to the status of the Reichsland and the régime introduced therein, see *infra*, chap. ix.

great German army.¹ In his speech of May 2, 1871, in the Reichstag, he went into this difficult question a little more fully. He referred to the antipathy of the population to their being taken over by Germany : " This antipathy exists, it is a fact, and it is our duty to overcome it by dint of patience. . . . We Germans are in the habit generally of governing with more good-nature, sometimes with a little clumsiness, but on the whole we are more benevolent, more human than French statesmen ; this superiority of the German régime will soon reveal itself and seduce the German hearts of the Alsatians. . . . Besides, we are able to grant the inhabitants communal and individual liberty, self-government, infinitely greater than they enjoyed under French institutions and traditions. . . . Thanks to German patience and benevolence, we shall succeed in gaining over the population, and that perhaps in less time than may be thought at present." With regard to the ways and means of beginning this task, he pointed out that only a provisional arrangement was then possible, that only empirical methods could in the circumstances be adopted : for the situation was an abnormal one, in that the territory was acquired by conquest, and was made the common property of a Confederation of sovereign princes and free towns—a fact, indeed, that was very rare in history, if not unparalleled. Two years later (May 16, 1873) the Chancellor again spoke in the Reichstag of the work of assimilation and absorption. He emphasised that it was necessary to combat in Alsace the prevailing sympathies for a past that gave the inhabitants many advantages and many glories, that it was incumbent on the Imperial Government to recognise the truly French sympathies of the country and to overcome

¹ H. Welschinger, *Bismarck* (Paris, 1900), p. 130.

PROPOSALS AS TO ITS FATE

them, despite the difficulty of the task, and above all to act in such a way as not to compromise the material security of Germany.

That Bismarck fully appreciated the difficulties involved and foresaw the troubles that would follow this forcible, arbitrary, and factitious annexation is evident from such reported conversations as the following (on the day following the capitulation of Paris) : " As you see, we are keeping Metz ; but I confess I don't like that part of the arrangement. Strassburg is German in speech, and will be so in heart ten years hence. Metz, however, is French, and will be a hotbed of dissatisfaction for a long time to come. The Emperor has too many foreigners for subjects as it is. We have had more than enough trouble with our Poles, though they have been benevolently governed, God knows ! And we shall have still more with these Lorrainers, who hate us like poison and will have, very likely, to be roughly handled, whereas the good old German Elsässer will be treated with the utmost consideration. They will soon like us better than they ever liked the Frenchmen, who were never weary of poking fun at them, gibing at their accent and generally holding them up to ridicule." [1] *(His doubts about Metz.)*

We shall see in subsequent chapters to what extent the German task succeeded, and how far the attempted assimilation and absorption failed.[2] In the meantime it is necessary to refer to the public protests against the annexation made by the representatives of Alsace-Lorraine in the National Assembly and by other notable deputies.

[1] *Conversations with Prince Bismarck.* Collected by H. von Poschinger. Edited by S. Whitman (London and New York, 1900 ; p. 98).
[2] See *infra*, chaps. ix and x.

CHAPTER VI

THE PROTESTS OF 1871 AGAINST THE ANNEXATION

Declaration of Alsace-Lorraine deputies—Submitted to the National Assembly—Various other protests—Debates in the Assembly on the proposed cession—Vote on the Preliminaries—Further protest of Alsace-Lorraine deputies—Demand from Germany—Effects of the annexation.

> *Thou hast consulted shame to thy house by cutting off many people, and hast sinned against thy soul.*
> *For the stone shall cry out of the wall and the beam out of the timber shall answer it.*
> Hab. ii. 10, 11.

AFTER the three weeks' armistice was concluded on January 28, 1871, the National Assembly was elected, and met at Bordeaux (February 12) for the purpose of deciding on the continuance or definitive cessation of hostilities, in view of the German demands as to the payment of an enormous indemnity and the cession of Alsace-Lorraine.

Protest of Alsace-Lorraine deputies in 1871.

On February 17, after the speech of M. Jules Grévy, who thanked the Assembly for the honour of electing him its President, M. Émile Keller, the head of the list of deputies for the department of the Upper Rhine, dressed in his officer's uniform, which was worn and dusty, read the celebrated declaration of protest against the proposed annexation of Alsace-Lorraine to Germany.[1] Before he read it, he said: " I am

[1] See H. Welschinger, *La Protestation de l'Alsace-Lorraine les 17 février et 1er mars 1871 à Bordeaux* (Paris, 1914), to which indebtedness for various particulars is acknowledged. Cf. also the same writer's *La Guerre de 1870 : causes et responsabilités* (Paris, 1910).

98

THE PROTESTS OF 1871 99

convinced that the proposition I am about to lay before you will receive your unanimous approval, for our honour and our national unity are at stake : on this point there can be no difference of opinion in a French assembly."

The solemn declaration, signed by all the representatives of Alsace-Lorraine (the departments of the Lower Rhine, Upper Rhine, Moselle, and Meurthe), has now become a noteworthy historical document ; so that it may be given here both in the original [1] and in an English translation :

"We, the undersigned French citizens, elected by the constituents of the departments of the Lower Rhine, the Upper Rhine, the Meurthe and the Vosges, and chosen by them to bring to the National Assembly of France the unanimous expression of the wish and will of the populations of Alsace and Lorraine, having previously met for and deliberated on the subject,

[1] " I. L'Alsace et la Lorraine ne veulent pas être aliénées.

" Associées depuis plus de deux siècles à la France, dans la bonne comme dans la mauvaise fortune, ces deux provinces, sans cesse exposées aux coups de l'ennemi, se sont constamment sacrifiées pour la grandeur nationale ; elles ont scellé de leur sang l'indissoluble pacte qui les rattache à l'unité française. Mises aujourd'hui en question par les prétentions étrangères, elles affirment à travers les obstacles et tous les dangers, sous le joug même de l'envahisseur, leur inébranlable fidélité.

" Tous unanimes, les citoyens demeurés dans leurs foyers, comme les soldats accourus sous les drapeaux, les uns en votant, les autres en combattant, signifient à l'Allemagne et au monde l'immuable volonté de l'Alsace et de la Lorraine de rester françaises.

" II. La France ne peut consentir ni signer la cession de la Lorraine et de l'Alsace. Elle ne peut pas, sans mettre en péril la continuité de son existence nationale, porter elle-même un coup mortel à sa propre unité en abandonnant ceux qui ont conquis, par deux cents ans de dévouement patriotique, le droit d'être défendus par le pays tout entier contre les entreprises de la force victorieuse.

" Une assemblée, même issue du suffrage universel, ne pourrait invoquer sa souveraineté, pour couvrir ou ratifier des exigences destructives de l'intégrité nationale. Elle s'arrogerait un droit qui n'appartient même pas au peuple réuni dans ses comices.

" Un pareil excès de pouvoir, qui aurait pour effet de mutiler la mère have resolved to set forth in a solemn declaration our sacred and inalienable right, so that the National Assembly, France, and Europe, who have before their eyes the wishes, the will, and the resolutions of our constituents, may not take, or allow to be taken for granted, an act of a nature to injure the rights of which a formal mandate has confided to us the guardianship and the defence.

" I. Alsace and Lorraine refuse to be transferred.

" Associated with France for more than two centuries, in good as in evil fortune, and unceasingly exposed to the blows of the enemy, these two provinces have

commune, dénoncerait aux justes sévérites de l'histoire ceux qui s'en rendraient coupables.

" La France peut subir les coups de la force, elle ne peut sanctionner ses arrêts.

" III. L'Europe ne peut permettre ni ratifier l'abandon de l'Alsace et de la Lorraine.

" Gardiennes des règles de la justice et du droit des gens, les nations civilisées ne sauraient rester plus longtemps insensibles au sort de leurs voisins, sous peine d'être à leur tour victimes des attentats qu'elles auraient tolérés. L'Europe moderne ne peut laisser saisir un peuple comme un vil troupeau ; elle ne peut rester sourde aux protestations répétées des populations menacées ; elle doit à sa propre conservation d'interdire de pareils abus de la force. Elle sait d'ailleurs que l'unité de la France est aujourd'hui, comme dans le passé, une garantie de l'ordre général du monde, une barrière contre l'esprit de conquête et d'invasion.

" La paix, faite au prix d'une cession de territoire, ne serait qu'une trêve ruineuse et non une paix définitive. Elle serait pour tous une cause d'agitation intestine, une provocation légitime et permanente à la guerre. Et quant à nous, Alsaciens et Lorrains, nous serions prêts à recommencer la guerre aujourd'hui, demain, à toute heure, à tout instant.

" En résumé, l'Alsace et la Lorraine protestent hautement contre toute cession. La France ne peut la consentir ; l'Europe ne peut la sanctionner.

" En foi de quoi nous prenons nos concitoyens de France, les gouvernements et les peuples du monde entier à témoin que nous tenons d'avance pour nuls et non avenus tous actes et traités, votes ou plébiscite, qui consentiraient abandon en faveur de l'étranger de tout ou partie de nos provinces de l'Alsace et de la Lorraine.

" Nous proclamons par les présentes à jamais inviolable le droit des Alsaciens et des Lorrains de rester membres de la nation française, et nous jurons, tant pour nous que pour nos commettants, nos enfants et leurs descendants, de le revendiquer éternellement, et par toutes les voies, envers et contre tous usurpateurs."

THE PROTESTS OF 1871

constantly sacrificed themselves for the national greatness; they have sealed with their blood the indissoluble ties that bind them to French unity. Being challenged by foreign pretensions, they affirm their unswerving loyalty in the face of all obstacles and dangers, under the very yoke of the invader.

" The citizens who have remained at home and the soldiers who have joined the colours unanimously proclaim—the former by their votes, the latter by fighting—to Germany and to the world the unalterable determination of Alsace and Lorraine to remain French.

" II. France may neither consent to nor sign the cession of Lorraine and Alsace. She cannot, without imperilling the continuance of her national existence, herself strike a mortal blow at her own unity, by abandoning those who have acquired by two hundred years of patriotic devotion the right to be defended by the entire country against the aggression of victorious force.

" An Assembly, even though elected by universal suffrage, cannot invoke its sovereignty to sanction or ratify demands that are destructive of the national integrity. It would be arrogating to itself a right which does not belong even to the people themselves assembled to vote under a plebiscite.

" Such an excess of power, which would result in the mutilation of the mother-country common to both of them, would expose to the just condemnation of history those responsible for it.

" France may suffer the blows of violence, she cannot sanction its decrees.

" III. Europe may not permit or ratify the abandonment of Alsace and Lorraine.

" Guardians of the law of justice and of the rights

of peoples, the civilised nations can no longer remain insensible to the fate of their neighbours, under pain of becoming in their turn victims of the outrages they have tolerated. Modern Europe cannot allow a people to be seized like a herd of cattle ; she cannot remain deaf to the repeated protests of the menaced populations. She owes it to her own preservation to forbid such abuses of force. She knows, moreover, that the unity of France is now, as in the past, a guarantee of the general order of the world, a barrier against the spirit of conquest and invasion.

" Peace concluded at the price of a cession of territory would be only a disastrous truce and not a definitive peace. It would be for all a cause of internal unrest, a legitimate and permanent provocation for war. And as for us, Alsatians and Lorrainers, we would be ready to make war again to-day, to-morrow, at any hour, at any moment.

" Finally, Alsace and Lorraine protest aloud against any cession. France may not consent to it ; Europe may not sanction it.

" In faith whereof we take to witness our fellow-citizens of France, and the governments and nations of the world, that we consider in advance as null and void all acts and treaties, votes or plebiscite, which consent to the abandonment, in favour of a foreign country, of all or part of our provinces of Alsace and Lorraine.

" We proclaim by this act that the right of the Alsatians and Lorrainers to remain members of the French nation shall ever remain inviolable, and we swear, on our own behalf as well as for our constituents, our children and their descendants, always to claim this right, by every means, against all usurpers."

Having read this declaration, M. Keller submitted

THE PROTESTS OF 1871 103

it to the Assembly for its earnest consideration, and reminded it of the painful situation of the provinces due on the one hand to their great suffer- ings in the war, and on the other to the menaced alienation from their mother-country. His last words, as M. Welschinger aptly remarks, were at once a cry of anguish and a cry of hope : " Behold, gentlemen, we are like the sailor who has let his vessel be sunk rather than surrender his flag. We stretch out our hands to you, do not refuse us yours ! " [1]

<small>Declaration submitted to the National Assembly.</small>

These words brought tears into many eyes ; but M. Thiers, whilst sharing the feelings of Keller, reminded the members of the Assembly of the urgent exigencies of the situation, that it was incumbent upon them to act as practical, serious men of affairs, and to make up their minds whether the peace negotiators were to be armed with full powers or not—for the one question to be determined upon was peace or war. After the sitting had been suspended for a short time, the following resolution was carried : " The National Assembly, welcoming with the profoundest sympathy the declaration of M. Keller and his colleagues, places its confidence in the wisdom and patriotism of its negotiators." Then M. Thiers was elected head of the executive.

We have already referred to the peace negotiations at Versailles which led to the conclusion of the Preliminaries on February 26, 1871. Whilst these negotiations were in progress the various groups of the National Assembly met to consider the course they should adopt. The extreme left was for continuing the war rather than submit to the humiliating terms demanded by the enemy. On

<small>Various other protests.</small>

---

[1] " Tenez, messieurs, nous sommes comme le marın qui a vu couler son navıre plutôt que de rendre son drapeau ; nous vous tendons la main, ne nous refusez pas la vôtre ! "

February 18 the party assembled under the presidency of Victor Hugo, and adopted an address, drawn up by Louis Blanc, which was delivered to the deputies of Alsace-Lorraine. It declared that neither the National Assembly nor the entire French nation had the right to make even a single Alsatian or Lorrainer a subject of Prussia ; it held in advance null and void every vote or plebiscite whereby any portion of Alsace or of Lorraine should be ceded ; it affirmed that, whatever might happen, the citizens of those territories remained the countrymen and brothers of the French people ; and it promised them, on behalf of the Republic " an eternal vindication." [1] This address was signed by thirty-eight deputies, including Victor Hugo, Louis Blanc, Edgar Quinet, and Clemenceau.

On February 28 M. Thiers submitted to the Assembly the Preliminaries of Versailles ; and at the next day's sitting, under the presidency of M. Grévy, the terms of peace were discussed. As soon as the proceedings commenced, one member rose to make a protest against all eventual cession of territory ; another demanded that the inhabitants of the provinces in question should be consulted ; a third denied the right to cede any territory at all ; a fourth handed his resignation to the President, saying that he could not be a party to the discussion of territorial cession ; and so on. In reply it was pointed out that the enemy was inexorable, and that it was an urgent necessity to arrest the invasion ; if the Assembly chose to renew the conflict by refusing to ratify the Preliminaries, Paris would be occupied, the invasion of France extended, and Heaven knew what further disasters might follow ; the Assembly was therefore urged not to abandon itself to a policy of desperation.

Debates in Assembly on proposed cession.

[1] Welschinger, *op. cit.*, p. 14.

Edgar Quinet said that till then the conquest had been only depredation, but if it were ratified by the Assembly it would assume the character of a right; Prussia wanted France to commit suicide, by means of a vote of the Assembly; Alsace and Lorraine were not only two French provinces, they were also bulwarks of France. Victor Hugo vowed that Alsace and Lorraine would remain French whatever might happen, and that France would never abandon her right and duty in regard to the provinces. " Non, la France ne périra pas, quelle que soit la lâcheté de l'Europe. Dès demain, la France n'aura plus qu'une pensée : se reconstituer, reprendre ses forces, ramasser son énergie, nourrir de saintes colères, élever sa génération ; ses petits deviendront grands ; former une armée qui sera un peuple tout entier, travailler sans relâche, étudier les procédés et la science de nos ennemis, redevenir la grande France, la France de 1792, la France de l'idée et de l'épée . . . Et puis un jour elle se dressera invincible."[1] He ended his speech on a humanitarian note, predicting a fraternal reconciliation : " France, one day victorious, would raise defeated Germany and say to her that they were sisters, and ought to act together as a single people, a single family, a single Republic." Louis Blanc said that history would ask Europe why she remained silent in the face of Prussian proceedings, the enormity of which exceeded all bounds. What could one expect of Prussia, who began with the robbery of Silesia and the partitioning of Poland ? Did not Russia see the German imperial eagle stretching its wings over the Baltic ? Had Austria forgotten Sadowa ? Did not Italy see the eye of Prussia on Trieste ? Had not the fate of Denmark warned Holland ? Did not England understand the designs

[1] Cf. Villefort, *op. cit.*, vol. ii., p. 49.

of Pan-Germanism ? Was it so long ago that in the interests of European equilibrium Belgium was placed under protection from invasion ?

Once more Keller appealed to the Assembly not to deliver up Alsace-Lorraine ; and he repudiated the treaty, which was for him a lie. " We wish to remain French," he said, " and we shall remain French ; no power in the world, no signature, either of the Assembly or of Prussia, can prevent us from remaining French. . . . Is it honourable to abandon populations who wish to remain French, and who, despite all, will remain French ? . . . This treaty, which it is proposed to ratify, is an injustice and at the same time a lie. . . . Before leaving this place I am bound to protest, as an Alsatian and as a Frenchman, against a treaty which is, in my eyes, an injustice, a lie, and a dishonour ; and, if the Assembly should ratify it, I appeal to God, the avenger of just causes ; I appeal to posterity, which will judge us one and all ; I appeal to all peoples, who cannot let themselves be sold like a wretched herd of cattle ; I appeal finally to the sword of men of mettle who will at the earliest possible moment tear up this detestable treaty ! "[1] Here Thiers exclaimed to Keller : " Give us means, not words." Keller did not reply, but another member, M. Tirard, got up and cried : " Levy *en masse* ! You ask for the means. Let the 750 representatives put themselves at the head of France, and you will save France ! " To which Thiers replied : " If you think you can get better conditions, send other negotiators, and you will thus take away a great burden from me. If you think you have military resources, produce them." A silence followed. All eyes turned towards General Chanzy, who remained silent. Then Thiers emphasised that France was not in a position to

[1] Welschinger, *op. cit.*, p. 18.

THE PROTESTS OF 1871

go on with the war, and fully explained the whole situation ; he impressed upon the Assembly his view that, if France decided to continue the war instead of accepting the terms imposed, she would be ruined and her future would be destroyed. He reminded his auditors that when France was mad enough to declare war in 1870, she was not prepared for it ; hostilities had gone on in a state of military disorganisation from the first ; and after the disasters that had been suffered in consequence it was no longer possible to offer successful resistance to the large duly constituted armies of the invader.

A vote was then taken on the Preliminaries ; 546 voted for their acceptance, and 107 for their rejection.

Vote on the Preliminaries.

Then M. Jules Grosjean read another protest in the name of all his colleagues representing the departments of the Lower Rhine, Upper Rhine, and the Moselle. It was as follows : [1]

" The representatives of Alsace and Lorraine have

[1] " Les représentants de l'Alsace et de la Lorraine ont déposé, avant toute négociation de paix, sur le bureau de l'Assemblée nationale, une déclaration affirmant de la manière la plus formelle, au nom de ces provinces, leur volonté et leur droit de rester françaises.

" Livrés, au mépris de toute justice et par un odieux abus de la force, à la domination de l'étranger, nous avons un dernier devoir à remplir.

" Nous déclarons encore une fois nul et non avenu un pacte qui dispose de nous sans notre consentement.

" La revendication de nos droits reste à jamais ouverte à tous et à chacun dans la forme et dans la mesure que notre conscience nous dictera.

" Au moment de quitter cette enceinte où notre dignité ne nous permet plus de siéger, et malgré l'amertume de notre douleur, la pensée suprême que nous trouvons au fond de nos cœurs est une pensée de reconnaissance pour ceux qui, pendant six mois, n'ont pas cessé de nous défendre, et d'inaltérable attachement à la patrie dont nous sommes violemment arrachés.

" Nous vous suivrons de nos vœux et nous attendrons, avec une confiance entière dans l'avenir, que la France régénérée reprenne le cours de sa grande destinée.

" Vos frères d'Alsace et de Lorraine, séparés en ce moment de la famille commune, conserveront à la France, absente de leurs foyers, une affection filiale jusqu'au jour où elle viendra y reprendre sa place."

delivered to the office of the National Assembly, before all peace negotiations, a declaration affirming in the most formal manner, in the name of these provinces, their will and their right to remain French.

<small>Further protest of Alsace-Lorraine deputies.</small>

" Given up, in contempt of all justice and by an odious abuse of force, to foreign domination, we have one last duty to fulfil.

" We declare once more null and void a compact that disposes of us without our consent.

" The vindication of our right remains ever open to all and each of us in such form and measure as our conscience shall dictate.

" At the moment of leaving these precincts where our dignity no longer permits us to remain, and despite the bitterness of our grief, the supreme thought we find in the bottom of our hearts is a thought of gratitude to those who for six months did not cease to protect us, and of unalterable attachment to the mother-country from which we are violently torn.

" We shall follow you with our prayers and we shall wait with perfect confidence in the future, till regenerated France resumes the course of her high destiny.

" Your brothers of Alsace and Lorraine, separated at this moment from the common family, will preserve for France, absent from their hearths, a filial affection until the day when she will come to take her place there again."

" C'était," comments M. Welschinger,[1] " le dernier sanglot des deux provinces arrachées à la France." In vain did the Assembly appeal to the protesting deputies to remain in their places; having thus resigned their positions, they left " sombres et silencieux." " Cette fin de séance eut un aspect funèbre." [2]

[1] *Op. cit.*, p. 21. [2] *Ibid.*

THE PROTESTS OF 1871 109

Several members of the Republican party, notably MM. Rochefort, Ranc, Benoit Malon, Félix Pyat, also sent in their resignations, saying they would not sit a single day longer " in an Assembly that had surrendered two provinces, dismembered France, and ruined the country." [1]

Such were the scenes—the eloquent speeches, the burning protests, the vows of brotherhood exchanged by those who were to be severed, the sobs of bereaved souls—that were witnessed on that memorable occasion when the representatives of France had thrust upon them for their acceptance the humiliating conditions demanded by an inexorable conqueror. " Will such scenes," observes M. Gabriel Hanotaux, " the lessons which they carry, and the duties which they impose, ever be effaced from the memory of the nation ? " [2]

After the ratification of the Preliminaries of Versailles the protesters saw clearly that the fate of their provinces was sealed ; and on March 24 M. Frédéric Hartmann turning towards Germany uttered these words, apt and precise : " By the fact that you have conquered us you owe us a legal status, a civil and political constitution in harmony with our traditions and our customs." This sentence enshrines the wisest policy—next to that of refraining from forcible annexation—which would in the circumstances have readily commended itself to statesmen possessing clear vision and sympathetic understanding. Whether it was through lack of these qualities or through the overweening arrogance and obstinacy of ungenerous and irate masters, the counsel was disregarded. Thus was perpetuated the Franco-German estrange-

Demand from Germany.

---
[1] For the protests made in the Reichstag in 1874 by the deputies of Alsace-Lorraine see *infra*, chap. x, *in init*.
[2] *Contemporary France*, English trans. (London, 1903), vol. i. p. 125.

ment, which did much to foster Germany's militarism and her resolve to acquire hegemony in Europe, to promote a sinister international diplomacy and intriguing political combinations, and so to prepare the way for the valley of the shadow of death of the present day.

An authoritative German historian, commenting on the fateful European politics consequent on the Franco-Prussian War, observes: " From the very outset the new structure of the German Empire was burdened as it were by a French mortgage, since every foreign foe could henceforth reckon unconditionally on French support. As in the past Frederick the Great had had to vindicate his conquest of Silesia in a seven years' war against a European combination, so Bismarck in his turn was painfully aware that the menace of a coalition hourly weighed upon his new creation. The great aim of his policy, from the first, was to prevent the formation of any such coalition." [1]

<small>Effects of the annexation.</small>

It appears that Bismarck himself admitted, a few years after the war, that the dismemberment of France was a blunder. In a despatch addressed to the French Minister for Foreign Affairs, November 14, 1879, M. de Saint-Vallier, the French ambassador at Berlin, reported a conversation he had with the German Chancellor. The latter is stated to have expressed himself to this effect : " One destroys a nation if one's power permits it, or if one's interest demands it ; one does not mutilate it with impunity . . . and history, the great instructor of statesmen, teaches us that one has always to repent it. In mutilating and humiliating Prussia, Napoleon caused the Steins and the Scharnhorsts to arise ; in taking from you Metz and part of Lorraine, the

---

[1] Professor Hermann Oncken, in *Cambridge Modern History* (Cambridge, 1910), vol. xii. p. 136.

Emperor, my master, and the militarists who inspired this resolve committed the greatest of political mistakes."[1]

In the light of an admission of this kind, and in view of the disastrous effects produced by a factitious and irrational dismemberment, we have now to examine the claims to Alsace-Lorraine that have been made from time to time in Germany, and the alleged grounds of its annexation.

[1] Nothing seems to have been said of Alsace, according to this reported conversation

CHAPTER VII

GERMAN CLAIMS TO ALSACE - LORRAINE — ALLEGED GROUNDS OF ANNEXATION : (*a*) HISTORICAL GROUNDS ; NATIONALITY AND RACE ; LANGUAGE

Historical grounds : Ranke's view—Mommsen's view—Treitschke's view—Early treaties—Appeal to the Holy Roman Empire—Difficulties in such contentions. Racial grounds : Names as a criterion—Claim untenable—Treitschke's arrogant pretensions. Claim on ground of language : Early struggles between languages—German dialect becomes predominant—Position of the *pays messin*. Principle of nationality—Attachment of Alsace to France—Principle of public right.

THE claims to Alsace-Lorraine laid by Germany are based on various grounds, *e.g.* historical considerations and previous ownership, nationality and race language, political necessity and German unity, military necessity and security, and finally (after 1870) the right of conquest. Before 1870 these claims were advanced on several noteworthy occasions. Thus during the Napoleonic wars, they were made by Prussian patriots in 1813 and 1815, when the Allied armies had penetrated into France. During the peace negotiations in the latter year the demand of the King of Prussia that France should be so dismembered was objected to by the Tsar, and the objection was acquiesced in. Prussia, however, did her utmost to maintain the anti-French movement, which had before been set on foot in Europe in consequence of the Revolutionary and Napoleonic régimes. Her writers and professors began to be more insistent on the pretension that Alsace and

German claims to Alsace-Lorraine.

GERMAN CLAIMS

Lorraine were really part of Germany and ought legitimately to be under German dominion. The claim was repeated in 1840, when Europe was nearly dragged into a general conflict as a result of the ambitious enterprise of the astute Mehemet Ali ; and it was reiterated in 1859 when Prussia was on the point of intervening in the conflict between France and Austria. Till 1866, France laughed at those demands ; but in 1867, when the Luxemburg affair aroused Prussian public opinion with regard to Alsace-Lorraine, she realised that the position was becoming serious. On the declaration of war in 1870 it was generally felt that the integrity of French territory was at stake. Alsace-Lorraine, well aware of the *franzosen-fresserei* of Germans and of their repeated demands, saw clearly that its destiny was now in question ; and only a few months after the outbreak of the war it realised that its fate was sealed.

Let us consider one by one the German claims to Alsace-Lorraine and the grounds alleged for the annexation.

In the first place, it was contended that the territory had been part of the German dominions until France got possession of it by force or fraud ; so that the claim thereto amounted to no more than the vindication of an old inalienable right. Accordingly the Germans long held that its annexation would be a mere restoration—a *zurückeroberung* (a recapture) as distinguished from an *eroberung* (a conquest). [Claims on historical grounds.]

This was in the mind of the eminent historian, Leopold von Ranke, when he addressed the following remark to Thiers in the autumn of 1870 immediately after the fall of Napoleon III : [Ranke's view.] " It is against Louis XIV that we have now to wage

8

war."[1] He was thinking of the French act of aggression whereby the provinces were wrested in the seventeenth century from a disunited Germany, and of the latter's necessity to undo that act.

Similarly, in 1870, in a series of letters addressed to the people of Italy, which were published in Milanese papers, Mommsen said, speaking of the German war aims[2] : " We ask something more than money. We claim territory ; not French territory, but German. . . . Melancholy is the tale of our neighbours appropriating Lorraine first, then Alsace. . . . The feeble policy of our forefathers betrayed our land, our faith, and our language." He emphasised that it was a question, therefore, of restoration and not of conquest : " Let France keep her French territory intact, whether always hers or not we will not ask. We desire no conquests; we want what is our own, neither more nor less."

<small>Mommsen's view.</small>

Treitschke, writing also in 1870 after the first German successes against France, said : " The thought which, after first knocking timidly at our doors as a shamefaced wish, has, in four swift weeks, grown to be the mighty war-cry of the nation, is no other than this : Restore what you stole from us long ago ; give back Alsace and Lorraine. . . . Why was it that, before the declaration of the war, the anxious cry rang through Alsace and Lorraine, 'The dice were to be thrown to settle the destiny of our provinces,' before a single German newspaper had

<small>Treitschke's view.</small>

[1] For a somewhat different interpretation of Ranke's words see *infra*, p. 139.
[2] *Letters on the War between Germany and France* (London, 1871). Letters I, II, and III, by T. Mommsen ; No. 1 published in the Milanese paper, *La Perseveranza*; Nos. II and III in the Milanese paper, *Il Secolo* (August 20 1870). The references are to the English translation issued under the above title.
[3] *Ibid.*, pp. 20, 21, 24, 29.

GERMAN CLAIMS

demanded the restitution of the plunder ? Because the awakened conscience of the people felt what penalty would have to be paid in the interests of justice by the disturber of the peace of nations."[1] This is not the true answer. The true answer is: because it was known that the Germans had long claimed the territory, that they regarded its eventual acquisition as only a restoration, that they did not make war for the vindication of honour and equitable reparation, but for territorial aggrandisement, that they coveted its mineral resources, and finally because Alsace-Lorraine was the most convenient French territory that could be annexed for geographical and commercial reasons.

Other claimants alleging these grounds are not so modest from an historical point of view. They refer even to such an ancient transaction as the Treaty of Verdun, A.D. 843, to show that Germany should extend to the Meuse. But as Germany then consisted of a great number of small States, and there was no consciousness of national unity whatever, it is a far-fetched and absurd contention for modern Germans to advance that the territories concerned formerly constituted part of the German "fatherland"; at an early date like this a German "fatherland" was not in existence, and it is a distortion of historical perspective to speak of it as such. Nor can we, on behalf of France, invoke the treaty of peace and alliance contracted at Vaucouleurs between Albert, King of the Romans, and Philip the Fair, whereby the former, with the concurrence of the prelates and nobles of Germany, agreed that the boundaries of France should be extended from the Meuse to the Rhine.[2]

Early treaties.

[1] *Germany, France, Russia, and Islam* (London, 1915), pp. 99, 100.
[2] This treaty is reported by the fourteenth-century chronicler, Guillaume de Nangis; modern edition by H. Géraud (Paris, 1843), vol. i. p. 308.

ALSACE-LORRAINE

The extravagant character and inadmissibility of the appeal to the Holy Roman Empire made by German writers become self-evident when we look at the constitution of this Empire. It was not a State in the modern sense of the term; it was an artificial and precarious Confederation that was held together with extreme looseness. It comprised the following: Central Europe; the United Provinces (Holland); the territories including the modern Luxemburg and the greater part of modern Belgium; about a third of modern France, including in the north (under Charles V) Flanders and Artois, in the north-east the territory between the Rhine and the Meuse (*i.e.* Alsace-Lorraine, etc.), in the east the Franche Comté and a part of Burgundy, in the southeast the territory between the Alps and the Rhône (viz. Provence, Dauphiné, Savoy, and Lyonnais); Switzerland; north and central Italy as far as Naples. This heterogeneous conglomeration of races, peoples, nationalities, kingdoms, duchies, countships, bishoprics, republics, free cities, etc., cannot be said to constitute a "fatherland" or a nation. In the later fifteenth century it contained some four hundred "States" or political units. Conflicts between them were frequent; and frequent were the appeals made by this or that ruler or league of rulers to foreign monarchs, notably to the kings of France and Sweden. In those days, too, national boundaries had not yet become fixed or stable; the feudal régime made impossible the very existence of nations and nationality. To belong to the Empire meant little more than the payment of tribute; it did not defend the weaker constituents from foreign raiders and plunderers. Before Alsace became French it, too, lacked a homogeneous political system; it was a miniature counterpart of

[marginal note:] Appeal to Holy Roman Empire.

GERMAN CLAIMS

the Empire itself in that it comprised a large number of dissociated units—bishoprics, free towns, self-governing republics, baronies, counties, and hereditary fiefs of the House of Austria. When Alsace became French this political heterogeneity began rapidly to disappear ; and Germany, in the modern sense of the term, was not in existence. Indeed, Alsace was part of France before such French territories as Lille, Nancy, Besançon.

Further, of this Holy Roman Empire—of which Voltaire aptly said that it was not an Empire, nor Roman, nor holy—Austria, and not Germany, was the successor.

In the Middle Ages Alsace, even though attached to this Confederation, sought inspiration from France for her culture, art, literature, architecture, scholarship. " As a fact," observes a recent Alsatian writer,[1] " Alsace, even in the Middle Ages, though it spoke a German dialect, was in the orbit of French culture. The Gothic artists who built Strassburg Cathedral came from the Île de France or had learnt their art there. The Alsatian authors who figure in German literature, such as Gottfried of Strassburg, and Fischart, imitated French authors, or initiated their German readers into the courtly life of France. Alsatian scholars studied in Paris, and at all periods many persons conversant with the French tongue were to be found in the cultivated classes." *Mediæval Alsace and France.*

However this may be, supposing that historical grounds be taken as the basis for modern territorial claims, the essential question at once arises—What date is to be regarded as the point of departure ? If former entities and political *Difficulties in historical contention.*

[1] P. A. Helmer, *Alsace under German Rule* (London, 1915), pp. 7, 8 ; *cf.* the same author's *France—Alsace* (Paris, 1916), pp. 36–96 : " L'Alsace sous le régime allemand."

attachments are to be re-established, which Europe is to be set up again (asks Fustel de Coulanges [1] in his effective reply to Mommsen's *Letters*)—that of the seventeenth century, or of the fifteenth, or that of the more distant epoch when ancient Gaul possessed the whole of the Rhine and when Strassburg, Saverne, and Colmar were Roman towns?

Could the German claim to Alsace on historical grounds be entertained, we should at once be confronted with a number of corollaries that would lead us into a maze of absurdities and impossibilities. If modern Germany is entitled to the possession of Alsace-Lorraine because it formerly belonged to the Holy Roman Empire, then she is equally entitled to the possession of Belgium, Switzerland, Northern France, Northern Italy, etc. Adopting the same reasoning, we should have to conclude that England has a legitimate claim to the United States, that Spain may advance a valid claim to the Spanish-American Republics, and so on *ad infinitum*.

Next we come to the question of race, kingship, and ethnical nationality, which, of course, does not necessarily coincide, in the case of a given territory, with the question of early historical association, but which may be, and often is, connected with it. German writers have asserted the claims of their country to Alsace-Lorraine on the ground that the population was of German blood; the following verse expresses this view:

Claims on racial grounds.

> Doch dort an den Vogesen
> Liegt ein verlornes Gut;
> Dort gilt es deutsches Blut
> Vom Höllenjoch zu lösen.

(There, hard by the Vosges, is a lost treasure; there German blood must be delivered from the yoke of hell.)

---

[1] N. Fustel de Coulanges, *L'Alsace, est-elle allemande ou française? Réponse à M. Mommsen* (Paris, 1870), p. 14.

GERMAN CLAIMS

It is pointed out that the Germanic origin of Alsatians is shown in the modern names of persons. An American observer[1] writes thus: "The originally Germanic character of the people of Alsace is plainly shown by the family names. Passing down Rufacherstrasse, a leading street in Colmar, I note these names on the door-plates and signs: Lange, Heilgendorf, Scherrer, Schultz, Weill, Schönbrod, Schaffer, Casper, Roths, Hacker, Didier, Werkemann, Bürger, Spira, Meyer, Pfleger, Wilberger, Klein, Schanzler, Becker, Luttin, Levy, Rueff, Moore, Geegert, Hidgen, Eglensdorfer, Heyne, Schoy, Kayser, Hild, Wertheim, Gerwig, Heimburger, Wyler, Burlen, Albrecht, Schuler, Helmer, Lentz, Blum, Matter, Engasser, Wittersheim.

Names as a criterion.

"In the directory of Mülhausen, the first forty-six names are Aab, Abegy, Abèle, Aberlen, Abermann, Aberth, Abraham, Abrahamsohn, Abry, Abt, Ach, Achenbach, Acker, Ackerer, Ackermann, Adam, Adams, Adelbrecht, Adelhold, Adis, Adler, Adloff, Adehung, Adolph, Adnau, Achen, Aeble, Aeby, Aegister, Aegler, Aeschmann, Agde, Agrippino, Ahr, Ahrens, Aicheler, Aischelmann, Aigle, Aichinger, Aigner, Ailuger, Albanesius, Alber, Albert, Albich, Albinus.

"But two of these (Abèle, Aigle) have a French origin, and one (Adams) is apparently English. Three (Agrippino, Albinesius and Albinus) represent the Teutonised Latin widely spread over Germany in an earlier day. It is worth noting that all the republican or nationalist leaders of Upper Alsace have German names, while in Lorraine, in several cases, German conservatism is marked by names unqualifiedly French."

[1] D. S. Jordan, *Alsace-Lorraine : A Study in Conquest*, 1913 (Indianopolis, 1917), pp. 36–8.

However this may be, from the character of names and from ethnical considerations generally it is possible to draw quite different conclusions. In regard to names there is undoubtedly a tendency for the conquered, subject, or alien inhabitants of a country to assume such names or so modify their own names as to make them similar or akin to those of the conquerors or of the native population as the case may be. One well-known instance will suffice as an illustration, viz. the case of the Jews : in England their names are frequently anglicised ; in Germany they are often germanised ; in Russia they are russified, and so on ; and yet they are all of the same race. Julius Cæsar says he found the territories that are now Alsace-Lorraine inhabited by Gauls ; the German invasions afterwards introduced another racial element ; and a certain fusion between them was also effected. The Celtic type, in fact, subsists in Alsace ; and in Lorraine it appears to predominate ; the presence of the Germanic type does not prove that the country is German. If this were so, we might argue that because the Goths left considerable Germanic traces in Spain when they invaded the country many centuries ago, therefore Spain is to be regarded as more or less germanised, and hence the modern Germans are entitled to lay claim to the parts of Spain thus affected. That the racial criterion cannot be adopted to support claims to territorial proprietorship or dominion is clearly shown by such examples as Belgium, with her Flemish and Walloon elements, and Switzerland, with her different ethnical constituents. If race is to be the determining factor, then Portugal should be absorbed by Spain, Scotland should be separated from England, Posen from Germany, Livonia and Riga from Russia, and so on.

We may apply, too, in regard to the racial claim

GERMAN CLAIMS

an argument similar to that we have already applied in reference to the historical claim, and effect in the former case, as in the latter, a *reductio ad absurdum*. Thus, Alsace was predominantly German before it became largely French; but it was Celtic or Gallic before it became predominantly German; before the Celtic inhabitants there were the prehistoric aborigines; and before the latter there were —presumably—apes. It is in view of such a resulting absurdity that Renan writes: " Avec la philosophie de l'histoire telle que la pratiquent les Allemands il n'y a de légitime de par le monde que le droit des orangs-outangs injustement dépossédés par la perfidie des civilisés." Difficulties in racial claims.

Though the Germans long claimed that Alsace-Lorraine was really a German country, and that the greater part of its population was of true German blood, yet when they "recovered" their "lost brothers" or "lost children" they imposed a large number of restrictions on them, and throughout denied their province the legal status of a German State on the ground that it was not German enough. There is thus the contradiction that Alsace-Lorraine was, on the one hand, wrenched from France because it was alleged to be overwhelmingly German, and was, on the other hand, refused equal treatment because it was strongly anti-German.[1] There is a further contradiction—the opposition of Germany to a plebiscite before the annexation, and the consent to allow the inhabitants an option as to their allegiance. It would therefore appear that it was not really their "lost brothers" and the long-lamented German blood that the Germans had sought to recover, but their country and its resources. Treitschke, however, has

[1] *Cf.* Novicow, *op. cit.*, p. 189.

his reply ready in defence of the annexationist policy—a reply inspired by arrogance and impaired by inconsistency and confusion of thought.

"In view of our obligation to secure the peace of the world," he exclaims, "who will venture to object that the people of Alsace and Lorraine do not want to belong to us? The doctrine of the right of all the branches of the German race to decide on their own destinies, the plausible solution of demagogues without a fatherland, shivers to pieces in presence of the sacred necessity of these great days. These territories are ours by the right of the sword, and we shall dispose of them in virtue of a higher right—the right of the German nation, which will not permit its lost children to remain strangers to the German Empire.[1] We Germans who know Germany and France, know better than these unfortunates themselves what is good for the people of Alsace, who have remained under the misleading influence of their French connection outside the sympathies of new Germany. Against their will we shall restore them to their true selves. . . . Before the nineteenth century closes the world will recognise that the spirits of Erwin von Steinbach and Sebastian Brandt are still alive, and that we were only obeying the dictates of national honour when we made little account of the preferences of the people who live in Alsace to-day."[2] The subsequent history of the provinces under the German régime shows (as we shall see later on [3]) that these high claims and confident predictions were not fulfilled.

<small>Treitschke's arrogant and untenable pretensions.</small>

[1] Treitschke is said to have admitted soon afterwards that the claim in regard to the racial origin of the Alsatians was a mere "swindle"; see *infra*, p. 138.
[2] *Op. cit.*, pp. 105, 106.
[3] See chap. ix, pp. 155 *seq.*

GERMAN CLAIMS 123

With regard to the German claim to Alsace-Lorraine on the ground of language, Mommsen declared[1] in 1870 that the population of Alsace was purely German, with the exception of a few French valleys in the Vosges—the latter comprising only 120 communes with 30,000 inhabitants, the remaining 917 communes with 1,035,102 inhabitants speaking German. "One of our most conscientious political economists calculated, before the war, that but a seventh part of the Alsatians understand French ; and again, but a small part of these use this language in domestic life. The country people and peasants universally speak nothing but German. . . . Here in these valleys you hear our songs and our legends ; and our literature has formed here a nucleus of opposition against Paris. . . ." As to so-called German Lorraine, including part of the department east of the Meurthe and the Moselle and the cantons of Saar, the same writer asserts that until 1751 it conducted all its official affairs in German, and it still preserved this language in its private life. " By the account of the French Minister of Instruction, made out in 1865, in 76 communes of the department of the Meurthe, out of 46,508 inhabitants only 6,870 could speak the French language ; whilst among those who attended the schools, in number 6,800, only 2,400 could be said to speak it correctly. . . . The city and canton of Thionville are completely German."

<small>Claim on ground of language.</small>

To this much too brief account given by Mommsen we may add the following observations both as a supplement and as a correction.[2] From the fourth

[1] *Letters*, etc., pp. 24 *seq.*
[2] *Cf.* C. Pfister, *La limite de la langue française et de la langue allemande en Alsace-Lorraine* (Paris, 1890) ; G. May, *La lutte pour le français en Lorraine avant 1870.—Annales de l'Est publiées par la Faculté des Lettres de l'Université de Nancy* (Paris ; Nancy, 1912).

century to the middle of the first century B.C. both
slopes of the Vosges (including the modern Alsace-Lorraine) were inhabited by Celtic tribes. During the Germanic invasions of the first century B.C. the Triboci established themselves in Lower Alsace among the Mediomatrici, a Celtic tribe. In 72 B.C. the Sequani, another Celtic people, occupying Upper Alsace and the modern Besançon, appealed for aid to the German chieftain, Ariovistus, who took possession of the country of the people he came to help. He was, however, expelled by Cæsar in 58 B.C.; but the Triboci remained. Thus a Germanic tongue was spoken from the frontiers of Sequania to the Sauer. From A.D. 100 to the middle of the fourth century Latin predominated. A little later the Germanic language, already spoken in Alsace, was brought into Lorraine by the barbarian soldiers in the Roman service and by barbarian colonists (the Alemanni). The incursions continuing, the Germanic element increased, and began to prevail over the Latin. After the recall of the Roman troops in the fifth century Alsace was invaded by the barbarians, and in the following century Latin almost disappeared from the country—except in one corner of the Vosges, at Orbey, Sainte-Marie-aux-Mines, and Schirmeck, where Latin took the form of a Romance dialect.[1] In Lorraine the earlier names were replaced by German in the fifth and sixth centuries.

Later, German made progress in Alsace; it predominated in the south near Oberlarg and Lucelle, and gained in the north in the valley of Sainte-Marie-aux-Mines. In the fifteenth century, however, French was the principal language in this valley, though in the following

[1] Pfister, *op. cit.*

century the German population increased—on the one hand there were the Saxon immigrants who came to the silver mines, on the other there were Calvinist refugees. Thus from 1560 to 1789 the Germanic patois supplanted French in these mining districts. In the upper valley of the Bruche a Germanic colony was brought by the Anabaptists of Salm ; but in the fourteenth and sixteenth centuries Swiss peoples, taking refuge in the Schirmeck district, reinforced the Romance element. Thus the progress of German, due to the immigrations, was comparatively small. French had gained a little in Lorraine, in the two upper valleys of the Sarre.[1] Its slow progress in Alsace was due to the neglect of Louis XIV, who, though concerned about religious unity, did nothing for extending the teaching of French ; not a word of French was taught, says M. Pfister, in the villages of Alsace and German Lorraine before 1789.[2] Only the upper classes among the urban populations spoke French, which they acquired in Paris, and not in the universities, which taught in Latin. Writing was done in Gothic, and not in Roman characters. Later, Louis-Philippe introduced French into the schools ; and Napoleon III made systematic provision for its use and teaching. Its expansion, however, was hindered by a portion of the clergy, who feared the language of Voltaire, and respected German as the language of the Catechism. Nevertheless, French advanced, especially in the towns ; but in 1870 it had not generally overtaken German.[3] After that date, as we shall see later, the latter language made further progress under the German régime. Had the annexation been deferred for a time there is no doubt that French would have become the predominating language.[4]

[1] Pfister, op. cit., p. 39.   [2] Ibid., p. 40.   [3] Ibid.   [4] May, op. cit., p. 8

In a word, before the union of Alsace to France, the Alsatians, or the greater part of them, spoke German, which continued after the union to be the predominating language of the province. Before the union of the Duchy of Lorraine to France the greater part of its population spoke French ; but in about a third of the territory, known as German Lorraine, very little French was spoken. After France acquired the Duchy the Germanic dialect continued to be used in German Lorraine in families, in business relationships, in schools and in religious services, but not for official purposes. Two points are here to be noted : first, German Lorraine would, till 1870, have been more appropriately described as German-speaking Lorraine, for the use of the language did not necessarily make the people German in thought, feeling, or usages ; secondly, their language (like that of Alsace) was not the classical German, but a Germanic patois.

Moreover, in 1871, Germany annexed not only Alsace and German-speaking Lorraine, but also a considerable portion of French-speaking territory, *e.g.* the *pays messin* : Metz always spoke French, though it is now predominantly German.

Position of the pays messin.

Mommsen admitted that to take this town from France could not be defended on the ground of language, sentiment, etc. "In possessing ourselves of Metz," he writes, "there will be a difficulty, as every one will see, in taking a French province, however small, ruled by French laws and sentiments, and making it German ; and public opinion, when it classes Metz with Alsace and German Lorraine, I think makes a mistake." [1]

From the above exposition of the language question, it can by no means be inferred that the use of a par-

[1] *Letters*, pp. 30, 31.

GERMAN CLAIMS

ticular language in a certain locality is either a valid criterion for determining nationality in the proper significance of the term (not merely in its ethnical sense), or an admissible basis for founding territorial claims. In the first place, the argument as to priority is here also applicable: from what date are we to start in asserting the predominance of this or that language in a given country? Secondly, if Germany might claim Alsace-Lorraine in 1870, because of the predominance of Germanic dialects in these provinces at that date, then she might just as legitimately have then claimed also (and may claim even now) various other countries or distinct parts of countries where Germanic languages prevail, e.g. Belgium (Flemish), Holland, a large part of Switzerland, Luxemburg and Austria. Similarly, England might claim the United States; and France might demand a great part of Switzerland, of Belgium, and of Canada. The use in a country of a common language no doubt tends to cement the nation; but it certainly cannot be taken as the characteristic test of nationality. That Germany can, when it suits her, disregard historical, racial, and linguistic considerations is shown by the annexation of a part of Poland, which was Slav in race and language. _{Language as a criterion.}

Nationality, indeed, depends much more on a people's common sentiment, aspirations, ideals, interests, remembrances, and desire for unity and for a common social life. Intention and will and actual facts are of far greater consequence than the fortuitous circumstances relating to distant and long-forgotten origins. It is for these vital reasons, and not in virtue of ethnographical and philological conclusions, that men are willing to live together, to fight side by side, to die for each other. The fact that _{Principle of nationality.}

the *Marseillaise* was composed and first sung in Strassburg and stirred the blood of its citizens possesses a greater significance than the fact that in this or that corner of the city a Teutonic dialect was spoken. To wrest a population from a country and a political system to which it is attached by ties of affinity, to which it wishes to remain attached, and thrust it against its will into another country and political system which it regards as alien can never be justified by inferences drawn from a state of things that existed in the past. Human beings are not chattels; no law and no morality, other than those of savages and barbarians, can treat one group of men as the objects of transactions, as the pawns of a game, carried on between other groups of men. The only sense in which the principle of nationality may legitimately apply is where a province or a population refuses obedience to a foreign pretender; it may not be invoked by a foreign pretender as a ground for forcible annexation. Thus the principle of nationality did not entitle Piedmont to conquer Milan and Venice; but it gave Milan and Venice the right to liberate themselves from Austria and unite themselves voluntarily to Piedmont. " Ce principe," said Fustel de Coulanges in 1870 to Germany, " peut bien donner à l'Alsace un droit ; mais il ne vous en donne aucun sur elle. . . . Il constitue un droit pour les faibles ; il n'est pas un prétexte pour les ambitieux." [1] Whatever Germanic elements of race and language Alsace may have possessed, it was for a long time French in its real nationality and its *sentiment de patrie*.

Even as long ago as 1709, at a critical moment for France resulting from the War of the Spanish Succession, the Prussian ambassador at the Court of France,

---

[1] *Op. cit.*, pp. 6, 7.

CHAPTER VIII

GERMAN CLAIMS TO ALSACE-LORRAINE — ALLEGED GROUNDS OF ANNEXATION : (*b*) NECESSITY ; CONQUEST AS CONFIRMED BY THE TREATY OF FRANKFORT

Claim on ground of necessity—Economic necessity · Outlet for overcrowded Germany ?—Natural deficiencies of Germany. Political necessity : German unity and the Reichsland. Military necessity : Frontier security—Mommsen on Metz. Conquest as confirmed by the Treaty of Frankfort : Prussia's territorial ambitions—Bismarck's admission in 1862—German views as to "right of conquest"—Recent growth of opinion as to conquest—Ground of illegitimacy of conquest—When conquest justified—International law as it existed in 1871. Binding force of Treaty of Frankfort—Supersession of one treaty by another.

HAVING examined in the preceding chapter the German claims to Alsace-Lorraine on the grounds of earlier association, race and nationality, and use of Germanic dialects, and having shown their fundamentally irrelevant and untenable nature, we have now to look at the claims based on the further grounds of, first, necessity, and, secondly, conquest as confirmed by the Treaty of Frankfort.

Claims on ground of necessity. The first of these grounds, necessity, may be looked at from three points of view—economic, political, military.

Economic necessity. With regard to the question of economic necessity, several German writers had urged, before the annexation of Alsace-Lorraine, that the additional territory would serve as a kind of colonial outlet for the rapidly increasing population in Germany. But this contention is rather fatuous, considering the principle of public right, whereby a population is entitled to be governed by the institutions that it accepts freely, and may not be detached from one State and attached to another without its voluntary consent. To claim a province on the ground that it once belonged to us is illegitimate ; a province and its people are not an object of possession to be restored—for they belong to themselves. The province is not *owned* by the State to which it is united ; it is simply associated with it. The only reason why France wished to retain Alsace was that Alsace valiantly showed its desire to remain with France. France, as Fustel de Coulanges said aptly, did not fight in 1870 to force it to remain with her ; she fought to prevent Germany from forcing it to leave her.[1]

[1] *Ibid.*, p. 16.

the revolutionary wars Alsatian patriotism gave France distinguished leaders like Kellermann, the victor of Valmy, and Kléber, the victor of Maestricht, Altenkirchen, and the hero of the Egyptian campaign; during the wars of the Empire, Alsace produced more generals and men than any other French province—such names as Rapp, Lefebvre, Sirhanun, Berckheim, Hengel, and others are a permanent record of the attachment of Alsace to its adopted country. "From that time," said Fustel de Coulanges in 1870, addressing himself to Germany, "Alsace has followed all our destinies; it has lived our life. All that we thought, it thought; all that we felt, it felt. It has shared our victories and our reverses, our glory and our mistakes, all our joys and all our sorrows. It has had nothing in common with you. In its eyes France is its fatherland, and Germany an alien country. . . . If your reasonings tell you that Alsace ought to have a German heart, my eyes and my ears assure me that it has a French heart."[1] He reminds the Germans, too, of the determined Alsatian resistance soon after the opening of the campaign and the reverses of the French armies; whether the valiant defenders spoke a Germanic tongue or not, they were the compatriots of the French and not of the Germans. Did the German soldiers who bombarded Strassburg, aimed at the cathedral, set fire to the New Temple, the library, hospitals and houses, feel that they were the countrymen of those they attacked so furiously and mercilessly?[2]

Voluntary fusion between French and Alsatians.

Principle of public right.

In conclusion, we may say, with the writer just quoted, that pretensions based on questions of language, race, origin, matter little in comparison with the claim resting on the supreme

[1] *Op. cit.*, pp. 10–11.   [2] *Ibid.*, p. 13.

GERMAN CLAIMS

Baron Schmettau, presented, in the name of his master Frederick I, a memorandum to the plenipotentiaries at the Hague, wherein he declared that the Alsatians were more French than the Parisians, that they were ever ready to take up arms on behalf of the King of France to repel the German invaders, and that they were united to France by such strong ties of affection that they would sooner convert their country into a desert than let Germans take possession of it. " L'Alsace n'est pas à comparer à la Franche-Comté au point de vue de l'utilité que les Hauts Alliés en peuvent retirer. Car, outre qu'il est notoire que les habitants de l'Alsace sont plus français que les Parisiens et que le roi de France est si sûr de leur affection à son service et à sa gloire, qu'il leur ordonne de se fournir de pistolets, de hallebardes, d'épées, de poudre et de plomb toutes les fois que le bruit court que les Allemands ont dessein de passer le Rhin, et qu'ils courent en foule sur les bords du Rhin pour en empêcher ou du moins disputer le passage à la nation germanique, au péril évident de leurs propres vies, comme s'ils allaient au triomphe ; en sorte que l'Empereur et l'Empire doivent être persuadés, qu'en reprenant l'Alsace seule, sans recouvrer la Franche-Comté, ils ne trouveront qu'un amas de terre morte pour l'auguste Maison d'Autriche et qui couvera un brasier d'amour pour la France et de fervents désirs pour le retour de son règne en ce pays, auquel ils donneront toujours conseil, aide et faveur dans l'occasion." [1]

Attachment of Alsace to France.

This union was definitively consecrated at the French Revolution, when a complete fusion between the French and the Alsatian people was effected. During

[1] G. de Lamberty, *Mémoires pour servir à l'histoire du XVIIIe siècle*, 14 vols. (Amsterdam, 1734–40), vol. v. p. 282.

GERMAN CLAIMS

comparatively small area of the provinces—about 5,600 square miles, as compared with Germany's 209,000 square miles.

Moreover, events after the acquisition of the territory showed that crowded Germany gained very little indeed in this respect. The immigrant Germans constitute a small part of the total population, except in Strassburg (which is about two-fifths German) and Metz (about three-fifths German); in such important industrial centres as Mülhausen and Colmar the native element easily preponderates. Even in Strassburg and Metz, as an American writer says, the germanisation in this respect is scarcely more marked than that of various manufacturing cities outside Germany, e.g. Milwaukee or St. Louis in the United States, or São Paulo in Brazil; with the development of German industries, Strassburg and Metz, like other German manufacturing towns, received a substantial accession of unskilled "cheap labour," much of it temporary, from Poland and Italy. The lands of Alsace still belong to the Alsatians.[1] Furthermore, it has been calculated, that in the twenty-five years after the annexation the total number of Germans who settled in Alsace-Lorraine, including the considerable body of officials and their families, was far less than that of the emigrants from Germany in a single year.[2]

As an outlet for over-crowded Germany.

The provision for an outlet for the crowded districts of Germany being necessarily insignificant, other economic reasons were advanced to show the necessity of incorporating the territory—the fertility of its soil and the favourable configuration of its surface were deemed to be an indis-

Natural deficiencies of Germany.

---
[1] Jordan, op. cit., pp. 63, 64.
[2] Cf. J. Heimweh, La Guerre et la frontière du Rhin (Paris, 1895), p. 84.

pensable compensation for the natural deficiencies of Germany. This is an argument to which Treitschke had recourse in the pamphlet issued in 1870 during the war.[1] "Our sober judgment," he said, " cannot refuse to admit that nature has dealt with our country much more like a step-mother than a mother. The singularly barren outline of our shore coast-line on the North Sea, and the course of most of our German rivers and hill-chains are just as unfavourable to political unity as they are to commerce. . . . But here, in Alsace, there is a real German district, the soil of which, under favouring skies, is rich with blessings such as only a very few spots in the Upper Rhenish Palatinate and the mountain country of Baden enjoy. The unusual configuration of the country has made it possible to pierce canals through gaps in the mountains —magnificent waterways from the Rhine to the basin of the Rhône and of the Seine—such as German ground scarcely ever admits. We are by no means rich enough to be able to renounce so precious a possession."[2]

An argument of this kind would be intelligible if it were a case of the contemplated acquisition of the provinces by fair, just, and pacific means, e.g. by purchase, exchange, etc. As it was, it was no more than the argument of a burglar who wants another's property. So that we need only say that neither the deficiencies of a country, in regard to its natural features or possessions, nor its inadequacy for accommodating its population, can possibly constitute a legitimate and valid reason, juridically or morally, for forcibly dismembering another country and seizing a part of it.

---

[1] *Was fordern wir von Frankreich ?* (Berlin, 1870). Eng. trans. in *Germany, France, Russia, and Islam* (London, 1915).
[2] English trans., *loc. cit.*, p. 113.

GERMAN CLAIMS 135

Next, as to the political aspect of necessity. Many Germans claimed that the acquisition of Alsace-Lorraine was essential for consolidating the German peoples and for effecting the unity of the Empire. "When our united strength," observes Treitschke, "has won that outwork of the German State, which is now in such mortal peril, the nation will have pledged its soul to the idea of unity. The resistance of the new province will strengthen the impulse of our policy towards unity, and constrain all sensible men to range themselves in disciplined loyalty behind the Prussian throne."[1]

<small>Political necessity.</small>

In reply to this contention we may say with Novicow, the Russian writer already referred to more than once, that the annexation of Alsace-Lorraine was not at all necessary for securing German unity, which, indeed, could have been established without the war of 1870. And even if such a war as that of 1870 was really necessary for attaining this object, it does not follow that the dismemberment of France was also indispensable. The conduct of the war by the German States in common was one thing; the spoliation of France was a totally different thing. Already, after the victory of Wörth and the capitulation of Sedan, the peoples of Bavaria, Würtemberg, and Baden were united against the "common enemy"; and hence it was possible to conclude a reasonable peace on the conditions soon afterwards proposed by Jules Favre, including the principle of "no annexation." It has been suggested that Bismarck insisted on the abandonment of the French provinces not for the purpose of increasing German territory, but with the view of establishing along the western German frontier such a fear of

<small>German unity did not depend on the Reichsland.</small>

[1] *Loc. cit,* p. 111.

renewed conflict as would necessitate and maintain the union of the German peoples. This view is superficially plausible, but far-fetched and inadmissible. The fear of a subsequent conflict with France could not have induced Bavaria, say, to enter a German Confederation, if she was really opposed to such a system. Had Bavaria been opposed to the establishment of such a system, and had she been resolved to preserve her separation and independence, she could easily have allied herself with France, as against the other German States that were bent on a union, in order to maintain and secure her political status. The South German States, indeed, had had no great love for Prussia; several times in the course of the nineteenth century they declared their preference for France. They agreed to form part of the German Empire, and remained in it, not because they feared a rupture with a reinvigorated France, but because such a policy was desired by them and was calculated to promote their interests. The theory that Alsace-Lorraine furnished the necessary cement for binding the Empire, in view of possible French aggression, involves a confession of the then non-existence of German nationality. "Dire qu'il [the Empire] se tient uni seulement par terreur de la France, c'est *nier* l'existence d'une nationalité allemande."[1] On the contrary, Germans of all States have always loudly proclaimed their German nationality; whatever German pretensions may be disputed, this claim needs no proof. So that it is absurd to suppose, as Novicow well remarks, that it needed French bayonets to preserve the strength of this sentiment of common nationality.

Further, apart from considerations of political

[1] Novicow, *op. cit.*, p. 25.

GERMAN CLAIMS

theory, dictates of public policy and national sentiment, actual events in the Franco-German War showed that the annexation of Alsace-Lorraine was not a *sine qua non* of German unity. We find, for example, that the arrangement between Prussia and Bavaria for the establishment of the Empire was concluded on November 25, 1870, and that the letter of the King of Bavaria to William I suggesting that the latter should assume the title and position of German Emperor was delivered on the following December 3. Thus the complete unity of Germany was already assured some three months before the Preliminaries of Versailles were signed, wherein the cession of Alsace-Lorraine was stipulated. King William was proclaimed Emperor at Versailles on January 18, 1871—an act which was at once a solemn recognition of unity on the part of the constituent members of the Empire, and an open declaration thereof to the world. To dismember France after this political achievement was not necessary—however auspicious and appropriate a conquest might seem to a newly created Emperor and a newly founded Empire. " The Emperor and I would be guillotined," Bismarck is reported to have said, " if we returned to Berlin without Alsace and Lorraine."

Finally, assuming that the annexation of Alsace-Lorraine *was* necessary for securing German unity, it does not by any means follow that the German States were entitled morally or legally to tear it away from France in order to promote their own interests.

The third aspect of the alleged necessity for the annexation relates to military security and self-defence. Thus Treitschke, speaking of the reparation that is to be exacted from " the disturber of the peace of nations," says : " What is demanded by

<small>Military necessity.</small>

justice is, at the same time, absolutely necessary for our security." [1] In his pamphlet of 1870 the German historian, like other clamorous German claimants, called for the annexation of Alsace-Lorraine (as has already been pointed out) for reasons of race and nationality. Two years later, however, in a conversation with M. Monod on the alleged German origin of the Alsatians, Treitschke is reported to have observed : " All this is a swindle. Even if the Alsatians had been Japanese, we would have annexed them just the same, because we had need of Metz and Strassburg from a strategic point of view." [2] Bismarck cared little for ethnological and linguistic arguments and for the kindred lucubrations of the German professorial class-room ; without resorting to any subterfuge he openly avowed the main, if not the only, reason for requiring the cession of the provinces—viz. military strategy. Metz and Strassburg were sally-ports from France into Germany ; therefore those, together with their surrounding territories, must be taken away from France. It has already been pointed out that he had, and for some time continued to have, doubts about Metz ; but he yielded to the demands of the military staff, who emphasised that the possession of this town was alone worth two army corps. From the open doors of Strassburg and Metz the French were said to have invaded German territory twenty-three times ; these doors must therefore be shut against them.

A German historian, whom we have quoted in the preceding chapter, has thus recently explained the true reason for the forcible acquisition of Alsace-Lorraine : " The motive for the annexations," he says, " is often misrepresented. Every-

Frontier security.

[1] *Op. cit.,* p. 100.
[2] G. Monod, *Allemands et Français* (Paris, 1872), p. 151.

GERMAN CLAIMS

one knows the famous words spoken by Leopold von Ranke, the historian, to Thiers in the autumn of 1870, after the fall of Napoleon III: 'It is against Louis XIV that we have now to wage war'; that is to say, we have now to fight against the country which has for centuries looked upon the defenceless condition of the Germans as the strongest bulwark of her own hegemony on the Continent. Bismarck's motive for the annexation lay in no faded memories of past imperial history upon which national enthusiasts dwelt, but in the real and pressing necessity for permanent military defence of German unity against all attacks from the west—a unity which had been threatened, so lately as 1866, by the preposterous demand of Napoleon III for the cession of Mainz and a portion of the left bank of the Rhine. This necessity alone impelled him to shift the frontier across the Rhine into the Vosges Mountains, for southern Germany had been long enough at the mercy of French artillery. For this reason too, and for this alone, he decided, almost under compulsion from the generals, to acquire the fortress of Metz, situated in the French-speaking area, in addition to Alsace, which, with the large German element in its population, might be expected to become gradually assimilated to the Empire. The annexation, far from being a deed done on the spur of the moment by the caprice of an individual, was the inevitable outcome for both nations of several centuries of their history. . . ."[1]

Mommsen, writing in 1870 when the annexationist demands were put forward on various grounds, pointed out that, whilst the annexation of Metz, unlike that of Alsace and German Lorraine, could not be justified by reason of nationality, senti- *Mommsen on Metz.*

[1] H Oncken, in *Camb. Mod. Hist.*, vol. xii. pp. 135-6.

ment, language, etc., it might none the less be justified on the ground of frontier security. He did not indeed state this conclusion explicitly ; he merely said that many Germans insisted thereon ; and he, for his part, preferred to leave the matter undiscussed and to rely upon the "able hands which hold the destinies of the two nations." [1]

Finally, we now have the declaration of William I himself, made in a letter, October 26, 1870, to the Empress Eugénie. (This letter was made public by M. Pichon at the beginning of March, 1918.) " After having made immense sacrifices for her defence," observed the German sovereign, " Germany wishes to be sure that the next war will find her better prepared to repel the aggression which we may be certain will be made as soon as France will have prepared her forces and formed allies. That alone is the deplorable consideration, and not a desire to enlarge our country, of which the territory is big enough, which obliges me to insist on the cession of territories which has no other object than to make more remote the point of departure of the French armies that in the future will come to attack us."

Having shown that neither economic nor political necessity could lawfully sanction the forcible annexation of Alsace-Lorraine, it remains to consider whether military necessity, in the sense explained above, could justify it—for it was this military necessity that constituted the bulwark of the German claims. The consideration of this question involves an examination of the broader question of conquest in general ; for after 1871 Germany held that, whatever validity her different claims possessed, the annexed provinces became hers by right of conquest, recognised and con-

[1] *Letters, loc. cit.,* p. 31.

GERMAN CLAIMS

firmed by the Treaty of Frankfort, which settled the question once for all in the eyes of international law.

The underlying impulse that led to the dismemberment of France was Prussia's lust for territorial aggrandisement. Seldom had the wars of Prussia been waged purely for the vindication of national honour or for the reparation of wrong; whatever the cause and whatever the ostensible purpose might be, the fundamental aim of her wars has frequently, if not invariably, been the acquisition of territory and the extension of dominion. In regard to political theory the modern German mind appears to have impregnated itself with Machiavellian conceptions: for Machiavelli and his disciples the predominant object of politics was the aggrandisement of the State, and for them war was merely a continuation of politics carried out by more violent and more drastic methods. This is the frankly avowed view of such German writers as Clausewitz, Lasson, Jähns, Von der Goltz, Treitschke, Bernhardi, and others. The glory, dignity, greatness, and prestige of a State are by them measured by the area of territory and the number of subjects governed. An idea of this kind was in the mind of the late Emperor Francis Joseph when he said on one occasion : " I want to end my reign with as many square kilometres as I began it."[1] What he lost in Lombardy and Venetia he made up in Bosnia and the Herzegovina. A victorious sovereign took possession of territory to show, too, that he had no fear of the vanquished; for to renounce conquests implied a respect for the rights of man—but mediæval and traditional records considered such respect as a " revo-

Prussia's territorial ambitions.

[1] Cf. *Le Matin*, January 24, 1909; cited Novicow, *op. cit.*, p. 28.

lutionary" tendency that must be repressed.¹ To this school of thought belonged the Prussian sovereign Frederick the Great, who once said : " Let us first take; we shall find jurists afterwards to legitimise our rights."

The territorial ambitions of Prussia were fully recognised by Talleyrand at the time of the Vienna Congress ; he realised her disposition to fasten on any pretext, to stop at no scruple, to measure law and right by her own interests in seeking to augment her dominions ; and he therefore emphasised the absolute necessity of preserving all the small States of Europe : " En Allemagne, la domination à combattre est celle de la Prusse : la constitution physique de sa monarchie lui fait de l'ambition une sorte de nécessité ; tout prétexte lui est bon, nul scrupule ne l'arrête, la convenance est son droit ; il est donc nécessaire de mettre un frein à son ambition en restreignant d'abord autant qu'il est possible son état de possession en Allemagne par la conservation de tous les petits états et par l'agrandissement des états moyens et en paralysant son influence par l'organisation fédérale."

Talleyrand on Prussian ambition.

Thinking of this Vienna settlement and of the Prussian annexationist policy, Bismarck observed in his noteworthy speech of September 30, 1862 : " Prussia must collect her strength for the propitious moment which has more than once been allowed to slip by. The frontiers assigned to Prussia by the Congress of Vienna are not good for a healthy and strong State. It is not by speeches and the votes of majorities that the questions of our time will be settled; it is by iron and blood." These words were a fitting prelude to the subsequent war

Bismarck's admission in 1862.

¹ Novicow, *ibid.*

GERMAN CLAIMS

enterprises of Prussia and her wholesale annexations. Bismarck found a worthy colleague in Moltke, who did not hesitate to declare that conquest was in conformity with the order of things established by God.

This view was elaborately set forth in 1871 by Adolf Lasson.[1] It is only in recent times, he says, that the "right of conquest" has begun to be doubted. The theory that conquest is robbery and brigandage is based on the principle of the inviolable character of frontiers. These ideas have a significance only in so far as States are considered the property of these sovereigns. In free States the condition of things is different. Each State that goes to war with another State puts its own existence at stake, and must therefore submit to the losses entailed by defeat. The conqueror is empowered to act towards the vanquished as he deems fit, because the latter would have proceeded in a similar manner had he been the victor. A conquest is justified only when it is in the interests of the conquering State; then it is as reasonable as any other measure that is dictated by the "reason of State."[2] It is really unnecessary to refute such arbitrary assertions and gratuitous assumptions, which are repugnant to civilised mankind and to the juridical consciousness of the family of nations; the reasoning based thereon is as fallacious as it is superficial. What difference is there between an autocratic sovereign making a conquest, and a republic making one? The evil inflicted is the same in both cases. Does the possession of liberty in a republic confer the right to violate the liberty of a neighbouring country? If a conqueror may do what he likes with the conquered, it means that

German views as to "right of conquest."

[1] A. Lasson, *Princip und Zukunft des Völkerrechts* (Berlin, 1871).
[2] *Ibid.*, p. 82.

the conquered becomes a *thing* of the conqueror: this is a negation of right, and not right. To speak therefore of a right of conquest is, strictly speaking, a contradiction : right as between States necessarily implies the existence of States, so that to put an end forcibly to the existence of a State is inevitably to step outside the sphere of right.[1]

To make up for the deficiencies of an abstract theory of conquest German writers point, in defence of the practice, to the various notable precedents furnished by European history. The French Revolution dealt a blow at the right of conquest, but in the wars of the Empire it was resumed. The succeeding half century (1815-1864), however, saw a markedly progressive movement. Many notable territorial modifications were, indeed, effected in this interval, for example, in the case of Greece, Belgium, the Danubian States, France, Italy; but these were all in conformity with the desire of the populations concerned, and were carried out in their interest. The more recent examples that Prussia could cite in 1871 were her own, viz. those of 1864 and 1866 ; but those created by Prussia's own proceedings could not legitimately be invoked by her as valid precedents.

<small>Recent growth of opinion as to conquest.</small>

The defenders of conquest and annexation ask, What law does international jurisprudence prescribe that prohibits the practice ? It is true there is no written law against it ; but modern nations feel that there is none the less an unwritten law, inasmuch as such a prohibition is of necessity implied in the universally recognised principle that States and peoples possess the fundamental and inalienable right to dispose of their own destiny.

<small>Written and unwritten law.</small>

[1] Cf. Novicow, *op. cit.*, pp. 208, 209.

GERMAN CLAIMS

This principle must have been recognised even in Germany after the events of 1848 and the parliament of Frankfort ; and subsequent events further enlightened European public opinion on the question. A plebiscite came to be regarded as an indispensable condition for sanctioning an annexation. Thus was the unity of Italy established, and thus were Nice and Savoy added to France. That the plebiscite in the case of the latter was not (as some German writers have contended) a mere piece of jugglery on the part of Napoleon III is shown by the loyalty and attachment of these provinces to France in the hour of her supreme agony in 1870 ; not only was there not the least sign of revolt, there was not even a protest against the annexation of 1860.[1]

The recognition by the modern world of the intrinsic illegitimacy of conquest and forcible incorporation is based ultimately on the axiom that a man, a group of men, or a nation cannot be the possession of another man, group of men, or nation—an axiom all the more applicable to and ineradicable from a society of Christian peoples. To deny this axiom is a negation of law and order, and amounts to an apotheosis of brute force and international anarchy. The advance of modern civilisation is irrevocably in the direction of liberty and equality ; a world catastrophe like the present may reveal here and there retrograde tendencies, but it has shown that nearly all the nations of the world are prepared to face slaughter and devastation rather than abandon their loyalty and devotion to the sacred cause of justice and right, freedom, and equality, rather than give up the right to dispose of their own destinies.

Ground of illegitimacy of conquest.

Further, if in the case of an annexation of another

[1] As to the question of plebiscite see further *infra*, chap. xvii.

State's territory and population, no assimilation or *moral* conquest has been brought about in a considerable period of time, the policy of the annexing Power stands condemned as much as its violation of the rights of the annexed population. To drag alien bodies within the circle of a State is a proceeding that is deprecated even by Treitschke. In a lecture on the nature of the State, he observed in reference to Napoleon's policy: " It was a sin against the spirit of history that the rich diversity of kindred peoples should be changed into the dreary uniformity of a world-empire. Such a naked policy of conquest in the long run destroys its own instruments . . . it is a huge blunder. . . . It presumes to take possession of countries which cannot be fitted into the national State as living members." And yet at other times he spoke with contempt of little nations, and of the expediency of more powerful neighbours to absorb them. We have already referred to the doubts and apprehensions of Bismarck in regard to the annexation of Metz and the *pays messin*. Many German writers have been mentioned as supporting the alleged right of conquest; there were other German publicists and writers, however—*e.g.* Bebel, Liebknecht, Mommsen— who declared in 1870 and 1871 that conquest is illegitimate and indefensible. Thus Mommsen defended the German demand for Alsace-Lorraine on the ground that it involved a restoration and not a mere conquest. " If this were a matter of conquest," he said, " the case might reasonably alarm the nations, for every conquest is a crime against the rights of nations—to trample upon one nation is to offend all. . . . If these French provinces, with a German nationality, belong again politically to Germany, there will be no infringement of

GERMAN CLAIMS

European political equilibrium."[1] We may concede that the eminent historian sincerely believed the annexation of Alsace-Lorraine to be no more than a "restoration," by reason of its earlier association, nationality, and language. The weakness and inapplicability of these grounds have already been shown. As to his statement that the annexation would not infringe European equilibrium, subsequent facts proved that his historical vision and judgment of policy erred most grievously : for there is scarcely any other act in European history that infringed and endangered the equilibrium to such an alarming extent.

As a last resource, Germans claim that even if conquest is unjustifiable generally, it is justified when there has been serious provocation on the part of the defeated State. Thus they hold that France was the aggressor in 1870, that she would have annexed German territory had she then been victorious, and that Germany was entitled to take possession of French territory as the reward of her victory and as the price of the aggressor's defeat. It has already been pointed out that Bismarck calculated that the French had invaded German territory on twenty-three separate occasions. He therefore felt doubly justified in taking away those districts which contained the sally-ports of invasion. In many quarters other than German it was believed that Louis Napoleon was really the aggressor, and that his conduct gave the victor —to use the phrase of the Duke of Argyll—"a right to annex conformably to the ancient acknowledged right of nations in successful wars."[2] Gladstone appears also to have been con-

When conquest justified.

[1] *Letters*, etc.
[2] Lord Morley, *The Life of W. E. Gladstone*, 3 vols. (London, 1903), vol. ii, p. 347.

vinced of "the deep culpability of France," and whilst he did not altogether differ from the Duke of Argyll, he condemned the "violent laceration" on the ground that the people of Alsace-Lorraine were attached to their country, and on general political grounds—viz. that such European complications would result therefrom as would imperil the peace of the Continent.[1] On the assumption that France was the aggressor, Treitschke does not hesitate to pronounce in favour of annexation —a pronouncement that is couched in extravagant language : "If a reckless robber-war like this is to cost that frivolous people nothing more than a war indemnity, the cynical jesters, who worship chance and fortune as the only governing powers among the nations, and laugh at the rights of States as a dream of kind-hearted ideologues, would be proved to be in the right. The sense of justice to Germany demands the lessening of France."[2]

We have now examined all the grounds of the German claims to Alsace-Lorraine—early association, nationality and race, language, economic necessity, political necessity, military necessity, conquest consequent on alleged French aggression—and we have already shown that all these grounds save the last are untenable.

As to the last, we must have regard to what the international law as it existed in 1871 said on the subject. This can be summed up briefly in a quotation taken from a recent work of the present writer[3] : "Perhaps the only cases where a right of conquest may be pleaded are

International law as it existed in 1871.

[1] Lord Morley, *The Life of W. E. Gladstone*, 3 vols. (London, 1903), vol. ii, pp. 346-8.
[2] *Germany, France, Russia, and Islam* (1915), p. 100.
[3] C. Phillipson, *Termination of War and Treaties of Peace*, pp. 30, 31.

GERMAN CLAIMS

where the people of a country are given to savagery, cannibalism, inhuman practices, or where in a war of self-defence it is found absolutely indispensable in the interests of general and more enduring peace to take away from an aggressive State a portion of its territory. As Fiore observes [1] : ' La conquête d'un territoire ne peut pas être par elle-même une condition suffisante pour exiger la cession du territoire conquis quand le droit du vainqueur n'existe pas. Le vainqueur pourra imposer cette cession, quand elle sera justifiée par des conditions évidentes de moralité, et par un interêt général d'assurer la paix.'" If a conquest, made on such grounds, is supported by the assent of the political and legislative authority of the country from which the territory is taken, by means of a treaty of peace signed as a bilateral transaction, then it is valid in the eye of international law, however it be deprecated and condemned by international morality and international politics.

Now we cannot enter here into the question of the Ems telegram and into the allegations that are sometimes brought forward that Napoleon was thereby wrongfully entrapped by Bismarck. In 1870 it was the belief throughout Europe that France was the aggressor, and that belief has generally prevailed since. Assuming, then, the belief to be founded on fact, we must conclude that the annexation of Alsace-Lorraine after its conquest, and its formal cession by the Treaty of Frankfort, was a valid act transferring the legal title of France thereto to Germany.

Conquest as recognised in a treaty.

Such an eminent authority as Lord Stowell maintained even that a treaty of cession was not indispen-

---

[1] P. Fiore, *Nouveau droit international public*, 2nd ed.; traduit de l'italien par C. Antoine. 3 vols. (Paris, 1880); § 1696.

sable to validate a conquest. Thus when Heligoland fell into British possession by conquest, and before its formal cession by the Treaty of Kiel, 1814, he held that the island in the circumstances became rightfully the property of the British Crown, and that a conqueror was entitled to alienate domains as soon as he acquired firm possession. "No point," he said, "is more clearly settled in the courts of common law than that a conquered country forms immediately part of the King's dominions."[1] This pronouncement must be taken subject to the qualifications implied in "firm possession": some time must elapse in order to allow the conqueror's claim to ripen, and to obtain or enforce definitively the acquiescence of the defeated country and the recognition of the conquest by third States. And such acquiescence and recognition are ensured by a treaty of cession, or a treaty of peace stipulating the cession of the territory concerned.

That conquest followed by such a treaty confers a good and lawful title has also been recognised by the American Courts.[2]

The same view is held by practically all international jurists.[3] We must add here, however, that due account must be taken of the recent development of universal public opinion—the father of public law—which is strongly against the forcible annexation of territory on any grounds whatever.

[1] *The Foltina* (1814), 1 Dodson, 450–51; referring to Campbell *v.* Hall (1774), Cowper, 208.

[2] U.S. *v.* Hayward (1815), 2 Gallison, 485; U.S. *v.* Rice (1819), 4 Wheaton, 246; American Insurance Co. *v.* Canter (1828), 1 Peters, 511.

[3] It is beyond the limits of our space to cite more than one or two leading modern representatives· J. C. Bluntschli, *Das moderne Völkerrecht* (Nördlingen, 1872); French translation by C. Lardy, *Le Droit international codifié*, (Paris, 1895), § 286; C. Calvo, *Le Droit international, théorique et pratique*. 6 vols., 5th ed. (Paris, 1896); vol. v. § 3141.

GERMAN CLAIMS

Further, the Treaty of Frankfort must be regarded as possessing binding force from the moment ratifications were exchanged (May 20, 1871) till the moment it is superseded by another formal treaty. No such formal treaty has yet been concluded; therefore, notwithstanding the existence of the present war, the Treaty of Frankfort retains its legal validity.[1] It does not belong to the class of treaties that are annulled *ipso facto* on the outbreak of war between their signatories, nor to the class of treaties suspended during the continuance of hostilities. A treaty of peace, involving a cession of territory, delimitation of boundaries, creation of servitudes, etc., is a dispositive or transitory treaty, which establishes a permanent condition of territorial rights, and cannot be affected by war between the parties thereto. From the point of view of international law and practice it is just as binding during war as treaties entered into expressly for the event of war, or general law-making treaties, like the Hague Conventions, the Declaration of Paris, 1856, the Declaration of St. Petersburg, 1868, or treaties effecting permanent international settlements, like neutralisation treaties, and so on. This is a well-established principle of international law: it is accepted and acted on by States, emphasised by jurists, and declared by courts of law.[2]

It appears to be thought in some quarters that a treaty imposing humiliating conditions, especially so on a great Power, is not a moral engagement which such Power is obliged to observe: whence it would follow that the Treaty of Frankfort, whereby France

Binding force of Treaty of Frankfort.

[1] As to the binding character of treaties of peace see Phillipson, *op. cit.*, pp. 162 *seq.* *Cf.* the declaration of the Bishop of Strassburg, *infra*, pp. 186, 187.

[2] As to the effect of war on different classes of treaties, see Phillipson, *op. cit.*, pp. 250-68.

was compelled to cede a portion of her territory—to her great humiliation—might be disregarded by her whenever she thought fit to denounce it. But nearly every treaty of peace imposes disadvantageous or humiliating terms on the defeated party; the element of disadvantage or humiliation does not, from the point of view of international law, vitiate such a transaction, whatever resentment and righteous indignation it may produce, whatever desire for retaliation it may engender. Unsatisfactory peace treaties have no doubt led to war in many cases; and it may be that a party that had previously felt itself humiliated managed, in the subsequent conflict, to gain such a success as to enable it to reverse the prior decision and to conclude a more satisfactory treaty. Here, however, it was not the unsatisfactory character of the first treaty that deprived it of binding effect; it simply fell to the ground as soon as it was formally supplanted by the second treaty accepted and signed by both disputants as a solution of their difference. The first treaty remained legally operative until it was thus formally supplanted by the second.

{margin: Is a humiliating treaty binding?}

Now international law does not demand that a nation, having been compelled through defeat to enter into an unfavourable transaction, should for ever remain contented therewith; it is not the business of international law to demand any such thing. It is entirely an affair of national policy and international politics. International law has not hitherto prescribed what grounds and causes are sufficient for undertaking a war—for resorting to this *ultima ratio* in order to redress a grievance. The Germans condemn the French *revanchegelüst*—hankering after "revanche,"

{margin: Supersession of one treaty by another.}

GERMAN CLAIMS

i.e. restitution, retaliation (not necessarily vengeance)—as a reprehensible aim on the ground that it is contrary to the settlement effected by the Treaty of Frankfort ; and yet they have themselves repeatedly declared that if they should one day be defeated and compelled to give up Alsace-Lorraine in a treaty reversing the dispositions of that of 1871, they would never rest content until they had once again wrested the territory from their conquerors. Recent pronouncements to this effect are familiar to all readers ; we may supplement them by recalling such a declaration as was made before the present war by Dr. Arendt, a deputy of the Reichstag [1] : " If Germany be one day conquered and Alsace retaken, the German people will never cease to claim Strassburg and Metz, as a sacred and patriotic duty, and will be prepared to fight for centuries in a war to the death." Thus in the eyes of the Germans it is reprehensible and dishonourable for the French to seek to reverse the Treaty of Frankfort, but for themselves it is a " sacred and patriotic duty " to seek to reverse such treaty as may eventually supersede that of 1871. In point of fact, the Treaty of Frankfort itself superseded in regard to territorial arrangements a number of earlier treaties—*e.g.* the treaties of Westphalia (1648), Nimeguen (1678), Ryswick (1697), Utrecht (1713), and Vienna (1815)—and is in turn liable to be superseded by the regular and legitimate method sanctioned by international law, viz. the conclusion of a new international engagement.

We must conclude, then, that the Treaty of Frankfort is at present binding, and that Alsace-Lorraine still belongs lawfully to Germany and will continue to do so until she cedes it to France or otherwise renounces

[1] Cf. Florent-Matter, *L'Alsace de nos jours* (Paris, 1908), p. 517 ; Novicow, *op. cit.*, p. 203.

her sovereignty over it. It is quite a different question, however, whether Germany has achieved a *moral* conquest over the provinces, and has dealt with the annexed people—formerly French citizens—in such a wise, just, and equitable manner as to absorb them into her political régime and national culture, and make the severance from France complete. This is the question to which we have now to address ourselves.

<small>When Alsace-Lorraine will cease to belong to Germany.</small>

CHAPTER IX

GERMAN RÉGIME IN ALSACE-LORRAINE

Military occupation, 1870-71—Status from February 1871 to June 1871—Dictatorship, 1871-3—The imperial constitution applied, 1874—Territorial Delegacy established, 1874—Council of State established, 1879—Application of the régime—Repressive measures—New constitution, 1911—Why autonomy refused—Precautions of Germany on outbreak of the present war—Why thorough germanisation not effected—The German official classes—The German immigrants—Pan-germanism—German methods compared with French.

FROM the middle of August 1870, when the Germans entered into the military occupation of Alsace-Lorraine, to February 26, 1871, when the Preliminaries of Versailles were concluded, stipulating its cession, the territory was placed under the authority of a military governor-general appointed by the King of Prussia, and was, conformably to international practice, subject to the martial and other law enforced by the former. During this interval it remained *de jure* French territory, though the sovereignty of France was suspended *de facto* and French law ceased to apply in so far as it was inconsistent with the provisional military law. (Military occupation, 1870-71.)

From the conclusion of the Preliminaries to the German law of annexation, June 9, 1871 (which came into force June 28, 1871), the régime of military occupation was no longer applicable; the rights of the acquiring State were derived from the formal cession; the status of the acquired territory with regard to third Powers was (Status from February 1871 to June 1871.)

155

156   ALSACE-LORRAINE

definitively fixed. It did not, however, become a constituent State of the German Empire under the German Constitution, which did not extend to it *in proprio vigore*.

The next was a transition period [1] of two and a half years—June 28, 1871, to December 31, 1873— during which the German Emperor was not the ruler (in the sense of being ruler of Prussia), but the dictator of the Reichsland (imperial territory), exercising the functions of an imperial organ. On December 30, 1871, an official known as an Oberpräsident was appointed ; he had an official seat at Strassburg, and acted under the direction of the Imperial Chancellor in matters of administration. He was not empowered to countersign ordinances of the Emperor, or to act as the representative of the Chancellor ; but he prepared the budget and the drafts of laws and ordinances for the territory, which had to be submitted to the Reichstag for approval.[2] Apart from legislative modifications made in this way, the existing French law remained operative for the time being.

Dictatorship 1871-3.

We may mention here that soon after the formal annexation an assembly of Alsatian notables in Strassburg appealed to the German Government to postpone the introduction of the law of military service into the transferred territory —for obvious reasons. But the appeal was rejected. Treitschke's observations in the Reichstag represented the view of the governing authorities, and amounted to a glorification of the German Army and

Law of military service introduced.

[1] For a convenient summary of the status and changes from 1871 to 1879, see B. E. Howard, *Alsace-Lorraine in its relation to the German Empire*, in *Political Science Quarterly* (New York, 1906), vol. xxi., pp. 447–74.

[2] *Cf.* P. Laband, *Das Staatsrecht des deutschen Reiches*. 3 vols. (Freiburg i. B., 1876–82), vol. ii. p. 218.

German military discipline as the unfailing source of the noblest virtues. " This wish," he said, " proceeds from the scanty knowledge of German life which still prevails in Alsace ; it proceeds in the first place from the vague idea that there may some day be a war with France, and the hearts of the Alsatians revolt against the thought of fighting against their old fellow-countrymen. But we cannot come to an understanding with the Alsatians until they give up such vague expectations, and learn to regard their present condition as one which will last for ever. Further, that wish proceeds from a confusion of the French and German military establishments. Our army is not an aggressive power intended within a measured interval to return home with a certain amount of military glory ; it is the nation in arms, it is the great school of courage, of manly discipline, of moral self-sacrifice on the part of the whole flower of the nation, and from this great school we do not wish to exclude the Alsatians at the outset. On the contrary, I say that the German law of military service should be introduced as soon as the economic conditions of the frontier territory admit of it." [1]

Under the law of June 25, 1873, Alsace-Lorraine was empowered to return fifteen members to the Reichstag at the next election. On January 1, 1874, the imperial constitution came into force and the dictatorship of the Emperor *ipso facto* ceased ; so that the law-making power was transferred to the ordinary legislature of the Empire. In the preceding year, however, it was enacted that when the Reichstag was not sitting the Emperor might, with the consent of the Bundesrat (the Federal Council), issue decrees having the force

The imperial constitution applied, 1874.

[1] *Germany, France, Russia, and Islam*, pp. 184-5.

of law, provided they were not incompatible with the constitution or with the existing imperial law. Though the legislative powers had thus been reshuffled, the dictatorial régime none the less remained in fact.

At the meeting of the Reichstag on February 18, 1874, the Alsace-Lorraine deputies presented a protest, in the form of a motion, against the annexation (we shall come back to this in the next chapter[1]); and—as a sequel to this protest—the Abbés Guester and Winterer moved in the Reichstag on the following March 3 that the dictatorial régime should be abolished. Bismarck, in reply, reminded the Alsatian representatives that the annexation was that of a conqueror, that they themselves were also responsible to some extent for the war, and that the kind of government to be given to the conquered provinces depended only on the will of the victor. " These gentlemen of Alsace," he observed, " complain that, during these three years, we have not made them happy, as they no doubt were under French domination. . . . But that was not exactly the object of the annexation. . . . I will beg these gentlemen of Alsace, in order to abate their wrath, to remember also a little the way in which annexation was arrived at. . . .. Each of them has his own 30,000,000th share of complicity and responsibility in the war which was declared against us. . . ." Bismarck did not confine his mockery and sarcasm to the Alsatian deputies, but directed his pungent observations also against the French Government and the French Assembly. " If such speeches, in the event of French victory, had been uttered at the Assembly of Versailles, we may be certain that, if not the majority, at least M. le President Buffet, with the cutting manner that is peculiar to him, would

[1] See *infra*, chap. x, *in init.*

soon have made liberty of speech an illusory privilege for the complainants." Bismarck concluded in favour of maintaining the dictatorial régime, and on a vote taken his view was supported by 196 against 138. The latter figure shows considerable progress in support of the amelioration of the status of Alsace-Lorraine.

On October 29, an imperial decree authorised the establishment of the Landesausschuss, *i.e.* a Territorial Committee or Delegacy, consisting of thirty members (ten for each of the three districts of Upper Alsace, Lower Alsace, and Lorraine), whose function was to advise on matters relating to local legislation and taxation, before bills were laid before the imperial legislature. The powers of this body were purely permissive—advisory, and not consultative. *Territorial Delegacy established, 1874.*

The results of the erection of the Territorial Delegacy being satisfactory, its functions were greatly extended by a law of May 2, 1877, whereby it became also a consenting body in regard to legislative projects, and could initiate territorial legislation. The legislature for the provinces now consisted of the Emperor, the Bundesrat, and the Landesausschuss (the approval of the Reichstag being no longer necessary). *Its functions enlarged, 1877.*

Next, under the law of July 4, 1879 (which became operative on October 1, 1879), a great change was made, which marked a notable stage in the movement towards autonomy. The administration was dissociated from the Imperial Chancellor; the office of Oberpräsident was abolished; and a Statthalter (governor) was appointed instead, the first to hold the office being Baron von Manteuffel. The latter, who represented the Emperor and not the *Progressive change in 1879.*

Imperial Chancellor,[1] was assisted by a Secretary of State, and three Under-Secretaries—the heads of the different executive departments; they were all appointed by the Emperor, and together constituted a "ministry for Alsace-Lorraine," with their offices at Strassburg, and to them were transferred some of the functions of the Bundesrat. The Territorial Delegacy was enlarged to fifty-eight representatives, thirty-four of whom were elected by the general councils of the three districts from their own members, four were appointed by the municipal councils of Strassburg, Metz, Colmar, and Mülhausen, and twenty were elected by the delegates of the rural communes; and the powers of the Delegacy were extended.

A Council of State, possessing advisory powers, was established; it consisted of the Secretary of State, the Under-Secretaries, the President of the Supreme Court of the Reichsland, the chief attorney of this court, and from eight to twelve members appointed by the Emperor for three years; and was presided over by the Governor, or, in his absence, by the Secretary of State. There were thus six legislative and administrative institutions for Alsace-Lorraine: within the territory—the Governor, the Ministry, the Council of State, and the Delegacy; outside the territory—the Emperor and the Bundesrat.

Council of State established.

The normal mode of legislating for the territory involved a roundabout and complicated procedure: the bill was drafted by the local ministry; was submitted to the local Council of State; transmitted to the Prussian Ministry, who, having given what has been termed a "certificat d'innocuité,"[2] submitted it to the Emperor; sent back to the Governor

Roundabout legislation.

[1] Laband, *op. cit.*, vol. ii. p. 229.   [2] Wetterlé, *op. cit.*, p. 112.

for his counter-signature ; laid before the Bundesrat ; passed through three readings by the Delegacy ; again presented to the Bundesrat (by Prussia, as the presiding State of the German Confederation) for definitive ratification ; promulgated by the Emperor (if he did not veto the measure). Laws could also be made, however, without the intervention of the Territorial Delegacy, e.g. by decree of the Emperor with the consent of the Reichstag and the Bundesrat ; or even by decree of the Emperor with the consent of the Bundesrat, having the force of a provisional law. Thus no legislation of any kind was entirely within local control. The co-operation of the Delegacy was not essential, but only permissive ; and even when it was permitted to co-operate, the local ministry could appeal to the Reichstag (which, in fact, not infrequently interposed in the legislation of Alsace-Lorraine).

Such was the constitution and scheme of government that prevailed in Alsace-Lorraine for some thirty years. But the fundamental restrictions and disabilities imposed thereby did not affect the people so much as the mode and details of the application of the régime and the attitude of the governing authorities, especially so of the minor officials. *Application of the régime.*

Baron von Manteuffel, the first Statthalter, however, made during the tenure of his office (1879-87) a conscientious and persistent attempt to win over the population by mild methods and sympathetic treatment.[1] He realised that the annexed territory had once been French, and that time, patience and tact were needed for transforming the nationality of its population and gaining their voluntary *Manteuffel's success.*

[1] *Cf.* P. A. Helmer, *Alsace under German Rule* (London, 1915), pp. 15, 16.

allegiance. He respected their feelings, and took into account the differences of their outlook, their ways, education, culture, and religion. He was ever ready to associate with them, and to listen to their grievances. And yet, despite the respect and esteem which his generous and affable disposition procured him, the fundamental object of his governorship was, in the eyes of his fellow-Germans, far from being attained. As M. Helmer says : " The first Statthalter's successes were purely personal. His loyal and generous attitude was incomprehensible to his compatriots. Baron von Manteuffel's manner of approaching the Alsace-Lorraine problem, and the principles which inspired him in his efforts to win popularity, were contrary to the spirit of the German nation. Germany, which had tardily achieved unhoped-for power, knew nothing of chivalrous traditions, nor of respect for the personality, the rights and interests of others. The tact and delicacy of Manteuffel, the nobility of heart which made him defer to the sentiments of the vanquished, were foreign to the great majority of his people." [1] He was even accused by Germans of siding with the native population as against the immigrant officials ; and his countrymen demanded that his mild and indulgent administration should be replaced by a strict and uncompromising régime. He died in 1887, and was succeeded as governor by Prince von Hohenlohe Schillingsfurst, who was specifically instructed by Bismarck to adopt more rigorous methods towards the people of Alsace-Lorraine.

In the meantime various happenings in France pointed to the possibility of a new Franco-German war, the object of which would be to restore the lost provinces. The feelings aroused in France on the

[1] *Alsace under German Rule* (London, 1915), p. 16.

occasion of the visit of Alfonso XII of Spain (1883), and afterwards during the Boulangist movement (1886 and 1887), and by such incidents as the Schnaebele affair (1887),[1] met with a ready response in the Reichsland. However this may be, at the elections of January, 1887, Alsace-Lorraine once more returned to the Reichstag " protesting " members—following the examples of 1874, 1881, and 1884—in spite of the pressure exercised by the German authorities to bring about a different electoral result. Now, Manteuffel having gone, and the provinces proving recalcitrant in their attitude and repeatedly hostile in their elections, a period of repression commenced.

"Protesting" members returned to Reichstag by Alsace-Lorraine.

At the same time the Alsatian-Lorrainers began to realise that, what with the political vicissitudes in France, the absence of national unity, and the pacific policy of the greater part of French democracy, the dream of liberation was a hopeless one; accordingly they attached themselves to the movement for autonomy within the German Empire, and " Alsace for the Alsatians" became the guiding watchword.[2]

Autonomist movement.

For many years the repressive measures were applied systematically and persistently to every side of social life, public activity, and exterritorial relationships. When the new governor was pressed to adopt severe methods, he made the following comment in his note-book : " It seems that at Berlin they want to drive the annexed population to desperation and to open revolt, in order to suppress the civil power and set up again the military dictatorship."[3] Numerous edicts were issued—*Abwehrgesetze* (laws of

Repressive measures.

---

[1] As to these see *infra*, pp. 217, 221.   [3] Wetterlé, *op. cit.*, p. 36.
[2] See *infra*, chap. x.

protection), known locally as "lois d'exception"—for the purpose of combating the influences emanating from France. Newspapers were from time to time suppressed, e.g. the *Union, Odilienblatt, Colmarer Zeitung, Mülhauser Volksblatt, Echo de Schiltigheim, Lorraine Sportive*. Clubs and societies were arbitrarily dissolved, e.g. the "sport" clubs of Metz, the souvenir societies for the decoration of French graves, the Alsatian Society of Mechanical Construction (its head being a Frenchman), as well as various singing, music, and gymnastic societies. Restrictions were imposed on correspondence, the movements of excursionists, the performance of French plays. Ardent "nationalists" (e.g. M. Antoine and M. Lalance) and also sympathetic visitors from France or Switzerland, were imprisoned, banished, or expelled.

Lois d'exception.
Newspapers suppressed.
Societies dissolved.
Censorship.

The Alsatians and Lorrainers who had emigrated from their country in pursuance of the right of option conceded to them by the Treaty of Frankfort were not allowed to return except with permits, which were obtainable with difficulty and available only for very short periods. For some fifteen years the passport régime was enforced, which to a large extent isolated Alsace-Lorraine from the rest of the world,[1] and—what was the greatest of hardships—separated the native families from their numerous French relations. Von Caprivi, the successor of Bismarck, stated on June 10, 1890, that he had decided to maintain the passport regulations "in order to make still wider the barrier that separated France from Germany." French officers who crossed over into the Reichsland had to submit to rigorous

Passport system.

[1] Wetterlé, *op. cit.*, p. 31.

and humiliating formalities, whilst German officers moved about freely at Nancy, Belfort, and Toul. The natives were regarded with suspicion, their words and acts were watched, and the practice of espionage and delation was resorted to: "La délation avait en effet été érigée chez nous à la hauteur d'un principe de gouvernement." [1]

<small>Suspicion and espionage.</small>

The natives were excluded as much as possible from public functions; in case of disputes between them and the immigrants, judicial decisions sometimes unfairly favoured the latter. "Pour l'habitant autochtone de l'Alsace-Lorraine, il n'y avait plus ni justice, ni droit, ni liberté. Avec toutes les formes hypocrites de la légalité, on en faisait un paria dans son propre pays." [2]

<small>Exclusion from public functions.</small>

Most of the business orders of the administration were sent to Germany, and all kinds of devices and contrivances were adopted to get the industrial undertakings of Alsace-Lorraine into German hands. " . . . Malgré nos protestations indignées, toutes les commandes des administrations civiles et militaires allaient à des fournisseurs d'outre-Rhin; toutes les grandes entreprises industrielles, mines de fer, de charbon, de potasse, passaient aux mains de syndicats germaniques. L'affaire de Grafenstaden et l'enquête ouverte l'an dernier par les chambres de commerce sur la participation des capitaux étrangers aux affaires alsaciennes-lorraines, prouvèrent que les Allemands avaient même l'intention arrêtée de s'emparer des maisons existant avant la guerre de 1870." [3]

<small>Economic pressure.</small>

Furthermore, the University of Strassburg was thoroughly germanised. The children of the natives were discouraged to attend the intermediate and the higher schools. French instruction

<small>Educational measures.</small>

[1] Wetterlé, op. cit., p. 32.   [2] Ibid., p. 34.   [3] Ibid., p. 33.

in the secondary schools was limited, **and as far as possible had to be given through the medium of the German language.**

In the case of the elementary schools French was banished altogether, except in certain entirely French-speaking villages. The Government seemed to be determined to eradicate the use of the French language in the annexed provinces. Business signs and notices had to be written or printed in German, special permission being required for the use of French. Such words as *coiffeur, menu, restaurant, modes*, etc., etc., were banned; they had to be replaced by *friseur, speisekarte, restauration, moden*, and so on. A Strassburg trader was fined for using the foreign expression, *liquidation totale*, instead of the German form *totale liquidation*; after paying the fine he put up a notice, " Hier wird Deutsch gesprochen." [1] " The struggle against the French language," says Paul Déroulède, " is one of the most ridiculous aspects of the pangermanist campaign. French souvenirs, French monuments, French tombs, French cookery, French bills of fare, French visiting-cards, French teaching, French Christian names, French gymnasium suits, French bugles, excite the wrath of the pangermanists. They would even germanise red skirts and blue skies. They would raise between Alsace and France, her former country, a Chinese wall." [2]

Fight against French language.

In reference to the German policy directed against the French language and French culture in Alsace-Lorraine, a Swiss writer observes : " The old policy of the Allemanni in enslaving their conquered foes is revived in the nineteenth century. Not slavery in a

[1] Jordan, *op. cit.*, p. 52.
[2] Preface to H. Zislin, *Sourires d'Alsace* (Paris, 1913).

physical or economic sense, of course, but touching their purest, most intimate and most legitimate feelings. Slavery of the body may be more easily borne than constraint of the spirit." [1]

It was to this period of repression that the Alsatian deputy, M. Preiss, referred when he said in the Reichstag on one occasion " that peace reigned in Alsace-Lorraine—the peace of cemeteries." [2]

In the meantime the movement in favour of autonomy was advancing; and it was felt in Germany that the governing officials, who constituted a kind of " close oligarchy," [3] had by their meddlesome disposition and arrogant behaviour contributed not a little to the alienation of the inhabitants and to the progress of the " nationalist " cause. Accordingly the Emperor intervened personally, and put an end to the ascendancy of the official circle. The Secretary of State, Von Puttkammer, was dismissed; and Von Koeller was appointed in his place, with instructions to inaugurate a policy of conciliation and pacification. The latter did much to restrain the interference of the officials and to allay the general irritation. The dictatorial abuses were to a large extent removed, and " exceptional laws" were repealed. The new Government, interposing little in public life, and leaving it to the free play of the party organisations, thus countered the political opposition to the sovereign authority and reduced it to comparatively small dimensions. " If the national question," says a leading observer, " had been a mere outcome of the political situation, it might have been supposed that germanisation had now been achieved." [4] But, owing to the insolent and

The official oligarchy.

Von Koeller's régime.

---

[1] A. Gobat, *Le Cauchemar de l'Europe*, cited by Jordan, *op. cit.*, p. 53.
[2] Wetterlé, *op. cit.*, p. 143. [3] Helmer, *op. cit.*, p. 21. [4] *Ibid.*, p. 27.

contemptuous attitude of the German immigrants and the consequent conflicts between them and the native population, Alsatian disaffection was nourished and demands for autonomy were renewed.

Next Von Koeller was replaced by Baron de Bulach, an Alsatian statesman, " qui crut devoir inaugurer immédiatement, pour se faire pardonner ses origines, la politique de la ' main forte.' " He became the tool of Herr Mandel, a Bavarian, the Under-Secretary of State for Foreign Affairs, a harsh man devoted to the strict and undiscriminating application of the written law—" un Bavarois dur et grossier, le type du légiste qui ne connaît que la loi écrite et l'applique sans ménagements." [1] The policy adopted was a resumption of the high-handed régime, which had met with failure throughout ; and before long there was an open rupture between the ministry and the Territorial Delegacy. Various incidents contributed to this : *e.g.* the prohibition of the performance of Racine's comedy, *Les Plaideurs*, the stormy debates on the Kubler motion relative to the teaching of French in the elementary schools, the affair of Noisseville and the Weissenburg monument (1908),[2] the expulsion of the Swiss Wegelin for causing the *Marseillaise* to be played in a Mülhausen restaurant, the trials of the native artists and caricaturists Hansi and Zislin, the closing of the students' club, the incident of the play in *The Daughter of the Regiment* at the Colmar theatre, and finally the indignation aroused in the Territorial Delegacy by the observation of the Secretary of State : " The Empire owes you nothing." Proceedings such as these could not but give rise at the meetings of the Landesausschuss to bitter and excited discussions, " que l'incapacité du Secrétaire

margin: Baron de Bulach's régime.

[1] Wetterlé, *op. cit.*, p. 116.   [2] See *infra*, p. 198.

d'État et l'impertinence de M. Mandel transformaient en scènes scandaleuses "—as an eye-witness says.[1] In these circumstances the Secretary of State urged upon the Governor, Count von Wedel, that, in view of the difficulties of the political position in Alsace-Lorraine, it was essential to modify its constitution in such a way as to get rid of the nationalist opposition. <small>Efforts against the nationalist movement.</small> The nationalist programme contained four fundamental demands: (1) that Alsace-Lorraine should be made a State of the German Empire ; (2) that the executive authority should be vested in an independent head, either prince or president ; (3) that a legislative body should be established within the State, with powers similar to those possessed by the legislative bodies of the other German States ; and (4) that the interposition of the Emperor, the Reichstag, and the Bundesrat in legislation exclusively relating to Alsace-Lorraine should be abolished.

The Imperial Chancellor, Herr von Bethmann-Hollweg, expressed himself in favour of reform. At the end of 1910 a Government Bill, approved by the Bundesrat, was laid before the Reichstag. <small>Government Bill, 1910.</small> Its main proposals were : (1) that Alsace-Lorraine should remain an imperial territory (Reichsland) ; (2) that the Emperor should continue to exercise sovereign authority, as the agent of the confederated States, through his representative, the Statthalter, at Strassburg ; (3) that the legislative powers of the Bundesrat and Reichstag in matters relating exclusively to the territory should be abrogated ; and (4) that two chambers—an upper and a lower—should be established, the second of which was to be elected by manhood suffrage.

In the Reichstag debates on the Bill there was a

[1] Wetterlé, p. 117.

conflict between the autonomists and the conserva ives, who also objected to the provision for manhood suffrage. The measure was referred to a special committee, who suggested amendments to the effect that the territory should be constituted a State of the Empire and that the Statthalter should hold office for life. The latter point was rejected by the Government; and in regard to the former a compromise was accepted whereby Alsace-Lorraine, though not raised to the precise status of a State, should be allowed three votes in the Bundesrat, which were not to count either in favour of any Prussian proposal except when Prussia gained a majority without them, or (whether for or against) in the case of any proposal to amend the imperial constitution. The amended Bill was passed, May 31, 1911, and the new constitution came into force on the following September 1.

Various progressive features were thus introduced; the rights of the population were very considerably enlarged. As before, the Kaiser was vested with the supreme executive authority. The Statthalter, appointed and dismissable by the Emperor, exercised as his representative the executive power, together with all the rights that were formerly in the hands of the Imperial Chancellor. He was also empowered to appoint and instruct the three delegates at the Bundesrat. Imperial decrees and orders could not have the force of law without his signature. No bill could become law without the assent of the Emperor and the two Chambers. He was empowered to summon, adjourn, and dissolve them. The Upper Chamber was to consist of twenty-three members: five permanent ex-officio, viz. the Bishops of Strassburg and Metz, the Presidents of the two Protestant Consistories, and the President of the Court

New constitution enacted, 1911.

of Appeal; the rest being elected members representing the University, the Jewish Consistory, the municipal councils, and the commercial, agricultural, and industrial associations. But the Emperor could, at the instance of the Bundesrat, appoint twenty-three others for the duration of the parliament—a serious defect that prepared the way for subservience to the imperial authority. The Lower House was to consist of sixty members elected by direct and secret ballot by male German citizens of twenty-five years of age who had resided for at least three years in Alsace-Lorraine (one year in the case of teachers and officials). The annual budget was to be submitted first to the Lower House, and was to be accepted or rejected in its entirety by the Upper House. If the former refused to vote supplies, the Government was empowered (as before) to raise taxes and issue treasury bonds.

The constitution could be modified only by the Reichstag and the Bundesrat, so that it rested on a precarious foundation. The Strassburg Government depended virtually on Berlin: for the Emperor appointed the Statthalter, and could dismiss him at discretion, and the latter instructed the Bundesrat Delegates; and the composition of the Upper Chamber was to a great extent subject to the Emperor's pleasure—" la composition du Sénat plaçait nos institutions parlementaires au-dessous de celles des pays les plus rétrogrades."[1] M. Wetterlé thus sums up the position of Alsace-Lorraine under the Constitution of 1911, considering it most unfavourable, despite the reforms, real and apparent, introduced: " Nous restions, en théorie comme en fait, terre d'empire, propriété collective des États, colonie, jouissant, mais provisoirement seule-

Position of Alsace-Lorraine under it.

[1] Wetterlé, *op. cit.*, p. 122.

ment, du droit de s'administrer elle-même sous la souveraineté du roi de Prusse. Nous étions livrés pieds et poings liés au bon vouloir des pouvoirs législatifs et de l'exécutif de Berlin."[1] Similarly M. Novicow regards the constitution as a deception —"trompe-l'oeil"—as a "manifestation of political hypocrisy scandalously practised recently on so large a scale": though it provided a senate, a chamber of deputies, universal suffrage, representation on the Bundesrat, etc., it did not give the essential thing, viz. the right of the people to manage their affairs as they deemed fit.[2]

Why the Imperial Government has refused Alsace-Lorraine autonomy is a question that can be readily answered. It is because of the persistence of French feelings in the provinces, especially among certain of the political leaders, and the imperfect germanisation of the territory and people as a whole. "L'unique raison," remarks M. Sembat,[1] "qui a suspendu jusqu'ici l'octroi de cette autonomie, c'est la persistance des sentiments français dans les provinces annexées. L'administration allemande en prend, à la fois, alarme sérieuse, et texte commode aux exagérations patriotiques et au maintien des mesures arbitraires." In February 1910 it is reported that the Secretary of State said to the deputies of the Territorial Delegacy at Strassburg: "Have the courage to declare that, being Alsatians, you are Germans, and you will receive autonomy at once." The constitution of 1911 shows that the deputies were not prepared to make such a declaration.[4]

Why autonomy refused.

Herr von Bethmann-Hollweg, in the course of a

---
[1] Wetterlé, *op. cit.*, pp. 122-3.   [2] Novicow, *op. cit.*, p. 160.
[3] M. Sembat, *Faites un roi, sinon faites la paix* (Paris, 1915), p. 170.
[4] Novicow, *op. cit.*, p. 173.

speech in the Reichstag March 14, 1910, recognised the necessity of conferring on Alsace-Lorraine a larger measure of political independence; but he emphasised that the formula of the nationalists—" Alsace for the Alsatians "—could not be put into practice so long as their leaders affected to ignore the German character of the population, and were disposed to gallicise the provinces contrary to the considerations of history and ethnography. Again, in the Prussian Upper Chamber Herr Wedelpissdorf said on April 5, 1911 : " The debates that have taken place in regard to a constitution for Alsace-Lorraine have aroused in us a deep anxiety, for we are of the opinion that the inhabitants of this country have not yet become German enough in order that it may be, without danger, constituted a confederate State." [1]

This opposition of the German Government on the one side and the alienation of sections of the people on the other constitute a dilemma which may be expressed thus. Germany says to Alsace-Lorraine : " I will not give you freedom until I am sure of your love." To which Alsace-Lorraine replies : " I cannot love you till you set me free." [2] Germany evidently does not think it safe to bestow on the Reichsland the complete liberty and rights of an autonomous State until the whole of the people are thoroughly imbued with the spirit of " Deutschtum," have fully absorbed German traditions and culture, and have become responsive to official discipline and amenable to the ubiquitous exigencies of a paternal Government. So far—till the outbreak of the present war—Alsace-Lorrainers have not, in the eyes of the governing classes, merited a higher category than that of second-class Germans—

[1] *Indépendance Belge*, April 7, 1911 ; cited by Novicow, p. 173.
[2] Jordan, *op. cit.*, p. 3.

"Deutsche zweiter Klasse"—to use an expression sometimes heard in Alsace.

With regard to the requirement of the German Government that the Alsace-Lorrainers should become fit for liberty before it is conferred upon them, we may recall the wiser and more generous view of Gladstone. The great Liberal statesman, writing to Mr. Forster (April 12, 1882), on the occasion of the Irish land disturbances, observed : " It is liberty alone which fits men for liberty. This proposition, like every other in politics, has its bounds ; but it is far safer than the counter doctrine—wait till they are fit."[1]

A few months before the outbreak of the war it was thought in Berlin that a severer régime than that of Count von Wedel was necessary ; accordingly the latter was replaced by Dallwitz von Roedern, who —in the words of M. Wetterlé —" was to substitute rods of iron for rods of wood, and to resume in Alsace-Lorraine the reign of terror, so that the difficulties resulting therefrom might provoke the annexation of the imperial territory to Prussia."[2] It was, indeed, frequently advocated in German conservative and military circles that the Kaiser should be made Landesherr (sovereign) of Alsace-Lorraine and that, it should be annexed to Prussia. Threats have more than once been made officially that this plan might be resorted to on account of the continued indocility of sections of the population and the agitation of parliamentarians and other national leaders.

Thus in May 1912, after the Mayor of Strassburg had made a complaint in regard to some industrial

Régime under Dallwitz von Roedern.

[1] Lord Morley, *Life of Gladstone* (1903), vol. iii. p. 58.
[2] Wetterlé, *op. cit.*, p. 127.

injustice to the city, the Emperor is reported to have replied: "Listen; so far you have known only my good side. If this situation lasts we shall suppress your constitution and annex you to Prussia."[1] In the following year, after the Zabern affair,[2] Herr von Jagow remarked that in Alsace-Lorraine his countrymen appeared to be in an enemy country. *The Kaiser's threat, 1912.*

Finally, a word remains to be said on the precautions and proceedings of the Imperial Government on the outbreak of the present war.[3] It is stated that lists had been prepared containing the names of Alsatians and Lorrainers whom it was thought necessary to remove and keep under surveillance. One list contained the names of some three hundred persons who were to be arrested for preventive purposes on the eve of the mobilisation and handed over to the military authorities. Many of them fled. A second list contained a number of suspects who were regarded as less dangerous but whom it was thought advisable to remove from the Reichsland; they were accordingly taken away to various German towns and placed under police supervision. As for the territory generally, a rigorous régime was introduced. Foreign news was admitted only through the medium of German papers. Nearly all the local newspapers were suppressed or ceased to appear. A strict censorship was imposed on private correspondence. To leave Alsace was almost impossible; those who obtained special authorisation were subjected, before proceeding to a foreign country, to a sort of quarantine—" une sorte de quarantaine préalable "—in a German town. Restrictions were *Precautions of German Government on outbreak of the present war.*

[1] Jordan, op. cit., pp. 58, 59, note. [3] Lichtenberger, op. cit., pp. 74, 75.
[2] See infra, p. 198.

imposed on the movements of the population. The use of the French language was entirely forbidden, even in private conversation. The least mark of sympathy shown towards the French—even kindness to the French wounded—was punished. The property of fugitives was confiscated, and their relatives were treated as suspects. On the declaration of war thousands—it is stated—fled, and enlisted under the French flag, some in Algeria, Morocco, or with the forces sent to Turkey, others in France.

We may conclude this chapter with a few words, supplementary to the various indications already given above, to explain why the German Government has not succeeded in Alsace-Lorraine in its endeavours to germanise thoroughly the population—to bring about their *entwelschung* ("deforeignisation"). The Germans have not infrequently attributed their failure to their hesitation, and, above all, to their leniency in administration; they have thought it a mistake to permit of the least compromise in Lorraine with French sympathy, and in Alsace with Swiss republican ideals. Some of the Statthalters, *e.g.* Manteuffel, Zeppelin, Von Koeller, have therefore been censured for paying heed to local opinion.[1] Others, however, have taken an entirely contrary view, and have thought that the failure was really due to the excessive severity imported into the administration, advocated as it was by the militarists and the pangermanists; and they have held that the Imperial Government and the local ministries have erroneously considered Alsace-Lorraine responsible for or identified with the occasional chauvinistic or *revanchard* manifestations in France.

<small>Why thorough germanisation not effected.</small>

[1] *Cf.* Jordan, *op. cit.*, p. 55.

RÉGIME, 1870—1914

The reason given by the latter critics is undoubtedly the right one. The fundamental deficiency of the rulers was a lack of tact and sympathy, the indispensable attributes in a conqueror who would win loyalty from the conquered. The absence of these qualities means the use of an undiscriminating coercion, which in its turn alienates the sympathy and good-will of the governed; it is the reciprocally spontaneous good-will alone that is the true cement of nationality and the controlling force of allegiance. The Germans have, admittedly, produced great works of philosophy and psychology; but in practice they have failed to grasp the very essentials of national psychology. They appeared to believe, if we may judge of their proceedings in the Reichsland, that constraint is the father of adherence and affection; whereas—to use the words of Novicow[1]—to force people to love is as impossible psychologically, as it is impossible geometrically to force a triangle not to have three angles. The ignorance of the very essentials of social science on the part of Bismarck and Moltke and their successors led them to commit the radical mistake of substituting for the earlier false principle " cujus regio ejus religio," the equally false principle " cujus regio ejus natio."[2] Force provokes antipathy, hatred; it can never produce national organic amalgamation. To show the conquered that he is weak and cannot liberate himself, whilst the conqueror is powerful and if need be can crush him, is a policy that can never result in a natural fusion—it is at most an " assimilation caporaliste."[3] This is recognised by such a writer as Herr Naumann, who observes in his recently published well-known work: " Prussia took

Fundamental deficiency of the rulers.

[1] *L'Alsace-Lorraine*, p. 153. [2] *Ibid.*, p. 159. [3] *Ibid.*, p. 156

compulsion in one hand and material prosperity in the other, and demanded loyalty in exchange. She brought about much good, but found no way to the heart of the people." [1]

The introduction of a large number of German minor officials aggravated the difficulties of the situation. Bismarck had himself fully realised the necessity of importing into the territory as few as possible ; but what he saw clearly in 1871 immediately after the formal annexation, was forgotten later on. The most unsympathetic, arrogant, and interfering of all the official caste were the Prussians ; they were devoid of tact and understanding, and withheld as much as possible from social relations with the people. Many of the lesser posts were filled by non-commissioned officers who were accustomed to the harsh and rigorous discipline of Prussian barracks. Karl Blind, an observer and publicist of wide experience, whilst favouring the cause of the Germans, emphasises this mistake : " Had the Berlin Government sent into the newly acquired provinces officials of a less hard type than many of those who came from Prussia, had more South Germans been appointed who better understood the kindred Alsatian character, the reconciliation would have made still quicker progress." [2]

The German official classes.

The non-official German immigrants were naturally of the same metal as their official brethren, although they were not in a position to inflict administrative hardships. The hostility, open or concealed, between them and the native population was due to the same fundamental causes as have been

The German immigrants.

---

[1] F. Naumann, *Central Europe*, English trans. (London, 1916), p. 79.
[2] *Alsace-Lorraine and William II.* (*with personal recollections*), in *Fortnightly Review*, vol. lxxviii. (1902), pp. 257 seq., at p. 258.

mentioned above. The immigrants generally assumed an attitude of superiority ; they thought they came as enlightened missionaries, devotees of the vaunted Kultur, to bring the light to a benighted country and true civilisation to a backward and inferior race. There were naturally marked differences between the newcomers and the old inhabitants : the former were believers in force and in ready obedience to bureaucratic regulations, they were hustlers, and were not endowed with a sense of humour ; the latter were profoundly democratic, easy-going, they appreciated the ridiculous side of things, and were not infrequently moved to laughter at the bombastic pretentiousness of their new neighbours. The Germans invariably preserve wherever they go their distinctive national characteristics—their manners, customs, prejudices— and they seem as incapable of being assimilated as of assimilating. " The self-conscious isolation of the German," says Sir Thomas Holdich, " his unbending belief in his own high destiny, added to a certain want of the magnetic attraction due to perfect tact and manners, militates against his success as a colonist, as much as his tactless appreciation of the worst form of Prussian militarism foredoomed the failure of peaceful administration in Alsace and Lorraine, and rendered the annexation of these two provinces a great blunder."[1]

No wonder, then, that for a long time the immigrants were not received in the native families, and that marriages between Germans and Alsatians or Lorrainers were very rare ; so that, despite the comparatively large immigrant population of 300,000 as against the native population of 1,800,000, there has not been any

[1] Sir Thomas H. Holdich, *Political Frontiers and Boundary-making* (London, 1916), pp. 24, 25.

fusion, or even real contact, between the Schwob[1] and the Welsche (or Französling).[2]

The greatest deficiency of all in the governing classes in Alsace-Lorraine is their incapacity to appreciate the spirit of the people, to understand their regrets, their hopes, their tradition, and their aspirations. This incapacity is intensified by the pangermanists' reactionary, autocratic, and militarist conceptions, according to which a conquered population, if not conforming promptly and voluntarily to the standard set before them, should be subjected to the drastic methods of a Procrustean régime. Thus the writer of an article that appeared in the *Elsässer Courier*, a German paper of Colmar, makes the following pronouncement: " Were I Emperor, there would be a dictator, not a Statthalter, in authority. No student should enter the University of Strassburg till he had spent two years at a University elsewhere in Germany. All private schools should be closed, and all public schools should be taught in German. There should be no public meetings in which French is spoken, and no private gatherings save in the presence of a German official. No newspapers should be printed in French, and each paragraph in French should have by its side a German translation. Each citizen, as he comes of age, should declare his eternal allegiance to Germany. He should give his pledge not to buy secretly any newspapers, books, or periodicals in French. All this under pain of expulsion from the land."[3]

It is this pangermanism that has throughout been in Alsace-Lorraine the obstacle to assimilation, peace,

[1] An Alsatian name for a German.
[2] A German name for the anti-German native.
[3] D. Frymann, *Wäre ich Kaiser*, an article published in the *Elsässer Courier* (Colmar), as copied from the *Strasburger Post*, July 1913; quoted by Jordan, pp. 32-3.

RÉGIME, 1870—1914 181

and good understanding, as it has been in Europe generally the obstacle to international amity and security. An Alsatian writer emphasises this in no uncertain accents. " Pangermanism is the exotic," he says, " which ruins the colour of Alsace. . . . It is evident that the only obstacle to the definite germanisation of Alsace is the pangermanist alone, the odious pangermanist under all his disguises, the pangermanist journalist, the pangermanist functionary, the pangermanist magnate, the pangermanist pedagogue, the pangermanist ecclesiastic, the pangermanist policeman, the pangermanist higher officer, the pangermanist subaltern, the pangermanist industrialist, the pangermanist trader. There is also the feminine pangermanist, and we have to call on all the vestiges of gallantry remaining to us from French times to induce us not to speak of her. That is all to her profit. When the last pangermanist shall be put under the sod, on that very day Alsace will find herself germanised as if by enchantment and with the best grace in the world. On that same day we shall have seen, sure as the dawn arises, the United States of Europe, to which the pangermanists constitute the sole obstacle, the day when international fraternity between States will efface them or leave them to retain only a conventional and administrative significance." [1]

A point of great importance to note is that these pangermanist aims and tendencies are resisted in Alsace-Lorraine even by the German Alsatians and Lorrainers, the immigrants' sons who were born in the territory ; many of them are devoted adherents of the nationalist movement.[2] This strong opposition to the Prussian

[1] J. Froelich, *Le pangermaniste en Alsace* ; quoted by Jordan, *op. cit.*, pp. 108-10.
[2] See the next chapter.

régime has been persistently offered in Upper Alsace, and in its two principal towns, Colmar and Mülhausen ; and also in Eastern Lorraine, which is Germanic by blood and speech. Indeed, the American writer to whom we have frequently referred goes so far as to say, as a result of his personal inquiries made in the Reichsland in the year before the war, that the political unrest there appeared to be more freely expressed by the inhabitants of Germanic origin than by those of French blood.[1]

In 1874 a distinguished Prussian publicist and writer issued a work[2] in which he examined the German policy inaugurated in the conquered country, and compared it with the methods adopted by the French. In view of the systematic exclusion of the French language, he asks what part can the French-speaking Alsatians play in the public life of Alsace. A language cannot be imposed on a people, he emphasises, without taking into consideration their antecedents, sympathies, needs, relationships, and the education of generations ; the obstinate war made by the German Government on the French language will be condemned by history as a crime against the most sacred rights of humanity.[3] He points out—with accuracy and notable impartiality —that the French Government, from the annexation of Alsace to France till the Revolution, pursued a different policy : it respected the institutions, the manners, and customs of the people ; it left them nearly all their own laws and traditional usages ; and it never attempted to substitute by force French for German. That was why France since 1789 obtained

(marginal notes: German methods compared with French.)

[1] Jordan, *op. cit.*, p. 41.
[2] G. Rasch, *Die Preussen in Elsass und Lothringen* (Braunschweig, 1874) ; French translation (Paris, 1876).
[3] *Ibid.*, chap. xii. p. 163 (Fr. ed.).

the cordial attachment of the annexed population, and their devotion to French nationality. (It may be added that, for saying these things, the author was sentenced to four months' imprisonment, and the book was confiscated and suppressed.)

More recently the German ministerial Director, Herr Althoff, whilst asserting (after the notorious fashion of Herr Houston Chamberlain) the supremacy of his countrymen in every other sphere, admits their political incapacity—the one failing. " We Germans," he is reported to have said to Prince von Bülow, " are the most learned nation in the world, and the best soldiers. We have achieved great things in all the sciences and arts ; the greatest philosophers, the greatest poets and musicians, are Germans ; of late we have occupied the foremost place in the natural sciences and in almost all technical spheres, and in addition to that we have accomplished an enormous industrial development. How can you wonder that we are political asses ? There must be a weak point somewhere." This passage has been cited by Prince von Bülow,[1] the German ex-Chancellor, as an argument against the institution of manhood suffrage in Prussia ; the German people, he declared, are incapable of self-government. How can people govern others, we may well add, if they cannot govern themselves ?

Political incapacity.

[1] Prince von Bülow, *Imperial Germany*, English translation (London, 1916), p. 161.

CHAPTER X

VIEWS AND ASPIRATIONS OF ALSACE-LORRAINE—THE NATIONALIST MOVEMENT

Protest of the Alsace-Lorraine deputies in the Reichstag, 1874—Why autonomist movement began—Aim in social and intellectual life of the people—Method of the nationalist leaders—Differentiation between autonomists and protesters—Socialist party; anti-clerical campaign—Democrats leave the Catholic party—National Union formed, 1910; its programme—Manifesto against the Constitution of 1911—" Home rule" demanded, 1913—Before present war, memory of 1871 fading in Alsace-Lorraine—Did Alsace-Lorraine desire reunion with France?—Noisseville affair; Saverne affair—Attitude of the people towards France and Germany—Distinctive personality of Alsace-Lorraine—The new generation and France—Doubtful indications as to feelings and desires of the people—Attitude of Alsace-Lorrainers at outbreak of the war—Declarations of the two Chambers, 1917—Conclusions.

THE first fifteen years of the history of Alsace-Lorraine under German domination may be described as " the period of protest," and the subsequent period may be designated " the era of young Alsace," when the autonomist movement was set on foot and developed, the watchword being " Alsace for the Alsatians." First, then, as to the period of protest.

On February 18, 1874, at a meeting of the Reichstag, a protest against the annexation was submitted, in the form of a motion, by fourteen out of the fifteen deputies of Alsace-Lorraine. The spokesman was M. Teutsch, an Alsatian advocate.[1] He desired to express himself in French, but was compelled to use German. The declaration he read was subjected to repeated

Protest of the Alsace-Lorraine deputies in the Reichstag, 1874.

[1] His speech is reprinted in French in Patiens, *L'Alsace-Lorraine devant l'Europe* (Paris, 1894), Appendix, Note B.

NATIONALIST MOVEMENT 185

interruptions, shouts, and sarcastic outbursts of laughter ; and he was more than once called to order. The principal passages are as follows [1] :

" The people of Alsace-Lorraine, whose representatives we are at the Reichstag, have entrusted to us a special and most grave mission, which we are anxious to fulfil without delay.

" Your last war, which terminated to the advantage of your nation, undoubtedly gave it the right to reparation. But Germany exceeded her right as a civilised nation in compelling France to sacrifice a million and a half of her children.

" In the name of the Alsatian-Lorrainers, sold by the Treaty of Frankfort, we protest against the abuse of force of which our country was the victim.

---

[1] " Les populations d'Alsace-Lorraine, dont nous sommes les représentants au Reichstag, nous ont confié une mission spéciale et des plus graves, que nous avons à cœur de remplir sans retard.

" Votre dernière guerre, terminée à l'avantage de votre nation, donnait incontestablement droit à celle-ci à une réparation. Mais l'Allemagne a excédé son droit de nation civilisée en contraignant la France vaincue au sacrifice d'un million et demi de ses enfants.

" Au nom des Alsaciens-Lorrains, vendus par le traité de Francfort, nous protestons contre l'abus de la force dont notre pays a été la victime.

" Si, dans des temps éloignés et relativement barbares, le droit de conquête a pu quelquefois se transformer en droit effectif, si aujourd'hui encore il réussit à se faire absoudre, lorsqu'il s'exerce sur des peuples ignorants et sauvages, rien de pareil ne peut-être opposé à l'Alsace-Lorraine. . . . En admettant, ce que nous ne reconnaissons pas, que la France ait eu le droit de nous céder, le contrat que vous nous opposez n'a pas de valeur. Un contrat ne vaut, en effet, que par le libre consentement des deux contractants. Or, c'est l'épée sur la gorge que la France saignante et épuisée a signé notre abandon. Elle n'a pas été libre, elle s'est courbée sous la violence, et nos codes nous enseignent que la violence est une cause de nullité pour les conventions qui en sont entachées.

" Vous le voyez, Messieurs, nous ne trouvons dans les enseignements de la morale et de la justice rien, absolument rien, qui puisse faire pardonner notre annexion à votre empire, et notre raison en cela s'accorde avec notre cœur. Notre cœur en effet se sent irrésistiblement attiré vers notre patrie française. Deux siècles de pensée et de vie en commun créent entre les membres d'une même famille un lien sacré, qu'aucun argument, et moins encore la violence, ne saurait détruire."

"If, in distant and relatively barbarous ages, the right of conquest was sometimes transformed into an effective right, if at the present day again it receives absolution when applied to ignorant and savage people, nothing of the kind can be urged against Alsace-Lorraine. . . . Even admitting—what we do not recognise—that France was entitled to cede us, the contract which you impose upon us has no validity. A contract, is, indeed, valid only by the free consent of the two contracting parties. Now, it was with the sword on her throat that France, bleeding and exhausted, signed our abandonment. She was not free, she was bent by violence, and our codes teach us that violence renders null and void agreements vitiated by it.

"You see, gentlemen, we find in the teachings of morality and law nothing, absolutely nothing, that can justify our annexation to your Empire, and in that respect our reason is in accord with our feelings. Our hearts indeed feel that they are irresistibly drawn to our French fatherland. Two centuries of thought and life in common create between the members of the same family a sacred bond, which no argument, and still less violence, can destroy."

On the following day, however, Mgr. Raess, Bishop of Strassburg, made a counter-declaration on behalf of himself and his co-religionists to the effect that they had no intention of repudiating the Treaty of Frankfort, which was concluded between two great Powers: "Messieurs, pour prévenir des commentaires fâcheux, qui pourraient nous atteindre, moi et mes co-religionnaires, je me trouve en conscience obligé de déposer ici une simple déclaration : les Alsaciens-Lorrains de ma confession n'ont aucune intention de mettre en question le traité de Francfort,

View of the Bishop of Strassburg.

conclu entre deux grandes puissances. Voilà ce que je voulais dire dés le début."

This counter-declaration called forth the next day a public letter from M. Pouquet, the deputy for Sarreguemines, who stated that the Bishop of Strassburg had spoken in his own name only, and not on behalf of his co-religionists. A warm controversy then ensued in the newspapers published in Alsace-Lorraine. In the *Journal d'Alsace* of February 21 a communication appeared from Mgr. Raess, who sought to explain his position and to amplify his previous statement. The following is the principal passage : " As I could not purely and simply regard the Treaty of Frankfort as being of no account, and not wishing to accept it purely and simply in all its consequences, I, in order to preserve an open and free field for the discussion, chose a means and an expression which, whilst respecting the treaty, would not prevent us from bringing out and attacking its deplorable consequences for Alsace-Lorraine, and would allow us to remain in the Reichstag to defend our rights and effectively present our grievances and our wishes. Thus I have kept within the Christian and Catholic doctrine which teaches us in its ethical books, in the apostolic constitutions and in the *Syllabus* (of which every one knows the name and only a few know the contents and value), that an individual may not, at his will, tear up treaties regularly concluded between individuals, towns, and nations. All this does not prove that I have ever been sympathetic towards the annexation of Alsace." [1]

At the subsequent elections in 1881, 1884, and 1887 " protesting " members, as in 1874, were sent to the

---

[1] *Mémorial diplomatique* (1874), p. 152 ; F. Klein, *L'Évêque de Metz: Vie de Mgr. Dupont des Loges* (Paris, 1899), p. 376 ; cited by Hanotaux, *Contemporary France*, Eng. trans. (1905), vol. ii. p. 431, note.

Reichstag by the annexed provinces, notwithstanding the pressure exercised by the German Government to secure the return of less hostile representa-
<small>Why autonomist movement began.</small> tives. The régime of repression was accordingly introduced in good earnest in Alsace-Lorraine, and germanising measures rapidly multiplied. What with the unsettled state of France and the pacific aims of French democracy, the Alsatians and the Lorrainers came to realise that their hope of liberation from the yoke of the conqueror was vain, and that therefore their only political salvation lay in the establishment of their territory as an autonomous State within the German Empire.

The formula " Alsace for the Alsatians " gradually assumed a wider scope ; from the sphere of practical <small>Aim in social and intellectual life of the people.</small> politics it was imported into the various spheres of social and intellectual life of the population. The aim was to preserve their essential characteristics, their own individuality, and their particular cultural aptitudes and aspirations, so that the German attempt at *entwelschung* might be defeated or neutralised. Some sections of the people devoted themselves to the promotion of national literature, the fine arts, painting, drawing, engraving, design, the decorative arts, architecture, and so on ; the Alsatian plays of Stosskopf,[1] written in dialect and performed by amateurs, depicted the contemporary life of the provinces. Others rallied round such journals as the *Revue Alsacienne Illustrée*, which encouraged contact with and sympathy for French culture—not, however, with a view to gallicising the population, but rather to graft on the natural soil such congenial elements as could be extracted from the intellectual, spiritual, and æsthetic

---

[1] *Cf.* Lichtenberger, *op. cit.*, p. 36.

NATIONALIST MOVEMENT 189

resources of the former mother-country; for it was recognised that the mass of the people was of a mixed culture, neither French nor German in a distinctive sense. All these tendencies were manifestly opposed to the policy of germanisation, and fostered the spirit of nationalism or particularism.

The method adopted by the nationalist leaders was founded in political opportunism, which at once took cognisance of actual facts and conditions and implied no sacrifice of feelings and ideals. Hence they agreed to establish in the Reichstag, as well as in the Territorial Delegacy, alliances with the Catholic centre and the Social Democrats amongst the German parties, for the purpose of attaining certain practical aims, *e.g.* the removal of the dictatorship, the emancipation of the press, and so paving the way to self-government as the great goal. And these efforts were ably seconded by journalists, humorists, and cartoonists, who set forth the claims of the governed and the ridiculous pretensions, together with the odious practices, of the governing authorities. The fundamental point of view of the active nationalists has been summed up thus : " Whether our aim is possible in our life-time or not, that is not our concern. It is our right, and so it becomes our duty as free men, to speak. A lesson of our history is this. We have endured the Huns, the Vandals, and the Pandours, and Alsace is still Alsace. Let us hope for better days, my children ; for the future, do not forget, belongs to the good God and not to the ugly fellow who presides over the Pangermanist League." [1]

Method of the nationalist leaders.

In course of time the autonomists became more or less differentiated from the protesters, and a certain antagonism even grew up between them ; the latter

[1] Quoted by Jordan, *op. cit.*, pp. 113, 114.

remained opposed to germanism and to the German régime, whilst the former were less uncompromising, and were prepared to arrive at an accommodation with the Imperial Government, to act loyally in union with it, and to make the annexed territory a true and genuine constituent of the Empire on the basis of internal self-administration. This twofold division did not remain throughout clearly defined; political thought could not adjust itself precisely, during the course of its development, to this dual classification. Different parties arose, their groupings and composition being somewhat complicated.[1]

Differentiation between autonomists and protesters.

At the elections of 1891 and 1893 the Socialist party, imported from Germany, made its appearance, and its activities intensified the political struggles and contributed much to modify the clearness and simplicity of the former issues. Its immediate purpose was to break up the union of Alsace-Lorrainers.

Appearance of Socialist party.

As a result of its establishment a violent anti-clerical campaign was inaugurated; this compelled the Catholics to form themselves into the Volkspartei (popular party), which soon became the Landespartei (national party). The latter asserted itself in 1896, when, owing to the Reichstag's rejection of the elected candidate, M. Poehlmann, the Kreisdirector of Schlestadt, M. Spiess, the former mayor of the town, offered himself as candidate of the Catholic party and was elected by a considerable majority, in spite of government pressure exercised against him. At this time, too, the Liberal Democratic party, though not yet properly constituted, manifested its existence.

Anti-clerical campaign.

In 1897 the Democrats left the ranks of the Catholic

[1] *Cf.* Wetterlé, *op. cit.*, p. 146.

NATIONALIST MOVEMENT 191

party; and after this separation, another distinctive group was established, viz. the Liberals, who were "de nuance gouvernementale," and anti-Catholic. The elections of the following year brought out the rivalries of the various parties and combinations; but on the whole the predominating feeling was hostility to the repressive régime of the Imperial Government. In all these political conflicts religious dissension played a great part; though about 80 per cent. of the population was Catholic, there were among the remainder vigorous Protestant centres in the larger towns. Still, natives and German immigrants combined more and more in their demands for autonomy, which the Imperial Government persistently refused to grant, on the ground (as we have already seen) that the provinces were not yet sufficiently German. *Democrats leave the Catholic party.*

In 1910 was formed the National Union, which contained representatives of various parties, and whose object was to stimulate the native population in favour of the national movement and against the policy of germanisation. The Liberal and Socialist sections, however, offered strong opposition to this new association. The fundamental demands of the autonomists in general have already been pointed out in an earlier chapter.[1] The complete programme of the National Union of Alsace-Lorraine, which was formally adopted on June 27, 1911, is an elaboration of these demands and is to the following effect: *National Union formed, 1910.*

1. The constitution of Alsace-Lorraine should be that of an autonomous State within the German Empire, and should possess all the rights of a confederated State equally with the other *Its programme.*

[1] See *supra*, p. 169.

constituent States. The guiding motto must be: " Alsace-Lorraine for the Alsatian-Lorrainers."

2. In the work of public administration the officials should speak the languages spoken in the provinces ; they should understand and take due cognisance of the intellectual life of the people, their traditions, their customs, and habits. More offices should be given to natives, though vested rights might well be left undisturbed.

3. Taxes and the national expenditure should be diminished ; the budget of Alsace-Lorraine should be used mainly in the interests of the population of the territory ; and the benefits acquired by the Empire from the railways of Alsace-Lorraine should be shared with them.

4. In the public educational institutions children should be allowed to learn French ; family traditions and the traditions of the country should be respected; and books should not be introduced nor lessons given which might cast any disadvantageous or deprecatory reflections on the ancestors of the scholars and their parents.

5. As for the military question, Alsatians and Lorrainers should be permitted to perform their military service in their own province ; soldiers should be allowed to speak their own language, and should not be compelled to substitute German for it.

6. The economic questions of the territory should be solved more in its own interest.

7. The national individuality of the country and the people should be respected, and their right to preserve and promote their individuality by every means should be recognised. Regard should be paid to their use of two languages, their relation to two different civilisations, and their desire to remain in

NATIONALIST MOVEMENT 193

contact with the literature, arts, intellectual life, sports, and worldly life of the two nations from whom they derive so many of their characteristics. They should be at liberty to visit their friends and relations who emigrated, and the formalities and restrictions imposed on the latter during their stay in the territory should be abolished. They should enjoy the right to pay respect as they thought fit to the tombs of the fallen, whatever flag they fought under. In return for the loyal submission of the people to the order established, they claimed respect for their remembrances and traditions, and the unrestricted liberty to maintain them.

On June 11, 1912, the National Union issued from Strassburg a manifesto directed against the constitution of 1911.[1] It declared that the imposing of a new constitution on the people, against their will, was a retrograde step, and brought them no nearer to autonomy; and it demanded that the country should be placed on a footing of equality with the other States of the Empire, for the people did not deserve to be treated as an inferior race. The exceptional situation was intolerable. Hence it was decided to establish a National Party in Alsace-Lorraine, with the object of preserving the individuality of the territory and the people, and of acquiring the position of an autonomous State within the German Empire.

Manifesto against the constitution of 1911.

It is to be noted that after 1911 the Reichstag parties obtained considerable support from leading Alsatians and Lorrainers, e.g. M. Hoeffel, deputy of Saverne; M. Vondersheer, deputy of Schlestadt; M. Grégoire, deputy of Metz; M. Ricklin, deputy of Altkirch-Thann. M. Wetterlé severely censures the latter's

[1] See *supra*, p. 170.

attitude, which is regarded as having greatly facilitated the Imperial Chancellor's task.[1] In more recent years the German Government gradually gained over several others of the Alsace-Lorraine leaders ; and in 1917 (as we shall presently see) we find that solemn declarations were made in the Upper and Lower Chambers expressing loyalty and firm adherence to Germany.

In 1913, again, Alsace-Lorraine asked for "home rule " ; thus, M. Georges Weill, the Socialist deputy of Metz, pleaded for it in the Reichstag, December 4, 1913. Whereupon it was argued by some Germans that the demand was made not in the interest of the territory and its population, but simply because of a desire to be on the same footing with the constituent States of the Empire.

Alsace-Lorraine asks for "home rule" in 1913.

At the Social Democratic Conference of Jena, 1913, the Alsatian Socialists present submitted a resolution claiming for their country republican autonomy ; this resolution was unanimously confirmed on July 5, 1914, by the Alsace-Lorraine Socialist Congress held at Strassburg.

Republican autonomy claimed.

There is no doubt that before the present war the memory of 1870-1, if not entirely obliterated in Alsace-Lorraine, had been fast fading. As a recent French writer observes[2]: "Il est d'ailleurs trop vrai que, jusqu'à ces derniers temps, la pensée de l'Alsace-Lorraine et, en général, les souvenirs de 1870 avaient grandement perdu de leur puissance sur les masses. Elles avaient appliqué à leur manière le mot malheureux de Gambetta, *Il faut y penser toujours et n'en parler jamais.* Elles n'en parlaient jamais et n'y pensaient pas davantage."

Before the present war memory of 1871 fast fading in Alsace-Lorraine.

[1] *Op. cit.*, p. 125.
[2] Général Palat, *L'Alliance franco-allemande ou la guerre* (Paris, 1914), p. 133.

NATIONALIST MOVEMENT 195

M. Jacques Preiss, formerly deputy for Alsace-Lorraine in the Reichstag, and previously one of the most vigorous protesters against the annexation, emphasised in an address[1] delivered on February 17, 1913, that his countrymen were strongly opposed to war as a means of settling the question, that they did not desire their rights and liberties to be defended by violence or menaces, and that all they wanted was autonomy. By way of summing up our considerations regarding the autonomist movement and the predominating views that were held by the leaders of political thought in Alsace-Lorraine before the present war, we may set forth the following passages from the address referred to above :

"Alsace-Lorraine wants autonomy. She adopts the motto : 'Alsace for the Alsatians.' She claims to be put on an equal footing with the other parts of the Empire. She wants her own government and her own legislative body, both to be independent in the same degree as those of the Grand-Duchy of Baden, of Mecklenburg, and of the little principality of Reuss, the younger branch. She wishes to govern herself, to regulate her home affairs in her own way, to live her own life, according to her characteristic tastes and traditions. She wishes her particular individuality to be respected, just as that of Baden, Bavaria, and the other States of the Empire is respected. We have the same duties and the same burdens as the other parts of Germany, and we ought in common justice to have the same rights and the same liberties.

Summary of aims and ideals.

"At home no one listens to us, no one understands. That is why we have decided to bring our just claims

[1] See Bourdon, *L'Énigme allemande*, pp. 467 *seq.* ; English trans., pp. 353 *seq.*

before the pacific tribunal of European public opinion, which has so strongly asserted its great ideas of justice and solidarity with regard to the Balkan peoples. And no one shall hinder us from expressing ourselves wherever we may think it useful and necessary. It ought to be known in the civilised world, that in the centre of modern Europe there is an oppressed people, who, although of an ancient and highly civilised race, and passionately addicted to peaceful industries, is yet deprived of the essential conditions of a normal and honourable existence.

"The German Empire holds Alsace-Lorraine in virtue of the Treaty of Frankfort, concluded between France and Germany. Alsace-Lorraine has never adhered to this treaty. Her word has never been pledged in favour of this treaty. Her consent has always been withheld. Not only has Alsace-Lorraine never accepted or ratified this treaty, but she has formally protested against her cession to and incorporation with Germany. These are the plain and simple facts.

"There are jurists who declare with much learning that all that counts for nothing, that there is no Alsatian question, that it has been definitively settled by the Treaty of Frankfort. Let us leave these good people to their gentle babblings and stick to facts. The protest of Bordeaux and Berlin is an historical fact. This historical fact is so clear, so striking, so dazzling, and so charged with moral significance, that in any case it would need an equivalent act on the part of the people of Alsace-Lorraine, an equally clear, obvious, and open manifestation, showing a will and sentiments entirely opposed, in order to efface it and blot it out of our history. . . .

"Let the people of Alsace-Lorraine, then, be con-

NATIONALIST MOVEMENT

sulted as to their nationality, and, provided they have a free vote, we shall accept this as a sovereign decree. ... Above all written law and formal treaties imposed by force of arms, there is the natural right of a people to decide its own nationality. ..."

It is to be observed that, in view of the earlier portion of this extract, the later passage as to choice of nationality does not appear to mean a choice as between French and German nationality, *i.e.* between remaining a part of the German Empire or returning to France, but a choice as between the existing position of the Reichsland and the status of a confederate State of the German Empire, with all the rights of autonomy and self-government. An ardent Alsatian patriot like M. Wetterlé [1] holds that this autonomy aimed at is to be only a stepping-stone to another goal, namely, reunion with France; others look upon it as an advance towards the achievement of complete independence. But whether or no this be the real view at present of the majority of the Alsatians and Lorrainers, there is no evidence that such was their view before the present war.

The measures of repression adopted by the Imperial Government and the brutal proceedings of the German officials in Alsace-Lorraine no doubt alienated the people, and turned many of them to France. But there is no doubt also that those who in such circumstances turned their eyes to their mother-country fully realised that it was powerless to come to their assistance, and that their yearnings and sentiments thus provoked were but a natural, though ineffective, reaction to the oppression suffered by them. Similarly, the

Did Alsace-Lorraine desire reunion with France?

[1] *Op. cit.*, p. 108.

occasional anti-German outbursts, *e.g.* in 1908 and in 1913, indicated the hostility of the people to the German régime and the offensive militarism ; they were not necessarily manifestations of a widespread determination or even desire to effect a reunion with France. Warm sympathies and cherished recollections connected with France were evoked ; but we cannot conclude therefrom that the predominant aim of the people as a whole was to bring about an incorporation with France.

Thus in 1908, in the case of the Noisseville affair, when Count Zeppelin, the Statthalter, authorised the erection of a monument to French soldiers who fell at Noisseville, large masses of the Lorraine people assembled to witness the dedication, sang the *Marseillaise,* and otherwise gave vent to sympathy for their former country. That the Germans were a little alarmed at this manifestation and much more irritated thereby is not surprising ; that they determined to tighten their grip on the territory and to wean the people from francophil tendencies by all manner of severe measures is true ; but the conclusion drawn from this incident by certain Alsace-Lorraine patriots is scarcely warranted.

<small>Noisseville affair.</small>

Again, in 1913, in the Saverne (Zabern) affair, when a Prussian subaltern aroused the hostility of the local population by abusing Alsatians before his men, the general indignation excited was against the insolent and contemptuous attitude of the Prussian military hierarchy, and merely showed that the germanisation of the people was by no means achieved and that their subjection was not acquiesced in. Indeed, it was incidents like this that provoked the disaffection and resistance of the people much more acutely than did the systematic measures adopted

<small>Saverne affair.</small>

NATIONALIST MOVEMENT 199

by the Imperial Government for the purpose of bringing about the *entwelschung* of the provinces. No wonder, then, that Herr von Jagow afterwards observed, in a letter that was made public: "The officers stationed in Alsace-Lorraine have the impression of living in an enemy country." Officers swollen with arrogance and haughtiness, and nourishing a profound contempt for civilians, will always find themselves in an enemy country wherever there are traditions of liberty and equality before the law.

The Alsatians in general have no leanings towards the neo-germanic culture or to the German political conservatism; they are democratic and republican in temperament, and opposed to the régime of paternalism, and everything in the German polity that savours of the *ancien régime* and dynastic loyalism, and demands subservience to officialdom and militarism.[1] It is the arrogance and persecuting spirit of the conquerors, rather than what is German in itself, that arouse their antipathy and disaffection. The peasantry as a whole concern themselves little with the question whether they are more French or more German, or with the questions of broader politics; they show no enthusiasm for problems of this kind; what they prefer, above all, is to be let alone, to be allowed to go on in their own way, and to be less interfered with in regard to the exactions of military service. They are not really dissatisfied, and not hostile to the German administration, whose thorough and systematic methods they appreciate, as conducing to the agricultural as well as to the industrial progress of the country. On the other hand, the old

(Attitude of the people towards France and Germany.)

[1] *Cf* Lichtenberger, *op. cit.*, p. 42.

Alsatian and Lorraine aristocracy and bourgeoisie are in favour of French culture and the French language, which they endeavour to maintain despite the ubiquitous restrictions imposed. But there have been numerous defections among the bourgeois classes; more and more of them have associated themselves with the national movement, and have set their minds on national self-realisation as against any possible amalgamation with France. Thus we may say that the intimate feelings of the great majority of the population before the present war can be pretty adequately expressed by the following three lines of current doggerel:

"Français ne peux, (Frenchman I can't be,
Prussien ne veux,   Prussian I won't be,
Alsacien suis."   Alsatian I am).[1]

Agitation to return to France was temporary and restricted. The agitation to return to France was temporary and restricted. The "Ligue Patriotique" established in Strassburg, with the object of effecting the restoration of the provinces to France, contained only a few hundred members, and already in 1894 there was very little active propaganda; so that its fundamental aim assumed the form of a mere *vœu*, or pious aspiration. Writing in 1915, MM. Lichtenberger—anti-German as they are—express a doubt whether the Alsatians, if given the choice, would prefer French to German administration.[2]

Position of the mass of the people. It is necessary to take cognisance of the fact that, notwithstanding occasional anti-German ebullitions, the mass of the people have fallen into line with the German régime and have taken full advantage of the benefits it offered. To mention but one instance: "Is it not a noteworthy

[1] Jordan, *op. cit.*, p. 83.   [2] *Op. cit.*, p. 87.

sign," asks Karl Blind, " that in these once French provinces—which are situated inland, high up in the south of Germany—the number of seamen, cadets, and officers who have, of their own free will, entered the German fleet should have risen during the last eight years [1884-1902] from 145 to 1,750 ? This number is nearly twice that which would correspond to the number of the population of Alsace-Lorraine, as compared with the remainder of Germany." [1]

The French Socialist deputy, M. Sembat, who is well acquainted with the popular tide of feeling, doubted in 1913 whether Alsace-Lorraine was anxious to be restored to France at all. He points out that, with the passing of time, great material and moral modifications have been brought about in the territory ; that the constant influx of immigrants, who are not all detested by the native population, has inevitably made a profound difference. He emphasises that a distinction must be drawn between the Alsace-Lorraine of to-day and that of 1871, that the temper of Alsace-Lorraine forty years after the annexation is not to be judged from the charlatanism of grief of the French boulevards, from the barrel-organ exhibitions of Parisian alleys, or from the myths of café-concerts. " Quelle est aujourd'hui la volonté de l'Alsace-Lorraine ? " he asks. " Je ne dis pas de l'Alsace-Lorraine de 1871, de l'Alsace-Lorraine en deuil, à genoux, éplorée et telle que l'éternisent, en statues de pierre, les sculpteurs patriotes. Je dis de l'Alsace-Lorraine d'à présent, de cette région si pleine de vie, si active, si prospère, si industrieuse et qui n'a rien, je vous assure, des allures languissantes et geignardes que lui prêtent les mythes de nos cafés-concerts."

Temper of Alsace-Lorraine after forty years of annexation.

[1] *Fortnightly Review* (1902), vol. lxxviii. p. 259.

We must recognise the truth that Alsace and Lorraine, originally different in many respects, acquired through their common destiny a common spirit, and have developed, in the twenty-five years before the present war, a distinctive personality, and their own particular ideals of nationalism and self-government. Thus Alsace-Lorraine is neither French nor German; it is itself. Through the failure to grasp this fundamental point, both France and Germany have in the past made many serious mistakes and have been misled by unfounded assumptions and grave misconceptions. If Alsace-Lorraine has any noticeable affinity with any neighbouring country at all, it is perhaps with Switzerland.[1]

<small>Distinctive personality of Alsace-Lorraine.</small>

Account must be taken, too, of the fusion between natives and immigrants, and of the rise of the younger generations in the country. A considerable proportion of the immigrants—the *Eingewanderte*—are now in the second generation; and many of them have contracted marriages with the native stock. It has, indeed, been calculated that over 12 per cent. of the annual number of marriages are "mixed"; and that 28 per cent. of the children born are either entirely German or the issue of these mixed marriages. It is a mistake to suppose that all these immigrants are bullies, arrogant interlopers, and devoid of all agreeable qualities. Even such an ardent patriot and uncompromising censor of the German régime as Maurice Barrès sees fit to portray a fine immigrant type in Asmus, in his novel *Colette Baudoche*. Colette marries Asmus; what is her position thereafter with regard

<small>Fusion between natives and immigrants.</small>

[1] Jordan, *op. cit.*, p. 76.

NATIONALIST MOVEMENT 203

to the contending claims in Alsace-Lorraine, and to whatever *revanche* aspirations may be cherished in France? Can she desire war to bring about a liberation of the provinces? The voice of Colette Asmus, says M. Sembat,[1] has frequently been heard in Mülhausen.

Moreover, the new generation does not regard France as its " patrie " ; nor, indeed, does it, for the most part, regard Prussia or any other State whence the older generation came as its *vaterland*. The Alsatian-born sons of the immigrants consider themselves as Alsatians ; and many of them are in fact vigorous leaders in the autonomist movement. They live and think as Alsatians, and speak the Alsatian dialect.[2] This assimilation by the new environment is more thorough and striking in the case of the sons of the South German immigrants ; for there is a far greater kinship between the latter and Alsatians than between the North Germans and the Alsatians. With regard to the position of this new generation and the question of assimilation, M. André Lichtenberger relates an illustrative anecdote of peculiar significance : At Strassburg two boys—one an Alsatian, the other the son of an immigrant—began to quarrel in the street. " You pig of a Prussian," cried the first. Whereupon the other exclaimed indignantly, " That is not true ! My father was a Prussian, but I am an Alsatian." [3]

The new generation does not regard France as its " patrie."

Furthermore, in our effort to ascertain the true feelings and desires of the people of Alsace-Lorraine

[1] *Op. cit.*, p. 160.
[2] *Cf.* H. Albert, in *Renaissance latine*, October 15, 1903, p. 70 ; referred to by Novicow, *op. cit.*, p. 167.
[3] *Le Matin*, March 26, 1911 ; cited by Novicow, *op. cit.*, p. 167.

ALSACE-LORRAINE

as a whole, we must take care not to be misled by various indications of a doubtful character.

Doubtful indications as to feelings and desires of the people. First, there is the question of language, to which reference has already been made.[1] Of the total population of Alsace-Lorraine, viz. about 2,000,000 (1,500,000 in Alsace and 500,000 in the annexed Lorraine), it appears that only about one-sixth of them are of French origin or speak French or a French dialect as their mother-tongue.

Language.

The greater part of the lower classes understand French even when they do not speak it in their homes; whilst the educated classes generally, excepting the immigrants, speak French by preference. Thus before 1870, says Karl Emil Franzos, about one-third of the bourgeoisie of Strassburg could speak and write French; another third did not write it, but understood it and spoke it more or less; the remaining third used only the Germanic dialect. But at the beginning of the twentieth century, notwithstanding a long period of German domination, about half of its population speak and write French, whilst a quarter of its population do not know it at all.[2] Thus French has advanced in many quarters, despite the opposition offered thereto by the governing authorities. Roughly speaking, the boundary between the French and German languages in Alsace follows the summit line of the Vosges. Herr Werner Wittich, a professor at the University of Strassburg, points out that on the whole the upper and middle classes of the towns, as well as the gentry of the country, and the people of the world, prefer French for their usual speech and communication, though they may speak the

[1] See *supra*, pp. 38, 123.
[2] Cited by Florent-Matter, *L'Alsace-Lorraine de nos jours* (1908), p. 193.

Germanic dialect to their servants and workmen. We may say, then, that at least four languages and dialects are spoken in Alsace-Lorraine, viz. French, German, a Germanic dialect, and a French dialect (or at least a form of French which differs very much from the standard French of educated Frenchmen). However this may be, we cannot infer from this distribution of languages, or from the preference shown here or there for French, conclusions as to political preference and attachment on the one hand, and aversion and disaffection on the other. For, in the first place, the use of a language is determined by geographical and hereditary circumstances ; and, secondly, the preference for French is for the most part due to the preference for French literature, culture, and social life. The international diplomacy of the past has preferred French to German because it was simpler, more elastic, more pleasing, and in all respects more suitable for intercourse, not because the government of the French was preferred to that of the Germans.

Nor can we infer political preferences from the character of the names of the inhabitants. In certain localities, as has already been shown,[1] Ger-   Names of man names predominate ; but it may well inhabitants. be that many of these names have deliberately been adopted conformably to the dictates of prudence or the exigencies of business.

Another source of error as to the temper and requirements of the people of Alsace-Lorraine is to be found in the productions of imaginative Novels and literature. Reference has been made to a poetry not a certain novel of Maurice Barrès. But it safe guide. would be altogether unscientific, to say the least, to

[1] See *supra*, p. 119.

place too great reliance on the constructive imaginings of novelists : it is not the aim and purpose of novelists and other artists to portray a people, and their circumstances, in general, but only particular characters and situations, which may well diverge far from the so-called average type, and the usual prevailing conditions. M. Barrès depicts in a masterly manner the strength of French sentiment in certain places, for example, in Metz ; but he does not deal with the powerful autonomist currents which well-nigh swept aside in many parts of the country the previously cherished French feelings and predilections. Nor are we on surer ground when we consider the passionate outbursts of native poets, such as Edgar Reyle of Metz, who exclaims in his *Gloria Victis* (1908) :

"La Patrie, oh! c'est tout! quoi qu'on puisse dire.
C'est la mère commune et l'immortel amour ;
Honte ou mépris à ceux qui la renient un jour ! "

Again, the outpourings of the chauvinistic journals of the contending parties cannot be regarded as representing a widespread public opinion ; we can readily understand, from our own experience of political journalism and pamphleteering, that the views expressed therein are frequently no more than the views of the individual writers, and are not necessarily shared by considerable sections of the community.

Newspapers.

Further, one or two writers have suggested that the fact that children and others in Alsace-Lorraine sometimes exclaim " Vive la France ! " serves to show the prevailing sentiment and leaning of the people. It may as well be argued that because Englishmen occasionally call out " Good old Ireland! " therefore they are in favour of Home Rule, or prefer Ireland to England.

Exclamations of " Vive la France ! "

NATIONALIST MOVEMENT 207

Finally, censors of the Germans and partisans of the French have pointed out that the native Alsatian women adopt the fashions of Paris rather than those of Berlin. But do they do so to mark their political preferences or to indicate their national grievances? It is not unreasonable to conclude that they do so because the Paris fashions are " smarter " and more becoming.

<small>French fashions of women.</small>

In conclusion, we may refer to the attitude of Alsace-Lorrainers at the outbreak of and during the present war. The autonomist movement before the war was based on the acceptance of the territorial *status quo*, and on the recognition that Germany was capable of preserving it, and that France was and would probably remain powerless to alter it; the Treaty of Frankfort was thus regarded by the advocates of autonomy as incapable of abrogation *de facto*, and as recording and sanctioning a territorial adjustment which was a *fait accompli*. But the declaration of war and the accession of powerful allies to the side of France opened a new prospect to many Alsatians and Lorrainers—a prospect that had hitherto existed, if it existed at all, in the margin and not in the focus of their consciousness. It seemed as though the earlier dream of reunion with France might, after all, become a reality; and the steadfast devotees of the mother-country began once again, and with greater vigour and ardour, to declare their claims to the world.

<small>Attitude of Alsace-Lorrainers at outbreak of the war.</small>

Several political leaders of the Reichsland went over to France and openly repudiated their allegiance to Germany. The deputy for Metz in the Reichstag, a Social Democrat who had been one of the autonomist leaders, fled to France and announced there that the *pays messin* was looking forward to reincorporation with its former country. M. Blumenthal, the mayor of Colmar, also fled and made a similar announcement in regard to Upper Alsace. The Abbé Wetterlé, a former deputy of the Reichstag and of the Alsace-Lorraine chamber, who has recently delivered numerous eloquent public lectures ardently advocating the restoration of Alsace-Lorraine to France, stated in the *Écho de Paris*, August 28, 1914, that he had been in favour of autonomy because he had neither hoped nor expected that the provinces would be regained by war; but that, war having broken out, the whole situation was thereby at once changed, thus making possible the reannexation of the territory to France.

During the course of the war declarations were made from time to time by representatives of various Alsace-Lorraine societies expressing a wish that the provinces should return to France.[1] Thus the Ligue Patriotique des Alsaciens-Lorrains, which was established in London in November 1914, aims at " a speedy reunion with France, so desirable and necessary for historical and economic reasons," and has issued several pamphlets in support of its object.

Again, after the outbreak of hostilities, many Alsace-Lorraine soldiers have deserted from the German Army. The Paris newspaper, *Le Matin*, of August 22, 1917, stated : " The desertions which have taken place since 1914 in tens of thousands in the regiments recruited in Alsace-Lorraine, the 3,000 years of imprisonment imposed in the space of a year on inhabitants of Alsace-Lorraine suspected of sympathy for France, suffice to illustrate the feelings which the two provinces cherish in regard to Ger-

[1] See *Le Matin* (Paris), August 22, 1917.

NATIONALIST MOVEMENT 209

many." Similarly, M. Georges Weill, a Strassburg Alsatian who represented Metz in the Reichstag, asserted, in a lecture delivered in Essex Hall, London, November 17, 1917, that in the few months after August 1914 more than 16,000 Alsatian-Lorrainers deserted from the German Army.[1]

We have already referred to the German proceedings and rigorous precautionary provisions adopted in the provinces on the eve of the mobilisation and after the commencement of the war—the preparation of lists of suspects, the restrictions on free movement and on the use of French in conversation, the censorship of news, the transportation and internment of many persons of doubtful German loyalty, etc.[2] That the military authorities were alarmed and were determined to apply the most drastic measures to cases of hostility or disaffection goes without saying. Thus, a Bavarian general is reported to have issued a proclamation, at the time his troops were crossing the Rhine, wherein he observed : " You are entering an enemy country, and you must bear yourselves accordingly." Similarly, the proclamation of General Gaede at Kaysersberg said : " The country pleases me, but its inhabitants will have to be destroyed."[3]

Attitude of the German authorities on outbreak of the war.

On the other hand, account must be taken of the pronouncements made in June 1917 by both Chambers of Alsace-Lorraine affirming their desire to perpetuate their union with the German Empire, and emphasising that what the people had before the war been striving for was autonomy within the Empire. Thus Dr. Ricklin,

Declarations of the two Chambers, 1917.

[1] *Observer*, November 18, 1917.
[2] See *supra*, p. 175.
[3] Wetterlé, in *Fortnightly Review*, November 1917, p. 799.

14

the president of the Second Chamber, said in the presence of the Statthalter: " The Germans, and in particular we, the inhabitants of Alsace-Lorraine, will never forget that the Kaiser, by proffering the hand of peace, evinced his readiness to put an end to the calamities, moral and material, which have broken in upon our land. We bless every act calculated to abridge the war, were it only for a day, and we put away from us everything which, undertaken ostensibly for the purpose of changing our lot, in reality protracts the struggle, and, together with it, our sufferings. The people of Alsace-Lorraine, in its overwhelming majority did not desire war, and therefore did not want this war. What it strove for was the consummation of its political status in the limits of its dependence upon the German Empire ['in seiner Zugehörigkeit zum Deutschen Reich'], and, that settled, to resume its peaceful avocations. In this respect the war has changed nothing in our country. We make this confession aloud and before all the world. May it be everywhere heard, and may peace be speedily vouchsafed us!"

The speaker of the First Chamber, Dr. Hoeffel, expressed himself to the same effect. The following is the principal passage of his speech: " Alsace-Lorraine in particular has felt how heavily the war presses upon us all; but selfless sacrifice is here, too, taken for granted. Our common task has knit the imperial provinces more closely together than before, and has also drawn more tightly their links with the German Empire." [1]

The Abbé Wetterlé, however, maintains that the above pronouncements are not representative of the

[1] These passages are quoted by Dr. E. J. Dillon, in *Fortnightly Review*, September, 1917, p. 344, referring to the *Frankfurter Zeitung*, June 10, 1917.

NATIONALIST MOVEMENT

opinion of the provinces, and therefore do not possess the importance which has been attached to them. He says that before the opening of the spring session, the Imperial Chancellor, Herr von Bethmann-Hollweg, proceeded to Strassburg in order to obtain from the local parliament declarations of loyalty to Germany, and that he was accompanied by the Socialist deputy, Herr Sudekum, who was to endeavour to win over the extreme left—eleven out of sixty deputies. But they refused to associate themselves with the proposed collective declaration. The Imperial Chancellor approached the bishops of Strassburg and Metz (Mgr. Fritzen and Mgr. Bentzler)—*ex-officio* members of the Upper Chamber—but could not obtain from them a pledge of attachment in the name of their diocesans. "The bishops thus refused to alienate themselves, by a declaration which would have been severely condemned, from the sympathies of their subordinates."[1] (As to this conclusion we may say, in passing, that it scarcely possesses logical cogency, inasmuch as it involves a begging of the question: for we are not sure whether the declaration would have been condemned, and what the sympathies of their subordinates were.) Further, the same writer points out that Dr. Ricklin is an *arriviste* and a turncoat, owing his appointment of president of the Second Chamber to the agrarians whose cause he had always espoused; and that Dr. Hoeffel was an opportunist throughout, being one of the senators directly nominated by the Emperor, and that his speeches have not received wide approval.[2] Apart from this personal stricture it is true that the Upper Chamber, considering its

<small>Whether these declarations are representative.</small>

---
[1] *Fortnightly Review*, November 1917, p. 796.
[2] *Ibid.*, p. 798.

extraordinary composition,¹ can hardly be the interpreter of popular views and feelings.

The only fair and safe inference deducible from the above account of the secession of several political leaders of Alsace-Lorraine, the declarations of refugees, the precautionary measures of the German Government taken in the territory, the desertions from the German Army, the proclamations of military commanders, the pronouncements made in the territorial Chambers, and the criticism thereof by ardent patriots, is that some people in Alsace-Lorraine were, after the outbreak of the war, desirous of being united again to France, and that others were desirous of remaining within the German Empire, especially if autonomy were conceded to them. What the proportion of these or those people is in regard to the total population cannot be estimated; whether the views of the one side or the other represent the views of a decisive majority cannot be affirmed.

Conclusion deducible therefrom.

Moreover, we must take into consideration an important factor affecting the determination of these views, viz. the vicissitudes of the war and the expectations of victory on the part of the Allies or the Central Powers. No one can imagine that, in the event of the overthrow of the latter, the native Alsatians and Lorrainers will deliberately and voluntarily choose to continue their association with Germany. On the other hand, are we justified in assuming that, if Germany should eventually triumph, those same people would still prefer to go over to a defeated France? The best way to ascertain the sense of the population is by asking, without threats or pressure, each citizen to express his true sentiments and wishes; and the best time and circumstances in which to ascertain

¹ See *supra*, p. 170.

this is not when one or other alliance of belligerents is being worsted or has been vanquished, but when neither side can properly claim an outstanding victory, and when the terms of peace can be arranged by negotiation and compromise instead of being dictated at the point of the bayonet by a victorious belligerent.

Thus it is submitted that the most rational and reliable guidance for settling the destiny of the provinces is to be found in the preponderating opinion and wishes of the population as they were expressed for years before the present war, and not in the uncertain, unnatural, and temporary conditions introduced by the war, nor under the influence of passions and fears engendered thereby. But if it be thought that the sense of the majority of the people may have entirely or substantially altered for good as a result of the present conflict, then it becomes necessary to ascertain it clearly and accurately by means of a justly contrived plan [1]; it would be unfair and unsafe merely to assume that it has changed in a contrary direction. What the desires of the great majority of the people were before the war we have attempted to set forth in the previous pages; by way of supplement we have now to consider the views and feelings in France with regard to Alsace-Lorraine, as they, too, existed before the war and after its outbreak.

---

[1] See *infra*, chap. xvii.

CHAPTER XI

VIEWS AND FEELINGS IN FRANCE AS TO ALSACE-LORRAINE

Three phases of French feeling—*Revanche* ideal—Evanescence of *revanche* ideal · contributory causes—Pacific policy of French democracy— Why *revanche* ideas were passing away—Disturbing currents in France since 1871—France and the question of nationalities—Recent national policy of France—Von Bulow's view of the French temper— French views after outbreak of the war—British view—Why France determined to recover Alsace-Lorraine—Whether recovery would be " restoration " or conquest—Status of Alsace-Lorrainers in France during the war.

OF the views and feelings in France with regard to the lost provinces there are three phases : first, passionate resentment at the laceration and a determination to effect a *revanche* (that is, to " get even " with Germany) ; secondly, the evanescence of the *revanche* ideal ; and thirdly, the sudden recrudescence of this ideal on the outbreak of the Great War.

<small>Three phases of French feeling.</small>

The famous declaration of the deputies of Alsace-Lorraine in the National Assembly is said to have been drawn up by or under the direction of Gambetta. The latter, who had proved himself for a space a mighty protagonist in the desperate struggle against the invaders, after the annexation gave utterance to a dictum which has been variously interpreted. His " n'en parlons jamais, pensons-y toujours " has been taken by some people to be a counsel of acquiescence in the accomplished fact. But there is little doubt that he really meant the.

<small>Revanche ideal.</small>

contrary—viz. silent preparation for the day when France would be in a position to make her actions speak louder than her words. Indeed, he emphasised that, failing the deliverance of the captive, there would be no peace in Europe and order and revival in France : " Il n'y aura de paix en Europe, d'ordre et de renaissance en France, que le jour où nous aurons délivré la captive. Préparons-nous sans phrases, et n'ayons jamais d'autre pensée que la reprise de notre bien." [1]

Ardent souls like Paul Déroulède gathered round them a League of Patriots and persistently endeavoured to maintain the *revanche* aspirations in the forefront of the French national life and policy. To men like these, whose longing for restitution was unwavering and all-absorbing, nothing could possibly be an adequate compensation for the territorial spoliation, except the actual recovery of what had been taken away. The acquisition of new colonies could not in their eyes make up for the loss. Thus, Déroulède, putting what he conceived to be his country's indefeasible national duty before all projects of a colonial policy, exclaimed to Jules Ferry : " Moi, j'ai perdu deux enfants ; et vous, vous m'offrez vingt domestiques." Similarly, masterly and eloquent writers such as Maurice Barrès did much to nurture and advance the old ideal. These efforts found support at the tribune, in the press, and on the stage.

And so for a long time the wound remained open; grief, rancour, and vows of retaliation were widespread in France, and were common to all parties and all sections of the people. As M. Sembat says : " Des cris déchirants, d'abord, au moment où le fer nous coupa un morceau de nous-mêmes ; puis d'éclatantes lamentations, mêlées à des clameurs de haine, et à

[1] H. Galli, *Gambetta et l'Alsace-Lorraine* (Paris, 1911), p. 28.

des serments de revanche ; enfin, de longs et pénibles gémissements, dont le temps assourdit la plainte. Ces cris, puis ces clameurs, puis ces plaintes sortaient de nos cœurs, de tous nos cœurs. Pas un Français, pas un seul, du royaliste au communard, du cagot à l'athée, qui au lendemain de la guerre ne les ait poussés de toute son âme."[1] The most poignant element in the disaster that gave rise to this national passion was the fact that France had in 1871 paid for her liberation from the invaders by the sacrifice of a group of her loyal citizens.[2] But we can by no means be certain that, even if the provinces and their population had soon afterwards been restored, France would have ceased cherishing a hope of retaliation, in view of the deep humiliation caused by her signal defeat and the exorbitant ransom of five thousand millions of francs. The history of the world shows that, when one State, relying on its superior brute force, acts unconscionably towards another, it not infrequently sows the wind to reap the whirlwind.

With the passing of time and the economic recuperation and growing prosperity of France, these *revanche* ideals began to lose ground generally ; practical-minded people recognised the uselessness and inexpediency of maintaining their devotion to them, they felt that the lost provinces could never be recovered forcibly by France, which was being overwhelmingly surpassed by Germany in the increase of population and in military and naval armament and organisation. Indeed Gambetta, who died a few weeks before the conclusion of the Triple Alliance was made public, and his opponent Jules

<small>Evanescence of *revanche* ideal.</small>

---

[1] *Faites un roi, sinon faites la paix* (1913), p. 148.
[2] *Cf.* Lichtenberger, *op. cit.*, p. 15.

FRENCH ATTITUDE

Ferry, were disposed to come to an understanding with Germany. In certain limited circles, however, there were still those who adhered to the old ideal, and at every opportunity gave vent to their feelings. Moreover, various public events, notably in the eighties, stirred up France, and showed that the anti-German sentiment was but latent, and that the *revanche* aspirations still possessed some strongholds in the country. [Contributory causes.] In September 1883 Alfonso XII of Spain came to Paris on his way home after his visits to the Austrian and to the German Emperors. When it was announced that the latter had made him colonel of a regiment of Uhlans garrisoned at Strassburg, the taking of which city was being celebrated in an ostentatious manner on the very arrival of Alfonso, protests were made in the Paris press, and the King was hooted as he drove through the streets with President Grévy. At the instance of the Extreme Left, General Thibaudin, the Minister of War, refused to meet " le roi uhlan." In 1886, with the advent of General Boulanger, a more vigorous military policy was inaugurated, which aroused a good deal of enthusiasm in France, and alarmed Bismarck, who, regarding Boulanger as the coming dictator for a war of retaliation, asked the Reichstag for an increased vote for the German Army, and sought to safeguard his country by the establishment of alliances. In April 1887 the Schnaebelé incident produced a grave Franco-German tension. The arrest of the French commissary-special, who had stepped over the frontier to effect a certain arrangement with the corresponding German official, was considered an outrage in France, but was justified by Bismarck before the Prussian Landtag in a speech in which he said it was impossible to live at peace with so bellicose a nation as the French. The whole proceeding was thought in France to be a trap laid by the Imperial Chancellor, with the object of provoking the French to adopt such a hostile attitude as would precipitate war. On the accession of William II, in the following summer, friendly overtures were made to France, but were not accepted. In February 1891 the young Emperor's mother came to Paris ; and her visit to various scenes of German triumph gave rise to an outburst of anger in the French press, which showed that the old fire was still smouldering. Again, anti-German feeling was revealed in France on the conclusion of the Franco-Russian *entente* in July 1891 ; and later, in 1905, on the occasion of the Franco-German conflict in Morocco. In regard to the latter affair, Mr. Bodley says : " The impression was current in France that Germany wished to give the French nation a fright before the understanding with England had reached an effective stage [the Anglo-French convention had been signed on April 8, 1904] ; and it was actually believed that the resignation of Delcassé averted a declaration of war. Although that belief revived to some extent the fading enmity of the French towards the conquerors of Alsace-Lorraine, the fear which accompanied it moved a considerable section of the nation to favour an understanding with Germany in preference to, or even at the expense of, friendly relations with England." [1]

The mourning figure of Strassburg in the Place de la Concorde of Paris symbolises the abducted daughters of the Vosges ; and it is in the presence of the Alsatian maid that the boulevards have continued more or less to cherish dreams of a *guerre de revanche,* of a *guerre d'honneur,* and have continued to respond in

[1] Art. *France,* in *Encyclopædia Britannica,* vol. x. (1910), p. 904.

their imagination to the traditional call of the *patrie mutilée*, and to the supposed appeal of the lost children.

But, despite such adventitious and sporadic manifestations, the overwhelming majority of the French people were for a long time before the present war sceptical as to such Alsatian sympathies, and were rather inclined to promote a pacific policy and the democratic interests of the country. *Pacific policy of French democracy.* And, as has already been pointed out in the preceding chapter, the Alsatians and Lorrainers themselves had long been doubtful as to the capacity, will, or inclination of the mother-country to embark on the perilous adventure of reconquest. Thus the ideals and aspirations which the events of 1870–71 had brought into being, and which were nurtured for some years afterwards, were beginning on all sides to pass away; and what with the autonomist movement and the era of Young Alsace inaugurated in the annexed provinces, the great majority of Frenchmen began seriously to doubt whether the lost children would be really disposed to return to France, even if they were relinquished by their conquerors. There is a pretty general agreement that Alsace-Lorraine would have been quite satisfied with the status of an autonomous State within the German Empire, and was in any case opposed to war as a means of effecting a solution [1]; so that France came to acquire the reasonable view that she ought to be satisfied, if the provinces themselves were satisfied. And General Palat, writing in 1914, expresses a widespread view when he says: " Pour notre modeste part, nous croyons que, si l'Alsace-Lorraine était satisfaite de cette autonomie restreinte, nous aurions mauvaise

[1] *Cf.* Sembat, *op. cit.*, p. 162.

grâce à être plus royalistes que le roi. . . . Cette solution, nous l'accepterions donc de grand cœur." [1]

Why were the old *revanche* ideas passing away? In the first place, as we have just pointed out, because it was realised that Alsace-Lorraine had been developing an individuality of its own, was striving to secure autonomy within the German Empire with which it was so closely allied economically, and was very probably unwilling for various reasons (which are to be considered later [2]) to be placed under French administration. Secondly, account must be taken of the internal dissensions in France, the disquieting political vicissitudes, and the consequent need that was felt everywhere for securing and cementing the unity of the country on a basis of peace and progress.

Why revanche ideas were passing away.

It is circumstances such as these, says a recent writer, that kept the question of Alsace-Lorraine dormant in the minds of Frenchmen: "The distracting influence of civil quarrels, colonial diversions, that vague terror of Cæsarism following a successful war which long haunted the diplomacy of the Republic, a widely diffused prosperity counselling comfortable acquiescence, the emasculate theories of internationalists, the fact that the centre of gravity in French politics has shifted to a part of the country which its immunity from invasion and its happy climate predisposed to an amiable materialism—all these causes contributed to keep the question of Alsace-Lorraine dormant in French minds." [3] But this dormancy practically amounted, except in a small minority of

---

[1] *L'Alliance franco-allemande ou la guerre* (Paris, 1914), pp. 145, 146.
[2] See *infra*, chap. xii.
[3] F. Y. Eccles, *Alsace-Lorraine* (Oxford Pamphlets, 1914–15).

FRENCH ATTITUDE

cases, to evanescence, if not to non-existence. These exceptional cases were for the most part the allies of the Royalist and clerical parties; but the mass of the nation, faithful and uncompromising republicans, discountenanced the *revanche* imaginings for the reason—amongst others—that their effective application would almost inevitably necessitate a revival of monarchical or personal rule. This is the fundamental point of view expounded in M. Sembat's widely circulated publication, to which we have already referred more than once. That the fear, however, was a mistaken one, is proved by the long period of war of incomparable magnitude waged by a united French nation. But would there have been this unity, initial warlike determination, and subsequent fighting persistence if France had not been supported from the very first by some of the mightiest Powers in the world?

It is difficult to give an affirmative answer to this question when we consider the numerous disturbing currents in French public life after the Franco-German War. First of all, there were the reactionary and monarchical projects associated with President Macmahon; then came the Boulangist movement, with its futile and paltry heroics, and its speedy collapse; next the Panama affair; the Dreyfus affair, and the anti-Semitic movement; anti-clericalism; to all of which being added the uncertain gyrations of foreign policy (from 1879 to 1894 there were no less than fourteen changes in the office of Minister for Foreign Affairs). The Dreyfus affair—with its revelations of military scandals, the conflict produced between pseudo-patriotism and anti-militarism, and the fear of republicans that it involved an attempt on the part of

Disturbing currents in France since 1871.

the army chiefs to introduce an ultramontane régime in France, whereby Jews, Protestants, and even all liberals were to be excluded from citizenship—intensified the doubt in reasonable men's minds as to the potentiality of the *revanche* policy, and the wisdom of continuing to talk of a " war of revenge." Moreover, the anti-clerical struggle, produced by the Dreyfus affair, had also a markedly chilling effect on Alsace-Lorraine, with its Catholic population amounting to 80 per cent. of the total number. To all these circumstances must be added this important consideration—the recognition of France that she was being hopelessly outstripped by Germany in the accumulation of armies, warships, and belligerent resources generally ; due account must also be taken of such matters as the development of socialism, the gravitation of the Catholic party towards the Centre party, the rise of other parties ; and, finally, we must remember the industrial expansion and the emergence of economic questions, together with the indubitably predominating desire of the nation for peace.

Further, as one of the ablest English writers on French public life and thought has pointed out, France in the pre-war period ceased to care about the question of nationalities : " It no longer troubles itself on the subject of nationalities.

France and the question of nationalities.

Napoleon III, who had more French temperament than French blood in his constitution, was an idealist on this question, and one of the causes of his own downfall and the defeat of France was his sympathy in this direction with German unity. Since Sedan little has been done in France to further the doctrine of nationalities. A faint echo of it was heard during the Boer War, but French sympathy with the struggling Dutch republics of South Africa

FRENCH ATTITUDE 223

was based rather on anti-English sentiment than on any abstract theory."[1] The same writer observes that the debates in the Chamber and the Senate on the Separation Bill (which became the Separation Law of December 9, 1905, coming into force January 1, 1906), convinced him that the age of theories and ideas was gone in France.[2] He says that the French nation at the beginning of the twentieth century had undergone a rapid transformation of character.[3] The electorate were affected chiefly by material concerns; " the strife of conflicting doctrine was assuaged under the more animating influence of material interest."[4] " . . . The idealistic causes which were at work in 1830, in 1848, and in 1871 are never heard of now. . . . The influences, which are now active, to rouse the revolutionary elements in the nation, are the living wage, the working day of eight hours, and the regulation of strikes. . . . The France of the young century is not the France of the last years of the old."[5]

To these observations may be added the testimony of a leading French historian. Summing up the recent national policy of France, at least till 1909, M. Bourgeois says, after pointing out the successful French colonial policy: " . . . France has shown great anxiety to associate herself with all the plans concerted between the Powers at the two Peace Conferences of the Hague, and with all efforts to prevent wars by arbitration treaties, while diminishing by international legislation their risks and deadly consequences. The restoration and development of her resources, commercial, agricultural, and colonial, a foreign defensive policy

<small>Recent national policy of France.</small>

---

[1] J. E. C. Bodley, art. *France*, in *Ency. Brit.*, vol. x. (1910), p. 904.
[2] J. E. C. Bodley, *The Church in France* (London, 1906), pp. 5, 7.
[3] *Ibid.*, p. 5.   [4] *Ibid.*, p. 9.   [5] *Ibid.*, pp. 10, 12.

directed towards the maintenance of her safety and the Balance of Power—these, and these alone, have been her general aims, her instinctive and national policy." [1] Thus the *revanche* ideas were fast passing away. Speaking of the military organisation after 1871, and the financial burdens on the people, the same writer observes : " It is evident that the sacrifices, once eagerly undertaken by the nation for its safety, appear less urgent and more burdensome to the more recent generations which have not experienced the danger, and are not actuated to the same degree by the bitterness of defeat and the desire of revenge." [2]

In concluding this section of the chapter we may set forth the remarkably different estimate of French aims and attitude recently made by Prince Bernhard von Bülow, Imperial Chancellor, 1904–9 :

Von Bülow's view of the French temper.
" The resentment against Germany might well be called the soul of French policy; the other international questions are more of a material nature, and only concern the body. It is a peculiarity of the French nation that they place spiritual needs above material ones.

" The irreconcilability of France is a factor that we must reckon with in our political calculations. It seems to me weakness to entertain the hope of a real and sincere reconciliation with France so long as we have no intention of giving up Alsace-Lorraine. And there is no such intention in Germany. There certainly are many individual points in which we can see eye to eye with France, and in which we can co-operate, at any rate, from time to time. We must always endeavour to preserve polite, calm, and peaceful relations with France. But beyond that we should

---

[1] E. Bourgeois, *The Third French Republic*, in *Camb. Mod. Hist.*, vol. xii. (1910), chap. v. p. 133.   [2] *Ibid.*, p. 97.

not pursue any will-o'-the-wisp delusions, otherwise we may meet with the fate of the astronomer in La Fontaine, who, while gazing at the stars, fell into the pit which lay at his feet, but which he had not seen. In this case the pit is called *Le trou des Vosges*.

"Also, as regards France, we must not hope too much from attentions and amenities—the small change of international intercourse. In saying this we do homage to the proud patriotism of a great nation. The resentment against Germany lies too deep in the hearts of the French for us to be able to overcome it by cheap expressions of friendship. France was never so hard hit, not even after the catastrophic defeats of 1812–15, as by the war of 1870–71. In France there is no comprehension of the fact that what seems to them the brutal severity of a conqueror was really a matter of national necessity to us Germans. Perhaps in course of time the French nation will grow reconciled to the decisions of the Peace of Frankfort, when it realises that they were and are irrevocable. But so long as France thinks she perceives a possibility of winning back Alsace-Lorraine, either by her own unaided efforts or with the help of others, so long will she consider the existing arrangement provisional and not final.

"The French have the right to claim understanding for this feeling with which the majority of the people are deeply imbued. It is a proof of a lively sense of honour if a nation suffers so keenly from a single injury to its pride that the desire for retribution becomes the ruling passion of the people. It is quite true that for many centuries France was responsible for the spirit of unrest which troubled the history of Europe. We had to fortify our position in the west in an enduring manner, so as to safeguard our peace from fresh disturbances. The remedy has not been altogether unavailing, not only so far as Germany is concerned, but for the whole of Europe. . . . We wish to prevent the return of such times as those of Louis XIV and of Napoleon I, and for our greater security have therefore strengthened our frontiers against France.

". . . The policy of revenge is supported by the unshakable belief of the French in the indestructibility of the vital power of France. This belief is based on all the experiences of French history. No nation has ever recovered so quickly as the French from the effects of national disasters; none have ever so easily regained their elasticity, their self-confidence, and their energy, after grievous disappointments and apparently crushing defeats. . . .

" When we consider our relations with France, we must not forget that she is unappeased. So far as man can tell, the ultimate aim of French policy for many years to come will be to create the necessary conditions, which to-day are still wanting, for a settlement with Germany with good prospects of success. If we soberly realise this truth, we shall be able to adopt a proper attitude towards France. Indignant tirades against the incorrigibility of the French are in very bad taste, as are futile attempts to propitiate them. The German ' Michel ' has no need again and again to approach the coy beauty with flowers in his hand; her gaze is riveted on the Vosges. Only an acceptance of the irrevocability of the loss of 1871 can accustom France finally and without restriction to the state of affairs fixed in the Peace of Frankfort. . . ."[1]

The above statement of the German ex-Chancellor

[1] *Imperial Germany*, English translation (London, 1914), pp. 70–74, 86.

needs little comment. It is obviously an entirely erroneous estimate, and an extraordinary misinterpretation of occasional and sporadic *revanche* manifestations as constituting the national policy of France. There is no doubt that pronouncements like this are meant to serve as a justification to the German people of the German Government's military and naval preparations and as a blind—for Europe in general—to cover the instinctive and insuperable aggressiveness of the pangermanists and the German military classes. The essential facts are that Germany had long been preparing for war, that she was a nation armed to the teeth and fully equipped in every conceivable manner, that she was ready to strike anywhere at a moment's notice, that her military projects were prearranged in every detail and were to be carried out according to programme ; that France did not desire and was not prepared for war, and that she indeed took up arms in August 1914, not because she wanted to recover Alsace-Lorraine, but because she was obliged to protect herself against this German aggressiveness, and was anxious to remove the constantly growing German menace which made life on the Continent well-nigh unbearable. To what extent the old *revanche* ideas and feelings were revived after the war had thus been precipitated we have now to consider.

His estimate erroneous.

At the session of the French Chamber, August 4, 1914, M. Viviani made but a brief allusion to Alsace-Lorraine : " L'Allemagne n'a rien à nous reprocher. Nous avons consenti à la paix un sacrifice sans précédent en portant un demi-siècle, silencieux, à nos flancs, la blessure ouverte par elle."

French views as to Alsace-Lorraine after outbreak of the war.

In November 1914 General Joffre said at Thann to the Alsatians amongst whom he found himself: " Notre retour est définitif, vous êtes Français pour toujours. La France apporte, avec les libertés qu'elle a toujours représentées, le respect de vos libertés à vous, des libertés alsaciennes, de vos traditions, de vos convictions, de vos mœurs. Je suis la France, vous êtes l'Alsace ; je vous apporte le baiser de la France."

This declaration was confirmed by President Poincaré at Saint-Amarin, February 12, 1915 : " Je viens confirmer aux populations d'Alsace les déclarations que leur a déjà faites le général Joffre. La France, heureuse d'ouvrir les bras à l'Alsace si longtemps et si cruellement séparée d'elle, ne doute pas que la victoire n'assure bientôt la délivrance des provinces qui lui ont été arrachées par la force ; et tout en respectant leurs traditions et leurs libertés elle leur rendra leur place au foyer de la patrie."

On December 23, 1914, at an extraordinary session of the Chambers, it was proclaimed that France was determined to fight on and not lay down arms until the outrage of 1871 was avenged and the provinces torn from her by force were reunited to her.

Similarly, M. Viviani, in the Chamber of Deputies on February 18, 1915, reaffirmed the resolve of France to prosecute the war " jusqu'à la libération morale de l'Europe," and demanded the return of Alsace-Lorraine : " Depuis quarante-quatre ans, messieurs, d'une façon permanente et plus vivement, j'allais dire plus tendrement depuis le début des hostilités, l'Alsace-Lorraine, sous toutes les formes, a manifesté son attachement au foyer français. Elle a préparé elle-même, par son héroïque fidélité, le retour à la patrie mutilée, si bien que, lorsqu'au jour venu, nous pourrons pour ainsi dire resserrer les bras autour d'elle, nous pourrons dire qu'elle nous est revenue non pas par le fait d'une conquête, mais d'une restitution." In regard to such pronouncements as this, we may say that France may have justifiably held that she had a moral right to endeavour to recover the lost provinces ; but we must add, with all due submission, that, conformably to the evidence adduced in this chapter, the claim as to Alsace-Lorraine having all along prepared itself for reunion to France can scarcely be substantiated.

On June 5, 1917, the French Chamber of Deputies adopted the following resolution by 453 votes against 55 : " Contresignant la protestation unanime qu'en 1871 firent entendre à l'Assemblée Nationale les représentants de l'Alsace-Lorraine, malgré elle arrachée à la France, elle déclare attendre de la guerre, qui a été imposée à l'Europe par l'agression de l'Allemagne impérialiste, avec la libération des territoires envahis, le retour de l'Alsace-Lorraine à la mère patrie et la juste réparation des dommages." The following day the French Senate too declared amongst the aims of the war " la restitution de l'Alsace-Lorraine."[1]

In a government statement made in the Chamber by M. Painlevé on September 18, 1917, it was said that " if France pursues this war it is neither for conquest nor vengeance," and one of her aims was proclaimed to be " the disannexation of Alsace-Lorraine."[2]

The following day M. Ribot, the Minister for Foreign Affairs, said : " We did not enter the conflict with

---

[1] *Bulletin des informations parlementaires. Publications du parlement interallié.* (No. 1. 1 juillet, 1917.)
[2] *Daily Telegraph*, September 19, 1917.

warlike designs. For forty-five years we desired peace, notwithstanding the bleeding wound in our side. And to-day, after all the French blood that has been shed during this long struggle which was imposed upon us, what do we want? Justice. France does not wish to do violence to any one. She only demands justice. . . . When we demand before the world the restoration of Alsace-Lorraine, we are the champions of violated right, and we claim from the world the indispensable preface to a durable peace, namely, reparation for the injustice which was done forty-five years ago, and which for forty-five years has weighed upon the world. If that is not done, nothing is done. (Loud cheers.) It would merely mean a truce for some years; whereas we shall not have made all our sacrifices in vain if we found peace on what is eternal—on justice and right." [1] The same minister observed on October 12, 1917, that an agreement by Germany to restore Alsace-Lorraine to France is " a condition precedent to a peace founded on justice," and he added: " There would be no peace which would guarantee our children from a renewal of such a terrible war, if the injustice of Alsace-Lorraine were not repaired." [2]

From time to time various other political leaders, such as M. Barthou, and more recently M. Clemenceau, have expressed themselves to the like effect. And in every case the idea of holding a plebiscite to determine the wishes of the population concerned was repudiated—when it was mentioned at all—as being at once unnecessary and in the circumstances insulting.

The French Socialist party, however, recognised the expediency and justice of resorting to a referendum on the ground that all oppressed populations were

[1] *Daily Telegraph*, Sept. 21 1917.   [2] *Times*, October 15, 1917.

FRENCH ATTITUDE 231

entitled to determine their own destiny, and held that the question of Alsace-Lorraine was not a purely territorial question, but a question of right. At the Congress of December 1915 the following resolution was passed by 2,759 votes against 72 and 92 abstentions : " Pas de paix durable sans que soit rendue aux populations opprimées de l'Europe la libre disposition d'elles-mêmes et sans que soit rétabli entre la France et l'Alsace-Lorraine, au nom d'un droit que le temps n'a pas prescrit, le lien que la brutalité de la force avait seule tranché en 1871, malgré la protestation socialiste de Bebel et de Liebknecht au sein de la nation allemande elle-même. Ce droit établi, la France saura se montrer prévoyante et juste en demandant à l'Alsace-Lorraine elle-même d'affirmer à nouveau, solennellement, comme le firent ses représentants à l'Assemblée de Bordeaux, sa volonté d'appartenir à la communauté française."

There is no need to give more references to the numerous and repeated French declarations on the subject, which have been consistent and unanimous. This openly expressed aim of France was accepted by the British Government and by authoritative spokesmen here, who have more than once declared their determination to support France so long as she laid claim to Alsace-Lorraine. Thus Mr. Lloyd George, the Prime Minister, said on October 11, 1917 : " However long the war may last, however great the drain upon our resources, this country intends to stand by her gallant ally France until she has redeemed her oppressed children from the degradation of a foreign yoke." [1] At the beginning of 1918, however, the Prime Minister made use of markedly modified expressions, when he said that the

British view.

[1] *Daily Telegraph*, October 12, 1917.

ALSACE-LORRAINE

Alsace-Lorraine question will have to come up for "reconsideration," along with other territorial questions, at the peace negotiations. And President Wilson expressed himself to the same effect.

We see, then, from the above pronouncements that France's resolve to recover the lost territories is based *Why France* on four main grounds—(1) to wipe away the *determined* bitter humiliation of having been forced to *to recover* *Alsace-* surrender a portion of her country and *Lorraine.* people contrary to their will, (2) to vindicate right and justice, (3) to give effect to the longings of the "lost children," and (4) to ensure the maintenance of European peace. The first reason is of course perfectly intelligible, and commends itself to all who possess any self-respect ; the second is also admissible if it be construed in the sense of *moral* right and justice, for—as we have shown in an earlier chapter [1] —the *legal* right and justice in regard to the possession of Alsace-Lorraine is undoubtedly on the side of Germany in the eye of international law and usage, through the sanction of the deliberately concluded Treaty of Frankfort ; the third is questionable, as we have already been obliged to infer from ample evidence ; the fourth reason is much more questionable.

With reference to these grounds suggested in the French claim, two points need to be emphasised—for *Whether* we must ever be mindful of the fact that *recovery* the Allies have from the first been fighting *would be* *" restora-* on behalf of law and order, and have re-*tion " or* peatedly protested against the signal viola-*conquest.* tions of international law committed by the Germans. In the first place, the French and others hold that the return of Alsace-Lorraine to France

[1] See *supra*, pp. 149 *seq.*

would be a "restoration" and not a conquest, and that the provinces have never formed part *de jure* of the German Empire. Secondly, it is contended that the German declaration of war in 1914 *ipso facto* abrogated the Treaty of Frankfort. The second point we have already dealt with, and have submitted that the contention is legally untenable.[1] As to the first point, we may say, briefly, that if Germany consents to return the provinces before the Allied forces have militarily occupied them, have ousted the Germans from them, and have determined to take them away permanently, such return will amount to a "restoration" in the proper sense of the term; but if Germany is compelled, through the military occupation by her opponents, to give up the territory, then the acquisition by France thereof is a result of conquest and annexation. Accordingly, if the formula "no annexation" is accepted by the belligerents, it necessarily implies that Germany is to retain Alsace-Lorraine.

Finally, a word must here be said regarding the status of Alsace-Lorrainers in France during the present war. If it be true that they (*i.e.* the annexed people and their descendants, not the German original inhabitants and immigrants) have always desired to return to France and that they have never ceased to be Frenchmen at heart, it follows that the moment they set foot on French soil they should be treated as Frenchmen and not subjected to discriminative regulations. Thus M. Helmer says that, in view of the Alsatian protests before the National Assembly at Bordeaux and the attitude of the population of the provinces for forty-four years, the "annexés" ought

<small>Status of Alsace-Lorrainers in France during the war.</small>

[1] See *supra*, pp. 151 *seq*.

to be considered simply as Frenchmen, even before the reunion resulting from victory.[1] Similarly, M. Barrès observes in the preface to the latter's book: " Il ne peut y avoir de doute que, même durant cette guerre et avant la réunion qu'amènera la victoire, les annexés doivent être considérés comme des Français." [2] The actual facts, however, do not correspond to these views. Whilst the " annexés " do not appear to be treated in France exactly like alien enemies, yet the régime applied to them—*e.g.* the insistence on the use of permits for residence, their internment, and various other restrictions—constitutes such a discrimination as amounts practically to a denial of their alleged status. " Décidément," observes M. Helmer, " la situation des Alsaciens n'est vraiment pas enviable." [3] No doubt precautions must be taken in these days. Whether or not it is expedient to do so, the actual treatment in France of the " annexés " and the theoretical claims advanced on their behalf are obviously incompatible.

Having already given an account of the nature of the Alsace-Lorraine question, the character of the country and people annexed, their history, the annexation in 1871, the claims of Germany to the provinces, the German régime therein, the views, feelings, and national movements in the Reichsland, the views and aspirations of France before and after the outbreak of the present war, we have now to address ourselves to our concluding task, viz. to examine the suggested solutions of the question and to show which it is best to adopt in view of the present complicated circumstances and conflicting claims and interests.

[1] P. A. Helmer, *France-Alsace* (Paris, n.d.), p. 123.
[2] Ibid., p. x.   [3] Ibid., p. 142.

CHAPTER XII

SOLUTIONS SUGGESTED : (*a*) REANNEXATION TO FRANCE

Reannexation followed by referendum suggested—German pronouncements as to Alsace-Lorraine—Forcible reannexation not a true solution; inherent difficulty—Various other difficulties: Frontier—Grouping of Alsace-Lorraine within political framework of France—The language question—The legal system—The industrial organisation—The commercial system—Fiscal legislation—The religious question—The educational system—Position of immigrants and the younger generation—The previous nationalist movement—Other difficulties. Interregnum suggested for smoothing over difficulties.

ONE of the solutions suggested as a settlement of the Alsace-Lorraine question is the reannexation or retrocession of the territory to France. This reannexation may assume one of two forms: it may be a forcible recovery, consecrated by the treaty of peace, as a result of a sufficiently decisive victory enabling the Allies to dictate terms; or it may be a voluntary cession on the part of Germany before such victory be gained. Each case assumes the willingness of the population of Alsace-Lorraine to accept and abide by the result. For the present we may eliminate this element of willingness or opposition, as we shall consider it later.

Reannexation, without being made subject to this latter qualification, has been advocated and claimed by many. Reference has already been made to the official French and British views. Some Frenchmen—for example, M. Albert Thomas,[1] the well-known Socialist—have brought forward a modified proposal, viz. that first

Reannexation followed by referendum suggested.

[1] *Times*, Jan. 22, 1918, p. 5.

the territory should be returned to France, and afterwards a referendum should be organized "under the ægis of a society of nations," for ascertaining the will of the population thus transferred. The intention here is obviously on the one hand to atone as far as possible for the wrong done to France in 1871, and on the other to apply the principle of the self-determination of populations—a principle that has recently been more than ever emphasised.

The main difficulty to be overcome is the opposition of Germany; for we cannot suppose that she will restore the territory voluntarily. The Germans are just as determined to hold Alsace-Lorraine as they are to hold Berlin. To overcome this determination by force of arms will mean to break the Central Empires into fragments and to annihilate the Germanic population. To achieve such a result would necessitate such unspeakably appalling slaughter, destruction, and sacrifice on all sides as would leave Europe a shambles and without any population at all. Is the result worth the cost? Only an unreasoning fanatic could answer this question in the affirmative.

However shallow and insincere German pronouncements in general may be, there can be no doubt that the reiterated declaration not to give up Alsace-Lorraine is meant in grim earnest. Thus Baron von Kühlmann, the Foreign Secretary, said in the Reichstag on October 9, 1917, in reply to Mr. Asquith's speech at Leeds, September 26, 1917, asking whether Germany was ready to restore what she took away from France in 1871: "There is but one answer to the question—Can Germany in any form make any concessions with regard to Alsace-Lorraine? The answer is, No, never. So long as a single German

German determination and pronouncements as to restoring Alsace-Lorraine.

SOLUTIONS: REANNEXATION

hand can hold a gun, the integrity of the territory handed down to us as a glorious inheritance by our forefathers can never be the object of any negotiations or concessions. I am sure that, whether on the Right or on the Left, you will stand for that with equal resoluteness and equal self-sacrifice. I am not of those who think that a candid statement of such a fact might be detrimental to the rise of a clear and sincere will for peace. On the contrary, I think such a will can only prosper and be fruitful on a ground of absolute clearness. Therefore I think it necessary to state emphatically, with all possible conciseness and clearness, as against all other questions which have of late so markedly come to the fore in public discussion, and which have taken up so much space, that what we are fighting for, and will fight for to the last drop of our blood, is not fantastic conquests, but before all the integrity of German soil." [1]

Similarly, a little later during the Kaiser's visit to Rumania, he is reported by the *Neue Freie Presse* of Vienna to have remarked in regard to M. Painlevé's speech in the French Chamber: " The maiden speech of the new French Premier has just been brought to me. So M. Painlevé wants Alsace and Lorraine again? Good! He can fetch them." [2]

In 1881 the Emperor William I said: " Germany would leave her eighteen army corps and her 42,000,000 people on the battle-field rather than surrender a single stone of the territory won in 1870."

It is of interest here to recall a statement made a year before the outbreak of the present war by the Berlin Professor of History, Dr. Hans Delbrück, who emphasised the absolute impossibility for Germany to

[1] *Daily Telegraph*, October 11, 1917.   [2] *Ibid.*, October 19, 1917.

give up the provinces or exchange them for other territory, and gives various reasons (which have already been dealt with in preceding chapters) why she insisted on the cession in 1871 and why she must retain them. He said to an interviewer that it was a mere waste of time to discuss the question of restoration; and he is reported to have expressed himself to the following effect : " I can conceive of no other single question within the scope of international politics, with the possible exception of disarmament, on which the German nation would chorus a more thundering ' No,' than of surrendering the conquered provinces. Alsace-Lorraine's connection with the Empire is the very last word of irrevocability. We might as well be asked to surrender Prussia as to give up the territory bought and paid for at Gravelotte, Mars-la-Tour, St. Privat, and Sedan. Restoration of Elsass-Lothringen is not debatable for us in any form whatever. No proffer of territory in exchange anywhere on the face of the globe could induce the German Government even to consider such a transaction. The anti-German sentiment there is a nebulous and vanishing force. It is kept up for the most part by clerical agitators. Compare the condition of the Roman Catholic Church in France and in Germany, and you will find, with me, that it is very likely that these men would be just as anti-French as they are now anti-German were the tricolour to supplant the black-white-red of Imperial Germany. Alsace-Lorraine now has a parliament of its own under a constitution which grants the inhabitants of the provinces the maximum of political liberty and self-government.[1] France is confined to Metz and the adjacent frontier regions. Alsace and Lorraine were German long

[1] We have seen in chaps. ix and x that this was not so.

SOLUTIONS: REANNEXATION 239

before they were French. Our folk-song literature is replete with songs of Strassburg.[1] Goethe attended the University there. When we took Alsace-Lorraine in 1871, we regained what was our own. Why did we retake it? Because the safety of German territory demanded it. France openly coveted the left bank of the Rhine. What else was the real underlying cause of Napoleon's war? Alsace-Lorraine had to be taken if that part of our fatherland west of the Rhine was to be permitted to develop in peace and safety as an integral part of the German nation. Sir Joseph Compton Rickett tells us that the restoration of Alsace-Lorraine would be the end of *revanche*. . . . It would be the very beginning. The French would say: 'If the Germans are supine enough to abandon Alsace and Lorraine, they will not be strong enough to resist pressure still further east.' Our defensive position, instead of being stronger, would be incomparably weaker after we had scuttled out of Metz and Strassburg. We should be in exactly the same perilous military situation as we were in before 1870. This is a state of things not even the most rabid Social Democrat would tolerate. . . . It would be a pitiable politician and a sorry strategist who would begin putting the national house in order for the great emergency by abandoning the ' watch on the Rhine.' " [2]

One more German view may be referred to—that of Maximilian Harden. Writing early in 1916, he said: " If people think in France that the re-establishment of peace is possible only through the restitu-

[1] "O Strasburg, meine Strasburg
Du wunderschöne Stadt,
Die seit zwei hundert Jahren
So viel gelitten hat."
[2] *Daily Mail*, August 20, 1913.

tion of Alsace-Lorraine, and if necessity compels us to sign such a peace, the seventy millions of Germans will soon tear it up."

Many Germans are fond of enlarging on the argument, referred to by Dr. Delbrück, that their country *The German argument that the annexation was paid for with German blood.* paid with its blood for the acquisition of the territory. To retrocede Alsace-Lorraine, they say, would be an act of treason committed against those who died for the fatherland. But a plea of this kind is untenable ; it is very nearly like saying that, because a burglar lost his life in taking another's property, therefore the ownership of the property must not be questioned when it is found in the hands of the burglar's sons or associates. Because our forefathers have shed their blood for an error, asks Novicow, must we persevere in that error ? To do so would mean to do evil to the living in order to please the dead. Fidelity to the ideas of ancestors, if these ideas were or have become false, is obviously an anti-social attitude. The ancestors of the present Germans burnt witches ; is that a reason why the Germans of to-day should do so ? This is not the way, says the last-mentioned writer, to acquire a " place in the sun " : it is possible to fight and kill and steal for the purpose of acquiring a place in the sun, and yet actually live in a fog.[1]

However little importance be attached to such German pronouncements and arguments as those set *Difficulty inherent in solution by forcible re-annexation.* forth above, there can be no doubt that a forcible retrocession of Alsace-Lorraine to France cannot be a true solution ; for a true solution necessitates an amicable accommodation and voluntary agreement of the parties con-

[1] Novicow, *op. cit.*, pp. 319, 320.

SOLUTIONS: REANNEXATION 241

cerned. In the present case there are: France, Germany, Alsace-Lorraine, and the rest of Europe (more correctly, perhaps, the rest of the civilised world). If, by reason of a decisive defeat, Germany felt constrained to abandon the territory, her resulting grievance would be a far greater menace to the peace of Europe than the grievance of France proved to be after 1871; a society or partnership of nations together with disarmament agreements could not then possibly be established; the existence of a festering sore in the very heart of Europe would render impossible frank and healthful international relationships, and would perpetuate those sinister shadows, suspicions, and fears which it is the business of a salutary régime to remove and prevent.

Moreover, in addition to this great difficulty attending a forcible restoration of the provinces there are various other difficulties that are incidental both to this kind of annexation and to amicable cession. Many simple persons believe, says M. Wetterlé, that nothing is easier than the reassimilation of Alsace-Lorraine to France, that French legislation may at a single stroke of the pen supersede the existing German legislation, that French officials may immediately supplant the existing German officials, and that, generally, a transformation may at once be effected as by a magic wand. Ardent enthusiast as he is for the restoration of the territory, this Alsatian patriot cannot but admit that the problem is a very complicated one, that the long period of German régime, legislation, organisation, and systems have set up an ever-widening barrier between France and Alsace-Lorraine, and have caused their habits, customs, and interests to diverge—" s'éloignant tou-

Various other difficulties.

jours davantage l'une de l'autre et créant dans deux populations, qui avaient perdu tout contact administratif, des habitudes, des mœurs, des intérêts divergents.' [1]

The return of Alsace-Lorraine to France within its geographical limits as existing before the Franco-German War would, of course, mean a restoration of the former boundary between France and Germany—a defective boundary that proved such a stumbling-block to the two nations and was more than anything else responsible for the outbreak of the war of 1870.[2] Strassburg and Metz were, in German eyes, sally-ports into Southern Germany, which therefore felt itself to be at the mercy of French artillery and French invaders. The fact that after their transference to Germany they became sally-ports into France shows that the frontier arrangement of 1871 was defective, not that the frontier existing before then was good; so that to substitute the former boundary for the present one is merely to substitute one evil for another. The truth is, indeed, that it is not so much faulty boundary adjustments that prove to be intrinsically disastrous and fatal, as the accumulation of armament and territorial lust. However this may be, the point we would here urge is that the retrocession of Alsace-Lorraine to France would involve the very serious disadvantage of putting back again an untenable line of demarcation between the two countries.

Former frontier untenable.

If the provinces were returned to France, how would they be grouped within her political framework? Before the cession of 1871 they comprised three departments—Haut-Rhin, Bas-Rhin, Moselle with parts of Meurthe. Considering the development of an

[1] *Op. cit.*, p. 290.   [2] See *supra*, pp. 138 *seq.*

SOLUTIONS: REANNEXATION 243

Alsace-Lorraine personality and national individuality during the last half-century (as has already been shown),[1] would it be a satisfactory and expedient arrangement to split the territory again into three minor departments, and, in view of the profound divergences that prevail, to reinstate them in a country where government and administration are so highly centralised? *Grouping of Alsace-Lorraine within political framework of France.* Alsatians and Lorrainers have long held that a status of this kind would be most undesirable, if not practically impossible. What other bonds of incorporation could be established? The fundamental difficulty is due to the conflict between the principle of centralisation, and the principle of self-government for which the people have long been striving and preparing themselves. MM. Lichtenberger observe that, as Upper and Lower Alsace have many affinities and common interests, it would be desirable to maintain the existing Alsatian unity, and effect a division into two departments, Haut-Rhin and Bas-Rhin, to which the country would soon accommodate itself.[2] The advocates of reannexation, whilst usually admitting the great difficulties involved, are too much disposed to gloss them over with a stroke of the pen, and to say glibly and in an off-hand manner, that a proper political adjustment would soon be effected, that a satisfactory accommodation would soon be arrived at, and so on.

The language question is another obstacle. We have already pointed out that the great majority of the population speak a German dialect, and that in many parts of Alsace-Lorraine French is neither spoken nor even known. *The language question.* M. Wetterlé himself admits that the working classes

[1] See *supra*, chap. x.   [2] *Op. cit.*, p. 89.

generally, who constitute the greater part of the people, now speak no other tongue but their German patois—" en étaient arrivés à ne plus parler que leur savoureux dialecte." [1] It is difficult to imagine that France would agree to adopt such a policy as was provided by Article V of the Peace of Vereeniging, May 31, 1902, whereby Great Britain consented that Dutch should be taught in public schools in the Transvaal and the Orange River Colony, if the children's parents desired it.

The substitution of French law for the existing German legal system would be attended by many serious disadvantages. It is obvious that, in case of reincorporation, the German law could not remain permanently; at most it could be allowed to remain in force for a given period—for the purpose of making the transformation gradual and interfering as little as possible with the vested rights, the executory contracts, and the material and moral interests in general of the population, just as Germany allowed French legislation to continue for a limited period after the annexation in 1871, before introducing the imperial law. Owing, however, to the much more developed state of the country at present, the period permitted would have to be of very considerable length, during which the various intimate relationships between France and the acquired territory would be made difficult. With regard to this change of public institutions and law, MM. Lichtenberger remark that the problems as to when French law should be resumed, how far German law should be retained and necessary exceptions introduced, or whether French law should be introduced with special exceptions, must all be solved " avec discernement et sans parti-pris " [2];

The legal system.

[1] *Op. cit.*, p. 292.   [2] *Op. cit.*, p. 112.

SOLUTIONS: REANNEXATION 245

that for the law of real property and mortgages a transition stage is indispensable ; that the various associations, such as limited companies, co-operative societies, commercial registers, should be preserved ; and that throughout " il faut procéder avec tact, et mesure." [1] It is, therefore, evident that very tight knots will be met with in all these matters.[2]

The industries of the provinces have undergone, under the German régime, a complete transformation ; and their products go for the most part to German purchasers and consumers. The labour legislation has been systematic and comprehensive, and either differs considerably from or has no counterpart in French legislation. In the case of the working classes German social legislation is admittedly far more progressive than the French [3] ; they enjoy benefits that are beyond the reach of the French proletariat, and great numbers of them have warmly espoused the social democratic cause. The insurance schemes for workmen have proved to be most beneficial, and, as M. Wetterlé himself admits, they have created rights " qui ne sauraient être écartés d'un geste dédaigneux." [4] Nearly all the German immigrants, with the exception of the officials of the country districts, are found in the towns : thus the 60,000 immigrants of Strassburg form about 35 per cent. of the total population of the city ; in Metz there are some 36,000 immigrants as against 30,000 natives, that is 55 per cent. of the population ; and in the mining district of Thionville in Lorraine the immigrants form

The industrial organisation.

[1] Op. cit., p. 113.
[2] For the effects of annexation, see Phillipson, *Termination of War and Treaties of Peace*, where several chapters are devoted to the subject.
[3] Cf. Jean Longuet (a French deputy), in *The Nation*, January 5, 1918 ; p. 456.
[4] Op. cit., p. 293.

60 per cent. of the total number. The reannexation of Alsace-Lorraine to France would undoubtedly mean the expulsion or withdrawal of this immigrant population ; so that serious economic disturbances would thereby be brought about. Furthermore, an enormous amount of German capital has come into the territory, especially for the purpose of developing the mining and metallurgical industries [1] ; whether it remained in the country or were expropriated it would constitute a disturbing factor in the existing economic system.

The business circles in the towns of Alsace-Lorraine, as in the towns of Germany in general, are always opposed to radical changes. It has already been pointed out that in 1909 some 80 per cent. of the exports of the provinces went to Germany, and 80 per cent. of their imports came from Germany ; and that even in regard to the remaining 20 per cent. Belgium—and not France—took the first place. Thus, if Alsace-Lorraine left the German Zollverein its commerce would suffer a great loss. The commercial organisation and methods are essentially German. Indeed, from the point of view of economic conditions, Alsace-Lorraine is very closely, if not inseparably, bound up with Germany.

The commercial system.

Till 1895 the French fiscal legislation was in force ; after that date a complete change was effected. The most vigorous opponents of German rule cannot but admit the great improvements made in the modes and incidence of taxation, as well as in the whole range of industrial and commercial legislation, and recognise that all these reforms have become part and parcel of the life and activities of the people. " Toutes ces réformes," says M. Wetterlé, " dont l'opportunité et la justice étaient reconnues par

Fiscal legislation.

[1] See the next chapter on the Franco German coal and iron problem.

SOLUTIONS: REANNEXATION 247

une population intelligente et réfléchie, étaient entrées profondément dans nos mœurs."[1]

The religious question, again, is one of the greatest difficulty. We have already pointed out[2] that the great majority of the population—indeed about 80 per cent.—are Roman Catholics, that the régime of the French Concordat of 1801 still obtains in Alsace-Lorraine, and that the elementary schools have remained confessional; so that in this respect the attitude of the people, devoted as they are to their religion, is diametrically opposed to the French separationist régime and anti-clerical spirit. The great teaching and charitable Orders of the Roman Church are recognised by law. As the writer just referred to observes, there is an "antinomie totale entre les habitudes et coutumes de la France et celles de l'Alsace-Lorraine."[3] The crisis of the "Kulturkampf" has long ago passed away, so far as these provinces are concerned; they remain attached as strongly as ever to the old traditions of worship and ecclesiastical organisation. The Protestant sections of the community, too, would be opposed to any changes tending to break up the collaboration between Church and State, or to interfere substantially with the prevailing conditions. Even the most vigorous opponents of Germany are agreed that an attempt to secularise education and to substitute a lay staff for the existing *congréganistes* would provoke the strongest resistance.

Apart from this religious difference in elementary education, there are striking discrepancies between the French and German systems of higher instruction. For example, in the case of the *baccalauréat* the curriculum and the standard

_{The religious question.}

_{The educational system.}

---

[1] *Op. cit.*, p. 294.   [2] See *supra*, p. 40.
[3] *Op. cit.*, p. 297. *Cf.* Lichtenberger, *op. cit.*, pp. 116 *seq.*

vary to a very large extent ; and the courses, methods, and requirements of university studies in general differ materially. Moreover, various German qualifications and diplomas, having no equivalent in France, have already been acquired by students and continue to be awarded at the University of Strassburg. Thus, M. Wetterlé points out that, in case of reannexation, it would be found difficult to regulate the legal status of doctors, solicitors, notaries, chemists, *philologues*, referendaries, and assessors, who possess German degrees. Furthermore, in regard to education in general, due account must be taken of the fact that Alsace is " un pays de culture mixte," [1] and that its very foundations are more Germanic than Gallic.

In addition to all these difficulties, one must mention that created by the position of the immigrants and the younger generation, who constitute a considerable proportion of the population.[2] More than 12 per cent. of the marriages year by year are " mixed " ; and nearly 30 per cent. of the children born are either entirely German or the issue of these mixed marriages. If the provinces were wrested back from Germany, no satisfactory adjustment of the position of these immigrants and their families could be effected ; indeed, there would inevitably be a repetition of the emigration and expulsions of 1871, and consequent perpetuation of grievances, resentment, and hatred rendering impossible an amicable accommodation between France and Germany.

Immigrants and younger generation.

Again—and this is a matter of the greatest consequence—the nationalist movement in Alsace-Lorraine, as we have shown fully in a previous chapter,[3] has taken

[1] Lichtenberger, *op. cit.*, p. 114.
[2] *Cf.* the official statistics given in *Die Bevölkerung Elsass-Lothringens* (Strassburg, 1908).
[3] See chap. x.

SOLUTIONS: REANNEXATION 249

such a powerful hold of the people that it will certainly be impossible to eliminate it by the union of the provinces to France with her centralised government and administration. The people have firmly and definitely pledged themselves to autonomy; for nearly thirty years their strivings and aspirations have unswervingly aimed at that object ; it is difficult to see how such object could be realised if the territory were incorporated within the framework of France ; whereas it is capable of full and complete realisation within the framework of the German Empire. Another solution consonant to the autonomist movement would be the establishment of entire political independence ; but this solution likewise means no reannexation to France. *The previous nationalist movement.*

As to other kinds of difficulties and differences, M. Wetterlé himself admits that " la liste pourrait en être considérablement allongée." [1] For example, there would be the expulsion of public officials, or the special regulation of their position; many of these are recognised by the Alsatians and Lorrainers as possessing conspicuous ability.[2] And there would be a great variety of further questions and claims, the adjustment of which would undoubtedly create difficulties through the clash of conflicting interests.[3] *Other difficulties.*

In consequence of all these difficulties incidental to reannexation, it has been suggested that, after the return of the provinces to France a sort of interregnum, or transition stage, with provisional legislation, should be allowed in them for a specified or indefinite period, in order that the more *Interregnum suggested.*

[1] *Op. cit.*, p. 298.
[2] *Cf.* Lichtenberger, *op. cit.*, p. 100.
[3] For many other kinds of questions that would have to be solved, see Phillipson, *Termination of War and Treaties of Peace*, pp. 290 seq.

striking differences introduced by the German régime might be smoothed over, the acquired rights and interests safeguarded as much as possible, and the assimilation to France facilitated. But this suggestion, like the entire proposal of reannexation, fails to take into account two most vital considerations : first, the autonomist movement established and developed during a whole generation, and, secondly, whether the population are in favour of reunion with France (*i.e.* the question of a plebiscite). To disregard these important considerations is to revert to the old arbitrary proceedings, which are to-day condemned by all the civilised peoples of the world as being contrary to the essential and inalienable right of national self-determination.

Accordingly, a plebiscite must be the condition precedent to the adoption of any course that can be regarded as a satisfactory solution in the case of a people like the Alsace-Lorrainers who possess a national consciousness and a national individuality. This question of a plebiscite, the reasons for resorting to it, its use in previous cases of annexation, and the difficulties involved in it will be dealt with in our final chapter ; in the meantime we have to consider certain other proposals that have been advanced for solving the Alsace-Lorraine problem, *e.g.* the establishment of Alsace-Lorraine as an autonomous State within the German Empire, the establishment of the provinces as an independent neutralised State, and the partition of the disputed territory or other readjustment of the existing frontiers. But before considering these proposals we must deal very briefly with the Franco-German coal and iron problem in reference to retrocession.

CHAPTER XIII

REANNEXATION AND THE FRANCO-GERMAN COAL AND
IRON PROBLEM

Commercial basis of the war—German declaration in 1915 as to economic needs—Coal and iron in modern war—German need of coal and iron—German demands as to Briey and Longwy—Coal resources of France and Germany—Iron ore in Lorraine—Iron resources of Germany—Effect of depriving Germany of the Lorraine ore.

IN this chapter, following on the consideration of the various difficulties incidental to the proposed retrocession of Alsace-Lorraine to France, we may conveniently turn our attention to the special Franco-German coal and iron problem, which has frequently been raised during the last two or three years. The essential question here is whether retrocession would bring about a satisfactory solution of this problem.

The present war is to a very large extent commercial in its origin, in its means, and in its objects. In regard to its origin, it has been pointed out [1] that the intensive and continuous over-production in Germany was preparing the way for an industrial cataclysm, if she failed to increase the number and importance of her outlets, in view of the fact that her principal customers were beginning to consider it necessary to protect themselves against her pacific penetration; another such revolution might bring with it an internal crisis, because the rise

Commercial basis of the war.

[1] *Cf.* M. Alfassa, *Le fer et le charbon lorrains* (Paris, 1916). (Preface by A. Lebon, a former French minister.)

in the cost of necessaries was far greater proportionately than the rise in wages. In the conduct of the war the commercial aspect is obvious—it is a war of machines and shells; the nations are specially organised to promote and accelerate the output of the essential industrial products, the practice of blockades is established by the belligerents for the very purpose of interfering with their enemies' commercial and industrial activity. Thus the object of the war, too, has a commercial basis, seen on the one hand in the resolution of the Allied Conference held in Paris, June 17, 1916, to the effect that the Allies should ensure their commercial independence with regard to the Central Empires, and, on the other hand, in the declarations contained in the confidential memorandum presented to the German Imperial Chancellor, May 30, 1915, by the six leading industrial and agricultural associations of Germany.

The Germans, believing at the latter date that they were about to secure a military triumph over their adversaries, declared in the following manner some of their economic aims, and particularly their intentions as to the necessary acquisitions of new coal and iron districts : " Nothing but the economic and military weakening of our adversaries will obtain for us the peace we desire—as a commencement Belgium, which lies so near our industrial centre, must in the monetary, financial, and postal sense become subject to the laws of the Empire. Her railways and waterways must be closely connected with our own communications. As regards France, it is of vital importance, both from the point of view of our relations with England, and from that of our maritime future, that we should possess the coast region to as far as the Somme. The ' Hinterland' should be of an extent sufficient to ensure their

<small>German declaration in 1915, as to economic needs.</small>

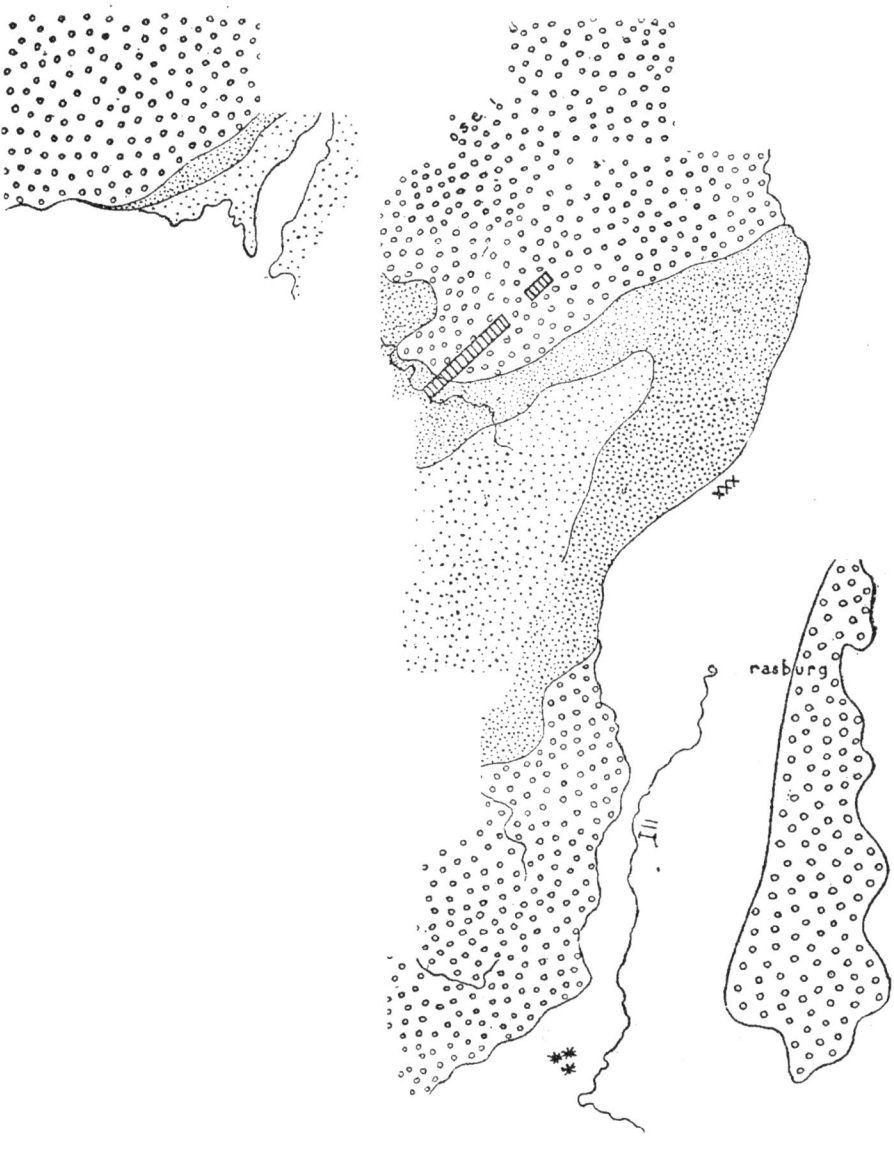

GEOLOGICAL SKETCH-MAP OF ALSACE-LORRAINE.

1. Upper Jurassic clays and limestones. 2. Middle Jurassic clays and limestones with the iron-containing beds at their base, shown by the black line. 3. Triassic marls and limestones. Between these and the Middle Jurassic limestones lies the Lias clay, left white on the map. 4. Triassic grits. 5. Ancient sedimentary or crystalline rocks of the Vosges, Black Forest and Rhine Highlands. The Rhine Rift Valley is chiefly floored by recent deposits, and is left blank on the map, but patches of Triassic and Jurassic rocks occur at its margins. Scale about 1 : 2,000,000. (*In part after Barré*)

COAL AND IRON PROBLEM 255

full importance to the ports forming the outlets for the canals behind them. In addition, it is self-evident that the fortresses of Verdun and Belfort, and the forts west of the Vosges lying between them, could not be left in French hands. By the acquisition of the line of the Meuse and of the French coast the iron-producing district of Briey, as well as the coalfields of the North and the Pas de Calais, would be acquired." [1]

The importance of coal and iron for carrying on a modern war is emphasised : " Territorial annexations, such as those of the mineral and coal regions, would not merely extend our industrial power. They represent military necessities, as is proved by the following consideration. The monthly production of pig-iron in Germany has risen since August 1914 to about a million tons—in other words, it has all but doubled. The production of steel exceeds one million tons per month. It must be added that neither pig-iron nor steel is abundant ; but if this is true of Germany it is still more true of neutral countries. The manufacture of shells requires a quality of iron and steel such as would not formerly have been believed. For cast-iron shells alone, which are an inferior substitute for those in steel, an average production of 4,000 tons of iron per day has been necessary.[2] If our production of pig-iron and steel had not been doubled, the war could not have been continued. As the material for the manufacture of these quantities of pig-iron and steel, the *minette* of Lorraine becomes more and more important, for this mineral is the only one that we can produce in rapidly increasing quantities. At this moment *minette* represents from 60

Coal and iron in modern war.

Translation as given in *Fortnightly Review*, November 1917.
[2] In 1916 the output increased enormously ; the monthly average of pig-iron was 1,150,000 tons ; and that of steel was (towards the end of the year) between 1,400,000 and 1,500,000 tons.

to 80 per cent. of our manufacture of pig-iron and steel. If the production of *minette* were imperilled the war would be as good as lost. Nor should it be forgotten that the large production of steel from *minette* provides the only source, when the import of phosphates is blocked, from which German agriculture can obtain the phosphoric acid that it requires." [1]

It is therefore urged that the acquisition by Germany of further coal and iron resources is imperative : " The security of the German Empire in a future war imperiously requires the possession of all the mines of *minette*, including the fortresses of Longwy and Verdun. The possession of the large quantity of coal, and especially of coal rich in bitumen, which abounds in the northern basin of France, is at least as important as that of iron ore for the decision of a war. Belgium and Northern France produce together over forty million tons a year. It appears to be true that the systematic production of coal from the Belgian mines has had during the present war the greatest influence in inducing several of our neighbours to preserve their neutrality. Coal, then, is one of the most decisive means of political influence in the world. Industrial neutral States are obliged to obey the belligerent which can best assure their needed quantity of coal. This we are unable to do of our own resources, and it is to Belgian coal that we are looking to prevent our neutral neighbours from being completely dependent on England." [2]

German need of more coal and iron.

Professor Hermann Schumacher of Bonn, one of the signatories of the annexationist manifesto, holds that it is essential to modify the Franco-German frontier in such a way as to assure for Germany adequate supplies of coal and iron and deprive the enemy of

[1] *Fortnightly Review*, Nov. 1917.   [2] *Ibid.*

COAL AND IRON PROBLEM 257

them. " Without the Lorraine ore," he says, " we should not be able to supply iron and steel necessary for the war. The Treaty of Frankfort gave us all Lorraine. A mistake was committed, for the geologists consulted by Bismarck were mistaken. It is known since 1880 that, as against the previsions of Bismarck, the Briey basin, which continues that of Longwy, is one of the richest parts of France. To-day we can correct this mistake, since we have occupied from the beginning of the war and we hold firmly in our hands the second raw material of war industry—coal. Just as we could not prosecute the war if we had not the rich Lorraine soil, so we could not prosecute it victoriously if we had not the rich coal-fields of Belgium and Northern France. As we know to-day what signify munitions in a war, we must tell ourselves that it is necessary for the life of our people, for peace and for war, to possess these sources of war and commercial power." [1]

Similarly, in the Prussian Diet, February 21, 22, 1917, in the course of a debate on the importance of completing the economic frontier by the inclusion of Briey and Longwy, it was said that Germany could not allow the French to be in possession of these districts, that it would be fatal for her in the next war, when she would be again blockaded, and must obtain the steel for her guns. Nor could she count on promptly occupying the industrial districts of France and Belgium on the declaration of war, as she had done on this occasion, for experience would teach the English and the French to take preventive measures. Therefore it was a question of life and death for Germany. Prince Schönaich Carolath, the leader of the National Liberal

German demands as to Briey and Longwy.

[1] *Le Temps*, 28 août 1915.

party, though an annexationist, did not support these extravagant demands, and some of the National Liberals, led by Professor Brandenburg, the president of the party in Saxony, declined to associate themselves with such an extremist policy. But Count Westarp, the leader of the Conservatives, repeated the demand for Briey and Longwy in the Reichstag, March 27, 1917. The German Socialists were opposed to these views, and the masses of the German population paid little heed to these annexationist proposals.

However this may be, Germany has long been attracted towards iron—the symbol of and key to material force. As a recent French writer aptly says: "L'Allemagne, créature et adoratrice de la force, ne pouvait pas ne pas être attirée vers le fer, instrument et moyen de la force."[1] She is aware that she has ample supplies of coal—it has been calculated that her resources would suffice for about a thousand years. Besides her rich Westphalian coalfields, she possesses the Sarre basin and other coal regions which she acquired by the Treaty of Paris, November 1815, the Convention of Frankfort, 1819, and the Treaty of Frankfort, 1871. The Sarre basin lies on the right bank of the Moselle between this river and the Rhine, and it occupies a region about 100 kilometres long by between 30 and 35 kilometres wide—45 kilometres being in Rhenish Prussia and the Bavarian Palatinate, 45 in Alsace-Lorraine, and 10 in Meurthe-et-Moselle. We may here recall that in July 1815 a memorandum was laid before the Prussian plenipotentiaries on their way to the Paris Peace Conference by one Herr Böcking, commissioner of the Sarre mines. He explained that

Coal resources of Germany and France.

[1] F. Engerand, *Les Frontières lorraines et la force allemande* (Paris, 1916), préface, p. 1.

the cession of the Sarre coalfield to Prussia would compel France to import her steel from the latter country and lower her import duties, to the advantage of German industries. Such turned out actually to be the result; and the French industries of the Moselle region declined accordingly. Indeed, had it not been for the importation of coal from Great Britain, France would have found herself in a disastrous condition.

It is thought in some quarters in France that if Germany retroceded Alsace-Lorraine to France and remained in possession of the Sarre coalfields, Germany would continue to enjoy industrial predominance; and therefore it is urged that France should also regain the Sarre basin, because of the proximity of this coalfield to the Lorraine ironfields, and the great distance of the British coalfields from the latter. Such a solution is obviously as inexpedient as it is impossible, for it would reduce Germany to a condition of economic ruin—and such intention has been repeatedly disclaimed on the part of the Allies.

<small>Iron ore of Lorraine.</small>

Even in the case of the mere retrocession of the territories annexed in 1871 the iron resources of Germany would be so diminished that she would not have enough within her own country not only for military purposes, but for commerce and peaceable manufactures. In addition to the German pronouncements given above we may refer to the statement of Herr Hermann Wendel, the German majority Socialist deputy, to the effect that to take away the iron of Lorraine from Germany would be " to force the German metal industry to its knees "; and Herr Hue, of the German Miners' Federation, observed in the Prussian Diet that it would also mean " the ruin of the German coal industry." To obviate such contingencies it has been suggested by certain French writers and publicists that, as Germany without Alsace-Lorraine would still have more coal than France, she would be able to exchange her surplus for French iron. It is thought, too, that in such a case it will be necessary to establish " the economic exterritoriality of the Thionville district," *i.e.* owing to the inadequacy of the French coal supplies and the fear of overproduction, the factories of annexed Lorraine will have to be excluded from the French market.[1] Others point out that it is only by depriving Germany of her iron ore that the military menace on the Continent will be removed. " Laisser la sidérurgie allemande florissante," says M. de Launay : " c'est lui permettre, après la guerre, de reconquérir aussitôt le marché mondial en écrasant la concurrence débile de nos usines ruinées et pillées, de nos flottes fatiguées et amoindries ; c'est lui fournir le moyen de préparer une prompte revanche."[2]

In 1910, at the International Geological Congress at Stockholm, in the course of an investigation into the world's iron resources, it was calculated that German Lorraine contained 1,830 million tonnes, to which those responsible for the report tacitly added 270 million tonnes of Luxemburg as forming part of the Zollverein, that the rest of Germany had only 700 million tonnes, whilst the amount of the ore of French Lorraine was estimated at 3,000 million tonnes.[3] Now, looking at the rate of consumption, we find that in the last normal year, 1913, Germany used up 42 to 43 million tonnes, comprising 21 million tonnes obtained from annexed Lorraine, 7 million tonnes from the rest of Germany,

Iron resources of Germany.

---
[1] Alfassa, *op. cit.*, p. 38.
[2] L. de Launay, *Le problème franco-allemand du fer*, in *Revue des Deux Mondes*, July 15, 1916, p. 345.
[3] *Ibid.*, p. 335.

COAL AND IRON PROBLEM 261

and the remainder imported from abroad (*e.g.* Sweden and Spain).[1] That is, the pre-war total resources of Germany, viz. 2,800 million tonnes, would last only about sixty-five years, assuming that there would be no annual increase in the consumption. In point of fact, since August 1914 Germany's production of pig-iron and steel has doubled in amount ; otherwise she would have found it impossible to continue the war. Had her Lorraine supplies been seriously interfered with, the war would by now certainly have been ended. Hence—among other reasons—her determination not to abandon any portion of the annexed provinces, and if possible to add thereto other neighbouring territory rich in minerals.

The great metallurgical development of Lorraine, like the progress in the Alsatian industries, is due to German brains, energy, and capital ; and any solution that deprived Germany of the *minette* would not be to the economic advantage of Europe generally, and would inflict on a great industrial nation an unparalleled economic disaster, whilst the interests of peace would not thereby be advanced. Indeed, the future peace of Europe would be more than ever jeopardised ; for it is nothing more than absurd to imagine that the potential labour, the industrial instincts, the business organisation, the commercial impulse, the economic progress of one of the greatest nations of the world could be suppressed by doubtful military victories, by factitious combinations of States, or by an unnatural policy of exclusion. The iron-mines of Lorraine work in close association with the coalfields of the Rhine basin ; and the Prussian State Railways make reduced charges to the Lorraine manufacturers as a compensation for their inland

Effect of depriving Germany of the Lorraine ore.

[1] *Comité des Forges de France. Circulaire* No. 655, p. 13.

position ; so that to put an end to such desirable co-operation would entail great loss. The solution of the Franco-German coal and iron problem can be effected by establishing a régime of free trade if Alsace-Lorraine remains within the German Empire (say, as an autonomous State), or by setting up the provinces as an independent State ; but it is very doubtful indeed whether a satisfactory solution can be reached by retroceding the territory to France, unless the economic organisation and system of commercial relationships of Western Europe be altered in such a way as to ensure a supply of coal and iron equally and impartially to those who are in need thereof.

CHAPTER XIV

SOLUTIONS SUGGESTED : (b) AUTONOMY WITHIN THE GERMAN EMPIRE

The nationalist ideal—Alsace-Lorraine can no longer remain a Reichsland —German view in 1898—Swiss view—French views—Recent German opinion—German Socialist view, 1917—Form of autonomous government—Position of Alsace-Lorraine as an autonomous State—Autonomy followed by plebiscite suggested.

As we have already fully described the autonomist movement, there is no need to do more here than add a few observations by way of supplement.

The establishment of Alsace-Lorraine as an autonomous State within the framework of the German Empire would be the fulfilment of the nationalist object, which has been aimed at by the great mass of Alsatians and Lorrainers for some thirty years. This would make of the provinces —which have hitherto constituted only a Reichsland, that is, common imperial territory, as the sinister symbol of conquest—a new federal unit, empowered to draw up its own constitution (subject, like every other German State, to certain limitations imposed by the imperial constitution), to choose its own government and administration, which would be directly responsible to the people, and to a very great extent make its own law. *The nationalist ideal.*

In a previous chapter [1] the demands of authoritative Alsace-Lorraine leaders have been set forth ; and we

[1] See chap. x.

have seen that they have repeatedly claimed autonomy within the Empire and have asserted that that was all they and the people wanted. Had the Germans possessed clearer foresight and greater political wisdom they would, even in their own true interests, have paid regard to the wishes thus expressed and to the increasing nationalist movement, and would have set up the régime and political structure required. Such an amicable accommodation may well have facilitated the *rapprochement* between France and Germany, and so may have done much to promote the public peace of Europe. However this may be, it is clear that Alsace-Lorraine can no longer remain a Reichsland after the conclusion of this war ; and when a solution is sought the consistent and reiterated demands for autonomy cannot be eliminated.

Alsace-Lorraine can no longer remain a Reichsland.

The Alsatians and Lorrainers were not alone in demanding autonomy for their provinces. They were supported by writers and publicists in various countries. Only one or two need be mentioned here as representative. Thus, Moritz von Egidy, an officer of the Prussian Army, delivered a number of lectures in several German towns, September-December, 1898, on the Tsar's peace manifesto, in the course of which he urged that the Reichsland question should and could be solved by applying the principle ' Alsace-Lorraine for the Alsace-Lorrainers,' and conformably thereto granting an autonomous government to the people.

German view in 1898.

MM. Lichtenberger, who maintain that Alsace-Lorraine would have been satisfied with autonomy within the German Empire, refer [1] to the view expressed by a Swiss impartial observer,

Swiss view.

[1] *Op. cit.*, p. 52.

SOLUTIONS: AUTONOMY 265

M. Albert Bonnard. In an article in the *Bibliothèque Universelle* of Lausanne, the latter said that a particularist (or nationalist) Alsace, having acquired her liberty, would be proud and jealous of her status and would be contented with it, as she would be enabled to proceed in her own way and develop her own individuality.

As to France, we have already shown that before the recent *revanche* recrudescence consequent on the outbreak of the war she would have willingly accepted the autonomist solution for Alsace-Lorraine, on the ground that the overwhelming majority of Alsatians and Lorrainers had made it their definitive goal. The following words have been quoted on a previous page, but they may be recalled here on account of their special appropriateness: " Pour notre modeste part, nous croyons que, si l'Alsace-Lorraine était satisfaite de cette autonomie restreinte, nous aurions mauvaise grâce à être plus royalistes que le roi. . . . Cette solution, nous l'accepterions donc de grand cœur." [1]

French views.

This view has also found supporters recently among leading German thinkers. Thus, Professor Wilhelm Förster, the astronomer of Berlin, whilst justifying the annexation of the provinces on the ground of frontier security, said in 1913, that in his opinion the difficulties of Germany with regard to France and Alsace-Lorraine could be removed by giving the latter as large a measure of independence as is possible within the German confederation. " Since France in 1866," he observes, " demanded the whole left bank of the Rhine, and in 1870 attacked Germany by force of arms, it became

Recent German opinion.

---
[1] Général Palat, *L'Alliance franco-allemande ou la guerre* (Paris, 1914), pp. 145, 146.

clear that Germany must, for her own security, extend her borders across the Rhine and not leave the powerful fortress of Metz on her frontier any longer in French hands. But Germany has throughout treated the people of Elsass-Lothringen in embittering fashion. By this means the painful influence of the conquest over the feelings of the French people has been kept alive and constantly renewed. In spite of this, a vote by the people of Alsace-Lorraine would now (Sept. 1913) probably show a majority in favour of remaining part of Germany. This would mainly be on economic grounds, as the fruit and wine industry of Elsass-Lothringen is in closer relations to the interests of Germany than to those of France. How can the relations between Germany and France be made better? Certainly through giving the people of Elsass-Lothringen the greatest possible independence, with freedom to continue to use the French language and the like. To this end, there must rule between Germany and France, and for that matter through Europe generally, a higher socio-political relation than at present. This should begin with a customs-union and with parliamentary control. The International Court needs organisation and expansion in power until its jurisdiction includes the whole earth." [1]

Similarly, Professor Rudolf Eucken of Jena observed in September 1913: "Elsass-Lothringen is for us Germans no longer a question. The land, the seat of an old German race, is a piece of Germany; in its language and its customs, German. We Germans are sensitive to all discussion of this question by foreign people as a revival of the French restlessness towards this problem. Inside of Germany I wish to see granted to Elsass-Lothringen all possible inde-

[1] Quoted by Jordan, *op. cit.*, pp. 26, 27.

SOLUTIONS: AUTONOMY 267

pendence; but this is a problem for ever and wholly German." [1]

Further, quite recently the opinion in favour of autonomy within the Empire has been gaining ground in Germany.[2] At the German Socialist Conference at Würzburg, October 14-17, 1917, Herr Scheidemann declared: "We demand complete autonomy for Alsace-Lorraine, but also demand that Alsace-Lorraine shall remain part of the German Empire." [3] *German Socialist view, 1917.*

In the event of adopting this autonomist solution, it has been suggested that a difficulty would arise in regard to the kind of government to be introduced into the newly constituted State, *i.e.* whether republican or monarchical. Some writers think that it could not be republican, or even monarchical (failing the necessary traditions). But the determining factor in this respect is, or should be, the will of the people. In Alsace-Lorraine, however, public opinion has not been unanimous on the point. Probably the clerical group, representing the Catholic and the Lutheran sections of the population, would prefer a monarchical form of government, for example, like that of the Grand Duchy of Baden; whilst the Alsatian Radicals, Socialists, and other nationalists would be in favour of a republic, and regard the free cities of Hamburg, Bremen, and Lübeck as analogous precedents. Indeed, for great numbers of Alsatians the very word "autonomy" implies a republican organisation within the framework of the German Empire. *Form of autonomous government.*

If Alsace-Lorraine becomes an autonomous State—

[1] Quoted by Jordan, *op. cit.*, pp. 27, 28.
[2] *Cf. Deutsche Revue*, June 1917, referred to by Dr. Dillon, *Fortnightly Review*, September 1917, p. 345, note.
[3] *Daily Telegraph*, October 17, 1917.

either republican or monarchical—what will be its position within the confederation? The latter now comprises four kingdoms, six grand duchies, five duchies, seven principalities, three free towns, and the Reichsland. Sovereignty is vested in the imperial government.[1] The Bundesrat (Federal Council), which represents the totality of the co-ordinated German States, is the embodiment of that sovereignty. The powers of government are divided between the imperial authorities and those of the State. In the case of the former they are specifically limited; in the case of the latter they are unlimited and residual. The legislative power of the Empire takes precedence in regard to such matters as the rights of citizenship, the army and navy, currency, weights and measures, tariffs, patents, copyright, fluvial and canal navigation, etc. On the other hand, a very wide domain is reserved to the States themselves, *e.g.* the determination of their own forms of government and the laws of succession, the relations between Church and State, all questions relating to their internal administration, the framing of their budgets, the control of public instruction, the making of laws as to land tenure and highways, the adoption of police regulations, etc. Justice is administered in the name of the particular State concerned and not in that of the Empire; and the judiciary is appointed by the State. The execution of imperial measures, except within the restricted spheres, devolves upon the officials of the respective States.

Thus, if Alsace-Lorraine were made an autonomous State it would enjoy a large measure of legislative and administrative independence, it would be able to develop to a very great extent its own personality, and

[1] *Cf.* F. A. Ogg, *The Governments of Europe* (New York, 1913), pp. 205 *seq.*

would at the same time possess the various advantages of membership of a great Empire. Its traditions as well as its interests could be safeguarded; and, being of a mixed Franco-German culture, it would serve as a bond of union between the two neighbouring peoples who have so long been at loggerheads. Sometimes a fear has been expressed that the newly established government might not work harmoniously with the Imperial Government; but there is no ground for such apprehension, and no plausible consideration has been advanced in support thereof. The Reichsland is no longer regarded as a guarantee or pledge of German unity; and to set it up as an autonomous State is not necessarily to impair German security.

We have more than once put forth the contention, and submitted evidence for it, that before the present war Alsace-Lorraine would have been fully satisfied with autonomy. Now it may be thought that, in consequence of the war, various complications have supervened, rendering that conclusion less certain. In these circumstances a plan suggested by Novicow in 1913 may well be adopted as a feasible expedient, *i.e.* the establishment of autonomy, to be followed ten or fifteen years later by a plebiscite.[1] He says that if the population vote then in favour of France, Alsace-Lorraine should be retroceded; but the referendum in Lorraine must be distinct from that in Alsace, and the decision of one province is not to be binding on the other. If the date of the plebiscite is fixed ten or fifteen years in advance, the population will remain conscious of a period of transition and hence they will adapt and prepare themselves accordingly. This arrangement, of course, assumes that no undue influence will in the

Autonomy followed by plebiscite.

---
[1] *Op. cit.*, p. 353.

meantime be exercised by the German authorities. How to ensure the prevention of such pressure is the main difficulty. In the first place, such pressure would be minimised or promptly revealed in the case of a completely autonomous State ; secondly, the Imperial Government might give an earnest of its good faith by permitting a neutral commission to remain in the territory for the purpose of exercising a certain surveillance until the referendum has been completed.[1]

[1] See further the final chapter as to the question of plebiscite generally.

CHAPTER XV

SOLUTIONS SUGGESTED : (c) ALSACE-LORRAINE AS AN INDEPENDENT STATE

Proposed neutralisation—Suggested in 1870—German objections—Population to be consulted—Resolution of League of Peace, 1884—Form of independent government—Various matters for adjustment—Advantages of creating an independent Alsace-Lorraine : Meeting the wishes of the people—*Revanche* obviated—Fusion of Germanic and Gallic elements —Military service difficulties removed—Bond of union between France and Germany—Would be a " buffer " State. Future international co-operation and treaties.

IT has frequently been proposed of late that the Alsace-Lorraine problem should be solved by erecting the provinces into an independent State. Such a plan would manifestly necessitate the neutralisation of the new State under the guarantee of the society of States or league of nations, whose establishment is an indispensable condition for securing the future peace of the world. It may be said, with the example of Belgium before us, that little confidence can be placed in the plan of neutralisation. But the flagrant violation of a law or engagement will not induce law-abiding and honourable citizens and nations to forswear all law and engagements, and to consent to abandon themselves to a condition of chaos and lawlessness. *Ubi societas ibi ius.* Where there is human life, where there are groupings of human individuals—be it clans, tribes, nations, States—there must inevitably be some governing law. The fact that the neutrality of Belgium was unconscionably dis-

Proposed neutralisation.

regarded in 1914 by a powerful State is no argument that the neutralisation of small States is useless. The best answer is to continue to neutralise small States —especially so those situated between greater States— and reinforce the underlying international engagement by more potent sanctions than have hitherto been available—and the most powerful safeguard is the formation of a " partnership of nations " together with the creation of an international court, empowered to take cognisance of international claims and differences and to enforce its judgments by means of an international army or police, by the imposition of economic restrictions, and similar measures that will influence a refractory State. But this régime implies a general pacification, a considerable disarmament, and an alliance of the nations on the basis of amicable co-operation and mutual good, and not for the purpose of bolstering up a precarious equilibrium. The main thing is to assure a whole-hearted acceptance of the fundamental principle ; the details necessary for its application can then be easily elaborated by negotiation. The present upheaval of the world, with its unparalleled slaughter and devastation, will surely serve as a drastic *katharsis,* a purgation for men and States, and will be a perpetual and convincing proof to all of the folly—indeed of the suicidal policy—of aggressions, of interfering with weaker neighbours, and of infringing the rules of established law and the dictates of public morality.

This proposal to neutralise Alsace-Lorraine is not new. It was brought forward as far back as 1870 by Suggested Count Agénor de Gasparin, that zealous in 1870. advocate of religious liberty. The view was afterwards adopted by various writers and publicists. One of the most enthusiastic supporters was M. Tachard,

SOLUTIONS: INDEPENDENCE 273

who was French by birth, Alsatian by adoption, and German by education. During the régime of Gambetta he was the French ambassador in Belgium, and in that capacity advocated his proposal at many of the European Courts. He was so attached to the idea and so firmly convinced of the salutary effect of setting up another buffer State between France and Germany, that he declared that his sole desire was to have the word *tampon* (buffer) inscribed on his tombstone.

We have already referred to Bismarck's speech in the Reichstag, May 2, 1871, when he discussed the policy of annexation and various expedients suggested as substitutes for it. Amongst these was the neutralisation of the conquered provinces; but he rejected this plan on the ground that the people would not be in a position to safeguard and defend their neutrality, and that, in the event of a renewed conflict between France and Germany, their French sympathies and interests would lead them to take the side of the former. Similarly, Treitschke repudiated the proposal; he pointed to the " disgusting spectacle " of the " Luxemburg nation," and maintained that the neutralisation of Alsace-Lorraine would be a certain means for enabling France to recover her lost territory [1] Other German opponents recalled the territorial transformations of the Revolutionary and Napoleonic periods, and asked their countrymen to remember the conduct of France, who on one occasion set up an " Independent Rhenish Republic " on the left bank of the Rhine, and afterwards, when she felt stronger, simply annexed it, with its three million inhabitants. But what was difficult of achievement in 1871 is much easier nowadays. During the last half-century the world has more than ever become convinced of the

German objections.

18   [1] See *supra*, pp. 89, 90.

utility and necessity of small States, of the illegitimacy and unwisdom of conquests, and of the right of peoples to determine their own destiny.

Whatever course be adopted as a solution of the Alsace-Lorraine problem—reannexation to France, establishment of autonomy within the German Empire, or the creation of an independent neutralised State—the population of the provinces should first be consulted and given an opportunity to express their will either by means of a referendum or by a vote of their specially elected representatives. To do so would be to vindicate in a triumphant manner this principle of national self-determination, and to recognise in the form of a striking and exemplary precedent this fundamental principle of public right. It is realised, and now asserted everywhere, that people are no longer like chattels, liable to be made the object of transactions between other contending nations. No one is entitled to neutralise the provinces in spite of them and without their consent; their free consent is indispensable to render the act of neutralisation valid, legitimate, and binding. The solution that is sought is not to be merely a settlement of an industrial or economic difference as between France or Germany, nor is it to be simply an adjustment of conflicting claims to the possession of a certain amount of territory. The solution must be such as will satisfy justice, reason, the conscience and desire of a compact population, and the interests of France and Germany and Europe in general.

[margin: Population to be consulted.]

At the general assembly of the members of the International League of Peace and Liberty, held at Geneva September 7, 1884 (at which, however, no German members appear to have been present), a resolution

SOLUTIONS: INDEPENDENCE

was passed affirming that the Alsace-Lorrainers possessed the inalienable right of choosing their own government, that the Franco-German hostility is due to the annexation of 1871, that the consequent state of armed peace is detrimental to the two nations and to Europe generally, that the provinces during their subjection to Germany (1871–1884) repeatedly claimed the right to dispose of themselves, that the security of Germany (the principal reason given by her for the annexation) will be attained by neutralising the annexed territory under the sanction and guarantee of the European Powers, and that all disputes arising out of such arrangement shall be submitted to a court of arbitration. The following is the text of the resolution, which is at present of great interest and significance:

Resolution of League of Peace, 1884.

" 1. Considérant que le droit des Alsaciens et des Lorrains de s'appartenir à eux-mêmes et par conséquent de choisir ou de constituer librement le gouvernement qu'il leur convient de se donner, est indiscutable, inaliénable, et imprescriptible;

" 2· Considérant que la seule cause d'hostilité qui existe entre la République française et l'Empire allemand est la situation faite à l'Alsace et à la Lorraine par les articles 1, 2 et 3 du traité signé à Francfort le 10 mai 1871 entre l'Allemagne et la France;

" 3. Que l'état de paix armée, qui est la conséquence de cette situation, est également dommageable pour les deux nations et pour toute l'Europe;

" 4· Que la seule raison donnée par l'Allemagne pour stipuler l'annexion était la nécessité d'assurer la sécurité;

" 5. Que depuis treize ans que l'Alsace et la Lorraine sont passées sous la domination allemande la manifestation constante de leurs sentiments, la rigueur croissante des mesures administratives et politiques prises à leur égard, l'attitude gardée par les députés qu'elle envoie au Reichstag, leur persévérance à réélire ces députés démontrent que leur volonté de disposer librement d'elles-mêmes est aussi ferme qu'elle l'était au lendemain de l'annexion ;

" 6. Que la neutralisation des territoires annexés, quelle que soit d'ailleurs la juridiction politique sous laquelle se rangeraient leurs habitants, donneraient à l'Allemagne une sécurité plus grande et plus réelle que ne le peut faire une possession toujours précaire qu'elle ne maintient que par la force ;

" 7. Qu'il est de l'intérêt commun de la France, de l'Allemagne, de l'Alsace, de la Lorraine, de l'Europe que cette neutralisation soit sanctionnée et garantie par tous les peuples européens ;

Par ces motifs :

" L'assemblée émet le vœu suivant :
" La France et l'Allemagne abrogeront d'un commun accord les articles 1, 2, et 3 du traité conclu à Francfort le 10 mai 1871.

" Le peuple alsacien et le peuple lorrain seront mis en situation de choisir librement l'une des trois solutions suivantes :

" 1. Annexion définitive de l'Alsace et de la Lorraine à l'Allemagne.

" 2. Retour de l'Alsace et de la Lorraine à la France.

" 3. Constitution de l'Alsace et de la Lorraine en un ou deux états indépendants et autonomes.

" Quelle que soit la décision du peuple alsacien et du peuple lorrain, cette décision fera loi pour l'Allemagne

SOLUTIONS: INDEPENDENCE 277

et pour la France et dans tous les cas entraînera la neutralisation des territoires alsaciens et lorrains.

"Le traité à intervenir entre la France, l'Allemagne et les autres Puissances contiendra une clause en vertu de laquelle toutes le difficultés auxquelles pourrait donner lieu son exécution, seront soumises en dernier ressort à un tribunal arbitral." [1]

Having regard to the tendencies, aptitudes, and traditions of the Alsace-Lorrainers, we may safely conclude that, if they voted in favour of the independence and neutralisation of their provinces, they would prefer a republican to a monarchical system of government. In that case the name of the newly constituted State might well be The Alsace-Lorraine Republic, which is much more appropriate than the designation, which has been suggested, of The Rhenish Republic. Under this solution of neutralisation, the fortresses of Strassburg and Metz would be dismantled, and no others would be permitted to be constructed. That is to say, the neutralisation would imply disarmament, as in the case of Luxemburg, and would not be like the neutralisation of Belgium and Switzerland, which are obliged to maintain standing armies. We have to bear in mind that the provinces in question are together less than the size of Yorkshire. The best way to safeguard this disarmament would be for France and Germany to disarm their respective frontier zones, to an extent agreed upon, adjacent to Alsace-Lorraine. Thus there would be between the two Powers a threefold disarmed sphere, which would minimise, if not

Form of independent government.

[1] *La neutralité de l' Alsace-Lorraine. Compte rendu de l'Assemblée Générale des membres de la ligue internationale de la paix et de la liberté. Tenue à Genève le 7 sept.* 1884. (Bâle, 1884.)

render impossible, the occurrence of those "incidents" that so often prepare the way for an open rupture.

The various matters of adjustment consequent on the creation of a new State out of a portion of another State could be provided for by international convention; and if need be an international commission might be appointed to supervise their execution. Thus the right of option of nationality would be stipulated, allowing such inhabitants as desired it to retain their allegiance to Germany or to transfer it to France instead of assuming the new allegiance on the establishment of the new State. Every precaution must be taken to safeguard the rights of the minority, and in suitable cases to offer adequate compensation for the loss or interference with vested rights and interests. A certain pecuniary compensation might be paid to the German Empire for such property as may be transferred with the territory, and for expenditure on public works, etc. In order to avoid economic dislocation the new State should be allowed, like Luxemburg, to remain within the Zollverein, and a Franco-German commercial alliance, including Alsace-Lorraine, would be one of the most satisfactory means of solving also the coal and iron problem. To establish the freedom of navigation of the Rhine—which is the direct route to the Sarre coalfields and the Lorraine ironfields—would be in the general interest, and would promote the commercial intercourse and pacific relationships generally between France, Germany, and Alsace-Lorraine, as well as other States, especially so when the Rhine-Danube canal becomes available for international navigation; and such freedom of navigation would be the better ensured by making Alsace-Lorraine an

Various matters for adjustment.

SOLUTIONS: INDEPENDENCE 279

independent State. There are many other questions that would necessarily arise for settlement : for example, those relating to treaties affecting the newly established State ; public law and administration, revenue laws, the official language of the State, religion, the position of officials, the armed forces, the courts of law, judicial proceedings pending, untried offenders ; public property of the State, charitable foundations, the state archives, the private domain of the State, unpaid taxes, private property of the German Emperor or other German sovereigns or princes ; the contractual obligations of the new State and apportionment of debts, concessions, and contracts other than public debts ; deposits, pensions, claims based on war losses ; private rights and private law. To facilitate the solution of all these questions regard may be paid to the various guiding precedents and established rules ; it is beyond our scope here to consider these separately ; so that it must suffice to refer to a work already cited in which they are fully and systematically dealt with.[1]

That the establishment of Alsace-Lorraine as an independent State would be attended by many signal advantages is obvious. It is highly probable that the great majority of the population, including the immigrants who have become definitely settled in the country, would now hail such a solution with delight.[2] Before the present war the desire of the generality was for autonomy within the German Empire ; but, what with the complications brought by the war, the revision of opinions it has occasioned, the manifestation of the democratic spirit in many parts of the world, and the universal assertion of the principle of national self-

Advantages of creating an independent Alsace-Lorraine.

---
[1] See Phillipson, *Termination of War and Treaties of Peace*, pp. 302-34.
[2] Cf. *La Nation* (an independent weekly paper of Geneva), June 16, 1917.

determination, it may well be that the former desire for autonomy has become transformed into a desire for complete independence. If this be so, the first and greatest advantage of such a solution would be that it conformed to the wishes of the population, who would thus be enabled to give free play to their deep local patriotism.

France, too, would be satisfied with this arrangement, assuming—as we may safely do—that it commended itself to the Alsace-Lorrainers; and the *amour-propre* of Germany would (or should) be little hurt thereby. The creation of an independent Alsace-Lorraine would partake of the nature of a compromise; so that, in view of the inveterate conflicting claims of France and Germany, neither Power could be considered as the vanquished party or as the outstanding victor, and hence neither party would feel the sting of humiliation or the need for *revanche*; neither party would be in the position to regard force alone as triumphant or as productive of good. As Dr. Fried, the distinguished German pacifist, has recently observed: "If we had not lost every claim to be considered as reasonable beings . . . in consequence of our three years' fight for trenches and rubbish-heaps, we should seek a way out of this fatal dilemma by a compromise which should primarily consider the interests of the population of the provinces, without giving the unconditional possession of them to either party. That would be a solution which would entitle neither France nor Germany to pose as conqueror, and would offer to each of them the possibility of ceasing to incur unspeakable sacrifice for the sake of a phantom."[1]

Meeting wishes of the people.

Revanche obviated.

[1] *Neue Zürcher Zeitung* (Swiss independent paper), June 24, 1917.

SOLUTIONS: INDEPENDENCE 281

Again, the fusion of the two elements—Germanic and Gallic—could continue apace without any heart-searchings and without any apprehension of ultimate difficulties, *e.g.* in case of a renewed Franco-German difference. The French emigrants who left the territory could freely return along with their families and descendants, and would be permitted either to retain their French allegiance or to accept the new citizenship; on the other hand, the German immigrants could remain if they thought fit to do so, and would no longer be deemed to be usurpers and interlopers. It is to be remembered that, even before 1871, the culture of the provinces was neither purely French nor purely German, but "mixed." Fusion of Germanic and Gallic elements.

Further, this solution would remove the great difficulties in regard to military service; before, the Alsatians and Lorrainers who were enrolled in the German armies and who had French sympathies or relations and friends in France, realised their particularly painful position in the event of the outbreak of hostilities between the two Powers. Such a condition of things encourages desertion and treason; and a Government adopting such a policy as to make this possible sows the wind to reap the whirlwind. Military service.

Then, too, an independent Alsace-Lorraine—with its bilingual people and its Franco-German civilisation—would, much more than under any other solution, serve as a permanent and salutary connecting-link between France and Germany, and through its instrumentality the great rival nations would find it easier to get rid of their inveterate differences, to reach a mutual understanding, and to inaugurate an epoch of true peace and amity—a consummation that would prove an inestimable Bond of union between France and Germany.

blessing to themselves, to Europe, and indeed to the whole civilised world ; for, unless it is brought about, a league of nations cannot be established. By virtue of its position as intermediary and bond of union it would exert a moderating influence on chauvinism on the one side and pangermanism on the other ; and through its traditions of freedom and newly acquired liberty it might well serve as a stimulus to the liberal movement in Germany, and a warning to would-be retrogressive reactionaries in France. Indeed, the country of Alsace-Lorraine, which has been a perennial cockpit of Europe, might appropriately offer its ancient city of Strassburg as the administrative seat of the League of Nations.

We have already mentioned the question of the free navigation of the Rhine, and the coal and iron problem which has aroused so much apprehension in Germany and such strong claims in France: the creation of an independent Alsace-Lorraine would make easy the settlement of both these difficulties. The new State, amicably disposed towards both Powers, and having intercourse with both, would need the markets of both, would welcome the capital of both, and would freely export coal and iron to both.

Finally, a neutralised Alsace-Lorraine would constitute a " buffer " State, and together with Belgium and Luxemburg would form a great neutral belt between France and Germany. The two Powers, no longer remaining in contact, would find it easier to disarm ; and both would thus be in a position to accept more readily the principle of general disarmament if introduced into the scheme of a League of Nations. We may here recall that in 1867 war would probably have broken out between France and Prussia in respect of the possession of the

Would be a " buffer " State.

SOLUTIONS: INDEPENDENCE 283

fortress of Luxemburg, had not Lord Stanley interposed to suggest the neutralisation of the duchy; and if Alsace-Lorraine had been a neutralised independent State in 1870 it is possible that the Franco-German War might have been prevented. (The neutrality of Belgium in 1914 was not on the same footing as Alsace-Lorraine would have occupied in 1870, had it then been a neutral country.) Despite the example of Belgium in 1914, the value of buffer States has been and will continue to be everywhere recognised. Persia has been an effective buffer between British and Russian interests, Afghanistan between Russia and India, and Tibet between India and Chinese Turkestan—although, it is true, these countries are in a different position geographically and economically from that of such territories as Belgium and Alsace-Lorraine. But Switzerland is also an independent and neutralised buffer State, and her neutrality has been respected in the present war. Those who object to the neutralisation of Alsace-Lorraine say, however, that the neutrality of Switzerland was not violated by the Germans simply because she possesses an efficient army, which she promptly mobilised for self-defence in case of attempted invasion; whereas Alsace-Lorraine, being so small a territory and possessing so small a population, could not be expected to maintain an army that would be similarly effective.

This view is certainly tenable if we take it for granted that after the present war a neutralised and independent Alsace-Lorraine would be protected by no more than a "scrap of paper," and would be left isolated by Europe in the event of an attempted invasion on the part, say, of the Germans or the French. On the contrary, the neutralisation scheme necessarily implies that after

Future international co-operation and treaties.

the war the civilised peoples of the world will effect a closer association—be it called league, society, or partnership of nations—that they will create more potent sanctions for international law, and that they will find a means for ensuring the observance of treaties and for dealing with a violator thereof. These requisite sanctions and guarantees are not the figments of theory; they have existed hitherto, and they were applied in the present war. If not, why is Great Britain fighting, and why has the United States entered the war—to mention only two of the belligerents? What is needed is to reinforce these sanctions and guarantees in such a way that a State preparing to violate international law or treaties will be certain that it will have the *whole* civilised world against it, that if it proceeds in its contemplated act or remains refractory it will be ostracised from the family of nations and excluded from all commercial intercourse, that it will even have to encounter the armed forces of the united world and suffer all the consequences of certain defeat. The future hope of mankind, then, lies in close international co-operation, which undoubtedly can be established; the lessons and results of the war make such organisation imperative, whatever be the destiny of Alsace-Lorraine, and whether this or that State is to be neutralised or not.

CHAPTER XVI

SOLUTIONS SUGGESTED : (d) PARTITION ; ALTERATION OF BOUNDARIES, ETC.

Partition proposals—Language as a basis—Suggested union of Alsace with Baden—Division among German States—Frontier rearrangement—The *pays messin* to France and the rest neutralised—Alsace-Lorraine as part of a Rhenish-Alpine Confederation—Boundary readjustment—Arbitration of the Pope suggested—Difficulties in these proposals : Division on basis of speech—Division on basis of sentiment—Division between German States—Lorraine as an independent State—Suggested confederation. The Rhine as a Franco-German boundary—Criticism of the view as to a Rhine frontier—Desideratum in fixing frontiers.

IN addition to the solutions considered in the preceding chapters, viz. the establishment of Alsace-Lorraine as an autonomous State within the German Empire, and the creation of a neutralised independent State, various schemes have been suggested which involve a partition of the territory or an alteration of its boundaries. {Partition proposals.}

Thus it has been proposed that Alsace-Lorraine should be divided into two parts—the predominantly French-speaking country, and the predominantly German-speaking country—that the former should be retroceded to France, and that the latter should continue to belong to the German Empire. {Language as a basis.} On one occasion Maximilian Harden expressed the view that such districts of the Reichsland as were conspicuously French in character and speech might be restored to France in exchange for an African colony. And quite recently at the German majority

Socialist Conference held at Würzburg, October 14-17, 1917, Herr Vetters of Giessen remarked that if it was simply a matter of the smaller French-speaking frontier districts, the Germans ought not to insist obstinately on retaining possession of them, if a great number of human lives could thereby be spared. Again, a more definite plan has been brought forward for separating Alsace and Lorraine as they are at present situated, and returning Lorraine to France, leaving Alsace to Germany. Further, it has been pointed out that, as Alsace would before the present war have probably voted, if the opportunity were offered, for inclusion within the German federation, and as French-speaking Lorraine—comprising only some 450 square miles—would probably have preferred to be incorporated with France, a division and partition might be effected accordingly; such arrangement would leave the germanised part of Lorraine, which might have preferred to be brought into close association with the Lower Rhine provinces for reasons of commercial intercourse and on the ground of linguistic affinity.

Alsace, too—or the greater part of it that is German —might then have chosen to be united to the Grand Duchy of Baden, with which it has many points of kinship. Baden is one of the best and most liberally governed of the German States; it is a cradle of German liberalism; its towns possess contented colonies of foreigners, and are becoming cosmopolitan in character; its arts, sciences, and social economy are in a progressive state of development. It is thought, therefore, that the Alsatians would have been quite satisfied with a union with Baden, and could have lived at peace, especially if many of the Prussian officials of Alsace were replaced by Alsatians and Badeners.

Suggested union of Alsace with Baden.

SOLUTIONS: PARTITION 287

Other partition schemes have quite recently been advanced in Berlin; *e.g.* that Alsace should be allotted to Bavaria, and Lorraine to Prussia; or that a threefold division should be made, assigning Lower Alsace to Bavaria, Upper Alsace to Baden, and Lorraine to Prussia. In support of such plans it is pointed out that, whilst Alsace is much more closely related to Bavaria or Baden than it is to Prussia, German Lorraine, on the other hand, has close commercial connections with Cologne, and better understands and can more easily accommodate itself to the nature and characteristics of the Prussians.

<small>Division among German States.</small>

A Swiss writer,[1] discussing in the summer of 1916 the question of a rearrangement of the Franco-German frontier, observes: " The coral rag summits of the [Lorraine] plateau are national strategical points which become doubly valuable by the erection of forts. The eastern edge of the Côtes Lorraine should become, from natural causes, the first defensive line of France against Germany." He maintains that no suitable dividing line can be found in Lorraine owing to its geographical position between two large river basins, *viz.* that of south-west Germany and that of the Seine. " The chalk, clay, and marl strata of Lorraine may be regarded as the eastern edge" of the latter, or as the western edge of the former. Now, as it is this natural formation which in the past determined the independence of this transition territory, established formerly as the buffer State of the Duchy of Lorraine, he therefore recommends the revival of such a State to be delimited in accordance with geographical exigencies.

<small>Frontier rearrangement.</small>

---

[1] *Basle Gazette*, August 27, 1916; referred to by Sir Thomas Holdich, *op. cit.*, pp. 110–11.

Again, it has been suggested that Alsace-Lorraine should be set up as an independent neutralised State, after giving Metz and the *pays messin* to France and effecting certain boundary modifications. The new State would comprise the territory on the left bank of the Rhine wherein the Germanic dialect predominated, and also —for the sake of securing territorial unity—Upper Alsace, where, however, the use of French is increasing amongst the bourgeois classes. The boundaries would then be, on the east, the Rhine; on the west, a line coinciding approximately with the present frontier, subject to certain rectifications, *e.g.* in regard to the district of the old commune of Raon-lès-Leau, after which the line would follow the course of the Sarre Rouge as far as its confluence with the Sarre, and then the course of the latter as far as its confluence with the Moselle.

The pays messin to France and the rest neutralised.

A remarkable proposal was brought forward in 1884 by a Saxon publicist [1] as a means of solving the widely felt difficulties in regard to the anomalous position of the conquered Alsace-Lorraine. Like many other German writers and politicians, he does not look with favour on the existence and multiplication of small States, and so he suggests that Alsace-Lorraine should be united to the neighbouring small States, Holland, Belgium, Luxemburg, and Switzerland, and that the whole should constitute a neutral Rhenish-Alpine Confederation. In this case the security of the frontiers of the German Empire might be ensured by causing the fortresses of Metz and Strassburg to be demolished, and by forbidding the construction of others.

As part of a Rhenish-Alpine confederation.

[1] M. Maass, *Was soll mit Elsass-Lothringen werden* (Leipzig, 1884), p. 45.

Writing in 1915, an English geographical authority [1] proposes such a boundary readjustment as amounts to an entirely French solution of the problem. He holds that the frontier should be determined by considerations of national sentiment, added to reasons of economic interests and geographical configuration. He points out that, whereas the forested Vosges form a real barrier in Alsace, yet French is steadily advancing towards the eastern slope, despite the fierce political hostility; and that, in view of all these circumstances, the eastern frontier of Alsace should be the Rhine, and such a reconstituted Alsace should go to France. In reference to the geographical features and the existence of German sentiment he says : " These include the lowland area of the Lorraine gate between the Hardt and the Vosges, the natural line of least resistance marked by the Zorn and the Kinzig valleys, and its complementary economic feature in the Rhine-and-Marne canal. This canal divides approximately the Alsace hop-lands from the Palatinate tobacco-lands, as the Saar divides the Lorraine hop-lands from the Palatinate grain-lands. So the frontier should run along the canal to the Saar, and then along the Saar to the point where the Moselle leaves the Luxemburg frontier. South of the canal and west of the Rhine there is no appreciable percentage of Germanic sentiment—in a population of 1,800,000 ; and it is better that the appreciable percentage of Germanic sentiment west of the Saar should come under a Power with a genius for assimilation than that the at least equally appreciable percentage of French sentiment should remain under a Power with no such genius." [2]

Boundary readjustment.

[1] L. W. Lyde, *Some Frontiers of to-morrow* (London, 1915), pp. 57–8.
[2] Ibid., pp. 57–8.

ALSACE-LORRAINE

Finally, as a way out of the seeming tangle a proposal has recently been brought forward by Herr Herzberger's organ, the Swiss paper *Neue Zürcher Nachrichten*, that the Alsace-Lorraine question should be submitted to the arbitration of the Pope, who would of course be able, subject to the limits of the submission, to choose from among the above-mentioned solutions.

Arbitration of the Pope suggested.

That all these proposals are attended by greater or lesser advantages there can be no doubt; but it is equally certain that they disregard or gloss over many outstanding difficulties and disadvantages, which would prove to be an obstacle to a satisfactory, equitable, and permanent settlement from the point of view alike of the provinces themselves, the two contending claimants, and the rest of Europe.

Difficulties in these proposals.

The division of the provinces on the basis of speech and the assignment of the French-speaking portions to France and the German-speaking districts to Germany would be impossible because— as we have shown in an earlier chapter— there is no clear line of demarcation between the two languages; if such an apportionment were attempted it would involve a chopping up of the country in such a fantastic manner that the result of the operation would be unmanageable for practical purposes. Moreover, great numbers of the people speak the two languages equally well; and many whose mother-tongue is the German dialect prefer French for cultural, literary, and social reasons. Indeed, language cannot safely be taken as the determining criterion for effecting a territorial division; it is not necessarily a true index of the sentiments, the sympathies, the aspirations,

Division on basis of speech.

BOUNDARY ADJUSTMENT 291

and the consciousness of national personality of a given population.[1] Such a partition would not satisfy either France or Germany ; and it would be certainly repudiated by the Alsace-Lorrainers. We have emphasised more than once that, speaking generally, the Alsace-Lorrainers are neither French nor German ; they are Alsace-Lorrainers with ideals of their own the fulfilment of which the great majority of them seek neither in France nor in Germany, but in Alsace-Lorraine. There is undoubtedly a certain difference between the Alsatians and the Lorrainers in respect both of physical and mental characteristics; but a common unfortunate destiny for well-nigh half a century—not to mention an earlier and happier association—has brought them intimately together and has welded them into an almost homogeneous people; the union is quite as close as, if not closer than, the union of the different elements of Belgium or of Switzerland. M. Heimweh points out that during the period of protest,[2] Upper Alsace, for example, which contained comparatively few French communes, returned protesting deputies to the Reichstag with the same persistence as Lorraine did, where half of the population were French ; that the evasion from military service, the enlistments in the foreign legion, the number of the fallen at Tonkin and Dahomey, were all divided pretty equally between all parts of the Reichsland; and that the emigration statistics during, say, the twenty years 1871–1890, show that there were just as many emigrants from the German-speaking districts as from the French-speaking localities.[3] Thus,

[1] On the question of language, see *supra*, chap. vii.
[2] See *supra*, chap. x.
[3] J. Heimweh, *La Guerre et la frontière du Rhin* (Paris, 1895), pp. 78–80 ; referring to the *Statistische Mittheilungen*, xxiii and xxiv (Strasburg, 1893–4), published by the Ministry of Alsace-Lorraine.

a partition based on language, or on earlier historical association, or on original nationality and race, whilst being ostensibly and superficially feasible and natural, would in reality be impracticable and artificial, and would amount to an arbitrary dismemberment of an organic whole. Furthermore, if a partition were effected, what would be the position of the part that remained German ? Would it be a diminished Reichsland, or would it be made an autonomous member of the German confederation ? Both alternatives give rise to difficulties.

Nor could a practical scheme of partition be arrived at on the footing of national sentiment and preference for France or Germany, for the reason—as in the case of the distribution of the two languages—that there is no definite dividing-line. The suggestion that Metz and the *pays messin* should be returned to France on the ground that this district is almost entirely French is weakened through the incorrectness of the reason given : for, in point of fact, Metz is not now predominantly French ; the old town may still be so, but the new town is nearly all German ; so that, speaking approximately, three-fifths of Metz as a whole may be said to be German. Besides, the French *revanche* sentiment would scarcely be satisfied with the acquisition of Metz alone, if the rest of Lorraine and the whole of Alsace remained in the hands of Germany ; for it is with Strassburg rather than with Metz that the French *revanche* sentiment—whatever there survived of it before the present war—had been associated.

The proposed division of Alsace-Lorraine between Prussia and one or two other German States (*e.g.* Bavaria and Baden) raises not only all the difficulties mentioned above, but the further difficulty in that it

[margin: Division on basis of sentiment.]

BOUNDARY ADJUSTMENT 293

would arouse the jealousy and dissatisfaction of the South German States; and the provinces, which have long been an unhappy object of contention in European conflicts, would become an unhappy scrambling-ground for German States. Division between German States.

To set up Lorraine alone as an independent buffer State also gives rise to the various disadvantages incidental to separation; besides, it creates the further difficulty in reference to boundary delimitation. Many of the fatal defects of the frontier established in 1871 would be continued. Lorraine as an independent State.

On the other hand, to do away as much as possible with small States altogether by combining Alsace-Lorraine with, say, Belgium, Luxemburg, Holland, and Switzerland, and so establishing a considerable confederation, is such an absurd proposal that it is not worth discussion. That the small nations have justified their existence in the world and that it is a supreme advantage from all points of view—political, legal, cultural—to let them remain and protect them is admitted everywhere, except perhaps among certain sections in Germany. Writers, militarists, and publicists such as Clausewitz, Lasson, Treitschke, Bernhardi, and so on, look with contempt on small States (as on small armies) and would readily, if permitted, bring about their extinction. Suggested confederation.

Lastly, the proposal to readjust the boundaries in such a way as to make the Rhine the dividing-line between France and Germany has certain important disadvantages. It was the fatal aim of Napoleon III to secure for France the frontier of the Rhine. Do those who advance this suggestion mean that only that part of The Rhine as a Franco-German boundary.

the Rhine which separates the present Alsace from Baden shall be the Franco-German boundary, or that the lower course of the river shall also form such a boundary? In the case of the former alternative—assuming all the benefits claimed for a river-boundary—only a comparatively small section of the Rhine (about a hundred miles) would furnish the boundary, leaving Lorraine and Northern Alsace with the same defective frontiers as existed before the war of 1870. The latter alternative implies the annexation to France of a considerable portion of Germany—the Palatinate and the Rhine Provinces—as well as interference with Luxemburg and Belgium. Even if Germany were overwhelmingly defeated and found herself at the mercy of France, there would be no valid reason, from the point of view of European policy, to take all this territory for the purpose of rounding off France. Moreover, what good reason is there, it has not inaptly been asked, to fix on the Rhine as the "natural" frontier of France rather than, say, the Elbe or the Oder, unless it be that the demand for the territorial extension of the Rhine is more modest and less impossible of realisation. But the fact that one claim is less extravagant than another does not necessarily make it a reasonable and legitimate one.

The question of the Rhine as a French boundary dominated the foreign policy of the Revolution and the Empire. It was an important feature of the negotiations of the Treaty of Bâle (1795), as well as of those of the Treaty of Campo Formio (1797) and of the Peace of Lunéville (1801), whereby France succeeded in acquiring the long-desired Rhine frontier. In November 1813 Metternich and Nesselrode declared at Frankfort to De Saint-Aignan, the French minister,

The Rhine in earlier European politics.

BOUNDARY ADJUSTMENT 295

that in their view the Rhine was one of the natural boundaries of France : " Que les souverains coalisés étaient unanimement d'accord sur la puissance et la prépondérance que la France doit conserver dans son intégrité, en se renfermant dans ses limites naturelles qui sont le Rhin, les Alpes, et les Pyrénées, et que si ces principes étaient agréés on pourrait neutraliser, sur la rive droite du Rhin, tel lieu qu'on jugerait convenable où les plénipotentiaires de toutes les puissances belligérantes se rendraient sur-le-champ." After the defeat of Napoleon, however, in 1814 and again in 1815, a territorial rearrangement was effected in order to secure European political equilibrium. Under the Peace of Paris, 1814, France was obliged to abandon the left bank of the Rhine ; and under the Treaty of Paris, November 20, 1815, she suffered further losses of territory—whereas Prussia gained considerable accessions beyond the Rhine, and, having thus acquired the hegemony in Germany, made a bid for the political hegemony on the Continent. A few months before his definitive downfall Napoleon is said to have remarked that the Rhine frontier is " un décret de Dieu "[1] ; but, thanks to his ambition, Europe was compelled to disregard such " decree," and bring about a different arrangement.

Several recent writers, maintaining that the Rhine is a natural boundary necessary for the security and independence of European countries, point to the great part it has repeatedly played in national struggles from the time of the Romans, and to the menacing predominance attained by the Power that took possession of the course of the river. Thus, a French historian writing soon after the

The Rhine in national struggles.

[1] Letter to Fleury de Chaboulon, March 1815 ; referred to by C. M. Savant, *Frontière du Rhin* (Paris, 1915).

Franco-German War, and foreseeing the approaching preponderance of Germany, observes : " Sur les rives historiques du Rhin et au pied des montagnes qui se reflètent dans ses eaux, bien des races humaines, des peuples européens se sont heurtés; et il semble que la domination, ou au moins la prépondérance en Europe soit attachée à la possession de ces hauts sommets d'où l'on descend partout et de ce fleuve qui arrose et quelquefois ravage les pays les plus divers. Quand les Romains atteignirent le Rhin ils arrivaient à l'apogée de leur puissance, et quand ils l'abandonnèrent, leur empire tomba. Le véritable centre de la puissance de Charlemagne, qui s'étendait de l'Eyder au Garigliano et du Raab à l'Océan, était, entre la Meuse et le Rhin, à Aix-la-Chapelle; et les empereurs allemands, ses héritiers prétendus, menacèrent souvent de là l'indépendance européenne. Louis XIV, en ramenant la France au Rhin, conjura cette menace. La première République française, qui prit toute la rive gauche du fleuve, assura tout à fait cette indépendance, et le premier Empire français, en passant sur la rive droite, la menaça de nouveau à son tour. Les traités de 1815, qui partagèrent plus ou moins équitablement les rives du fleuve entre plusieurs peuples, avaient établi sur ce point un équilibre un peu factice, mais qui dura longtemps. La nouvelle puissance, en reprenant violemment presque tout le cours du fleuve sur ses deux rives, redevient la plus formidable puissance de l'Europe. Pour l'indépendance et la sécurité des peuples, le Rhin doit être une limite." [1]

But this argument, to which certain events of past European history certainly lend colour, savours of the *post hoc propter hoc* fallacy. It cannot for a moment

[1] J. Zeller, *Origines de l'Allemagne et de l'empire germanique* (Paris, 1872), p. 2.

be supposed when we consider the course of history, say, during the last two centuries, that the establishment of the Rhine as a boundary between France and Germany would have ensured peace and arrested the territorial ambitions of this or that Power. Under Louis XIV, for example, little importance was attached to natural defences.[1] The cause of aggression is not the absence of a natural boundary like the Rhine, but, on the one hand, the absence of a properly constituted society of nations governed by an international law that cannot be set aside at discretion, and on the other hand the accumulation of armaments, and the obtuseness of peoples in their subservience to military fanatics. In these circumstances a natural boundary, involving a greater or less obstacle, is scarcely more effective than a purely artificial boundary of stakes and stones, protected by trenches and fortifications. Moreover, the contention that the Rhine is the most suitable Franco-German boundary is disputed by an eminent authority on boundary delimitation. Thus, Sir Thomas Holdich, writing in 1916, points out that it is the Rhineland fortresses, and not the Rhine itself, that protect the western frontiers of Germany from France,[2] and goes on to say: "Many people hope that the Rhine will be the new boundary between France and Germany. But the Rhine is no barrier from the military or political point of view. Its banks offer no serious means of defence, the population of the Rhine valley on either side the river being of the same ethnical type which spread down originally from Alpine regions. The western water-parting of the Rhine basin, where

Criticism of the view as to a Rhine frontier.

---

[1] *Cf.* C. Lecomte, *Les ingénieurs militaires en France pendant le règne de Louis XIV* (Paris 1904).
[2] *Political Frontiers and Boundary-making*, p. 129.

that water-parting is caused by the Vosges Mountains, lends itself far better to the ideal of a frontier barrier, and could readily be rendered impregnable by modern military engineering." [1] The same writer has observed more recently : " The Rhine boundary between Germany and France was unsatisfactory because the Rhine rift is connected by easy lines of approach from the German side, whilst France possesses no such easy approach lines from the Lorraine plateau, where the drainage, represented by the Meuse and Moselle, runs northward, whilst the plateau is buttressed on the east by the Vosges and the Hardt Mountains, which offer no such facilities. Thus the Rhine became geographically a German river, and has always been claimed as such by Germany. The Meuse-Moselle plateau has, historically, been an effective barrier between east and west because of this inaccessibility from the east, and also because of the character of its wild, uncultivated, and forest-clad uplands. It has, indeed, proved almost as great a barrier to French expansion as to German aggression." [2] This view is supported, from another standpoint, by Mr. J. W. Headlam, who states the results of his observation in the following terms : " No one, indeed, who has ever stood on the slopes of the Black Forest and looked across the magnificent valley, sheltered by the hills on either side, through which the Rhine flows, can doubt that this is all one country, and that the frontier must be sought, not in the river, which is not a separation, but the chief means of communication, but on the top of the hills on the further side." [3]

[1] *Political Frontiers and Boundary-making*, p. 290.
[2] Article in *New Europe*, February 8, 1917, p. 110, entitled *New Political Boundaries in Europe : Alsace-Lorraine*.
[3] J. W. Headlam, *Bismarck. Heroes of the Nations Series* (New York : London, 1899), p. 375.

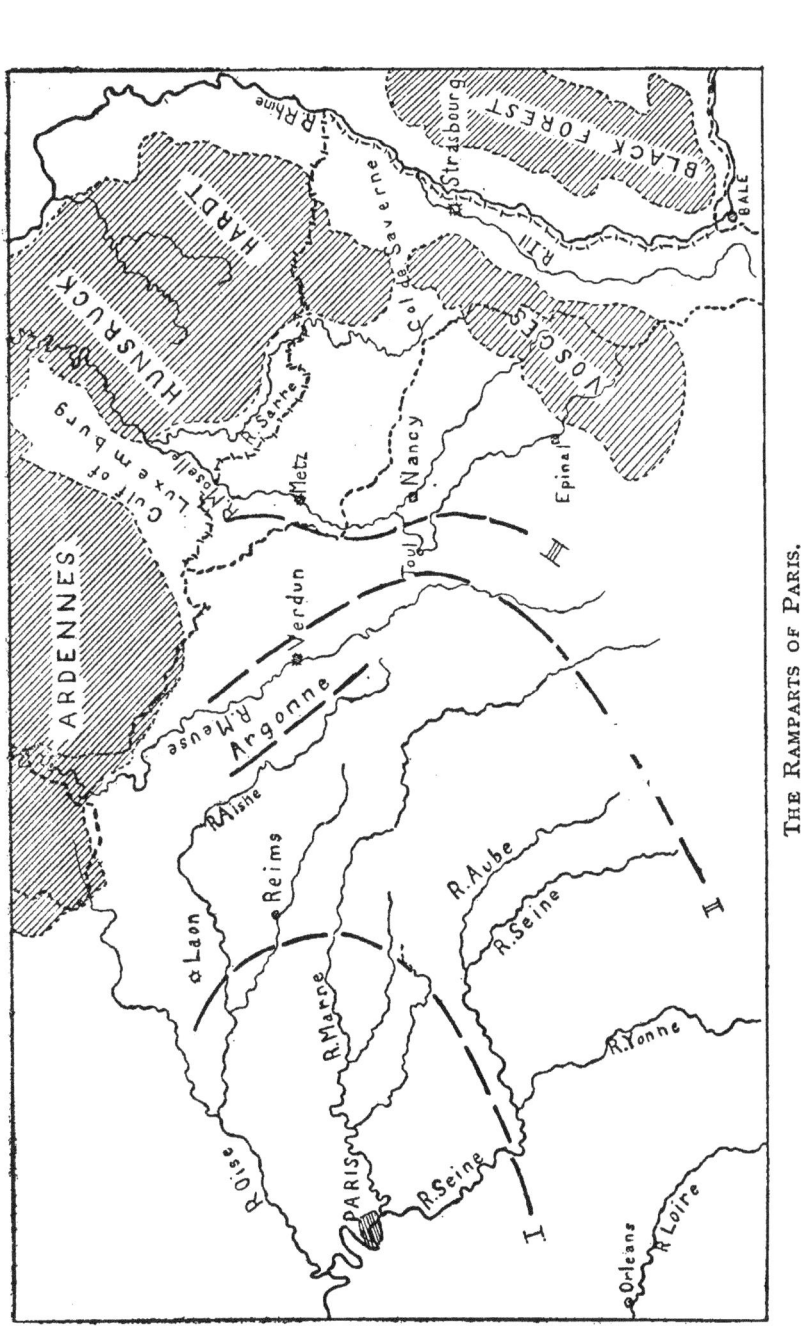

THE RAMPARTS OF PARIS.

The shading in this map shows the upland areas of N.E. France and the neighbouring regions. It will be seen that the 1871 frontier brought Germany across the low forested uplands (Low Vosges and Hardt) which extend from the plateau region of the High Vosges to the Hunsrück plateau, as far as the crest of the Heights of the Moselle near Metz, and beyond this point farther north. The broken lines indicate diagrammatically the outcrops of more resistant rock which constitute the natural defences of Paris from the east.

╀╀╀╀ Frontier of 1870.
‒ ‒ ‒ ‒ Frontier of 1914.

BOUNDARY ADJUSTMENT

The main desideratum in fixing the Franco-German boundary, as in adjusting the fundamental issue relative to Alsace-Lorraine, is to consult the wishes and circumstances of the populations directly concerned, and not to attempt to settle these questions merely by means of secret negotiations in a council-chamber and by the arbitrary and independent tracing of maps. A carefully and impartially organised referendum is, then, a condition indispensable to the eventual settlement. This has already been emphasised more than once in the preceding pages. A fuller consideration of the question of a plebiscite may, therefore, suitably conclude the present work.

Desideratum in fixing frontiers.

CHAPTER XVII

THE QUESTION OF A PLEBISCITE

Plebiscite for Alsace-Lorraine necessary—Examples of plebiscites—Cases of annexation without a plebiscite—Anglo-American practice—Juristic opinion—Grounds of support of plebiscite—Grounds of objection to plebiscite—Each case to be considered on its merits—Alsace-Lorraine a suitable case—Prevailing views as to self-determination of peoples—Alsace-Lorraine desirous to decide its own fate—Alsace-Lorraine ever against war as a solution—Opposition to plebiscite by France, Germany, and leading Alsatians—Criticism of objections—A real difficulty: presence of immigrants and absence of emigrants—Compromise necessary—Organisation of plebiscite—Persons who should vote—Probable result—Essential condition for the future.

THE key-note of this question has been expressed thus by a French writer [1] : " We may admit that France has only mediocre rights to Alsace-Lorraine, after having sold it to obtain peace. But those who have inalienable rights and have never been consulted, are the Alsatians and Lorrainers themselves." During the last hundred years the view has been gaining ground that the annexation of territory with a considerable population is illegitimate and invalid without their consent expressed on a plebiscite. A few precedents may here be recalled. An early instance is that of 1552, when Henry II of France, after taking from the German Empire the three Bishoprics, Metz, Toul, and Verdun, appears to have submitted their proposed annexation to a vote of the inhabitants. The Bishop

Plebiscite for Alsace-Lorraine necessary.

Examples of plebiscites.

[1] C Andler, *Le Prince de Bismarck* (Paris, 1899), p. 308.
[2] Phillipson, *Termination of War and Treaties of Peace*, pp. 282 seq.

PLEBISCITE 303

of Verdun said to his people, "que le roi de France était venu comme libérateur, qu'il voulait traiter les bourgeois comme de bons Français et que, bien éloigné d'user de mesures de rigueur, il en appelait au vote libre du peuple." [1]

The procedure was adopted, again, by the French Revolutionary Government in several cases.[2] Thus, during the war between France and Sardinia, 1792, General de Montesquiou having invaded Savoy and taken possession of Chambéry, September 24, the communes were asked to elect delegates (October 14) for the purpose of discussing and voting on the question of annexation. A great majority having voted in favour thereof, the Convention accordingly decreed, November 27, the union of Savoy to the Republic, of which it formed the eighty-fourth department.[3] On September 29, 1792, Nice was taken by General Anselme, who met with no opposition from the troops of the King of Sardinia; whereupon a local assembly was summoned, and it decided by a large majority in favour of annexation to France.[4] Similarly, after Mayence was entered by the French troops, October 21, 1792, and the greater part of the territory now forming Rhenish Bavaria was occupied, an assembly was constituted, and it resolved on union with France; accordingly the Convention decreed, March 30, 1793, that the towns and communes of Mayence, Worms, etc., were to become part of the French Republic.[5]

[1] Cf. E. Ollivier, L'Empire libéral (Paris, 1895), vol. i. p 165.
[2] J. Heimweh, Droit de conquête et plébiscite (Paris, 1896); R. de Card, Les Annexions et les plébiscites dans l'histoire contemporaine in Études de droit international (Paris, 1890).
[3] Cf. V. de St. Genis, Histoire de la Savoie (Chambéry, 1869), vol. iii. pp. 137 seq.
[4] J. B Toselli, Précis historique de Nice depuis sa fondation jusqu'en 1860, 4 vols. (Nice, 1867-9.)
[5] A Chuquet, Mayence (Paris, 1892).

Napoleon III, who proclaimed the right of peoples to choose their own masters, adopted the system of plebiscite in the case of the annexation of Nice and Savoy to France (treaty of March 24, 1860, Art. I.),[1] and in the cession of Venetia and its incorporation with Italy (treaty of October 3, 1866, plebiscite, October 21, 22). Other plebiscites established the union of Parma, Modena, Tuscany, and Emilia to Piedmont and Lombardy, March 11, 12, 1860 ; Sicily and the Kingdom of Naples to Italy, October 21, 1860 ; Umbria and the Marches, November 30 ; Rome and its territory, October 1870. Thus the principle of voluntary incorporation played a noteworthy part in the creation of a new Power—Italy.

Under the Treaty of Paris, August 10, 1877 (Art. I.) the island of St. Bartholomew (Antilles) was ceded by Sweden to France, subject to the express consent of its population.

In the treaty of peace of October 20, 1883, between Chile and Peru, it was stipulated that the territories of Tacna and Arica should remain in the possession of Chile for a period of ten years, and that at the end of this term a plebiscite should decide whether they were to remain definitively annexed to Chile or were to be restored to Peru. Numerous difficulties arose between the two States in regard to the organisation of the referendum ; negotiations between them were more than once commenced and then broken off.[2]

On the other hand, there have been several striking cases of annexations in which the plebiscitary procedure was not adopted : *e.g.* the dismemberment and

---

[1] G. Cogordan, *La nationalité au point de vue des rapports internationaux* (Paris, 1890), pp. 344-56 ; *Revue des Deux Mondes*, March 1, 1896.

[2] H. Bonfils, *Droit international public* (Paris, 1912), p. 372 ; *Revue de droit international* (Bruxelles), vol. xxix. (1897), pp. 660 seq.

partition of Poland in 1772, 1793, and 1795 ; most of the treaties concluded by Napoleon, notably the Peace of Tilsit (July, 1807), which deprived Prussia of an immense extent of territory ; the treaties of 1815—a counterblast to the Napoleonic conquests—which effected a great territorial readjustment in Europe ; the Treaty of Frankfort, 1871. It may be added that in the Treaty of Prague, August 23, 1866, between Austria and Prussia, it was stipulated (Art. V) that Austria should transfer to Prussia Schleswig and Holstein (the rights over which having been acquired by the Treaty of Vienna, October 30, 1864), with the condition that the population of the northern districts of Schleswig should be ceded to Denmark if, by a free vote, they expressed a wish to that effect. But Prussia refused subsequently to carry out this plebiscitary provision.

Cases of annexation without a plebiscite.

Anglo-American practice in the past has been against the plebiscite. The United States has nearly always refused to resort to the procedure in the case of her territorial acquisitions, whether they were forcible annexations or were the outcome of amicable cessions by means of negotiation. On one occasion the inhabitants of the Danish West Indies were allowed to vote on the question of annexing the islands to the United States ; but Mr. Seward, the Secretary of State, protested against this concession.[1] As for Great Britain, Lord Salisbury once declared in the House of Lords that " the plebiscite is not among the traditions of this country."[2]

Anglo-American practice.

Thus the practice of States has been far from uniform ; and this divergence of practice is reflected

[1] *Cf.* F. Bancroft, *Life of William H. Seward* (New York : London, 1900), vol. ii. pp. 483-5.

[2] (June 19, 1890). Hansard, 3rd series, vol. cccxlv. p. 1311. (In regard to the cession of Heligoland.)

in the opinions of international jurists. There is no room here to consider these in detail, but we may refer to one or two representative pronouncements. M. Acollas, who is a French civilian as well as a writer on international law, emphasises that there can be no legitimate dismemberment or annexation of a country without the free consent of the people who are to be separated and of those who are to be united thereby : " Il ne peut y avoir de démembrement légitime que par la volonté propre de ceux qui se séparent ; d'annexion légitime que par la volonté réciproque de ceux qui s'unissent." Bluntschli, who showed himself a staunch advocate of the progressive law of war as against the extravagant pretensions of Von Moltke,[2] observes that a cession of territory presupposes the recognition of the act by its people, that such recognition need not be express and voluntary, but may be tacit and involuntary, manifested by their submission and obedience to the acquiring Government by reason of considerations of necessity, although to secure voluntary adhesion is undoubtedly the best policy. Art. 286 of his notable work on international law is to this effect : " La validité d'une cession de cette nature présuppose pour le moins la reconnaissance par la population jouissant des droits politiques, laquelle habite le territoire cédé et passe à un nouvel État. Observation : La reconnaissance pour la population jouissant des droits politiques est indispensable parce que celle-ci n'est pas un objet

Juristic opinion.

[1] E. Acollas, *Manuel du droit civil. Commentaire philosophique et critique du Code Napoléon* (Paris, 1868) ; *cf.* the same writer's *Le Droit de la guerre* Paris, 1888).
[2] Von Moltke to Professor Bluntschli, dated Berlin, December 11, 1880 ; translated by Prof. Holland, *Letters to* The Times *upon War and Neutrality* (London, 1909), pp. 24–9 ; see also Phillipson, *International Law and the Great War* (London, 1915), pp. 138–41.

PLEBISCITE

privé de volonté et de droits qu'on puisse aliéner, mais un élément vivant de l'État et que l'opposition de la population rend la prise de possession pacifique impossible. Mais la reconnaissance de la nécessité suffit, et l'adhésion libre et joyeuse de la population, bien que désirable, n'est pas nécessaire. La nécessité à laquelle on se soumet contre sa volonté et en maugréant, mais en reconnaissant qu'on ne peut faire autrement, fonde elle aussi dans la vie politique un nouveau droit ; cette reconnaissance est déjà impliquée par l'obéissance, qu'on montre envers le nouveau gouvernement et dans la cessation de toute résistance. Par contre, l'adhésion libre constitue une approbation active de la cession. Sans aucun doute, il vaut mieux que l'État qui acquiert un nouveau territoire obtienne cette adhésion et qu'il ne soit pas obligé de se contenter provisoirement de la reconnaissance par nécessité." [1]

Those who support the practice of plebiscite maintain that the mere might of the stronger ought not to be allowed to prevail, that the circumstances in which we now live are different from those of earlier ages when might was deemed to be right, that the public opinion of the civilised world has manifestly changed, that the general democratic movement may not be disregarded, that popular suffrage is now almost everywhere the fount of political authority, that the sovereignty of the people is now the governing factor in the political and social life of nearly all civilised States, and that it is now being strikingly asserted in countries that were hitherto subjected to an autocratic or oligarchical government. *(Grounds of support of plebiscite.)*

Those who object to the practice hold that it is not likely to become a recognised part of international

[1] J. C. Bluntschli, *Das moderne Völkerrecht* (French trans.—*Le Droit international codifié*), § 286.

usage, in that it is not capable of acquiring universal applicability, that in some cases it may produce more evils than it is intended to avoid, that in a forcible annexation a powerful State will repudiate the procedure if it suspects that a vote of the people will be unfavourable, and will be disposed to resume hostilities for the purpose of effecting a complete subjugation of the recalcitrant parties, that the vote of a majority is not necessarily the best, that such a vote would force the minority—which might be almost equal in numbers to the majority—to accept a destiny contrary to its will (a condition of things which the very procedure is meant to obviate), and that there is no certainty that the people would give their votes freely, uninfluenced by malpractices and sinister motives. The opponents point further to the case of the American secession, as being analogous to a case of cession in regard to the will of the population ; they say that had the plebiscite been resorted to in 1861, there would, indeed, have been no American civil war, but also there would have been no United States— for a majority in the Confederate States of the South would undoubtedly have voted in favour of separation.

<small>Grounds of objection to plebiscite.</small>

However this may be, even if the universal applicability of the practice be doubtful, each case must be taken on its merits—for there certainly are cases in which the plebiscitary procedure would be eminently fitting, desirable, and practicable. Moreover, the present war has had a great influence on the world's opinion, and particularly on the conception of the interrelation and interdependence of States. Some of the objections to the plebiscite become untenable in view of the now accepted principle, which has in these days so strikingly been put into practice, that third Powers have the right

<small>Each case to be considered on its merits.</small>

to intervene in the affairs of two given States, when one of the latter violates the law of nations or is about to take an unconscionable advantage of the other, contrary to what is manifestly right and just. Other objections will lose their force if the contemplated league of nations becomes a reality.

Whatever cases may be cited as being unsuitable for the application of a plebiscite, there is no doubt that Alsace-Lorraine is a suitable case. On the one hand, there are two parties contending for its possession; on the other hand, there is a territory with a highly civilised population possessing a distinctive soul and personality and a view of their own. What is, therefore, necessary is to make their will known, and to give them an opportunity of formally registering it in favour of one of various courses: to remain within the German Empire as an autonomous State, to return to France, to become a neutralised independent State, or some other preferred solution. *[margin: Alsace-Lorraine a suitable case.]*

We have already referred to the various pronouncements of governments, ministers, and other publicists as to the necessity of the principle of self-determination of peoples—and the Alsace-Lorrainers undeniably constitute a " people " in every rational sense of the term. These pronouncements are supported by other views representative of increasing elements in democracy: *e.g.* by the British Labour Party,[1] by the French Socialist Party, and also by German Socialist circles—Herr Katzenstein (of Stralsund), supported by Herr Glattbach (of Mülhausen), brought forward a motion at the Socialist Conference held at Würzburg, October 14, 1917, on behalf of the Socialists of Nuremberg, Würzburg, and the sixth division of the Palatinate (repre- *[margin: Prevailing views as to self-determination of peoples.]*

[1] *Daily Telegraph,* October 31, 1917.

senting the most moderate section of the Majority Party) in favour of allowing a referendum to the people of Alsace-Lorraine. The American declaration of policy on this point announced on October 19, 1917, is to this effect : " President Wilson is determined to uphold the rights of small peoples, and adhere to the general principle that no people shall be forced to live under a ruler under whom they do not wish to live. Just how far this idealistic rule will be enforced depends entirely upon the conditions existing at the close of the war."

Alsace-Lorraine has throughout been desirous of deciding its own fate. Alike during the period of protest and during the national movement its people have time and again called for a plebiscite. Writing at a date midway between the Franco-German War of 1870 and the great war of 1914, one of Alsace-Lorraine's stoutest defenders repudiated the various proposals that had from time to time been advanced by friends of Alsace-Lorraine for settling the question, without consulting the people themselves. He observed that to suggest neutralisation, exchange for a French colony, purchase, or even pure and simple retrocession to France is to dispose arbitrarily, once more, of two provinces containing a million and a half of human beings ; that to proceed in this measure is to adopt the way of the Germans, who also thought they were doing the population a service by annexing them without letting them express their view. He asks the friends of his country to deny themselves the pleasure of thus giving happiness to the people, who, having learned by experience, desire to pronounce themselves on their own destiny. " Que nos amis veuillent donc bien renoncer à la satisfaction de nous octroyer le bonheur. Instruits par

PLEBISCITE 311

l'expérience, nous demandons à pouvoir prononcer nous-mêmes sur notre propre destinée."[1] Similarly, some twenty years later, and before the present war, M. Auguste Lalance, of Mülhausen, a former deputy of the Reichstag, urged that the people of Alsace-Lorraine should be permitted by means of a free vote to decide their own fate.[2] And so on with other representative views.

Indeed, Alsace-Lorraine has all along been most anxious that the question should be settled by pacific means, and that war on its account should be avoided. Mr. Jordan, who conducted a personal inquiry on the spot in 1913, says that in all Alsace he found only two persons who thought that the ultimate solution was to be found in war. *Alsace-Lorraine ever against war as a solution.* He writes in the following terms as expressing the views of leading Alsatians and the attitude of the majority of the population : " War is the worst possible solution of our problems, because war is no solution. With war there is never a solution of any question. Alsace has been part of Germany, of Austria, of France, and now of Germany again. If France should gain Alsace by war, it would be only the beginning of another war, and so on without end. . . . Every solution implying war is to be rejected. No definite solution could result from a Franco-German war, by which Alsace would find herself cut into two parts, each to destroy the other. A war, whatever its result, provokes always the desire of revenge, and leads to indefinite international disorder, in which the antagonism among different elements would be greatly intensified. . . . A Franco-German *entente* would necessitate for Alsace-Lorraine a govern-

[1] J. Heimweh, *Triple Alliance et Alsace-Lorraine* (Paris, 1892), p. 131.
[2] *Cf.* Bourdon, *L'Énigme allemande*, p. 471 ; Eng. trans., p. 357.

ment according to its own will. It would thus destroy the worst obstacle to the pacification of Europe, and open to civilisation new lines of progress." [1]

The only way to ensure the pacification of Europe, so far as it depends on the solution of the Alsace-Lorraine problem, is to give the Alsace-Lorrainers an opportunity of deciding their destiny definitively and formally by means of a plebiscite.

Now we have already seen that Germany is opposed to a plebiscite, not necessarily because she fears an adverse vote, but on the ground that there is legally no "question of Alsace-Lorraine," and that there is no lawful justification for a referendum, seeing that the provinces were transferred to her in perpetuity by the Treaty of Frankfort, and that they could no longer, after that act, concern any other Power but herself. On the other hand, the French, as well as certain leading Alsatians, object to a plebiscite for different reasons. In the first place, they hold that the return of Alsace-Lorraine to France would be merely a recovery or reunion, and not a cession or annexation: France is to regain her property just as stolen goods are taken from a thief and restored to the true owner. "La France," says M. Helmer, "reprend son bien, qu'elle retrouve dans la main du possesseur de mauvaise foi, comme je puis reprendre ma bourse à celui qui m'en a dépouillé." [2] Similarly, M. Wetterlé observes: " Who to-day would wish to sanction that insult should be added to injury in proposing to surround with ridiculous formalities the restoration to France of her property, the return of the Alsace-Lorrainers to the true mother-country? . . . I am

Marginal note: Opposition to plebiscites by France, Germany, and leading Alsatians.

[1] *Op. cit.*, pp. 96–8.   [2] *France-Alsace*, pp. 158, 159.

not in doubt as to the result of a referendum in Alsace-Lorraine if one were to be organised. By a crushing majority my compatriots would affirm their desire to be relieved for ever from those masters who have so cruelly tortured them. But it would be an attack on the honour of France to force her to make an electoral bid to regain the heart of her children, and on the honour of Alsace-Lorrainers to make them to put up their heart for public sale.''[1] The republican newspaper of Paris, Le Temps, condemned, in its issue of August 11, 1917, the submission of the majority to the minority French Socialists in accepting a plebiscite in their reply to the Stockholm *questionnaire*, on the ground that recourse thereto " would mean the casting of an odious doubt on the patriotic conscience of the Alsace-Lorrainers." The radical paper, Le Matin, of August 22, 1917, likewise rejects a plebiscite, and says that the people of the annexed provinces cannot admit that their character of Frenchmen should be questioned.

Again, it is contended that the protests of the Alsatian and Lorraine representatives made in 1871 do not now need confirmation, and that they are still applicable and valid.[2] " We will have," says M. Georges Weill, ex-deputy for Metz in the Reichstag, " no preliminary plebiscite, since that would be an abjuration of the protests of the past, an insult to our feelings, and a sanction of the greatest outrage of modern times."[3] A similar view is expressed by MM. Lichtenberger.[4] And M. Helmer holds that to agree to a plebiscite would be an admission that Alsace-Lorrainers might to-day deny the solemn and unani-

[1] *Fortnightly Review*, November 1917, pp. 799, 800.
[2] *Le Matin*, August 22, 1917.
[3] *The Observer*, February 3, 1918.
[4] *Op. cit.*, p. 83.

mous declaration of their deputies in 1871.[1] " La seule base certaine de la réunion de l'Alsace-Lorraine à la France doit être la manifestation de Bordeaux." [2]

Next, it is urged that the acceptance of a plebiscite would be a tacit recognition of the effects of violence.[3]

This would, too, assume the validity of the Treaty of Frankfort, which is considered by many Frenchmen and Alsatians to be null and void *ab initio*, and by others to have been abrogated on the outbreak of the present war.[4]

There is really no need to examine these objections in detail. The untenability of most of them has already been shown. It will be sufficient to say that Germany acquired a legally valid title to the provinces by the Treaty of Frankfort, which remains binding until it is superseded or modified by another treaty; that the declarations of 1871, whatever moral weight they had, had no such legal force as could invalidate the transaction solemnly and voluntarily effected by the declarants' recognised Government; that the return of Alsace-Lorraine to France would not be a " recovery " or " restoration " in the sense alleged, but an annexation—to claim otherwise is to prevaricate just as much as the Germans did in 1870 when they attempted to justify the dismemberment of France on the ground that it was necessary as a " protective guarantee "; that the violence of 1871 would be repeated if Alsace-Lorraine were annexed to France contrary to the wishes of the population ; and that the only way to find out what their true wishes are is to ask them, and to ask them cannot surely be an " impiety " or an " insult," when

_{Criticism of objections.}

---

[1] *France-Alsace*, p. 156.
[2] *Ibid.*, p. 164.   [3] *Ibid.*
[4] *Ibid.*, and also the view of M. Barrès, in the preface, p. ix.

PLEBISCITE 315

the object of asking them is merely to settle a disputed or doubtful point.

There is, however, another objection that has more force, viz. that a plebiscite would not be fair owing to the presence of German immigrants and the absence of Alsatian and Lorraine emigrants. In 1871 the population of Alsace-Lorraine was about 1,500,000. Under the Treaty of Frankfort the practice of option was adopted[1]; the native inhabitants (excluding women and minors) had to choose between French and German nationality by September 30, 1872. There were about 160,000 options, of which more than a half were annulled because they were not followed by effective departure within a reasonable time. The emigration of natives and the immigration of Germans began in 1871 and continued in the subsequent years. We may quote some figures from the Official Manual of Statistics of Alsace-Lorraine to show the loss in population during the first twenty-five years after the annexation :

A real difficulty—presence of immigrants and absence of emigrants.

From 1871 to 1875 the number of emigrants *exceeded* the number of immigrants by 70,970.
From 1875 to 1880 the number of emigrants *exceeded* the number of immigrants by 35,835.
From 1880 to 1885 the number of emigrants *exceeded* the number of immigrants by 59,312.
From 1885 to 1890 the number of emigrants *exceeded* the number of immigrants by 37,991.
From 1890 to 1895 the number of emigrants *exceeded* the number of immigrants by 34,534.
Thus, from 1871 to 1895 the number of emigrants *exceeded* the number of immigrants by 238,642.

[1] See Phillipson, *Termination of War and Treaties of Peace*, pp. 296 *seq.*

As these figures show only the difference between the number of emigrants and that of immigrants, it is clear that the actual number of emigrants was much greater than the numbers shown in the above table. It is roughly estimated that down to the year 1900 there were about 500,000 emigrants and about 300,000 German immigrants; and during the subsequent period the numbers on both sides increased to some extent, though not proportionately—perhaps 600,000 represents the approximate number of emigrants up to date (though a much larger number, even as high as a million, has been stated by M. Georges Weill [1]). In any event, allowing for errors in the estimate, it is contended that, to determine the true voice of Alsace-Lorraine, we must not confine ourselves to its present population, but we should also take into account the emigrants and their descendants. Furthermore, it is thought that it would be unfair and unjust to ask the large contingent of German immigrants to say whether the country in which they have settled should be French or German.

Thus the principal difficulties that arise relate, on the one hand, to the classes of persons who should be permitted to vote, and on the other to the organisation and supervision of the plebiscite machinery. A compromise appears to be the only way to overcome these obstacles; and such a scheme as the following would be an equitable one, and by its means a fair expression of Alsace-Lorraine opinion could be ensured.

Compromise necessary.

First, the entire organisation of the voting should be entrusted to a mixed commission including neutral

---

[1] *The Observer*, November 18, 1917; February 3, 1918. With the estimate of M. Weill we may compare that of MM. Lichtenberger, who give the number of emigrants, down to the year 1910, as 500,000; *op. cit.*, p. 17.

PLEBISCITE 317

members, or to an entirely neutral commission guaranteeing liberty and secrecy of the poll and protection from bribery, duress, and other irregular practices. <small>Organisation of plebiscite.</small>

Secondly, we have to bear in mind that the overwhelming majority of the population are Alsace-Lorrainers, and not German immigrants; and so, having regard to their solidarity, their consciousness of national personality, and their common destiny for nearly half a century, we must conclude that it would be better to poll the votes of the qualified population as a whole, rather than divide up the country into a number of territorial units and take the poll of each of these separately.[1] Subject to slight frontier emendations that may be shown to be imperative, Alsace-Lorraine should not be chopped up, but should stand or fall together—an inference that presents itself irresistibly from our previous exposition of the entire problem and its various implications.

Thirdly, the persons qualified to vote might include the following : (1) the domiciled native male inhabitants who are of legal age ; (2) the domiciled native unmarried women or widows who are of age (since the nationality of a wife is that of her husband, it would be either supererogatory or impolitic to give them separate votes) ; (3) the domiciled native male orphans who have reached military age, if this is lower than the ordinary legal age ; (4) the domiciled naturalised inhabitants of age who are neither of French nor German origin ; (5) German immigrants—men, unmarried women, and widows— who have established, say, a ten years' domicile ; (6) Alsatian and Lorraine emigrants—men, unmarried <small>Persons who should vote.</small>

[1] A division into small areas is suggested by A. J. Toynbee, *Nationality and the War* (London, 1915), pp. 42 *seq.*

women, and widows—who have emigrated, say, within the last ten years. The claim sometimes advanced that *all* the German immigrants should be disqualified, and that *all* the Alsace-Lorraine emigrants, and their descendants, should be qualified, is unfair, irrational, and inexpedient; for we have to determine the will of Alsace-Lorraine as it is at the date of the plebiscite, and not as it was in 1871. We know that in 1871 it went over to Germany most reluctantly; but in the period between then and now the country has in many respects been revolutionised; and it is its present view and feeling that we have to ascertain.

Fourthly, before resorting to this plebiscitary procedure it would be well to wait, say, two or three years, until the passions aroused by the war have been cooled a little, and the thoughts of the people have been collected sufficiently to allow of an undisturbed consideration of the choice to be made.

It is audacious at all times to indulge in prophecies, and especially so in the case of the present complicated problem, which the war has rendered all the more difficult. None the less, mindful of the facts, considerations, and conclusions presented in the foregoing chapters, we venture to express our belief that a plebiscite organised before the present war on the lines suggested would have resulted in favour of autonomy within the German Empire, and if organised now will result in favour of neutralised independence.

Probable result.

Be this as it may, whatever result is arrived at it will be only a dangerous, patched-up solution unless there be a general reconciliation of the warring peoples, and such a change in the position and relationships of the society of States as will more effectively safeguard international law and minimise the possibility of war.

Essential condition for the future.

INDEX

Abwehrgesetze 163
Acollas, plebiscite, on 306
Agénor de Gasparin, neutralisation of Alsace-Lorraine 272
Agriculture 43, 44
Albert, King of the Romans 115
Alfonso XII 163, 217
Alsace. *See also heads for various topics*
    French Revolution, at 59–60
    Middle Ages, in 55, 117
    part of Germany till seventeenth century 56
    Thirty Years War, in 56
    union with France 60
' Alsace for the Alsatians ' 163, 173, 184, 264
    significance of 188
Alsace-Lorraine *See also headings relating to the various topics*
    annexation in 1871, 20, 61 *seq.*
        See Annexation in 1871
    area of, in earlier history 19, 20
        when annexed by Germany 34
    attitude of, outbreak of the war, at 207 *seq.*
        towards France before the war 199 *seq.*
        See also Nationalist movement
    bone of contention, long a 19
    ' challenge-cup of Europe,' as 30
    claims of Germany to 112 *seq.*
        See Claims of Germany to Alsace-Lorraine
    cockpit of Europe, as a 30
    declaration of the two Chambers (1917), 209 *seq.*
    description of 34 *seq.*
    French attitude towards 214 *seq.*
        See French attitude towards Alsace-Lorraine
    history 49 *seq. See* History
    nationalist movement 184 *seq.*
        See Nationalist movement
    new generation, attitude of 203
    personality of 202

Alsace-Lorraine—*continued*
    position of, in earlier history 19
    problem of
        See Problem of Alsace-Lorraine
    proposals as to its fate after annexation 86 *seq.*
    protest of 1871 against annexation 98 *seq*
    protest of deputies (1874) 184 *seq.*
    régime in 155 *seq.*
        See Régime in Alsace-Lorraine
    status of 155 *seq.*
    views and aspirations of 184 *seq.*
        See Nationalist movement
    views and feelings of people, doubtful indications of 203–7
Althoff, quoted 183
Amnesty 83
Annexation in 1871, 61 *seq.*
    amnesty 83
    announcement of 63
    boundary commission 80–81
    canalisation of the Moselle 84
    ecclesiastical authority 83
    effects of 20 *seq.*, 110
    German attitude as to 79–80
    grounds for
        See Claims of Germany to Alsace-Lorraine
    imperial province, made an 94
    navigation on rivers and canals 84
    option of French subjects 82
    pecuniary deposits 83
    proposals as to fate of provinces 86 *seq.*
    protests against 65
        Alsace-Lorraine deputies in 1871, of 98 *seq.*
        Germany, in 86
        various other 103 *seq.*
    public records 83
    rights of inhabitants of ceded territory 81
    territorial lust of Germany 141 *seq.*
    various matters regulated 84–5

INDEX

Area 34
Arendt 153
Argyll, Duke of 147
Asquith, Mr., Alsace-Lorraine as cause of the war, on 29
    reannexation to France, on 236
Austria, aim in 1815, 60
Autonomy for Alsace-Lorraine, demand of 194-7
    French views 265
    government, form of 267
    movement for
        See Nationalist movement
    nationalist ideal 263-4
    plebiscite following 269-70
    position as autonomous State 268-9
    recent German opinion 265-7
    refusal of, reasons for 172-4
    suggested in 1871 93-4

Baden, suggested union of Alsace with 286
Bâle, treaty of 294
Ballon d'Alsace 37
Barrès 202, 205, 206, 215
    quoted 234
Barthou 230
Bebel 86
Beer, manufacture of 44
Belfort 77, 78, 79
    gap of 37
Benedetti 62
Berckheim 130
Bernhard of Saxe-Weimar 56
Bernhardi 141
Bethmann-Hollweg 169, 172, 211
Beust, Count von 66
Bismarck, Belfort, concession as to 70
    dictatorial régime in Alsace-Lorraine, on 158-9
    doubt as to territorial demands 67
    effects of annexation of 1871, on 110
    European intervention feared by 65
    Ferrières, at 63
    germanisation, view as to 95-6
    indemnity, concession as to 70
    Metz, doubts about 97
    neutralisation, on 273
    policy as to annexed provinces 88 *seq.*, 95
    political necessity of annexation, on 137
    proposed treaty with Benedetti published 62

Bismarck—*continued*
    Russian support secured by 66
    Schnaebelé incident, on 217
    territorial ambition of Prussia, on 142, 143
    Versailles, demands made at 68
    interview with Favre at 64
Blanc 105
Blind, attitude of mass of Alsatians to Germany 200-1
    official classes in Alsace-Lorraine 178
Blumenthal 208
Bluntschli, plebiscite, on 306-7
Böcking, Sarre mines 256-7
Bodley, change of French policy, on 222-3
    Franco-German conflict in Morocco, on 218
Boll, desideratum in solution of problem, on, 31
Bonnard 265
Bordeaux, National Assembly at 64
Boulanger 217
Boulangist movement 163, 217-18, 221
Boundaries 34
    See also Frontier
Bourgeois, French national policy, on 223-4
Brandenburg, Prof. 258
Bray, Count von 92
Briey, German demands as to 257
Bruno, Archbishop of Cologne 51
Brussels, negotiations at 73-5
Bucer 56
Budget 45, 46
Buffer State, Alsace-Lorraine as a 273, 282-3, 284-5
    value of 283
Bulach, Baron de 168
Bulow, Prince von 183
    French temper, on the 224-6

Campo Formio, treaty of 294
Caprivi, passport system in Alsace 164
Cateau-Cambrésis, treaty of 53
Catholic party 190
    anti-clerical campaign 190
    Democrats leave the 191
Censorship, imposition of 164
Chamberlain, Houston 183
Chanzy 106
Charlemagne 50
Charles IV 55
Charles V 53
Charles the Bald 51
Church and State, relation between 40, 41, 247

INDEX

Claims of Germany to Alsace-Lorraine 112 seq.
conquest 147. See Conquest
economic necessity 132 seq.
historical grounds 113 seq.
   difficulties in 117-18
   early treaties 115
   Holy Roman Empire appealed to 116
   Mommsen's view 114
   Ranke's view 113
   Treitschke's view 114-15
language, on ground of 123 seq.
   difficulties involved 127
military necessity 137 seq.
nationality, question of 127 seq.
political necessity 135 seq.
   criticism 135-7
public right, principle of 130-31
racial grounds 118 seq.
   difficulties involved 120, 121
   names as criterion 119
self-contradiction 121
territorial lust 141 seq.
Treaty of Frankfort, binding force of 151
Clausewitz 141
Clemenceau 230
Climate 37
Clovis 50
Coal 42
   See also Coal and iron
resources of Germany and France 258
Coal and iron, effect of depriving Germany of 261-2
   German declaration in 1915 252-6
   problem of 251 seq.
   war, in 251-2, 255-6
Communication, means of 44
Concordat 40
Condé 57
Configuration of surface 34, 35
Conquest, claims to Alsace-Lorraine based on 147
   German view as to 143
   illegitimacy of 145
   recent growth of opinion as to 144
   right of 186
   treaty, as recognised by 149
   Von Sybel on 91
Conrad the Red 51

Dallwitz von Roedern 174
Debt 45
Delbrück, reannexation to France, on 237-9

Democrats 191
Déroulède, quoted 166, 215
Dreyfus affair 221-2

Eckhart 56
Economic position 41 seq.
Education 46, 47
Egidy 264
Emigrants, Germany, from 133
   plebiscite, in case of 315
Ems telegram 61, 149
Entwelschung 176, 199
Eucken, autonomy, on 266
Expenditure 45
Exports 44

Fabert 53
Favre, Ferrières, at 63
Frankfort, at 75
   Preliminaries of Versailles, after 71
   Versailles, interview with Bismarck at 64
Ferrières, interview between Bismarck and Favre at 63
Ferry 217
Fiore, conquest, on 149
Fischart 117
Foreign labour 133
Förster, autonomy, on 265-6
France. *For various matters see separate heads*
Francis III 54
Francis Joseph 141
Franco-German War 61 seq.
Frankfort, Convention of (1819) 258
   negotiations at 75-7
   treaty of, 65, 185, 187, 232
   binding force of 151, 233
   provisions of 77 seq.
   Von Bulow on 225, 226
   whether abrogated by the war 151, 233
Franzos 204
Franzosen-fresserei 113
Französling 180
Frederick I 129
Frederick the Great 142
Free Imperial towns 55
French attitude towards Alsace-Lorraine 214 seq.
   disturbing currents in France since 1871 221-2
   Great War, after outbreak of 227 seq.
   nationalities, question of 222-3
   pacific policy of French democracy 219-20
   phases of French feeling 214

21

French attitude—*continued*
  recent national policy 223-4
  revanche ideal 214 *seq.*
    evanescence of 216 *seq.*, 220 *seq.*, 224
French Revolution, Alsace at 59
  fusion between France and Alsace 129
Fried, Alsace-Lorraine as cause of the war, on 29
  compromise preferable to slaughter 32, 280
Froelich, pan-Germanism in Alsace-Lorraine 181
Frontier, desideratum in fixing 301
  former, untenable 242
  rearrangement suggested 287, 289
  security of 138 *seq.*
Fustel de Coulanges, nationality, on 128
  nationality of Alsace, on 130

Gaede, General, proclamation of 209
Gambetta 194, 214, 216
  assumes dictatorship 63
George, Lloyd, restoration of Alsace-Lorraine 231
Germany, aggressiveness of 28
  For various matters see separate heads
Gladstone, annexation of Alsace-Lorraine, on 24, 147-8
  liberty, on 174
Glattbach 309
Gobat, repressive measures in Alsace-Lorraine 166-7
Goltz, Von der 141
Gortchakoff, circular of 67
' Gottesfreunde,' the 56
Gottfried 117
Grafenstaden affair 165
Granville, concludes treaties (1870) to protect Belgium 62
Great War, attitude of Alsace-Lorraine on outbreak of 207 *seq.*
  attitude of German authorities towards Alsace-Lorraine on outbreak of 209
  precautions of Germany in Alsace-Lorraine 175-6
  Treaty of Frankfort not abrogated by 151, 233
Grévy, 98, 104, 217
Grosjean 107
Guester, Abbé 158
Gustavus Adolphus 57
Gutenberg 56

Hanotaux, protests in 1871, 109
Thiers's efforts in negotiation 69

Hansi 168
Harden, partition, on 285
  restoration of Alsace-Lorraine 239-40
Hartmann, 109
Headlam, Rhine frontier, on 298
Heligoland 150
Helmer, Manteuffel's régime 162
  mediæval Alsace 117
  plebiscite, on 312
  position of Alsatians in France after outbreak of the war, on 233-4
Hengel 130
Henry I 55
Henry V 51
Hervé, progress under German rule, on 47, 48
Herzberger 290
History 49 *seq.*
  Alsace, French Revolution 59
    Middle Ages 55
    part of Germany till seventeenth century 56
    Thirty Years War 56
    union with France 60
  Charlemagne 50
  Germanic invasions 49
  Lorraine, of 51 *seq.*
    annexations to France 52
    cession to France 54, 55
    French invasion 54
    Middle Ages, in 51, 52
    sixteenth century 52, 53
  Merovingian period 50
  Roman period 49
  union with German Empire 51
Hoeffel, declaration in First Chamber 210, 211
Hohenlohe Schillingsfurst, Prince von 162
Holdich, German characteristics 179
  Rhine frontier, on 297
Holy Roman Empire 116-17
Home Rule
  See Autonomy; Nationalist movement
Hue 259
Hugo, protest against annexation in 1871 104, 105

Immigrants, attitude of 178
  fusion with natives 202-3
  number of 179
  plebiscite, in case of 315
  younger generation, position of 248
Imports 44

Independence for Alsace-Lorraine,
  advantages 279 seq.
  bond of union between France
    and Germany 281-2
  buffer State, would be a 282-3
  fusion of Germanic and Gallic
    elements 281
  government, form of 277
  matters for adjustment 278-9
  military service difficulty removed 281
  neutralisation proposed 271 seq.
  revanche obviated 280
Industries 41 seq.
International law, in 1871 148
International League of Peace and
    Liberty 274-7
Iron
  See also Coal and iron
  effect of depriving Germany of
    261-2
  German resources 260-61
  Lorraine, in 42, 259

Jagow, attitude of Alsace-Lorraine
    175, 199
Jähns 141
Joffre, restoration of Alsace-Lorraine
    228
Jolly, suggested division of Alsace-Lorraine in 1871, 92
Jordan, Alsace-Lorraine against war
    as solution 311
  Alsatian names, character of 119
Julius Cæsar 49

Katzenstein 309
Keller 98, 103, 106
Kellermann 130
Kiel, treaty of 150
Kléber 130
Koeller, régime under 167-8
Kühlmann, Alsace-Lorraine in relation to the war, on 29
  reannexation to France, on
    236-7

Labour Party 309
Lalance 311
Lamberty, attachment of Alsace to
    France 129
Landesausschuss 159
  See Territorial Delegacy
Language 38-40
  division on basis of 290-92
  index of feelings and desires of
    the people, as 204-5
  partition, in regard to 285-6
  question of 123 seq.
  reannexation, in case of 243-4

Lasson 90, 141
  conquest, on 143
Launay, German coal and iron supplies, on 260
Laussedat, boundary commission
    80-81
  negotiations with Bismarck, on
    76-77
League of Free Cities 55
Lefebvre 130
Leopold 54
Liberal democratic party 190
Lichtenberger, attitude of Alsatians,
    on 200
  autonomy, on 264
  education, on 47
  law in case of reannexation 244
  new generation, attitude of 203
  plebiscite, on 313
  unity of Alsace, on 243
Liebknecht, protest against annexation in 1871, 86
Ligue Patriotique 200, 208
' Lois d'exception ' 164
Longwy, German demands as to 257
Lorraine. See heads for particular
    topics
  cession to France 54-5
  Middle Ages, in 51
  sixteenth century, in 52
Lothair 50
Louis XIV, annexation of Strassburg 59
  natural defences under 297
Louis the German 51
Lunéville, Peace of 294
Lyde, boundary readjustment, on
    289

Maass, Rhenish Alpine Confederation suggested 288
Machiavelli 141
Macmahon 221
Malon 109
Mandel 168
Manteuffel, régime under 159, 161-2,
    163
Manufactures 41 seq.
Marseillaise, the 60, 128, 168, 198
Mehemet Ali 113
Merlin of Douai 60
Metternich, Rhine boundary, on
    294-5
Metz. See also Pays messin
  annexation of, Mommsen on
    139-40
  Bismarck's doubts about 97
  German element in 133

INDEX

Military service, introduction in Alsace-Lorraine 156
Minerals 37, 42, 43
Minette 255, 256
Moltke 143
Mommsen, claims of Germany to Alsace-Lorraine, on 114
conquest, on 146
language, claim on ground of 123
Metz, annexation of 126, 139–40
Monod 138
Morocco 218
Munster, treaty of 57, 60

Napoleon, Rhine frontier, on 295
Napoleon III 145, 147, 149
plebiscite, adoption of 304
Rhine frontier, aim as to 293
National Assembly, debates on cession 104 *seq.*
National Union, formation of 191
manifesto against the Constitution of 1911, 193
programme of 191–3
Nationalist movement 184 *seq.*
attitude towards France and Germany 199 *seq.*
autonomists and protesters distinguished 189–90
autonomy demanded 194–7
efforts against 169
method adopted 189
National Union 191–3
parties in 189–92
why began 188
Nationality, option of 82
principle of 127 *seq.*
Naumann, German attitude towards Alsace-Lorraine 177
Near Eastern Question, distinguished from Alsace-Lorraine question 21
Nesselrode 294
Neutralisation of Alsace-Lorraine 271 *seq.*
Bismarck's view 89–90
German objections to 273–4
Treitschke's view 90
Newspapers, suppression of 164
Nimeguen, treaty of 58, 153
Noisseville affair 198
Novicow, constitution of Alsace-Lorraine 172
German unity and Alsace-Lorraine 135
plebiscite following autonomy 269

Oberpräsident, appointment of 156
office abolished 159

Oncken, effects of annexation of 1871, 110
frontier security 138–9
Option of nationality 82
Otto the Great 51

Painlevé, restoration of Alsace-Lorraine demanded 229, 237
Palat, Alsatian demand of autonomy 219
Panama affair 221
Pangermanism 31, 180–1
Paris, Peace of (1814) 295
Treaty of (1815) 258
(1856) 66
(1877) 304
Partition of Alsace-Lorraine 285 *seq.*
difficulties 290 *seq.*
language as basis 285–6
suggested in 1871, 92
various forms of 286 *seq.*
Passport system 164
Paulsen, no question of Alsace-Lorraine 25
Pays messin 126, 146
See also Metz
Petroleum 43
Pichon 140
Plebiscite, Anglo-American practice 305
appropriateness of, for Alsace-Lorraine 309
autonomy followed by 269–70
compromise necessary 316
condition of annexation, as a 145
demand by Alsace-Lorraine 310–11
difficulty in 315
examples of 302–4
juristic opinion on 306–7
necessity for 250, 274, 302
omission of, cases of 305
opposition to 312 *seq.*
grounds of 308
validity of 314
organisation of 317
persons who should vote 317
support of, grounds for 307
Treitschke's view 90, 91–2
Poehlmann 190
Poincaré (President), reannexation 228
Population 37, 38
characteristics of 38
Postal service 45
Potash 43
Pouquet 187
Pouyer-Quertier 75

INDEX

Prague, treaty of 305
Preiss 195
    repressive measures in Alsace-Lorraine 167
Problem of Alsace-Lorraine 19 *seq.*
    aspects of 24
    French view as to 26
    German denial of 25
    Great War, as cause of 27
    Near Eastern Question distinguished from 21
    origin of 21
    solution of 30 *seq.*
        See Solution of problem
    solutions suggested 235 *seq.*
        See Solutions suggested
    third States concerned in 22
Public right 130–31
Public works 45
Pyat 109

Quinet, cession of Alsace-Lorraine in 1871, 105

Raess, Mgr. 186
Ranc 109
Ranke, historical claims of Germany 113, 139
Rapp 130
Ratisbon, treaty of 58
Reannexation to France, coal and iron problem 251 *seq.*
    commercial system 246
    difficulties involved 240 *seq.*
    educational system 247–8
    fiscal legislation 246
    German attitude 236 *seq.*
    Great War, attitude of Alsace-Lorraine before 197 *seq.*
    industrial organisation 245
    interregnum suggested 249
    language question 243
    legal system 244–5
    mixed population 248
    modes of effecting 235
    nationalist movement as affecting 249
    plebiscite following 235–6
    political grouping 243
    religious question 40, 41, 247
Reason of State 143
Referendum. *See* Plebiscite
Régime in Alsace-Lorraine, Bulach (Baron de), under 168–9
    censorship 164
    Council of State established 160
    Dallwitz von Roedern, under 174
    dictatorship (1871–3) 156
    economic pressure 165

Régime in Alsace-Lorraine—*continued*
    educational measures 165–6
    'exceptional' laws 164
    exclusion of natives from public functions 165
    failure, reasons for 177 *seq.*
    germanisation not effected 176 *seq.*
    Government Bill (1910) 169
    Great War, precautions on outbreak of 175–6
    Hohenlohe Schillingsfurst, under 162
    imperial constitution applied (1874) 157
    Koeller, under 167–8
    language, conflict as to 166
    legislation, methods of 160–61
    Manteuffel, under 161–2
    military occupation (1870–1) 155
    nationalist movement, efforts against 169
        See also Autonomy; Nationalist movement
    new constitution (1911) 170 *seq.*
    newspapers suppressed 164
    official classes 167, 178
    passport system 164
    progress in many respects 47
    repressive measures 163 *seq.*
    societies dissolved 164
    Statthalter appointed 159
    status from February 1871 to June 1871, 155
    suspicion and espionage 165
    Territorial Delegacy 159–61
        See Territorial Delegacy
Religion 40
Religious question 40, 41, 247
Renan, racial claims of Germany 121
Revanche 21, 31, 32, 33, 176, 214 *seq.*, 239, 265
    See also French attitude towards Alsace-Lorraine
Revanchegelüst 152
Reyle 206
Rhine as a boundary 293 *seq.*
    difficulties 297–8
Ribot, restoration of Alsace-Lorraine 229–30
Ricklin 209, 211
Rochefort 109
Rudolf III 55
Russia, *entente* with France (1891) 218
Ryswick, treaty of 54, 59, 153

Saint-Aignan 294
St. Odilia 50
Saint-Vallier 110

Salisbury, Lord, plebiscite, on 305
Saverne affair 175, 198
Scheidemann, autonomy, on 267
Schmettau 129
Schnaebelé incident 163, 217-18
Schönaich Carolath 257
Schongauer 56
Schucking, German agressiveness, on 28
Schumacher, German need of coal and iron 256-7
Schwob 180
Sembat, attitude of Alsace-Lorraine 201, 203
autonomy, refusal of 172
French feeling after annexation in 1871, on 215-16
Seward, plebiscite, on 305
Sirhanun 130
Socialists, Alsace-Lorraine, in 190
Congress (1914) 194
France, in 230
self-determination, on 309
Germany, in, annexation proposals 258
autonomy, on 267
Conference at Würzburg (1917) 286
self-determination, on 309
Societies, dissolution of 164
Solution of problem, desiderata in 30, 31, 33
difficulties in 31
justice the fundamental point in 33
Solutions suggested, arbitration of the Pope 290
autonomy within the German Empire 263 *seq.*
See Autonomy for Alsace-Lorraine
Confederation, to form part of a new 288
division among German States 287
frontier rearrangement 287, 289
independence for Alsace-Lorraine 271 *seq.*
See Independence for Alsace-Lorraine
partition between France and Germany 285 *seq.*
See Partition of Alsace-Lorraine
pays messin to France and rest neutralised 288
plebiscite in 302 *seq.*
See Plebiscite
reannexation to France 235 *seq.*

Solutions suggested—*continued*
See Reannexation to France
Rhine as boundary 293 *seq.*
union of Alsace with Baden 286
Spiess 190
Stanislaus Leszczynski 54
Statthalter 159
Stowell, conquest, on 149-50
Straits Convention (1856) 66
Strassburg, German element in 133
seventeenth century, in 58
University of 47
germanisation of 165
Streams in Alsace-Lorraine 37
Sturm von Sturmeck 56
Sybel, conquest, on 91

Tachard, Alsace-Lorraine as a buffer State 272
Talleyrand, Prussian ambition, on 142
Tauler 56
Telegraph service 45
Telephone service 45
Territorial Delegacy, composition of 159, 160
establishment of 159
functions enlarged 159
legislation, part in 160-61
political alliances in 189
rupture with ministry 168
Territory, German lust for 141 *seq.*
Teutsch 184
Thibaudin 217
Thiers, head of the executive 64, 103
interview with Bismarck at Versailles 68
interview with German Emperor and Crown Prince 69
mission to European Powers 63
Preliminaries of Versailles submitted to Assembly 104
Thirty Years War 56
Three Bishoprics, the 51
Tilsit, Peace of 305
Tirard 106
Transport, means of 44
Treaties, binding force of 151-3
future international co-operation and 283-4
Treitschke, autonomy, on 94
claims of Germany to Alsace-Lorraine, on 114
conquest, on 146
military necessity of annexation, on 137-8
military service in Alsace, on 156-7
natural deficiencies of Germany, on 134

INDEX 327

Treitschke—*continued*
  neutralisation, on 90, 273
  partition, on 92–3
  plebiscite, on 90, 91–2
  political necessity of annexation 135
  pretensions of 122
Trouée de Belfort 37
Turenne 57

' Ubi societas ibi ius ' 271
Utrecht, treaty of 153

Vaucouleurs, treaty of 115
Verdun, treaty of 50, 115
Vereeniging, Peace of 244
Versailles, Preliminaries of 65, 70
  debate on 104 *seq.*
  provisions of 71–3
  vote on 107
Vienna Congress 142
Vienna, treaty of (1755) 54
  (1815) 153
  (1864) 305
Vincennes, treaty of 54
Viviani, reannexation of Alsace-Lorraine 227, 228
Vosges, as frontier 298

Wagner, plebiscite, on 92
Wedel, Count von 169
Wedelpissdorf, Alsatian demand for autonomy 173
Weill, Alsatian desertions from German army 209
  autonomy demanded in Reichstag 194
  plebiscite, on 313

Welsche 180
Welschinger, protest in 1871, 103, 108
Wendel 259
Westarp 258
Westphalia, treaty of 57, 153
Wetterlé, autonomy as a stepping-stone, on 197, 208
  Constitution of 1911, 171–2
  Dallwitz von Roedern's régime 174
  declarations of the two Chambers in 1917, on 210–11
  difficulties of reannexation 249
  industrial organisation in case of reannexation 245
  plebiscite, on 312
  reassimilation to France, on 241–2
  religious question, on 247
William I 137, 237
  reason for annexation, on 140
William II 175, 218
Wilson (President), ' reconsideration ' of Alsace-Lorraine question 232
  self-determination of nations 310
Wine, manufacture of 43
Winterer, Abbé 158
Wittich 204

' Young Alsace ' 219
  See Nationalist movement

Zabern. *See* Saverne
Zeppelin 176, 198
Zislin 168
Zollverein 278

PRINTED IN GREAT BRITAIN
BY HAZELL, WATSON AND VINEY, LD.,
LONDON AND AYLESBURY.

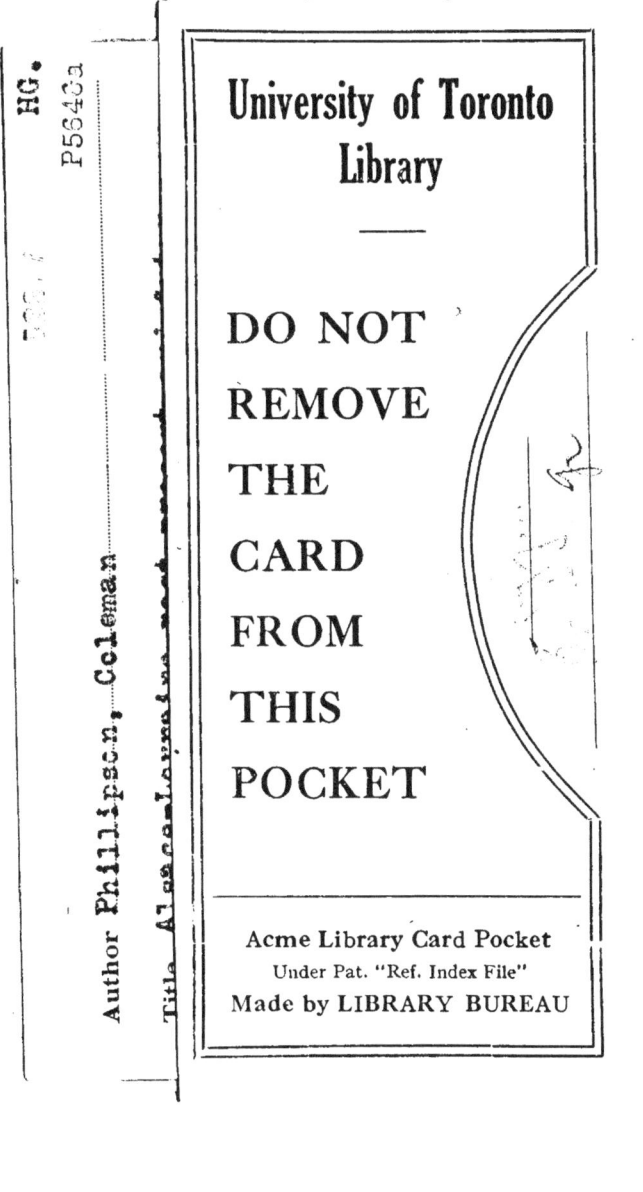

WS - #0018 - 190625 - C0 - 229/152/18 [20] - CB - 9780265367094 - Gloss Lamination